Elias G. Saba

Harmonizing Similarities

Islam – Thought, Culture, and Society

Volume 1

Elias G. Saba

Harmonizing Similarities

A History of Distinctions Literature in Islamic Law

DE GRUYTER

Winner of the 2018 BRAIS-De Gruyter Prize in the Study of Islam and the Muslim World

BRAIS
British Association
for Islamic Studies

ISBN 978-3-11-076327-0
e-ISBN (PDF) 978-3-11-060579-2
e-ISBN (EPUB) 978-3-11-060439-9
ISSN 2628-4286

Library of Congress Control Number: 2019946400

Bibliographic information published by the Deutsche Nationalbibliothek
The Deutsche Nationalbibliothek lists this publication in the Deutsche Nationalbibliografie; detailed bibliographic data are available on the Internet at http://dnb.dnb.de.

This volume is text- and page-identical with the hardback published in 2019.
Cover image: © Calligraphy by Osman Özçay. With friendly permission.
Printing and binding: CPI books GmbH, Leck

www.degruyter.com

Acknowledgements

This book is the fruit of years of intellectual labor. I have been fortunate to have had the help, guidance, and friendship of a great many people and institutions. This book is a refined and improved version of my dissertation. Paul M. Cobb and Jamal J. Elias provided exceptional help and mentoring during my graduate studies, as I wrote my dissertation, and having continued to do so in the following years. My dissertation advisor, Joseph E. Lowry, was an exemplary advisor. He provided constant encouragement and detailed critique.

This study would not have been possible without the help of a variety of grants. The Mellon-Mays Fellowship has provided years of financial support and provided me with a community that has been key to my academic success. I am also grateful for a residency at the American Center for Oriental Research through an ACOR-CAORC grant during which I was able to conduct much of the research that guided this book. At the University of Pennsylvania, I was able to succeed thanks to a Benjamin Franklin Fellowship, the Foreign Language and Area Studies Fellowship, a fellowship from the Communication within the Curriculum program, a Janet Lee Stevens Fellowship, and a grant from the Digital Humanities Forum.

I am grateful to the BRAIS – De Gruyter Prize 2018 committee for honoring my work. As I have refined this monograph, I have benefitted greatly from the help of Robert Gleave and A. Kevin Reinhart. Marc Herman and Nicolai Sinai provided wonderfully detailed feedback on the majority of this book. I also wish to thank Sophie Wagenhofer, Katrin Mittmann, and André Horn at De Gruyter for all of their editorial assistance.

I am grateful as well to those who have read sections of this work and/or have helped me refine my arguments. In particular, I thank Ṣalāḥ Abū al-Ḥājj, Roger M. A. Allen, Jeffery Arsenault, Kameliya Atanasova, Carolyn Baugh, Joel Blecher, Carolyn Brunelle, Talya Fishman, Angela Giordani, Ari Gordon, Cameron Hu, Ali Karjoo-Ravary, Nicholas Harris, Renata Holod, Murad Idris, Matt Keegan, Susan MacDougall, Christian Mauder, Christian Müller, Tilman Neuschild, David S. Powers, Raha Rafii, Yossef Rapoport, Ryan Rittenberg, Noel Rivera, Mariam Sheibani, Thomas Levi Thompson, and Amir Toft. I also wish to thank my colleagues at Grinnell College for their help and encouragement. In particular, I wish to thank Shanna Benjamin, Caleb Elfenbein, and Karla Erickson.

I also thank the helpful and accommodating staffs at the British Library, the Bibliothèque nationale de France, the Staatsbibliothek zu Berlin, the Suleymaniye Library in Istanbul, the Leiden University Libraries, the Garrett Library at

https://doi.org/10.1515/9783110605792-001

Princeton University, and the staff at the New York Public Library, particularly Thomas Lannon.

Finally, I thank Eiren Shea for unwavering emotional, intellectual, and editorial help during every stage of this book.

Contents

Introduction — 1
Legal Background — **3**
A Note on Genre — **6**
The Role of Genre in Islamic Law — **8**
Chapter Overview — **12**

Chapter One:
What Is a Legal Distinction? — 16
Defining Legal Distinctions — **17**
Premodern Definitions — **17**
Modern Understandings — **31**
Justifications for Legal Distinctions — **36**
Conclusion — **41**

Chapter Two:
A General History of Distinctions — 43
Furūq in Medicine — **45**
Furūq in Philology — **54**
Early Lexicographical Activity — **58**
Books of *Farq* — **61**
Farq and the Arabic Alphabet — **69**
Farq and *Furūq* in Other Fields — **73**
Farq in Philosophy — **74**
Farq in Ethics — **76**
Farq in Law — **77**
Conclusions — **79**

Chapter Three:
***Jadal* as a Source for Legal Writings: The Cases of *Khilāf* and *Furūq* — 81**
Disputation and Distinction — **82**
Farq in Theological Disputation — **84**
Farq in Legal Disputation — **87**
Disputational Theory and Practice (*Khilāf*) — **94**
Disputation in *Furūq* — **103**
Conclusion — **108**

Excursus: The Logic of Legal Distinctions — 110
Understanding Lexicographic Distinctions — 112
Understanding Legal Distinctions — 114
Concluding Thoughts — 117

Chapter Four:
Riddles and Entertainment — 119
Literary Salons, Learning, and Culture — 121
Literature and Practice of Legal Riddles — 132
Legal Distinctions as Play — 141
The Merging of *Alghāz* and *Furūq* — 144
Separating Riddles and Distinctions: The Case of Jamāl al-Dīn al-Asnawī — 148
Conclusion — 154

Chapter Five: A Bibliographic Survey of the Distinctions Genre — 157
Narrative Listing of Furūq Works — 165
The Fourth/Tenth Century — 166
The Fifth/Eleventh Century — 167
The Sixth/Twelfth Century — 171
The Seventh/Thirteenth Century — 172
The Eighth/Fourteenth Century — 177
The Ninth/Fifteenth Century — 180
The Tenth/Sixteenth Century — 182
Works of Indeterminate Date — 183
Historical and Geographical Trends — 185
A Note on Manuscripts — 187
Conclusion — 191

Conclusion — 194

Appendix I:
Bibliography of *Furūq* Works by *Madhhab* — 198
Shāfiʿī — 198
Ḥanafī — 203
Mālikī — 206
Ḥanbalī — 210
Shi'i Works — 212
Works Incorrectly Said to Be of Legal Distinctions — 212

Appendix II:
Chronological *Furūq* Bibliography — 215
Third/Ninth Century — **215**
Fourth/Tenth Century — **215**
Fifth/Eleventh Century — **215**
Sixth/Twelfth Century — **216**
Seventh/Thirteenth Century — **216**
Eighth/Fourteenth Century — **216**
Ninth/Fifteenth Century — **217**
Tenth/Sixteenth Century — **217**
Unknown — **217**

Appendix III:
The Manuscripts of *Furūq*-A: Table of Contents — 218

Appendix IV:
The Manuscripts of *Furūq*-B (Najm al-Dīn Naysābūrī, *attrib.*): Table of Contents — 221

Works Cited — 225
Manuscripts — **225**
Printed Sources — **226**

Index — 243

Introduction

What is the social history of Islamic legal literature? The answer to this question remains unclear. Even though the history and development of Islamic law have long formed the subject of extensive scholarly study, scholars have not discussed the rhetoric or aesthetics of law's literature. Most of the study of Islamic law has tended to focus on the legal system that is described in works of Islamic law, at the expense of the way that this system is expressed. Yet, change and dynamism in Islamic law also occurs through the ways in which legal knowledge is packaged, organized, and presented; in other words, through development and change in literary features, such as genre. A focus on Islamic law as a field of learning rather than as part of a legal system requires a greater focus on its literary characteristics.

Modern scholarship has generally divided the history of Islamic law into three periods: "early," "middle," and "modern." Most scholars have focused on the rise and early development of the Islamic legal tradition or the transition to multiple modern, national ones that selectively incorporate concepts from Islamic law. This division parallels the prevailing periodization of the history of Islamic societies generally. Marshall Hodgson divided that history into three broad periods, which he labeled "the Classical Age," "the Middle Periods," and "Gunpowder Empires and Modern Time."[1] Until recently, the middle periods have been sorely understudied. Wael Hallaq, arguably the leading western scholar of Islamic law, has referred to this post-formative period, from approximately 1250 to 1800, as "a virtual *terra incognita*."[2] This lack of scholarly attention is due to a belief that this period was one of legal and cultural stagnation. The scholars who do study this period, however, have shown that Islamic law underwent remarkable changes.

The misunderstanding about a so-called "middle period" of Islamic law relates, at least in part, to a misconception about the very nature of Islamic legal change. In arguments about development or lack thereof, scholars have attempted to look for changes or development in either the substantive rules of Islamic law (*furūʿ al-fiqh*) or in legal theory (*uṣūl al-fiqh*). Since Islamic law is understood as a legal system, it makes sense to look for development to occur in manuals of substantive laws or in the theoretical writings on legal interpretation. *Furūʿ al-*

1 Marshall G.S. Hodgson, *The Venture of Islam: Conscience and History in a World Civilization*, 3 vols. (Chicago: University of Chicago Press, 1974).

2 Wael Hallaq, *The Origins and Evolution of Islamic Law* (Cambridge: Cambridge University Press, 2005), 1.

https://doi.org/10.1515/9783110605792-002

fiqh and *uṣūl al-fiqh* are not the two halves of Islamic law, however; they are only two genres of Islamic legal literature.[3] In addition, Islamic law can also be understood as a scholarly discipline, concerned with the production and organization of a specific kind of knowledge. According to this understanding, promulgation of new substantive rules and advancements in legal theory are only two possible kinds of development.

This book traces the history of one understudied genre, that of legal distinctions, *al-furūq al-fiqhiyya*—the comparison of apparently similar fact-patterns that lead to different legal outcomes. Examining thirty-six works that belong to this genre, composed over a period of approximately six hundred years, allows us to understand the social and intellectual trends that drove the rhetoric of this genre. The beginnings of this genre can confidently be dated to the fourth/tenth century, though the earliest such work remains to be identified. The fifth/eleventh century saw a surge in works addressing legal distinctions, and the genre flourished in the seventh/thirteenth and eighth/fourteenth centuries. Books of legal distinctions were written in all four Sunni schools of law, although it found greatest currency in the Shāfiʿī school. In general, Shi'i jurists did not compose works of legal distinctions, although an early work is attributed to the Shi'i jurist Aḥmad ibn Muḥammad al-Barqī (d. third/ninth c.) and another work is attributed to the Zaydī author ʿAlī ibn Yaḥyā ibn Rāshid al-Washlī al-Yamanī (d. 777/1375–76).[4] The genre seems to have been particularly popular in large urban centers, with an original point of focus in Abbasid Baghdad and later in Mamluk Cairo. The manuscripts of books of legal distinctions show that these works were copied and recopied often and circulated widely.

This study emphasizes one literary manifestation of Islamic law. In particular, it looks to expand the study of genre within Islamic legal writing by carrying out a history of one particular genre. The genre of legal distinctions has received little scholarly attention. Nevertheless, its history is an important part of the development of Islamic law. This study shows the genre to be a valuable rubric for locating the relevance of later Islamic legal literature, and in particular highlights the intellectual and social background from which this genre emerged and the specific ways in which the genre of legal distinctions adapted to changing social patterns that affected the consumption of Islamic legal knowledge.

---

3 Admittedly, they may be the most important genres in Islamic legal literature. A legal system, of course, is made up of much more than legal theory and substantive laws. In addition, a legal system would need at least courts, a state, and enforcement mechanics. See Joseph Raz, *The Concept of a Legal System: An Introduction to the Theory of Legal System*, 2nd ed. (Oxford: Clarendon Press, 1980).

4 Unfortunately, neither work is extant.

Furūq literature offered a venue that allowed jurists to adapt the law in new packaging as a response to social demand for new and different forms of legal knowledge.

Legal Background

The Middle Periods of Islamic history witnessed the downfall of caliphal hegemony as well as the rise of non-Arabic Islamic culture. These political changes have led scholars to describe this period as one of scholarly stasis and cultural decadence. In the realm of Arabic literature, for example, the idea that Arabic writing entered a period of steep decline around the thirteenth century had been accepted for well over a century. R.A. Nicholson already took this as a given in his *Literary History of the Arabs* published in 1907, when he refers to cultural production in Arabic after the Mongol sack of Baghdad in 1258 as "a melancholy conclusion to a glorious history."[5] Ensuing scholarship assumed that it is possible to identify the precise moment the age of decline began and argued for various moments. In the *Cambridge History of Arabic Literature*, M.M. Badawi argued that the alleged decline began early in the sixteenth century and ended in the late nineteenth, declaring that "[t]he period is no doubt characterized by the absence of creativity and loss of vigour."[6] While the period of supposed decline is shrinking in size, Badawi does not question the decline narrative. It is only very recently that scholars of Arabic literature have begun to study this period in earnest. Joseph Lowry and Devin Stewart describe the period between 1350 and 1850 as "a period of time almost uniformly dismissed by scholars of Arabic literature as lacking in literary achievements."[7] Their volume, which surveys some major figures of this period, marks a radical shift in the reassessment of cultural production in Arabic.[8]

---

5 Reynold A. Nicholson, *A Literary History of the Arabs* (Cambridge: Cambridge University Press, 1907), 442.

6 Muhammad M. Badawi, "Introduction," in *Modern Arabic Literature: The Cambridge History of Arabic Literature*, ed. Muhammad M. Badawi (Cambridge: Cambridge University Press, 1992), 3.

7 Joseph E. Lowry and Devin J. Stewart, "Introduction," in *Essays in Arabic Literary Biography 1350–1850*, ed. Joseph E. Lowry and Devin J. Stewart (Wiesbaden: Harrassowitz Verlag, 2009), 1.

8 More recently, Thomas Bauer has put forth a convincing case for ambiguity as a central aesthetic notion in Arabic literature. The tolerance for, and even delight in, ambiguity was a central motivator of scholarly writing. See Thomas Bauer, *Die Kultur der Ambiguität: Eine andere Geschichte des Islams* (Berlin: Verlag der Weltreligionen, 2011).

Joseph Schacht, perhaps the most important twentieth-century scholar of Islamic law, reinforced this broad narrative of decline as the dominant conception of Islamic law. He held that creative development within Islamic law came to an abrupt stop around the middle of the fourth/tenth century. At this time, legal creativity ossified into a state of total rigidity, or as he called it, "*ankylose.*"[9] As evidence for the lack of creativity during this period, Schacht has pointed to several factors: the rise of commentary traditions, a decline in innovative legal reasoning, and, most importantly, a discursive commitment to adhering diligently to already-established legal interpretations, known in Arabic as *taqlīd.*[10] Schacht's interpretation of Islamic law amounts to the dismissal of the majority of Islamic legal history.

In a well-known article, Wael Hallaq challenged Schacht's ideas by adducing evidence of many legal scholars who, after the tenth century, offered new and inventive legal interpretations. His findings "suggest [that] developments in positive law, legal theory, and the judiciary have indeed taken place."[11] Elsewhere, Hallaq looked at the development of Islamic law through the incorporation of legal responsa, fatwas, into legal compendia, demonstrating the adaptability of Islamic law well into its supposed period of rigidity.[12] The suggestion that genres otherwise assumed to signify ossification in fact signify innovation challenged scholars to integrate new discourses to identify development and creativity within the history of Islamic law. Baber Johansen and David S. Powers have both demonstrated in greater detail how legal change and creativity were expressed through such responsa. Johansen argues that fatwas were not "chiefly responsible," but rather that commentaries on legal compendia also played a major role in changing legal doctrine.[13] Powers, meanwhile, argues that post-classical authors did adhere to already-established legal interpretations, "or, what we might call, adherence to the rule of law."[14]

---

9 Joseph Schacht, "Classicisme, traditionalisme et ankylose dans la loi religieuse de l'Islam," in *Classicisme et déclin culturel dans l'histoire de l'Islam*, ed. Robert Brunschvig and G.E. von Grunebaum (Paris: G.P. Maisonneuve et Larose, 1977).

10 Joseph Schacht, *An Introduction to Islamic Law* (Oxford: Clarendon Press, 1964), 71.

11 Wael Hallaq, "Was the Gate of Ijtihad Closed?" *International Journal of Middle Eastern Studies* 16 (1984), 33.

12 Wael Hallaq, "From *Fatwās* to *Furūʿ*: Growth and Change in Islamic Substantive Law," *Islamic Law and Society* 1 (1994): 29–65.

13 Baber Johansen, "Legal Literature and the Problem of Change," in *Islam and Public Law: Classical and Contemporary Studies*, ed. Chibli Mallat (London: Graham and Trotman, 1993), 30–31.

14 David S. Powers, *Law, Society, and Culture in the Maghrib, 1300–1500* (Cambridge: Cambridge University Press, 2002), 94.

Sherman Jackson rejects Schacht's assertion of "ossification," seeing the constraints of the tradition as an impetus for legal creativity, more so than what was possible without these limitations: "In fact, it may not be at all incorrect to say that *taqlīd* represents a more rather than less advanced phase of legal development."[15] Jackson interprets this respect for legal tradition as the parameters within and through which later jurists display their intellectual creativity. Norman Calder takes this idea to an extreme, arguing that Islamic law is, in fact, not law for this world at all, but rather a "brilliant imitation of reality, sharply characterised, precisely delineated, charmingly evocative."[16] With this statement, Schacht's formulation of Islamic legal history has been turned on its head. *Taqlīd* does not mark a nadir of any kind, but rather the beginning of an opening within legal literature for concern with the aesthetics of the law, and of the maturation of the craft of legal writing.

As previously noted, this scholarly debate is incomplete. It deals only with three genres of legal writing: legal theory (*uṣūl al-fiqh*), legal compendia (*fiqh*), and responsa (fatwas). There are other post-formative genres of legal writing that remain almost entirely unexplored. They include works on legal distinctions (*furūq*), cognate and similar legal cases (*al-ashbāh wa-l-naẓāʾir*), legal maxims (*qawāʿid*), legal riddles (*al-alghāz al-fiqhiyya*), and more. These genres are, further, interrelated. Many books, such as *al-Ashbāh wa-l-naẓāʾir* by Ibn Nujaym (d. 970/1563), contain extensive sections on all three of these topics. To date, there has been little scholarship dealing with any of these other genres. More significantly, the subject of this book, *al-furūq al-fiqhiyya*, has received almost no scholarly attention in the Western academy. Yaʿqūb al-Bāḥusayn and Necmittin Kızılkaya have, however, each written monographs, in Arabic and Turkish respectively, surveying the distinctions genre.[17]

This genre is, in fact, quite understudied: there are just two articles in European languages dealing specifically with such books and only a handful of mentions of them in other research. The first of the two articles on this subject, by

15 Sherman Jackson, *Islamic Law and the State: The Constitutional Jurisprudence of Shihāb al-Dīn al-Qarāfī* (Leiden: Brill, 1996), 227.

16 Norman Calder, *Islamic Jurisprudence in the Classical Era*, ed. Colin Imber (Cambridge: Cambridge University Press, 2010), 95.

17 Yaʿqūb ibn ʿAbd al-Wahhāb al-Bāḥusayn, *al-Furūq al-fiqhiyya wa-l-uṣūliyya: muqawwamātuhā shurūṭuhā nashʾatuhā taṭawwuruhā; dirāsa naẓariyya waṣfiyya tārīkhiyya* (Riyadh: Maktabat al-Rushd, 1419/1998); Necmettin Kızılkaya, *İslâm hukukunda farklar: Furûk literatürü üzerine bir inceleme* (Istanbul: İz Yayıncılık, 2016); in addition, see Muḥammad Abū l-Ajfān and Ḥamza Abū Fāris, "*al-Dirāsa*," in Abū l-Faḍl Muslim al-Dimashqī, *al-Furūq al-fiqhiyya*, ed. Muḥammad Abū l-Ajfān and Ḥamza Abū Fāris (Beirut: Dār al-Gharb al-Islāmī, 1992).

Joseph Schacht, was published in 1926. In this article, Schacht alludes to the potential importance of the genre of legal distinctions, but most of his comments are about the condition of two manuscripts.[18] The next article on this topic was published in 2000 by Wolfhart Heinrichs. Again, rather than analyzing *furūq* literature, he primarily provides an annotated bibliography of some *furūq* works. He repeats the call for its study and asserts that legal distinctions should be studied along with two other similar genres: legal maxims and cognate and similar cases. Such research "will lead to a fairer assessment of later Islamic legal culture."[19] Since Heinrichs wrote his article, there has been work done on the "cousins" of *furūq* literature—cognate and similar legal cases (*al-ashbāh wa-l-naẓā'ir*), and legal maxims (*qawā'id*)—but little on the *furūq* literature itself.

A Note on Genre

The idea of genre inspired the analysis in this study. It is therefore important to discuss what I mean by the word "genre" and how I use this term. While genres are commonly thought of passively, as "groups of works that belong together because they stand in the same tradition,"[20] genres are really the products of agency, of those who bring the texts together and those who construct and determine the contours of a tradition. In the *Princeton Encyclopedia of Poetry and Poetics*, Max Cavitch explains that "[t]he practice of grouping individual texts into distinct categories, called *genres*, is common to *writers* and *readers* of all periods."[21] Both authors and audiences play a role in determining the genre of a work with the result that shifting conceptions of different genres emerge over time.

The understanding of genre relied on in this study draws in part on formalist understandings. A formalist interpretation of genre, as explained by Tzvetan Todorov, is based on the idea of genre as a category or groupings to which texts can

18 Schacht is primarily concerned with presenting two manuscripts within this genre, one attributed to a Najm al-Dīn al-Naysābūrī (d. ?) and another by al-Sāmarrī (d. 545/1150). Joseph Schacht, "Aus zwei arabischen *Furūq*-Büchern," *Islamica* 2 (1926): 505–37.

19 Wolfhart Heinrichs, "Structuring the Law: Remarks on the *Furūq* Literature," in *Studies in Honour of Clifford Edmund Bosworth Volume I: Hunter of the East; Arabic and Semitic Studies*, ed. Ian Richard Netton, 332–44 (Leiden: Brill, 2000), 340.

20 Alastair Fowler, "Genre," in *Encyclopedia of Literature and Criticism*, ed. Martin Coyle et al. (Detroit: Gale Research, 1990), 151.

21 *Princeton Encyclopedia of Poetry and Poetics*, 4th ed., s.v. "Genre" (Max Cavitch). Italics added.

be ascribed. Tzvetan Todorov's ideas about genre are useful because of the change and dynamism that he detects in literary genres. On the origins of a genre, one of the central questions of the first part of this book, Todorov writes: "Where do genres come from? Quite simply from other genres. A new genre is always the transformation of an earlier one, or of several: by inversion, by displacement, by combination."[22] Genres should not be seen as static or stable, but rather as constantly changing. A genre can undergo change in itself, or it can change into a new genre. Todorov sees the origin of the novel arising from a massive series of generic transformations, arguing that "[t]he difficulty of the study of the 'origin of the novel...' arises only from the infinite embedding of speech acts with others."[23] Only a finite number of transformations, or embedded speech acts, can be accounted for. While it may not be possible to capture all of the transformations that gave way to the creation of a new genre, this methodology is quite useful for understanding Islamic legal genres.

Genre should also be understood as a Wittgensteinian language game,[24] meaning that "language [is] to be understood as an activity,"[25]or "recurrent acts of play in time."[26] This line of reasoning allows us to think of genre as a continuous activity, always open to change and improvisation, rather than a rigid category. A genre thus consists of "family resemblances," not "defining characteristics."[27] Each genre is beholden to its particular rules and these rules are liable to change over time, as the game plays out in a series of social and intellectual contexts. Understanding genre as a game is particularly useful when looking at premodern Arabic writers. These writers clearly had ideas of genres, as is evident in the title of works, the allusions made through titles of works, the ways authors used introductions to contextualize a given book, and in discussions of literature in prosopographical works. A flexible understanding of genre is necessary to study the life of any Islamic legal genre, as these were elaborated over centuries, across a wide geography, and by several authors belonging to different schools of thought. If one thinks of genre as a continuous activity, it is not surprising to find one set of genres in an early period evolving in multiple ways.

---

22 Tzvetan Todorov, *Genres in Discourse*, trans. Catherine Porter (Cambridge: Cambridge University Press, 1990), 15.
23 Todorov, *Genres*, 26.
24 Fowler, "Genre," 157.
25 Hans Sluga, *Wittgenstein* (Malden, MA: Wiley-Blackwell, 2011), 60.
26 Ludwig Wittgenstein, *On Certainty*, ed. G. E. M. Anscombe, trans. Denis Paul and G. E. M. Anscombe (Oxford: Blackwell, 1969), 68e, ¶519.
27 Fowler, "Genre," 157.

Genres can splinter off into new genres and genres can change their rules to adapt to new activities.

The Role of Genre in Islamic Law

This study builds on recent attempts by scholars to explore the full archive of Islamic law, a trend that has enabled scholars to better understand the development of Islamic law and the way Islamic legal thinking has transitioned into modernity.[28] These works, however, are not explicit attempts at studying genre broadly speaking. Rather, notions about specific genres and their function in Islamic law seem to guide much of the research they undertake. As Ahmad Ahmad notes, for instance, "[i]n fact, I am not aware of much treatment by Western scholars of any of the particular juristic genres that make up the corpus of Islamic legal writings as genres in their own right."[29] A treatment of particular juristic genres in their own right requires the existence of identifiable genres.

One issue that immediately arises when attempting to study one particular genre is how to define the criteria for inclusion in and exclusion from the genre, or, in other words, how to recognize works as being part of one genre. Previous studies have used a variety of methods for grouping works into genres. Ahmad himself seems to be confident of his ability to recognize a genre when he sees one, even though he does not tell us how he identifies specific genres.[30] Similarly, Intisar Rabb does not state her criteria explicitly, but it is clear from looking at her overview of the genre of legal maxims that she classifies works based on their content.[31] Another approach, taken by Khadiga Musam appears to be classification by title.[32]

---

28 In particular, I am indebted to Ahmad A. Ahmad's *Structural Interrelations*, which analyzed works of *al-takhrīj* and *al-qawāʿid*, Ahmed El Shamsy's "The *Ḥāshiya* in Islamic Law," on the *ḥāshiya* literature, Intisar Rabb's *Doubt in Islamic Law*, on *al-qawāʿid al-fiqhiyya*, and Khadiga Musa's "Legal Maxims as a Genre of Islamic Law," a study of *al-qawāʿid al-fiqhiyya* and *al-ashbāh wa-l-naẓāʾir.*

29 Ahmad A. Ahmad, *Structural Interrelations of Theory and Practice in Islamic Law: A Study of Six Works of Medieval Islamic Jurisprudence* (Leiden: Brill, 2006), 45.

30 Although he does note that "focusing on the significance of these different types of Islamic legal writing is more valuable than squeezing them into identifiable genres"; Ahmad, *Structural Interrelations*, 17.

31 Rabb, "Doubt's Benefit: Legal Maxims in Islamic Law, 7th–16th centuries," (Ph.D. Diss., Princeton University, 2009), 458–82.

32 Khadiga Musa, "Legal Maxims as a Genre of Islamic Law: Origins, Development, and Significance of *al-Qawāʿid al-Fiqhiyya*," *Islamic Law and Society* 21 (2014): 325–65. This is also the ap-

Ahmed El Shamsy has recently discussed legal genre in a study devoted to "the emergence of the *ḥāshiya* [supercommentary] genre in Islamic legal literature."[33] While El Shamsy does not include a theoretical discussion of genre or the role of genre in Islamic law, he attempts to state parameters for the genre of the *ḥāshiya*. The characteristic features of the genre include "an exercise in a specific kind of erudition,"[34] "a linguistic preoccupation,"[35] "the sheer scholasticism of many of the *ḥāshiya* authors' concerns,"[36] and "its [very concise] Arabic style."[37] The characteristics that El Shamsy describes are useful, but too broad as they apply to more than just the *ḥāshiya* texts. His list leaves out the most obvious shared feature of supercommentaries, a formal consideration, namely, that a *ḥāshiya* is a commentary on a previous commentary. This formal characteristic seems to be what El Shamsy is using in identifying works belonging to this genre, even though it is not part of his list of "characteristic features."

Wittgenstein's idea of a language game is particularly useful for the study of Islamic legal literature: instead of looking for rigid characteristics, one should look for the kinds of rules that each genre follows *qua* game.[38] Rules establish the parameters of a particular game and can be, but are not necessarily, strict or rigid. Certain games, such as chess, may have a detailed list of clearly defined unbending rules. Other games, however, such as playing with a ball, do not have any explicit or strict rules, but follow rules nonetheless.[39] The different features or characteristics can be thought of as limits within which genres can play. An adherence to certain rules, which may be both unwritten and flexible, makes genres recognizable, but perhaps indescribable.[40] Unwritten but recognizable

proach taken by Devin Stewart in his studies on Islamic legal theory. Devin J. Stewart, "Muḥammad b. Jarīr al-Ṭabarī's *al-Bayān ʿan uṣūl al-aḥkām* and the Genre of *Uṣūl al-Fiqh* in Ninth-Century Baghdad," in *ʿAbbasid Studies: Occasional Papers of the School of ʿAbbasid Studies, Cambridge 6–10 July 2002*, ed. James Montgomery, 321–49 (Leuven: Peeters, 2004).

33 Ahmed El Shamsy, "The *Ḥāshiya* in Islamic Law: A Sketch of the Shāfiʿī Literature," *Oriens* 41 (2013), 290.

34 El Shamsy, "*Ḥāshiya*," 296–97.

35 El Shamsy, "*Ḥāshiya*," 297.

36 El Shamsy, "*Ḥāshiya*," 297.

37 El Shamsy, "*Ḥāshiya*," 298.

38 Sluga, *Wittgenstein*, 61; Ludwig Wittgenstein, *Preliminary Studies for the "Philosophical Investigations": Generally Known as The Blue and Brown Books* (New York: Harper & Row, 1965), 25–26.

39 Sluga, *Wittgenstein*, 78–79; Wittgenstein, *Philosophical Investigations*, 83.

40 Here, the comparison with playing a game of passing a ball is particularly relevant. Passing a ball is a completely informal game, the rules of which can be malleable, but are generally intuitive to the participants. The rules of this game are never stable and cannot be definitively established, but those playing will nevertheless adhere to them during a particular game.

rules that authors and readers participated in suggest as well that they were aware of generic conventions.

The articles by Ahmad, El Shamsy, Musa, and Rabb also provide evidence for the usefulness of thinking about genre as a language-game. Genre is not just a function of packaging or presentation, but has profound consequences on understanding the content of a work and the context to which it may be responding. Both El Shamsy and Rabb find evidence of legal content being shaped by genre: they find thought and language conforming to the rules of particular language games. El Shamsy suggests that the development of supercommentaries was a way for jurists to cope with and comprehend the enormity of the legal literary tradition, "a product of the logical development of a discipline."[41] In seeing supercommentaries as a sort of end-point for a legal tradition committed to commentary, jurists were free to elaborate on any and all aspects of these texts. The rules for a supercommentary seem to allow for a great degree of freedom so long as the commentator follows a particular kind of text from start to finish. It was not simply the legal content that was important, but also the linguistic and intellectual concerns of the authors of these texts—they respond to these texts as scholars in addition to their responses as jurists. Rabb, meanwhile, finds that the maxim, "Avoid capital punishment in cases of doubt (*idraʾū l-ḥudūd bi-l-shubuhāt*)," underwent change as it moved from one genre to another. She argues that "[t]he sources indicate that the differences in the form of the maxim in the early period were a matter not of sequence, but of genre."[42] The changes inherent in this maxim were less of a function of historical than of literary context. The maxim changed as it played different generic games.[43]

---

41 El Shamsy, "*Ḥāshiya*," 303.

42 Rabb, "Doubt's Benefit," 61.

43 This maxim, which Rabb calls the *ḥudūd* maxim, appears almost from the start of Islamic legal literature. It is found, for instance, in works of substantive law such as the *Kitāb al-Āthār* by Muḥammad ibn al-Ḥasan al-Shaybānī (d. 189/804) and the *Kitāb al-Kharāj* of Abū Yūsuf (d. 182/798). The maxim also appears in the *Muwaṭṭaʾ* of Mālik ibn Anas (d. 179/795), in the recension of Yaḥyā ibn Yaḥyā l-Laythī (d. 234/848). Similarly, we can find the doubt canon in the the *Risāla* of Muḥammad ibn Idrīs al-Shāfiʿī (d. 204/820), a legal-theoretical work, and even in works of hadith such as the *Muṣannaf* of ʿAbd al-Razzāq (d. 211/827), the *Musnad* of Aḥmad ibn Ḥanbal (d. 241/855), and the Shiʿi *Qaḍāyā amīr al-muʾminīn ʿAlī ibn Abī Ṭālib* by Ibrāhīm ibn Hāshim al-Qummī (d. mid-third/ninth c.). Across these different types of literature, the *ḥudūd* maxim makes subtle, but noticeable difference in wording, scope, and source. The maxim is not always considered Prophetic, but slowly acquires status as a prophetic hadith over time. In its early history, the maxim is more amenable to changes in wording and interpretation; once the maxim becomes codified and included in works of *qawāʿid*, its role in Islamic law is stable and understood. See Intisar A. Rabb, "Islamic Legal Maxims as Substan-

One of the benefits of studying Islamic law from the vantage point of genre is that jurists seem to have seen themselves as participating in established genres, or discursive traditions. Despite the absence of a term for "genre" in the classical Arabo-Islamic tradition, several words in Classical Arabic, including *bāb*, *ʿilm*, and *nawʿ*, track this concept. Moreover, the concept of genre has proved productive for scholars who have used it as an analytical framework. Not all of the genres of Islamic legal literature are commensurate with one another, nor does it make sense to analyze them in a similar fashion. Not all genres function in a similar way. El Shamsy's study of supercommentaries necessitates his analytical focus on the formal features of a work.[44] Rabb, meanwhile, alerts us to the importance of content. It may seem obvious that content plays a role in the determination of genre, yet it is an important point that has been obscured in studies of Islamic law. Musa's focus on titles, meanwhile, reveals yet another way to think about genre. Title was one of the few explicit ways that premodern authors had of announcing their participation in one genre or another. Why and how this was accomplished may not always be straightforward, but titles should not be dismissed.

One result that can already be seen from treatments of genre is the overemphasis given to two genres of Islamic law, substantive rules (*furūʿ al-fiqh*) and legal theory (*uṣūl al-fiqh*).[45] It can seem, at times, that all Islamic legal writing can be included in one of these two rubrics. As Rabb writes, "[m]ost studies of Islamic law tend to portray a bipartite arrangement [of substantive legal rules and formalist jurisprudence]."[46] Such a portrayal leaves no room for legal literature that exists outside of this framework. Ahmad comes to a similar conclusion, claiming that legal distinctions and maxims "are but two examples of Islamic legal writing that cannot be subsumed under the rubrics of *fiqh* and *uṣūl al-fiqh*."[47] The present study adds to this trend in recent research attempting to overcome the *uṣūl-furūʿ* dichotomy.

It is not completely clear how and why authors chose to write in one genre instead of another, nor how and why genres were created, flourished, or waned. By tracing these issues for one particularly understudied tradition within Islamic

tive Canons of Construction: *Ḥudūd*-Avoidance in Cases of Doubt," *Islamic Law and Society* 17 (2010): 63–125; and *idem*, *Doubt in Islamic Law*, 48–66.

44 El Shamsy presumably takes these formal features as a given feature of supercommentary, and are not included in his list of generic considerations.

45 See also Ahmad, *Structural Interrelations*, 16.

46 Rabb, *Doubt in Islamic Law*, 20.

47 Ahmad, *Structural Interrelations*, 29.

law, this study suggests avenues of exploration that can be applied to other types of Islamic legal literature.

Chapter Overview

This history of the genre of legal distinctions is composed of four chapters and an excursus. Chapter One begins by asking what a legal distinction is, and what a book of legal distinction looks like. The theoretical question of the nature of a legal distinction is not one seriously taken up by the classical tradition. I have found only three such discussions, which are examined in this first chapter. The earliest and most in-depth is found in *al-Jamʿ wa-l-farq*, also known as *Kitāb al-Furūq*, by ʿAbdallāh al-Juwaynī (d. 438/1047), but there are also brief analyses in *ʿAlam al-jadhal fī ʿilm al-jadal* by Najm al-Dīn al-Ṭūfī (d. 716/1316) and *al-Manthūr fī al-qawāʿid* by Badr al-Dīn al-Zarkashī (d. 794/1392). From this survey, several aspects of legal distinctions emerge: the specific form of the comparison carried out in a legal distinction; its relationship to analogical reasoning; and the importance of formal disputation to the creation of the field of legal distinctions. The chapter then pursues this question from a different angle, by looking at books of legal distinctions themselves. The chapter closes with a look at the justifications given in books of legal distinctions for the composition of such works.

Having explored the definitions of this genre, the second chapter takes a wider view, looking at the literature on distinctions in the Arabic tradition generally. This second chapter focuses primarily on the genres of distinctions in linguistics and in medicine as parallels to the genre of legal distinctions. Distinctions in linguistics focused either on differentiating between letters of the Arabic language, often on phonological grounds, or on lexicographic distinctions in the sense of semantic differentiation between near-synonyms. This chapter finds that the genre of lexicographic distinctions was an important precursor to legal distinctions; it may perhaps even be said to establish some rules of the language game that is the genre of legal distinctions regarding the organization and presentation of information. In medicine, differential diagnostics also has a certain resonance with the genre of legal distinctions. This conclusion is complicated by the fact that although classical bio-bibliographical works seem to attest to a small but extant genre of distinctions works in medicine, only one work of this genre has survived, in various manuscripts and attributed to a variety of authors. Little, therefore, can be said about the genre or its conventions. Finally, the chapter closes by discussing other areas of intellectual inquiry that appear to have traditions of distinctions writing, such as ethics and philosophy. These works on distinctions, however, are not genres specific to these disciplines, but rather what I term applied lexicographic distinctions, by which I mean a work of lexicographic distinctions as applied to the technical vocabulary of a specific scholarly discipline—a comparison of words for the soul, for instance, or of giving advice and reprimanding. These works of applied lexicographic distinctions are important since they are found in almost all areas of Arabo-Islamic scholarship, and relevant to this study since they are even found in the field of law, but they are not examples of works of legal distinctions.

With these foundations in place, the third chapter looks for precursors to legal distinctions within other genres of Islamic law. Here, I locate one of the origins of legal distinctions, the discussions in manuals of disputation theory (*ʿilm al-jadal*) on a particular method of objection labeled *farq* ("distinction"). *Farq*, as a formal technique, is found in manuals of legal disputation, but not in manuals for disputations in philosophy or theology. It is an objection to the applicability of a legal rationale (*ʿilla*) of one legal ruling to a second ruling. A *farq*-objection is used to trap a debate opponent into admitting that his statement for the case at hand contradicts a known doctrine held by him or his legal school. Books of legal distinctions can be seen as attempts to organize possible *farq*-objections and the information necessary to overcome them. In this sense, *farq*-objections are used "offensively" in order to demonstrate contradictions while the genre of legal *furūq* contain the information necessary to defend oneself against such objections, thereby presenting a legal school's substantive doctrines as coherent in terms of the rationales that underlie them.[48]

After studying the disputational background of legal distinctions, a brief excursus analyzes in detail the logic of legal distinctions. This section attempts to define the relationship between lexicographic distinctions and legal distinctions in terms of the analytical framework employed in each genre. Although the resonances between these two genres are clear, there are significant differences in the reasoning employed in legal and lexicographic distinctions and, consequently, in the rules that each genre attempts to follow. In differentiating between near-synonyms, the genre of lexicographical distinctions is based on a fundamental similarity between the two words being compared. Legal distinctions, however, aim to demonstrate the fundamental dissimilarity between the two legal scenarios being compared. The analysis in this section establishes some of the rules that govern the genre of legal distinctions.

---

48 Ahmed El Shamsy, *The Canonization of Islamic Law: A Social and Intellectual History* (New York: Cambridge University Press, 2013); Joseph Lowry, Introduction to *The Epistle on Legal Theory* by Muḥammad ibn Idrīs al-Shāfiʿī, ed. and trans. Joseph E. Lowry (New York: New York University Press, 2013), xviii–ix.

Having established some of the parameters of the genre of legal distinctions, Chapter Four turns to works that potentially complicate our understanding of the genre of legal distinctions. In particular, this chapter studies the intersection between the genres of legal distinctions and that of legal riddles (*al-alghāz al-fiqhiyya*). There are obvious parallels between these two genres, and each of them seems to have affected the other, with some works of legal riddles being almost indistinguishable from works of legal distinctions and some works of legal distinctions presenting distinctions couched in the rhetorical style of riddles. This chapter locates the impetus for this convergence in the proliferation of venues at which legal knowledge could be performed—teaching sessions, literary salons, and the court of the ruler—and a growing taste, particularly in the Mamluk period in Cairo (seventh/thirteenth – tenth/sixteenth centuries), for the aesthetics of riddles. The role of performance is also important as it connects changes in literary style with social practice and different reading publics.

Finally, Chapter Five is a narrative bibliography of all known works of legal distinctions. The bibliographical work carried out in this chapter builds on previous catalogs. My survey locates thirty-six works that belong to this genre, and identifies the fifth/eleventh century and the seventh/thirteenth through eighth/fourteenth centuries as the peak period of composition in this genre. Chapter Five also discusses three books of legal distinctions, one Shāfiʿī and two Ḥanafī, that have various dubious attributions but no known author. In spite of the uncertainty about the authors of the two Ḥanafī works, they clearly belong to the genre and were copied and circulated to the same extent as other works in the genre whose authors are more easily identifiable.

The genre of *al-furūq al-fiqhiyya* presents a good subject for a case study of the emergence and maturation of a new and distinct genre in Islamic legal literature. A study of this genre ties the intellectual history of Islamic law together with the social display and consumption of Islamic legal knowledge. Specifically, it shows that the need for books of legal distinctions arose in part from the popularity of legal disputation and the usefulness of these works in overcoming *farq*-objections, which were common in the context of formal disputations. It also demonstrates a close link between legal distinctions and distinctions in other scholarly fields.

Taken together, these chapters demonstrate the way that legal writing was fully enmeshed in social and intellectual trends. The rise of legal distinctions treatises was due to the popularity of legal disputation—a kind of performance of legal knowledge. The shift in this genre towards a rhetoric of riddles tracks the popularity of posing and solving riddles in intellectual gatherings. The composition and production of particular books of law was a result of changing trends in the ways that legal knowledge was consumed by a certain educated public.

At the same time, this study reminds us that these literary changes in Islamic law were part of larger aesthetic trends. The rise of legal distinctions treatises closely follows the rise of lexicographical distinctions and perhaps medical distinctions. Changes in the aesthetics of scholarship during the Mamluk period are seen to operate in legal texts as well. These changes highlight that the literature of Islamic law was, in part, a literary endeavor subject to the same changes in aesthetic and rhetorical interest as other disciplines. For jurists in late Mamluk and early Ottoman Cairo, the form of Islamic legal writing was as important as their content. Understanding this literary dimension will help us to better understand their works, but also the ways in which they understood and conceptualized the discipline of Islamic law.

Chapter One: What Is a Legal Distinction?

This book explores the genre of legal distinctions in Islamic legal literature. Before formal works of legal distinctions appeared, however, authors writing in Arabic expressed abiding interest in other kinds of distinctions (sg. *farq*, pl. *furūq*), an interest that undoubtedly helped shape the legal genre at issue in this study. At least three distinct threads contributed to the rise of treatises addressed to legal distinctions: (i) the organization and systematization of substantive legal doctrine, (ii) the use of distinctions in non-legal contexts, and (iii) the use of *farq* as an objection in formal disputation (*ʿilm al-jadal*). This chapter focuses on the first of these threads, the organization and systematization of substantive legal doctrine. The following two chapters will address the second and third of these threads, respectively. Before delving into legal distinctions as a kind of natural result of the systematization of legal knowledge, however, this chapter addresses the issue of what legal distinctions are and how premodern jurists conceived of legal distinctions as both a concept and a genre.

While legal distinctions treatises abound in both print and manuscript, discussions of legal distinctions are quite scarce, in both the premodern tradition and in the modern scholarly study of Islamic law. Legal distinctions are both a genre of Islamic legal literature and a concept within Islamic law. In the words of the scholar Yaʿqūb al-Bāḥusayn, legal distinctions treatises list pairs of "legal problems that are similar in appearance, but contradictory in their ruling" (*aḥkām tatashābahu ṣuwaruhā wa-takhtalifu aḥkāmuhā*) and explain the distinctions that lead to the contradictory rulings.[1] First appearing in the Ḥanafī, Mālikī, and Shāfiʿī (but not Ḥanbalī) schools of law in the early fifth/eleventh century, these small legal works endeavored to show the inherent harmony governing the doctrinal complexities present in Islamic schools of law.[2]

In order to understand the purpose of these texts, this chapter will define the scope of legal distinctions (*al-furūq al-fiqhiyya*) and offer a typological explanation of their functions. My discussion relies on both premodern and modern discussions of legal distinctions. As a concept, legal distinctions seem to play the role of a kind of doctrinal gatekeeper, certain doctrines are preferred over others. Legal distinctions also play a role in legal disputation (*jadal*), as mentioned in the premodern discussions.

---

1 Yaʿqūb ibn ʿAbd al-Wahhāb al-Bāḥusayn, *al-Furūq al-fiqhiyya wa-l-uṣūliyya: muqawwamātuhā shurūṭuhā nash'atuhā taṭawwuruhā; dirāsa naẓariyya waṣfiyya tārīkhiyya* (Riyadh: Maktabat al-Rushd, 1419/1998), 14–15.

2 Ḥanbalī works of legal distinctions first appear in the seventh/thirteenth century.

https://doi.org/10.1515/9783110605792-003

After exploring premodern and modern definitions of legal distinctions, this chapter analyzes the ways in which works of legal distinctions are introduced. In these introductory comments, authors generally repeat similar themes alluding to the importance of their works for students of Islamic law. Legal distinctions are presented to us as supplementary works available to students. The discussions that elucidate the differences between two similar fact-patterns makes these works beneficial to law students. Given the reality of legal complexity, distinctions help to systematize and organize legal knowledge. Taken together, a relatively clear definition of legal distinctions emerges. As a genre, these texts contain comparisons of legal rulings and the legal reasoning undergirding these rulings.

Defining Legal Distinctions

Premodern works of legal distinctions are rarely self-conscious, that is, they do not explicitly discuss precisely what legal distinctions are. For us, however, it is important to understand what a legal distinction is and how it functions before analyzing the history of the genre of legal distinctions. First, this section covers premodern understandings of legal distinctions, focusing on three discussions, by Abū Muḥammad ʿAbdallāh al-Juwaynī (d. 438/1047), Najm al-Dīn al-Ṭūfī (d. 716/1316), and Badr al-Dīn al-Zarkashī (d. 794/1392). These three discussions all focus on the relationship between legal distinctions and legal disputation, a topic to which we shall return in Chapter Three, as well as the resolution of apparent doctrinal inconsistencies. We then turn to twentieth-century discussions of legal distinctions in the writings of Joseph Schacht, Yaʿqūb al-Bāḥusayn, Wolfhart Heinrichs, and Necmettin Kızılkaya. Taken together, these understandings of legal distinctions will guide our explorations throughout this book.

Premodern Definitions

Ironically, the paucity of premodern definitions of what constitutes a legal distinction appears to suggest a widespread and shared understanding of the topic among both authors and their readers. There is no need to spend time defining a concept if everyone already understands it. Indeed, works of legal distinctions themselves all share a similar conceptual framework and organization. This means that works of legal distinctions are recognizable, both in the way that they organize legal distinctions and in the rhetoric through which they present legal distinctions. That this shared understanding of legal distinctions can be seen from the earliest works in this genre suggests that the concept of legal distinctions predates the composition of legal distinctions treatises. Nevertheless, the discussions on the nature of legal distinctions that are preserved provide important insight into the way that legal distinctions have been understood historically.

Abū Muḥammad ʿAbdallāh al-Juwaynī

The earliest theoretical discussion of legal distinctions appears in a work of legal distinctions by Abū Muḥammad ʿAbdallāh al-Juwaynī, the father of the more famous Imām al-Ḥaramayn Abū l-Maʿālī l-Juwaynī (d. 478/1085). His *al-Farq wa-l-jamʿ*, alternatively known as *Kitāb al-Furūq*, begins with a lengthy introduction detailing his theory of legal distinctions. Al-Juwaynī's discussion is unique in its depth and breadth. He offers a threefold typology of legal distinctions. I shall explain this typology briefly, and then provide examples and further explanation of each type.

The first type of distinctions obtains when "there are two issues on which the legal school does not disagree, which have a similar appearances but a contradictory ruling."[3] What this means is a comparison of different laws that only appear to contradict, but do not, in fact, contradict.[4] This is the most basic and common kind of legal distinction, both in al-Juwaynī's treatise and in the genre of legal distinctions generally. The second and third type of distinction are rarer and both consider uncertainty regarding which legal consideration is favored in the *madhhab*. The second type of distinctions obtains "when two questions arise that appear to be the same and al-Shāfiʿī [(d. 204/820)] gave a categorical response to one of the questions and made the other ruling dependent on some factor" (*qaṭaʿa qawlahu bi-jawābihi fī iḥdāhimā wa-ʿallaqa qawlahu bi-l-ukhrā*).[5] This type of distinction involves understanding the particularities of the substantive doctrine of Muḥammad ibn Idrīs al-Shāfiʿī, the eponym of the

---

3 Abū Muḥammad ʿAbdallāh ibn Yūsuf al-Juwaynī, *al-Jamʿ wa-l-farq*, 3 vols., ed. ʿAbd al-Raḥmān ibn Salāmah ibn ʿAbdallāh al-Mazīnī (Beirut: Dār al-Jīl, 1424/2004), 1:39. *An yuṣādifa masʾalatayn lam yakhtalif al-madhhab fīhima wa-lā fī wāḥida minhuma wa-l-ṣūra mutashābiha wa-l-ḥukmān mukhtalifān.*

4 While the rulings contradict, the laws do not contradict since the appearance or fact-pattern are not equivalent. The nonequivalence of the issues removes the ground for comparison between them. They are simply different rulings for different issues. Since they are different and cannot be compared, they cannot contradict each other.

5 Al-Juwaynī, *al-Jamʿ wa-l-farq*, 1:39 – 41.

Shāfiʿī school. The distinction rests on those statements that al-Shāfiʿī stated as unconditional and those that he said were conditional. Finally, the third type of distinction is that in which "two questions come up which appear to be the same and our legal scholars have mentioned two legal considerations for one of them but given a categorical response for the other" (*tajtamiʿu masʾalatān dhakara mashāyikhunā wajhayn fī iḥdāhima wa-qaṭaʿū l-qawl fī l-ukhra*).[6] This is similar to the second type of distinction, except that it requires a familiarity with the doctrine of school authorities after al-Shāfiʿī.

Although this last group is by far the least common type of distinction, al-Juwaynī spends the most time describing it. There are two subdivisions within this third type: (a) "the two different considerations have equivalent weight" (*an yaqwā kull wāḥid min al-wajhayn*)[7] and (b) "one of the two considerations is weakened by the indicant in the case on which there is no disagreement" (*an yaḍʿufa aḥad al-wajhayn bi-dalīl al-masʾala allatī lam takhtalifū fīhā*).[8] The first subdivision decides between two rulings with equal epistemological value, that is, when there does not seem to be any criterion for preferring one ruling over another. The second evaluates two cases with different rulings and different epistemic values. Al-Juwaynī seems to be asking the following: how should a jurist measure a ruling reached by consensus that applies only indirectly to the case at hand as opposed to a directly relevant ruling on which there is no consensus?

Let us consider this classification more closely. The first type of legal distinction addresses a mistaken identity. In this case, the accusation involves two entirely separate legal issues, which have different rulings attached to them. In these cases, there is no disagreement. The supposed contradiction only arises when someone wrongly supposes two different issues to be the same legal issue. Al-Juwaynī argues that this is the most common kind of distinction, a claim evidenced by other legal distinctions treatises.[9] Al-Juwaynī gives the following example of this type of distinction:

> A ritual prayer is invalid if it is begun with a temporally prior intention, unless this intention is coterminous with the beginning of the prayer (*anna l-ṣalāt lā taṣiḥḥu bi-niyya mutaqaddama ḥattā takūna l-niyya muqtarana bi-awwalihā*).

6 Al-Juwaynī, *al-Jamʿ wa-l-farq*, 1:41.
7 Al-Juwaynī, *al-Jamʿ wa-l-farq*, 1:41.
8 Al-Juwaynī, *al-Jamʿ wa-l-farq*, 1:41.
9 Al-Juwaynī, *al-Jamʿ wa-l-farq*, 1:39. He says the *furūq* of this kind are "practically infinite" (*naẓāʾir hādhā l-qism akthar min an yuḥṣā*).

> A fast, however, is valid even if the intention to fast was made prior to the start of the fast (*wa-yaṣiḥḥu l-ṣawm wa-in kānat al-niyya mutaqaddama ʿalā l-ṣawm bi-l-zamān*).
>
> The distinction between these is the possibility to follow the statement of intention directly by the prayer and the clear inability to follow the statement of intention directly by the fast.[10]

In this example, the doctrinal difference centers on making an intention to perform a ritual act. In the first situation, one must make a mental resolution to pray in the moment before praying. In the second situation, one may make a mental resolution to fast long before the start of the fast. These two situations appear similar since they both involve affirming one's intention to perform a ritual duty. The rulings, however, seem contradictory because the allowable time between resolving to perform the duty and performing the duty differs. Confusion, according to a-Juwaynī, rests on the assumption that all ritual duties are legally similar; that is, confusion arises from assuming that the rules regulating ritual prayer are equivalent to those regulating ritual fasting. Only by first thinking that the acts of prayer and fasting must be alike can one err in this regard. Al-Juwaynī's distinction between these cases endeavors to show that these two rulings are not incongruent; it is the cases themselves that are dissimilar.

The next two kinds of distinction proposed by al-Juwaynī operate differently. These distinctions require determining correct precedent. Here, the apparently distinct situations really are similar in some way, and resolving the incongruity results from determining the relevant precedential opinions. Al-Juwaynī cites a case in which al-Shāfiʿī gives apparently conflicting opinions:

> Al-Shāfiʿī, may God be pleased with him, had two rulings in regard to a hired worker (*al-ajīr al-mushtarik*) in cases when the capital is destroyed while in his possession.
>
> One ruling is that the worker is liable for the value of the capital (*ḍāmin*). The other is that he is exempt from any liabilities (*barīʾ ʿan al-ḍamāʾin*).
>
> Thus, if someone hires a man as a worker to perform work in his workshop and something is destroyed while in the worker's possession, al-Shāfiʿī has stated categorically (*qaṭaʿa al-qawl*) that he is not liable, even though both of them are laborers.[11]

According to al-Juwaynī, al-Shāfiʿī said that a hired worker both is and is not liable for damages to the goods with which he is working. Al-Juwaynī presents these statements without further explanation or information. He does not contextualize this information nor explain where it was that al-Shāfiʿī made these

10 Al-Juwaynī, *al-Jamʿ wa-l-farq*, 1:39.
11 Al-Juwaynī, *al-Jamʿ wa-l-farq*, 1:40.

statements, in what text, on what basis, etc. He simply presents this contradiction as a known fact, although he will later offer a partial contextualization. Al-Juwaynī is addressing an audience expected to be familiar with the Shāfiʿī legal school and its doctrines such that the aforementioned matters do not need to be explained in full. This exposition, however, makes clear not only the contradiction inherent in al-Shāfiʿī's doctrine, but also how it manifests itself in an applied setting.

Next, Al-Juwaynī seeks to resolve the contradiction between the two rules, writing:

> The distinction between them is that an independent laborer (*al-ajīr al-mushtarik*) has possession of the countervalue that corresponds to the price of his labor. Thus, he can be held liable for the destruction of the good. A worker in a workshop, however, is not in sole possession, but rather the owner of the workshop has possession (*al-yad*) of what is in his workshop. Thus, the destruction of something in the possession of the worker (*fī yad al-ajīr*) is like the death of a slave in the possession of his owner (*fī yaday sayyidihi*) through phlebotomy or cupping during an operation. The phlebotomist is not liable.[12]

Al-Juwaynī distinguishes between two types of workers, arguing that an independent laborer is not equivalent to an employee in a workshop (*al-ajīr fī l-ḥānūt*) when it comes to damages. The former is liable for damages because he has the goods in his sole possession (*al-yad lahu*), while the latter is exempt because the goods remain in the store and therefore in the possession of the storeowner (*al-yad li-ṣāḥib al-ḥānūt*). Al-Juwaynī asserts that the determinant of liability in these situations is possession, not the legal status of the laborer as a hired worker.[13] In other words, whoever possess the goods is responsible for damages, not the one who committed the damage.

Al-Juwaynī compares this legal issue to the non-liability of a doctor when treating someone's slave. The doctor is not responsible for any damages to the slave because damages happen while the slave is in the care and custody of his master (*fī yaday sayyidihi*). This physician is thus legally equivalent to a worker in a shop. Despite the implicit general rule, that liability for damages due to negligence falls on whoever has possession of the damaged good, al-Juwaynī does not state such a general rule explicitly. Al-Juwaynī's discussion is not concerned with a systematic elaboration of doctrine, but rather with distinguishing between certain cases and positing an analogy between others. Indeed,

---

12 Al-Juwaynī, *al-Jamʿ wa-l-farq*, 1:40 – 41.

13 Indeed, this may also explain the seeming inconsistency in labelling one worker the worker in a workshop rather than a hired worker (*al-ajīr al-mushtarak*). This seeming incongruity also explains why I translate this term, *al-ajīr al-mushtarak*, differently in this passage.

it seems that al-Juwaynī locates an instance of apparent doctrinal contradiction in the work of al-Shāfiʿī and then resolves this contradiction through an appeal to the prevailing interpretations of the Shāfiʿī *madhhab.*

Although al-Juwaynī clears away the contradiction as a part of the authoritative doctrine of the Shāfiʿī legal school, his explanation ignores the potentially contradictory nature of the two statements attributed to al-Shāfiʿī. While there are several possibilities for harmonizing al-Shāfiʿī's two statements, al-Juwaynī seems uninterested in undertaking this specific task. Instead, his concern is with the coherence of the Shāfiʿī *madhhab* as developed over the centuries by later jurists. It may be the case that al-Juwaynī sees Muḥammad ibn Idrīs al-Shāfiʿī's substantive doctrine and the doctrinal elaborations of the legal school that bears his name as extensions of each other, such that resolving apparent contradictions found in the doctrine of the Shāfiʿī school implicitly performs the same work for the doctrine of its eponym. Nevertheless, it is worth noting that al-Juwaynī's interest lies primarily in the Shāfiʿī *madhhab* as an elaborated scholarly-legal institution rather than in explicitly defending the specific doctrines of Muḥammad ibn Idrīs al-Shāfiʿī. In other words, the authority or validity of the *madhhab* as expressed here lies in the rationality of its doctrine and is not tied to the explicit words and writings of its assumed founder.[14]

In this discussion, al-Juwaynī is concerned with establishing the absolute coherence of the doctrine attributed to Muḥammad ibn Idrīs al-Shāfiʿī. His discussion therefore avoids instances in which al-Shāfiʿī's doctrine may actually contradict. In part, this is a generic constraint; legal distinctions treatises serve to show the lack of internal doctrinal contradiction, and admitting the possibility of such contradiction would defeat the purpose of the treatise. For al-Juwaynī in this work, the fact that Shāfiʿī scholars have found a way to harmonize al-Shāfiʿī's statements is sufficient to show that al-Shāfiʿī's doctrine is not inconsistent or at odds with itself.

The third category in al-Juwaynī's heuristic is similar to the second. Instead of focusing on the teachings and doctrines of al-Shāfiʿī and the interpretations thereof, however, this category is concerned with the teachings and writings of other scholars affiliated with the Shāfiʿī *madhhab.* Since the first subcategory

---

14 Al-Juwaynī may have seen this distinction as trivial, since a legal school can be seen as a large-scale hermeneutic project to harmonize, expand, and perfect the ideas of its eponym. The way in which the *madhhab* is defended, however, is noteworthy. In other words, al-Shāfiʿī's doctrine and the doctrines of his students as recorded in writing seem to have been less important than the interpretations of those doctrines elaborated by the later Shāfiʿī *madhhab.*

here is equivalent to category two above, al Juwaynī omits a fuller discussion of it.[15]

Al-Juwaynī's discussion of his second subcategory (namely, that one of two seemingly contradictory realings turns out to be weaker than the other) is worth quoting in full because it reveals a great deal about how ramified legal thought had become already by the fifth/eleventh century. Al-Juwaynī defines this subcategory, but refrains from quoting any particular examples of this topic, perhaps because of their relative infrequency. It remains unclear whether we can infer from the lack of examples here that this particular sub-type was more theoretical than practical in his eyes.[16]

> The second subcategory obtains when the applicability of one of the two considerations is weakened by an indicant in the unanimously agreed-upon case. Maintaining a clear distinction then becomes impossible. In such a situation, one should strive to deem the weaker of the two considerations untenable and dismiss it, rather than strive to discover the basis for a distinction and rationalizing it, not even by extrapolating from the two considerations on the basis of the unanimous accepted ruling. Wayward speculation and farfetched extrapolations are rampant in this category. Expending great energy on invalidating weaker considerations is more important than both wayward speculation and rampant proliferation in authoritative legal considerations and extrapolating from them.[17] When we come across examples of this subcategory, we shall mention them but we have already explained the reasoning in these cases.[18]

Here, legal distinctions have become a methodology for reining in the growth of authoritative school doctrine. As the Shāfiʿī legal school developed, jurists continued to elaborate substantive law based on the doctrine and method laid out by Muḥammad ibn Idrīs al-Shāfiʿī. The more jurists pronounced their own particular opinions, the more unwieldy the totality of Shāfiʿī doctrine became. Al-Ju-

---

15 In other words, this subcategory is fully equivalent to category two, except the harmonization techniques are not applied to the substantive doctrine of al-Shāfiʿī, but rather to considerations of prominent Shāfiʿī jurists. Al-Juwaynī, *al-Jamʿ wa-l-farq*, 1:41.

16 It was, perhaps, aspirational as well.

17 This statement should be understood as promoting the rigor of the *madhhab* in order to prevail in a legal disputation, not necessarily as related to the desirability of *ijmāʿ*.

18 Al-Juwaynī, *al-Jamʿ wa-l-farq*, 1:41. I give a full transliteration of this passage because of the subtle ways it discusses legal epistemology and legal elaboration: *al-qism al-ākhir an yaḍʿufa aḥad al-wajhayn bi-dalīl al-masʾala llatī lam yakhtalifū fīhā. fa-yataʿadhdharu l-farq al-wāḍiḥ fa-shtaghil fī mithl hādhā l-mawḍiʿ bi-tazyīf aḍʿaf al-wajhayn wa-isqāṭihi. wa-lā tashtaghil bi-ltimās al-farq fa-yataʿadhdharu wa-lā bi-takhrīj al-wajhayn fī l-masʾala l-mujmaʿ ʿalayhā. wa-fī hādhā l-qism yakthuru l-taʿassuf wa-l-takhrījāt al-mustaḍʿafa. wa-ṣarf al-ʿināya ilā isqāṭ baʿḍ al-wujūh al-ḍaʿīfa awlā min al-taʿassuf wa-l-wulūʿ bi-stikthār al-wujūh wa-takhrījihā. wa-idhā ntahaynā ilā amthilat hādhā l-qism dhakarnāhā wa-mahhadnā hādhihī l-ṭarīqa fīhā in shāʾ allāh.*

waynī seems to suggest that legal distinctions are one way to slow this growth and that constraining the doctrinal growth of the school is a better use of jurists' time than developing their own particular doctrine.

Extrapolation (*takhrīj*) seems to have been one of, if not the, primary method of legal derivation after the onset of the so-called "regime of *taqlīd*."[19] The formalization of Islamic law involved the formalization of distinct legal schools following the doctrine of their eponyms, Abū Ḥanīfa l-Nuʿmān ibn Thābit (d. 150/767), Mālik ibn Anas (d. 179/795), Muḥammad ibn Idrīs al-Shāfiʿī, and Aḥmad ibn Ḥanbal (d. 241/855).[20] *Taqlīd* can perhaps be understood best as a discursive commitment to adhering diligently to already established legal interpretations set out by the earliest figures in a legal school. Discursive adherence implied a shift away from labeling one's own juristic techniques as *ijtihād*, independent legal reasoning, since one's legal reasoning should occur within the established bounds of the legal school.

Operating under the regime of *taqlīd* imposed certain strictures on jurists. Instead of independent legal reasoning, jurists called their reasoning extrapolation (*takhrīj*), based on the writings of previous authorities.[21] Later jurists based their reasoning and interpretations on the works of earlier master jurists. Extrapolat-

---

19 The idea of *taqlīd* has long been a subject of scholarly attention. *Taqlīd*, in this context, refers to the faithfulness on the part of jurists to the juristic authority of earlier jurists. On *taqlīd*, see Sherman Jackson, "*Taqlīd*, Legal Scaffolding and the Scope of Legal Injunctions in Post-Formative Theory: *Muṭlaq* and *ʿĀmm* in the Jurisprudence of Shihāb al-Dīn al-Qarāfī," *Islamic Law and Society* 3.2 (1996): 165–92; Mohammad Fadel, "The Social Logic of *Taqlīd* and the Rise of the *Mukhtaṣar*," *Islamic Law and Society* 3.2 (1996): 193–223; Ahmed Fekry Ibrahim, *Pragmatism in Islamic Law: A Social and Intellectual History* (Syracuse, NY: Syracuse University Press, 2015), 1–30. On *takhrīj*, see Wael Hallaq, *Authority, Continuity, and Change in Islamic Law* (Cambridge: Cambridge University Press, 2005), 43–56; *idem*, "*Takhrīj* and the Construction of Juristic Authority," in *Studies in Islamic Legal Theory*, ed. Bernard Weiss (Leiden: Brill, 2002), 317–35; and Ahmad A. Ahmad, *Structural Interrelations of Theory and Practice in Islamic Law: A Study of Six Works of Medieval Islamic Jurisprudence* (Leiden: Brill, 2006), 1–4, 49–72. See also Talal Al-Azem's recent work in which he argues for the importance of *tarjīḥ*, a process of rule-formation, through which precedential opinions are created and established, Talal Al-Azem, *Rule-Formulation and Binding Precedent in the* Madhhab-*Law Tradition* (Leiden: Brill, 2016).

20 Christopher Melchert locates the emergence of the legal schools in the fourth/tenth century. In his account, Ibn Surayj (d. 306/918) established the Shāfiʿī school, Abū Bakr al-Khallāl (d. 311/923) established the Ḥanbalī school, and Abū Ḥasan al-Karkhī (d. 340/952) established the Ḥanafī school. All three of these figures lived in Baghdad. The Mālikī school had a double history, according to Melchert. In al-Andalus, it was established by ʿĪsā ibn Dīnār (d. 212/827–28) and Yaḥya ibn Yaḥya al-Laythī (d. 234/849) in Toledo. The Eastern Mālikī school was established by Abū Bakr al-Abharī (d. 375/986) in Baghdad but only lasted seventy-five years. Christopher Melchert, *The Formation of the Sunni Schools of Law, 9th–10th centuries C.E.* (Leiden: Brill, 1997).

21 Hallaq, *Authority*, 43–56; Ahmed, *Structural Interrelations*, 1–4, 57–59, 189–92.

ing on the basis of earlier jurists gave later jurists a way to elaborate on substantive law and engage in legal reasoning. At the same time, they could argue that they were remaining within the institutional confines of their respective legal school. Modern scholars have tended to view this methodology as a kind of decadence, although recent scholarship has challenged this narrative of *taqlīd* as decay. More productively, *taqlīd* may be understood as a discursive, rather than practical, move, and may even described as merely amounting to "adherence to the rule of law,"[22] or as Ahmed Fekry Ibrahim puts it, "legal conformism."[23] Thus, *taqlīd* helps establish predictable rules.[24]

Extrapolating new opinions based on previous ones poses a problem for the discursive adherence expected in *taqlīd*. The problem is not merely the exercise of legal reasoning, but rather the infinite potential that extrapolation holds.[25] Al-Juwaynī utilizes the logic of legal distinctions in order to impose limits on doctrinal growth. This subset of distinctions serves to limit the speculative extrapolation, underscoring the importance of expending energy invalidating the weak points of legal doctrine.[26] By ensuring that Shāfiʿī legal doctrine is coherent, rationally derived, and appropriately citing source texts, al-Juwaynī is preparing Shāfiʿī jurists for formalized disputation (*jadal*) in which they can demonstrate the soundness and correctness of their school doctrine. Discussing distinctions in the context of disputations allows al-Juwaynī to present his distinctions both as ways to overcome the accusation of *farq qua* contradiction and potentially to make this charge himself against other Shāfiʿī jurists.

This treatment shows that, for al-Juwaynī, determining the distinguishing features—drawing a distinction—between what appear to be similar cases is helpful for resolving apparent contradictions. This comparative approach can

---

22 David S. Powers, *Law, Society, and Culture in the Maghrib, 1300–1500* (Cambridge: Cambridge University Press, 2002), 94.

23 Ibrahim, *Pragmatism*, 10.

24 See, among others, Wael Hallaq, "From *Fatwās* to *Furūʿ*: Growth and Change in Islamic Substantive Law," *Islamic Law and Society* 1 (1994): 29–65; and more recently, *idem*, *Sharīʿa: Theory, Practice, Transformations* (Cambridge: Cambridge University Press, 2009); Sherman Jackson, *Islamic Law and the State: The Constitutional Jurisprudence of Shihāb al-Dīn al-Qarāfī* (Leiden: Brill, 1996); and Norman Calder, *Islamic Jurisprudence in the Classical Era*, ed. Colin Imber (Cambridge: Cambridge University Press, 2010), among many other works.

25 Ahmed Fekry Ibrahim, "The Codification Episteme in Islamic Juristic Discourse between Inertia and Change," *Islamic Law and Society* 22 (2015): 157–220.

26 Al-Juwaynī, *al-Jamʿ wa-l-farq*, 1:41. A concern for controlling the growth of legal doctrine was a recurring topic in post-formative Islamic legal writing. See Hallaq, *Authority*, 236–41; and Norman Calder, "al-Nawawī's Typology of Muftis and Its Significance for a General Theory of Islamic Law," *Islamic Law and Society* 3.2 (1996), 137–64, especially 137–43.

also provide a method for reasoning through different kinds of ambiguous or uncertain legal issues. In his view, thinking through legal distinctions acts as a defensive and pedagogical intellectual maneuver serving to justify the doctrine of a particular legal school, by teaching the rationales for specific points of legal doctrine.

Al-Juwaynī's classification establishes a hierarchy between different types of legal distinctions. His hierarchy can be read in two separate ways. First, it helps him organize the different kinds of *furūq* according to epistemic criteria. The first type of legal distinction, between actually different, but apparently similar issues, involves no epistemic conflict, but clarifies the scope of applicability of two different laws. The second type, involving clear and ambiguous statements made by al-Shāfiʿī considers the opinions of the school's eponym; as the founder of the legal school to which the rest of the Shāfiʿī jurists adhere, his opinions enjoy epistemic authority over those of other jurists. And the third type tackles disagreements between later jurists, which carry the least authority. For the reader of his work, applying earlier rulings forms an essential part of the academic formation of a jurist.

In fact, this typology also tracks the educational formation of a jurist. The first type of distinction is the simplest. These involve understanding the correct ruling to apply to a particular situation. The second type is more complex and involves knowing how to judge between various foundational statements and doctrines. The third type is more specific and involves judging between the doctrine of previous scholarly authorities. In this way, al-Juwaynī's scheme progresses from a basic understanding of substantive law to that of the founder to that of the universe of different Shāfiʿī jurists.

Al-Juwaynī's typology pertains to the contents of his work, but more broadly seeks to classify Shāfiʿī doctrine. *Furūq* can serve to constrain doctrinal growth and thereby minimize the accusations of contradictions that may be lobbed at a Shāfiʿī jurist in the course of a formal disputation (*mujādala* or *munāẓara*). These were not merely hypothetical objections but instead correspond to the very ones found in recordings of real disputations and paradigmatic accounts in writing.[27] Thus, al-Juwaynī seeks to preempt accusations of contradiction by arguing that an opponent does not understand (i) the scope of applicability of seemingly overlapping rules, (ii) the nuances of al-Shāfiʿī's vast legal doctrine,[28]

27 On legal debates, see Chapter Three.

28 The history of al-Shāfiʿī's substantive legal doctrine is complex. Not only was his writing preserved and transmitted in slightly different versions by his students, but he is also said to have produced a version of his legal doctrine in Iraq and a different and revamped version in Egypt, the so-called old (*al-qadīm*) and new (*al-jadīd*) doctrines. For more on this issue, see Ahmed El

or (iii) how to reason through competing statements of substantive law by later Shafiʿī authorities. In other words, according to al-Juwaynī, non-Shāfiʿīs could accuse a Shāfiʿī of contradiction because the non-Shāfiʿī did not understand how to make the complexity inherent in the substantive doctrine of the Shāfiʿī legal school coherent. Of course, it should not be surprising for a Shāfiʿī scholar to claim that others do not understand the depth and complexity of Shāfiʿī doctrine. Nevertheless, al-Juwaynī's claim helps clarify the role of *furūq* in regulating school doctrine and in inter-*madhhab* disputation.

Najm al-Dīn al-Ṭūfī

A second discussion of *furūq* appears in Najm al-Dīn al-Ṭūfī's manual for legal disputation, *ʿAlam al-jadhal fī ʿilm al-jadal.*[29] This discussion, too, is couched in the terms of legal dialectics. Al-Ṭūfī's discussion of *furūq* appears in the section titled "Counter-Objections Based on *Qiyās*." The seventeenth kind of disputational objection based on *qiyās* is distinction (*farq*), which I refer to as a *farq*-objection. In his presentation, a *farq*-objection "discovers a characteristic in either the precedent case or the instant case that entails a specific legal ruling (*ibdāʾ waṣf fī l-aṣl aw al-farʿ yunāsibu mā khtaṣṣa bihi min al-ḥukm*)."[30] In other words, a *farq*-objection is a claim to a legally compelling similarity—a shared legal rationale—between two cases of law. Unlike al-Juwaynī's discussion, al-Ṭūfī understands *furūq* as primarily a disputational maneuver related to the proper exercise of legal reasoning. He continues his discussion with an explanation of how to recognize when a *farq*-objection may be lodged in a disputation. "The necessary condition for a distinction is that the two fact-patterns share multiple legally relevant characteristics, otherwise the difference between the two cases is a fundamental difference and an objection based on distinction would be ineffective."[31] According to this statement, in order to use a *farq*-objection, one must compare two situations that share several relevant characteristics. The similarities shared by two fact-patterns invite comparison and allow the possibility that they may be treated the same way legally. This discussion guides participants in debates in overcoming objections.

Shamsy, *The Canonization of Islamic Law: A Social and Intellectual History* (New York: Cambridge University Press, 2013).

29 I discuss the relationship between distinctions and disputation in Chapter Three.

30 Najm al-Dīn Sulaymān ibn ʿAbd al-Qawī l-Ṭūfī, *ʿAlam al-jadhal fī ʿilm al-jadal*, ed. Wolfhart Heinrichs (Wiesbaden: Franz Steiner Verlag, 1408/1987), 71.

31 Najm al-Dīn al-Ṭūfī, *ʿAlam al-jadhal*, 71.

It may seem that al-Ṭūfī's understanding of *furūq* is fundamentally different from that of al-Juwaynī. Al-Juwaynī is only partly interested in disputation, and focuses as well on the potential of *furūq* for disambiguating substantive legal doctrine. Despite the explicit focus on disputation, al-Ṭūfī's analysis is actually quite similar to al-Juwaynī's. The shared characteristics that enable comparison are legal rationales (*ʿilal*) that result in similar rulings. The differing characteristic (*al-fāriq*), however, is the actual legal rationale that gives one of the two compared fact-patterns a legal outcome distinction from the original fact-pattern. This is very similar to al-Juwaynī's first type of legal distinction, which involves distinguishing between two fact-patterns that share only a superficial resemblance. Further, even though al-Ṭūfī's discussion appears in the context of guidelines for formal legal disputations, he addresses the larger subject of legal *furūq* by offering a list of the treatises written on this subject. "Scholars have written many treatises on the distinctions between rulings (*al-furūq bayn al-aḥkām*)."[32] The treatises he lists are those discussed in this study, including al-Juywaynī's *al-Jamʿ wa-l-farq*.[33] He seems to understand these texts as an extension of distinctions *qua* disputational objections.

Badr al-Dīn al-Zarkashī

Finally, the Shāfiʿī scholar Badr al-Dīn al-Zarkashī includes a short discussion of legal distinctions in his *al-Manthūr fī l-qawāʿid*. Noting that "the law has many subdisciplines" (*al-fiqh anwāʿ*), the author addresses "knowledge of assimilation and distinction" (*maʿrifat al-jamʿ wa-l-farq*).[34] In his recounting, "among the best works written on this topic is the treatise by the scholar Abū Muḥammad [ʿAbdallāh] al-Juwaynī."[35] This is a telling account in that al-Zarkashī cites al-Juwaynī's treatise as one of the two principal legal distinctions treatises in the course of his discussion.

Al-Zarkashī seeks to detail the literature related to legal distinctions, writing:

---

32 Najm al-Dīn al-Ṭūfī, *ʿAlam al-jadhal*, 72.

33 Najm al-Dīn al-Ṭūfī, *ʿAlam al-jadhal*, 72–73.

34 Badr al-Dīn Muḥammad ibn Bahādur al-Zarkashī, *al-Manthūr fī l-qawāʿid*, 3 vols., ed. Taysīr Fāʾiq Aḥmad Maḥmūd and ʿAbd al-Sattār Abū Ghudda (Kuwait: Wizārat al-Awqāf wa-l-Shuʾūn al-Islāmiyya, 1402/1982), 1:69. In this phrase, distinction refers to distinguishing between apparently similar cases that are governed by distinct legal rationales. Assimilating refers to bringing together similar cases that are governed by the same legal rationale, that is, to assimilate different cases under one overarching rationale.

35 Al-Zarkashī, *al-Manthūr*, 1:69.

> The second type of knowledge is knowledge of how to assimilate and distinguish between cases. This was the basis for most of the disputations among the early scholars, so much so that one of them said, "Law is nothing other than distinction and assimilation" (*al-fiqh farq wa-jamʿ*).[36] Among the best works written on this topic are the treatises by the renowned Abū Muḥammad al-Juwaynī and Abū l-Khayr ibn Jamāʿa l-Maqdisī [(d. 480/1086)]. Any distinction that can be drawn between two cases is effective as long as the cases cannot be conjecturally assimilated to each other (*kull farq bayn masʾalatayn muʾaththir mā lam yaghlib ʿalā l-ẓann anna l-jāmiʿ aẓhar*).[37] The Imam [al-Zarkashī] said, "It is not sufficient to draw distinctions merely on the basis of one's whims. Rather, if two cases can be assimilated to each other in a way that seems more probable than drawing a distinction between them, then one should rule on the basis that they share a similarity. If the two cases are at odds, however, they should be held to be distinct."[38] The Imam also said, "Understand this well, for it is one of the foundations of the religion (*qawāʿid al-dīn*)."[39]

Al-Zarkashī, accordingly, foregrounds the centrality of legal distinctions within Islamic law. He dutifully lists *al-farq wa-l-jamʿ* (distinctions and assimilation) second in his list of subdisciplines of Islamic law. His subdisciplines are: (i) "knowledge of the substantive laws, both those mentioned explicitly in revelation and those known through legal reasoning";[40] (ii) "*al-farq wa-l-jamʿ*";[41] (iii) "the building of legal cases one on the other such that they all result from one underlying principle";[42] (iv) "difficult questions (*al-muṭāraḥāt*), i.e., obscure questions that are used to test one's intellect";[43] (v) "sophistical argumentation" (? *mughālaṭāt*);[44] (vi) "examinations" (*mumtaḥināt*);[45] (vii) "riddles";[46] (viii) "legal strategems";[47] (ix) "knowledge of individual scholars, [namely,] what spe-

---

36 The source of this aphorism is perhaps Najm al-Dīn al-Ṭūfī. See Najm al-Dīn al-Ṭūfī, *ʿAlam al-jadhal*, 71. See also Heinrichs, "Structuring the Law," 333.

37 This statement should draw to mind al-Ṭūfī's insistence on the importance of shared characteristics.

38 This statement is quite similar to al-Juwaynī's discussion of the typology of legal distinctions. In particular, this statement is reminiscent of his final type, wherein a jurist ought to compare the particular considerations held by prominent jurists of the Shāfiʿī school.

39 Al-Zarkashī, *al-Manthūr*, 1:69.

40 Al-Zarkashī, *al-Manthūr*, 1:69.

41 Al-Zarkashī, *al-Manthūr*, 1:69.

42 Al-Zarkashī, *al-Manthūr*, 1:69–70. Specifically, al-Zarkashī says, "*bināʾ al-masāʾil baʿḍahā ʿalā baʿḍ li-jtimāʿihā fī maʾkhadh wāḥid*." On the concept of legal scaffolding, see Sherman Jackson, "*Taqlīd*."

43 Al-Zarkashī, *al-Manthūr*, 1:70–71.

44 Al-Zarkashī, *al-Manthūr*, 1:71.

45 Al-Zarkashī, *al-Manthūr*, 1:71.

46 Al-Zarkashī, *al-Manthūr*, 1:71.

47 Al-Zarkashī, *al-Manthūr*, 1:71.

cific considerations each took on issues of substantive law";[48] and (x) "knowledge of the specific precepts (*ḍawābiṭ*) that assimilate and the maxims on which legal theory and substantive law depend."[49] This list, which al-Zarkashī uses to situate his work on legal maxims (*qawāʿid*), provides a fascinating insight into the prevailing conceptions of Islamic law in the ninth/fifteenth century.

Al-Zarkashī sees distinctions as a core component of Islamic law. Moreover, he sees distinctions as an area of knowledge separate from the knowledge of substantive law, which he refers to here as "rulings on legal cases" (*aḥkām al-ḥawādith*). Al-Zarkashī's list is also curious in that it does not use the terms *furūʿ* and *uṣūl*, the traditional bipartite division of Islamic law and legal writing, to denote broad categories of legal discourse.[50] It furthermore underscores the importance of al-Juwaynī's treatise on legal distinctions to the Shāfiʿī school and the centrality of disputations in the early rise of legal distinctions, at least for the Shāfiʿī *madhhab*. Al-Ṭūfī also makes a strong connection between legal distinctions treatises and *farq* as a kind of objection made in a legal disputation. Still, al-Zarkashī's discussion adds little to our understanding of what legal distinctions are.

These are the only three theoretical discussions of the genre of legal distinctions of which I am aware. Al-Juwaynī and al-Zarkashī are interested in discussing legal distinctions as a methodology of legal argumentation and legal reasoning. For them, the focus in this field is on resolving apparent contradictions. These three surveys of the place of legal distinctions are all brief. They do not discuss the relationship between theoretical understandings of legal distinctions and legal distinctions treatises nor do they provide information as to where and how legal distinctions texts were used.

---

48 Al-Zarkashī, *al-Manthūr*, 1:71.
49 Al-Zarkashī, *al-Manthūr*, 1:71. Here, *ḍawābiṭ* are understood to relate to one particular field of legal knowledge (purity, sales contracts, oaths, etc.). A jurist can know which *ḍawābiṭ* assimilate when the jurist knows which *ḍawābiṭ* relate to similar fields of legal knowledge.
50 At the end of his entry on *ḍawābiṭ* and *qawāʿid*, al-Zarkashī says "These are the true foundations of the law" (*wa-huwa uṣūl al-fiqh ʿalā l-ḥaqīqa*) (al-Zarkashī, *al-Manthūr*, 1:71). Dividing Islamic Law into either *furūʿ* or *uṣūl* seems to be traditional in the Western study of Islamic law, but it may not be a reflection of the ways in which the Islamic legal tradition has always understood itself. I hope to return to this in a future publication.

Modern Understandings

Most modern definitions and discussions of legal distinctions are quite limited in scope, although some offer a more substantial understanding of the role and history of legal distinctions than the premodern discussions. The majority of modern discussions appear in editors' introductions to printed editions of works of legal distinctions. These introductory essays typically list major works of legal distinctions and their authors, offering a short lexicographical discussion of the root *f-r-q* and its morphological derivates. These works tend to overlap with each other and provide a mostly descriptive discussion of a literary genre.[51] This section, instead, will deal with the major modern studies of legal distinctions, beginning with Joseph Schacht's important 1926 article, and then the works by Yaʿqūb al-Bāḥusayn, Wolfhart Heinrichs, and most recently Necmittin Kızılkaya.

Joseph Schacht wrote what seems to have be the first modern treatment of legal distinctions treatises.[52] Written in the early twentieth century, Schacht's short article is more concerned with introducing works of legal distinctions and understanding their role within Islamic law. His article is not directly engaged with studying the genre or the concept of legal distinctions.[53] In attempting to describe works of legal distinctions, he only repeats the definition given by the classical tradition, "the outward findings of the cases are similar, but the legal assessments differ."[54] Already, however, Schacht dismisses works such as Ibn Taymiyya's *al-Farq al-mubīn bayn al-ṭalāq wa-l-yamīn* as not truly fitting into the genre of legal distinctions.[55]

Yaʿqūb al-Bāḥusayn's *al-Furūq al-fiqhiyya wa-l-uṣūliyya: muqawwamātuhā shurūṭuhā nashʾatuhā taṭawwuruhā; dirāsa naẓariyya waṣfiyya tārīkhiyya* consti-

51 The major exception here is Muḥammad Abū l-Ajfān and Ḥamza Abū Fāris, "*Dirāsa*," in Abū l-Faḍl Muslim al-Dimashqī, *al-Furūq al-fiqhiyya*, ed. Muḥammad Abū l-Ajfān and Ḥamza Abū Fāris (Beirut: Dār al-Gharb al-Islāmī, 1992).

52 Joseph Schacht, "Aus zwei arabischen *Furūq*-Büchern," *Islamica* 2 (1926): 505–37.

53 He also provides lengthy excerpts in Arabic from the distinctions treatises entitled *al-Furūq ʿalā madhhab al-Imām Aḥmad ibn Ḥanbal* by Ibn Sunayna (d. 616/1219) and *Kitāb al-Furūq* attributed to Najm al-Dīn al-Naysābūrī to demonstrate the rhetoric of the genre. I discuss the work by al-Naysābūrī in Chapter Five, pp. 190–91.

54 Schacht, "*Furūq*-Büchern," 512: "die ihrem äußeren Tatbestande nach gleich, in ihrer juristischen Beurteilung aber verschieden sind."

55 Schacht, "*Furūq*-Büchern," 511. See also below and Chapter Two, pp. 77–79. In this study, such works are termed applied lexicographical distinctions and are understood as a separate, though related, form of legal writing.

tutes the first systematic study of the concept of legal distinctions.[56] Al-Bāḥusayn provides a brief theoretical discussion of the kinds of *furūq* writing that differs significantly from that of al-Juwaynī. Al-Baḥusayn finds two different kinds of distinctions in legal writing, legal distinctions (*al-furūq al-fiqhiyya*) and legal-theoretical distinctions (*al-furūq al-uṣūliyya*). In his understanding, legal distinctions focus on correctly determining the legal principles and rationales (*al-ʿilal*) on which rulings are based. Understanding the relevant legal rationale allows a jurist to rule on other cases by following the ruling in the example case. It seems, then, from al-Bāḥusayn's explanations that legal distinctions serve as a kind of test for the correct exercise of legal analogies (*qiyās*). His discussion emphasizes the role of legal distinction as a kind of natural progression of the organization and systematization of legal doctrine.

Al-Bāḥusayn explains that writings on legal distinction have taken different forms.[57] He lists two matters on which all legal distinctions treatises agree and a few in which they differ. According to him, all legal distinctions treatises discuss individual laws and the distinction(s) between them – sometimes they also discuss shared characteristics (*al-jāmiʿ*) – and they all "follow the traditional legal organization."[58] According to al-Bāḥusayn, however, they differ in their particular content. He sees four kinds of works that address legal distinctions: (i) some works discuss only substantive laws that are similar outwardly but have conflicting rulings and the distinctions between them (*dhikr al-furūʿ al-fiqhiyya l-mutashābiha fī l-ṣūra wa-l-mukhtalifa fī l-ḥukm maʿ bayān al-farq baynahumā*);[59] (ii) some discuss maxims (*qawāʿid*) and precepts (*ḍawābiṭ*) in addition to a discussion of legal distinctions;[60] (iii) some address distinctions relat-

56 Al-Bāḥusayn, *al-Furūq al-fiqhiyya.*

57 Al-Bāḥusayn, *al-Furūq al-fiqhiyya*, 79 – 82.

58 Al-Bāḥusayn, *al-Furūq al-fiqhiyya*, 79.

59 Al-Bāḥusayn, *al-Furūq al-fiqhiyya*, 79 – 81. He gives the following as examples of this kind of work: *al-Furūq* by Asʿad ibn Muḥammad al-Karābīsī (d. 570/1174 – 75), *ʿIddat al-burūq fī jamʿ mā fī l-madhhab min al-jumūʿ wa-l-furūq* by Abū l-ʿAbbās al-Wansharīsī (d. 914/1508), *al-Furūq al-fiqhiyya* by Abū l-Faḍl Muslim ibn ʿAlī l-Dimashqī (d. fifth/eleventh c.), and *Īḍāḥ al-dalāʾil fī l-farq bayn al-masāʾil* by ʿAbd al-Rahīm al-Zarīrānī (d. 741/1341).

60 Al-Bāḥusayn, *al-Furūq al-Fiqhiyya*, 81 – 82. He gives the following as examples of this kind of work: *Kitāb al-Munāqaḍāt fī l-ḥaṣr wa-l-istithnāʾ* by Muḥammad ibn al-Ḥusayn al-Fattākī (d. 448/1056 – 57) and *al-Istighnāʾ fī l-farq wa-l-istithnāʾ* by Badr al-Dīn al-Bakrī (d. ninth/fifteenth c.). Al-Bakrī's treatise is also known by the title *al-Iʿtināʾ fī l-farq wa-l-istithnāʾ*. It has been published twice, once under each name. Muḥammad ibn Abī Bakr al-Bakrī, *al-Istighnāʾ fī l-farq wa-l-istithnāʾ*, ed. Saʿūd ibn Musʿad ibn Musāʿid al-Thubaytī (Mecca: Jāmiʿat Umm al-Qurā, Maʿhad al-Buḥūth al-ʿIlmiyya wa-Iḥyāʾ al-Turāth al-Islāmī, Markaz Iḥyāʾ al-Turāth al-Islāmī, 1988) and *ibid.*, *al-Iʿtināʾ fī l-farq wa-l-istihnāʾ: Kitāb yabḥathu fī qawāʿid al-fiqh al-islāmī wa-furūʿihi*, ed.

ed to a specific legal issue;[61] and (iv) some larger works devote one section to legal distinctions.[62]

One noteworthy feature of al-Bāḥusayn's book is his discussion of the function of legal distinctions, in which he explains, normatively, how legal distinctions treatises ought to work.[63] His methodology here is interesting. First, he assumes that legal distinctions function in one of two ways. The first is "a distinction between the precedent case and the instant case (*al-aṣl wa-l-far'*), or between a case resulting from an analogy and the principal case (*al-maqīs wa-l-maqīs 'alayhi*)."[64] Here, legal distinctions function as a measure to control legal analogy and there is little difference between drawing a legal distinction and analyses of individual exercises of analogical reasoning. This is, perhaps, an overdetermination of the importance of analogical reasoning to the development and spread of substantive legal doctrine.

The second way in which al-Bāḥusayn claims that legal distinctions function is by elucidating "a distinction between a descriptive characteristic and a rule (*al-waṣf wa-l-ḥukm*)."[65] This second category, he says, overlaps with the first, and is related to the applicability of a specific ruling to a particular situation. Here, the descriptive characteristic is something broader than a legal rationale. He gives the example of the permissibility of *ẓihār* divorce for Muslims and non-Muslims (*al-dhimmī*). He says that the descriptive characteristic is the permissibility of divorce, the rule is the permissibility of *ẓihār*, the precedent case of that of the Muslim, and the instant case of the the *dhimmī*. In short, Muslims are permitted to divorce and also to divorce via *ẓihār*. *Dhimmī*s are also allowed to divorce, so one may think that they are allowed to divorce via *ẓihār*. This distinction

'Ādil Aḥmad 'Abd al-Mawjūd and 'Alī Muḥammad Mu'awwad (Beirut: Dār al-Kutub al-'Ilmiyya, 1991).

61 Al-Bāḥusayn, *al-Furūq al-fiqhiyya*, 82. Al-Bāḥusayn does not give any examples, but it seems that he is referring to the kinds of works that contain what I term applied linguistic distinctions, see Chapter Two.

62 Al-Bāḥusayn, *al-Furūq al-Fiqhiyya*, 82. Al-Bāḥusayn also does not give an example of this kind of treatise, but rather says that it happens in "texts on legal maxims (*mu'allafāt fī l-qawā'id al-fiqhiyya*)." This kind of discussion can be found in, for example, *al-Ashbāh wa-l-Naẓā'ir* of Ibn Nujaym al-Miṣrī (d. 970/1563).

63 Al-Bāḥusayn, *al-Furūq al-fiqhiyya*, 35–58.

64 Al-Bāḥusayn, *al-Furūq al-fiqhiyya*, 40.

65 Al-Bāḥusayn, *al-Furūq al-fiqhiyya*, 40.

has been drawn along the lines of a descriptive characteristic—Muslim or *dhimmī*—but the actual legal rationale is left unstated.[66]

His discussion of this second type of distinction, however, focuses only on distinctions as they appear in manuals of legal disputation (*jadal*), not in legal distinctions treatises. He treats both kinds of distinctions as if they were equivalent, even though the purpose of referring to a distinction in disputation is different from doing so in distinctions treatises.[67] In disputation, a *farq*-objection is an attempt to trap one's debate opponent in a doctrinal contradiction. One party makes a claim about the legality of one fact-pattern; the other party introduces a seemingly analogous fact-pattern with a different legal ruling. The similarity between the two cases, which al-Bāḥusayn refers to as the shared *waṣf*, is a surface-level similarity that may or may not be relevant to the legal rationale that engendered the original legal rule.[68] In a *furūq* treatise, a series of comparisons between apparently similar fact-patterns that engender differing rulings are brought forward in order to show the lack of doctrinal contradictions within a particular legal school. The analysis in books of distinctions focuses on seeing past the irrelevant situational similarities and highlighting the clearly distinct legal rationale in each fact-pattern. Al-Bāḥusayn assimilates a *farq* in the context of disputation and a *farq* in the context of the genre of legal distinctions in spite of their inherent dissimilarities. It is worth nothing that his discussion does not quote from any legal distinctions treatise, neither to supplement the theoretical component nor to give substantive examples.[69]

The second section of al-Bāḥusayn's book is on legal-theoretical distinctions. These distinctions are, according to him, entirely different from substantive legal distinctions.[70] His categorization parallels one made in the present study, which understands legal distinctions to be different from what I term applied lex-

66 While a *ẓihār* divorce is legally permissible, it is disapproved and requires a penance. The penance of non-Muslims is not accepted in Islamic law, and therefore *ẓihār* divorce is not applicable to non-Muslims.

67 See Chapter Three.

68 As discussed in Chapter Three, the way to overcome a *farq*-objection is to elucidate the distinct legal rationales in each of the two different fact-patterns. At some level, the equivalence in descriptive characteristics is a red herring since the only legally relevant equivalence is in the legal rationale.

69 The paucity of such discussions is likely the major reason for this lacuna.

70 This is a point on which Schacht, al-Bāḥusayn, Heinrichs, and Kızılkaya all agree. The present study also understands an important categorical distinction between these two kinds of works.

icographical distinctions. Al-Bāḥusayn's legal-theoretical distinctions are roughly equivalent to what I term an applied lexicographical distinction.[71]

Wolfhart Heinrichs sees legal distinctions as part of a larger complex of "inductive" reasoning in Islamic law, in conjunction with "*qawāʿid* [legal maxims], and *asbhāh wa naẓāʾir* [cognate and similar legal cases]."[72] He contrasts these three categories of inductive reasoning based on existing substantive laws with *uṣūl al-fiqh*, which he calls "a deductive and hermeneutical procedure trying to establish juridical determinations (*aḥkām*) by deducing them from a correct interpretation of the sources (Qur'an, Sunna, etc.)."[73] For Heinrichs, *furūq* is a productive branch of knowledge for so-called *muqallid*s in that works on *furūq* allow us to see "the *muqallid* as a thinking jurisprudent, not just a parrot."[74] His understanding of *furūq* as one part of a larger complex of understudied productive areas of Islamic law is useful. While al-Juwaynī discusses the use of distinctions for *limiting* the juristic production of rules, Heinrichs' statements nevertheless correspond to how jurists after al-Juwaynī understood the field of distinctions and related activities.

Finally, Necmettin Kızılkaya takes a more expansive view of legal distinctions. In his monograph, he contextualizes *furūq* literature within a broad scholarly context, looking beyond the confines of Islamic law. Kızılkaya's study is a survey of legal distinctions as a concept. In his analysis, *furūq* is one method for analyzing Islamic law, and he relates it to hermeneutic tools such as *ẓāhir* vs. *bāṭin*, *mabnā* vs. *maʿnā*, and *ṣūra* vs. *ḥukm*.[75] The concept of *furūq* in Islamic law, of course, is also related to *furūq* in other disciplines.[76] For Kızılkaya, perhaps the most important feature of *furūq* literature is the way that it tracks the development of juristic authority and the rise and fall of *ijtihād*.[77] The majority of his monograph, however, consists of brief discussions of the *furūq* literature as he sees it, with comments on all legal distinctions treatises and their authors.[78]

---

71 See Chapter Two, pp. 77–79 and Excursus, pp. 110–112.
72 Heinrichs, "Structuring the Law," 335. As discussed in the introduction, *al-ashbāh wa-l-naẓāʾir* refers to a genre of legal writing.
73 Heinrichs, "Structuring the Law," 335.
74 Heinrichs, "Structuring the Law," 340.
75 Kızılkaya, *İslâm hukukunda farklar: Furûk literatürü üzerine bir inceleme* (Istanbul: İz Yayıncılık, 2016), 28–32.
76 Kızılkaya, *İslâm hukukunda farklar*, 33–48.
77 Kızılkaya, *İslâm hukukunda farklar*, 89–120.
78 Kızılkaya, *İslâm hukukunda farklar*, 121–208.

We learn from all of the above discussions of distinctions, however, that legal distinctions treatises focus on apparently conflicting substantive laws within one *madhhab*. It is not necessarily problematic that two different legal schools will have different rulings for particular actions. This kind of normative pluralism was a well-accepted reality within Islamic law.[79] In and of itself, disagreements across legal schools does not engender the supposed systemic contradictions brought about by conflicting laws within one and the same legal school. Authors of *furūq* works are concerned, rather, with explaining legal contradictions that arise within a given school's doctrine.

Reading only the *furūq* literature, one may assume that, properly understood, a specific *madhhab* does not have any internal doctrinal contradictions. This, of course, is inconsistent with the understood history of Islamic law, in which differences and contradictions are widely acknowledged and even celebrated.[80] This outlook, in which contradictions or inconsistencies are a problem to be resolved, should not be imputed to those jurists who contributed to the genre of legal distinctions but rather understood to be a constraint of *furūq* writing.[81] ʿAbdallāh al-Juwaynī, as a scholar, certainly understood the doctrinal disagreements among jurists in the Shāfiʿī school. As an author of a work of *furūq*, however, his text must largely look past these disagreements to present a harmonious vision of the Shāfiʿī *madhhab*. While we may understand the function of legal distinctions, the reasons why jurists wrote works in this genre is addressed in the next section.

Justifications for Legal Distinctions

Legal distinctions treatises do not generally begin with a theoretical discussion of legal distinctions; instead, many authors introduce their works by saying that they are writing in response to a request from students or others interested in Islamic law. While such apologetic introductions are a common trope of medieval Arabic writing, the recurrence of these formulas remains instructive. Moreover, an examination of these justifications can give us insight into what it was that motivated jurists to write works of legal distinctions.

The earliest authors of these works portray the study of legal distinctions as a way to understand the subtleties of a school's doctrine and emphasize the im-

---

79 EI^2 s.v. "Ikhtilāf" (Joseph Schacht).

80 See Wael Hallaq, *Authority*.

81 Using Wittgenstein's terminology, it may also be said that assuming that one's *madhhab* is doctrinally harmonious is a rule of the game of legal distinctions.

portance of such unprecedented works on these grounds; that is, as a kind of natural result from the systematization of the legal school. Al-Juwaynī's introduction is noteworthy in this regard, in that he approaches the topic as if it were a new subject with which the reader is not necessarily familiar. He starts by saying:

> Legal problems can resemble each other outwardly but have contrasting outcomes (*qad tatashābahu ṣuwaruhā wa-takhtalifu aḥkāmhuhā*) because of legal rationales (*ʿilal*) that require different rulings. Those who seek true answers cannot do so without careful study of these legal rationales, which necessitates distinguishing what needs to be distinguished and assimilating what needs to be assimilated. Thus, through God's will, may He be exalted, and His providence, we have collected legal issues and distinctions in this treatise, some of which are more obscure than others.[82]

Al-Juwaynī begins his treatise by introducing the topic of legal distinctions with both a definition and a justification of the need for studying distinctions: distinctions enable one to understand legal rules with precision. It is clear that he sees legal distinctions as a way of understanding the intricacies of the doctrines of the Shāfiʿī school, but cannot take his audience's knowledge of the concept or genre of distinctions as a given. This implies that al-Juwaynī understood himself to be among the first Shāfiʿī scholars, if not the first member of the school, to write a treatise on legal distinctions.[83] Al-Juwaynī's detailed explanation of legal distinctions and his lack of reference to similar works is circumstantial evidence of the primacy of his work in the genre of legal distinctions. His view, however, that legal distinctions are a way of understanding the intricacies of Islamic law or of a legal school's doctrine is echoed in other works of this genre.

The introduction to *al-Nukat wa-l-furūq* by ʿAbd al-Ḥaqq al-Ṣiqillī (d. 466/1073–74) is similar. ʿAbd al-Ḥaqq, however, adds a mention of the intended audience of his work:

> A student of Mālikī law asked me for help in collecting the particular legal questions from *al-Mudawwana* and *al-Mukhtalaṭa*[84] that novice and beginning students need to learn, to-

---

82 Al-Juwaynī, *al-Jamʿ wa-l-farq*, 1:37.

83 There are some reports in the biographical tradition ascribing a treatise of legal distinctions to Ibn Surayj, although it is unlikely that he wrote such a work. See Abū Isḥāq al-Shīrāzī, *Ṭabaqāt al-fuqahāʾ*, ed. Iḥsān ʿAbbās (Beirut: Dār al-Rāʾid al-ʿArabī, 1970), 109.

84 *Al-Mudawwana* and *al-Mukhtalaṭa* are two of the foundational texts of the Mālikī legal school. Both texts were compiled by the Mālikī scholar Saḥnūn ibn Saʿīd (d. 240/855). *Al-Mudawwana* contains legal opinions from the school's eponym, Mālik ibn Anas, with some additions by Mālikī scholars from Ibn al-Qāsim (d. 191/806) through Saḥnūn. *Al-Mukhtalaṭa* primarily contains opinions going back to Saḥnūn himself. See Miklos Muranyi, *Die*

gether with issues that I find important to understand, distinctions between legal issues, and the differences between the rulings that would otherwise be impossible for students to know.[85]

In introducing his treatise with this claim, ʿAbd al-Ḥaqq notes that the intended audience for his work are students who are still learning the law. This should not necessarily be understood to mean something akin to first-year or introductory students, but rather that the treatise is not aimed at fully formed jurists. ʿAbd al-Ḥaqq's treatise is intended to be a part of legal education, as a supplement to the existing works of law. From his description, it could be of use to students studying formally in a madrasa or informally in study circles.[86]

ʿAbd al-Ḥaqq's *al-Nukat wa-l-furūq* is an early treatise in the genre of legal distinctions in which the author signals that this is a new form of legal composition. Nevertheless, ʿAbd al-Ḥaqq asserts that the existence of distinctions between similar laws has long been a part of Islamic law; "most of what I discuss," he writes, "is what I learned from my own teachers in their study circles (*majālis*)."[87] This trope of modesty suggests that the study of legal distinctions, or perhaps a comparison of similar points of substantive doctrine, formed a part of Mālikī legal study before ʿAbd al-Ḥaqq al-Ṣiqillī. His work, however, is the first Mālikī text in which this activity finds literary expression.[88]

The need to address students appears throughout the *furūq* literature. Abū Faḍl Muslim al-Dimashqī (d. fifth/eleventh c.) says that he wrote his legal dis-

---

Rechtsbücher der Qairawāners Saḥnūn B. Saʿīd: Entstehungsgeschichte und Werküberlieferung (Stuttgart: Deutsche Morgenländische Gesellschaft, 1999), 1–22.

85 ʿAbd al-Ḥaqq ibn Muḥammad al-Ṣiqillī, *al-Nukat wa-l-furūq li-masāʾil al-Mudawwana: Qism al-ʿibādāt*, ed. Aḥmad ibn Ibrāhīm ibn ʿAbdallāh al-Ḥabīb, (PhD Diss., Jāmiʿat Umm al-Qurā, 1416/1996), 148; *idem*, *Kitāb al-Nukat wa-l-furūq li-masāʾil al-Mudawwana wa-l-Mukhtalaṭa*, 2 vols., ed. Abū Faḍl al-Dimyāṭī Aḥmad ibn ʿAlī (Casablanca: Markaz al-Turāth al-Thaqāfī; Beirut: Dār Ibn Ḥazm, 2009), 1:23.

86 The Mālikī scholar Ibn Farḥūn reiterates the importance of ʿAbd al-Ḥaqq's work for students. He says that this "is a useful treatise for developing scholars who show promise (*al-nāshiʾīn min ḥudhdhāq al-ṭalaba*)." Although this seems to complement ʿAbd al-Ḥaqq's words, Ibn Farḥūn continues this with the following sentence: "It is said that he later regretted writing this work (*nadama baʿda dhālika ʿalā taʾlīfihi*), and that he withdrew many of the citations and comments he included therein, and corrected much of what he said." ʿAbd al-Ḥaqq was reported to have said: "Were I able to collect the work again and hide it, I would do so (*law qadartu ʿalā jamʿihi wa-ikhfāʾihi la-faʿaltu*)." See Ibrāhīm ibn ʿAlī ibn Farḥūn, *al-Dībāj al-mudhahhab fī maʿrifat aʿyān ʿulamāʾ al-madhhab*, 2 vols., no ed. (Beirut: Dār al-Kutub al-ʿIlmiyya, 2004), 1:174.

87 ʿAbd al-Ḥaqq al-Ṣiqillī, *al-Nukat wa-l-furūq*, 149; ed. Aḥmad ibn ʿAlī, 1:24.

88 It could very well be the case that interest in legal distinctions is part of a response to a greater necessity to have ready responses to charges of *farq* in formal disputation, but this is not stated by ʿAbd al-Ḥaqq.

tinctions treatise, again after being asked to do so, because "for someone who so wishes, memorizing them is very difficult since they cannot find a treatise dedicated to them but rather have to find them among multitudes of different treatises (*taḍāʿīf al-kutub*)."[89] Much later, Ibn Sunayna (d. 616/1219), who wrote one of the first Ḥanbalī legal distinctions treatises, echoes this theme. He states that he is writing his treatise in response to "repeated requests from one of his colleagues (*baʿḍ aṣḥābinā*)."[90] He likewise aims to address conflicting laws that make up the substance of legal distinctions and clarify "their legal indicants and rationales (*adillatahā wa-ʿilalahā*), to explain to a jurist the derivations of legal rulings (*ṭuruq al-aḥkām*) so that his legal reasoning (*qiyāsuhu*) for substantive rules might be in accordance with legal-theoretical principles (*al-uṣūl*) and so that they might form a coherent system (*muttasiq al-niẓām*)."[91] Consistent with al-Juwaynī, he asserts that the importance of understanding legal distinctions is not simply about understanding the scope of applicability of individual substantive laws, but also about refining one's understanding of the legal theoretical-underpinnings of Islamic law. In other words, legal distinctions treatises help jurists to understand how legal rationales (*ʿilal*) and analogical reasoning (*qiyās*) are applied. Legal distinctions provide an opportunity to reason backwards from very specific situations to the rationales behind those rules.

Social demand is not the only reason given, of course, for writing legal distinctions treatises. Often authors cite the need for a way to learn and understand obscure or difficult points of law. The Ḥanafī jurist Asʿad ibn Muḥammad al-Karābīsī (d. 570/1174–75), for instance, says about his legal distinctions treatise:

> These are legal issues (*masāʾil*) which I collected from treatises, questions regarding which the authorities of our *madhhab* have not agreed upon standard rulings and exceptions (*laysa fīhā qiyās wa-lā stiḥsān illā khilāf mashhūr bayn aṣḥābinā*) ... I intended to single out these cases, to aid in their memorization (*li-yusahhila ḥifẓahā*).[92]

The Shāfiʿī Jamāl al-Dīn al-Asnawī (d. 772/1370) takes a similar approach, although he situates his treatise within an existing legal-literary genre. He explains: "I have seen that other Shāfiʿī scholars have written texts (*li-aṣḥābinā*

---

89 Abū l-Faḍl Muslim al-Dimashqī, *al-Furūq al-fiqhiyya*, ed. Muḥammad Abū l-Ajfān and Ḥamza Abū Fāris (Beirut: Dār al-Gharb al-Islāmī, 1992), 62.

90 Muʿaẓẓam al-Dīn Abū ʿAbdallāh ibn Sunayna al-Sāmarrī, *Kitāb al-Furūq ʿalā madhhab al-Imām Aḥmad ibn Ḥanbal*, ed. Muḥammad ibn Ibrāhīm ibn Muḥammad al-Yaḥyā (Riyadh: Dār al-Ṣamīʿī, 1418/1997), 115.

91 Al-Sāmarrī, *Kitāb al-Furūq*, 115.

92 Asʿad al-Karābīsī, *al-Furūq li-l-Karābīsī*, 2 vols., ed. Muḥammad Ṭumūm and ʿAbd al-Sattār Abū Ghudda (Kuwait: Wizārat al-Awqāf wa-l-Shuʾūn al-Islāmiyya, 1402/1982), 1:133.

taṣānīf) about this subject (*ma'nā*) and I have discovered many tomes by them. Some are written exclusively on this topic, while others encompass a broader focus."[93] Al-Asnawī, writing within an already well-defined literary tradition, can no longer claim to be writing on legal distinctions because of the lack of such treatises. Instead, al-Asnawī says: "This topic (*bāb*) is very wide, encompassing both minimal and maximal discussions of issues, so I asked God for guidance in writing a treatise about this subject (*ma'nā*), following the abovementioned scholars."[94] In other words, he is consciously adopting the model set out by his predecessors and participating in a pre-existing tradition.

Muḥammad al-Baqqūrī (d. 707/1307–08) is in a position similar to that of al-Asnawī, participating in well-established tradition, influenced in the Mālikī school by Shihāb al-Dīn al-Qarāfī (d. 684/1285) and his *Furūq*. Al-Qarāfī's work is peculiar in that it is titled *al-Furūq*, but is not a work about legal distinctions at all.[95] Because of his importance within Mamlūk juristic culture and in the Mālikī legal school, it nevertheless became the focal point for further writings on legal distinctions among Mālikī scholars. Thus, al-Baqqūrī says the following in introducing his commentary on al-Qarāfī's text: "When I studied [al-Qarāfī's] *al-Furūq* ..., it became clear to me that al-Qarāfī, may God have mercy on him, was unable to organize it in a reader-friendly fashion because the work was published while he was still composing it and copies were distributed in this state. This stopped him from being able to change the text."[96] To solve this problem that al-Baqqūrī saw in al-Qarāfī's text, he composed his own work, an abridged and reorganized presentation of al-Qarāfī's work. The relative lack of organization and clarity is a problem that other Mālikī scholars also saw in al-Qarāfī's work; they therefore position their commentaries on his *Furūq* as correctives.

A final an example from a treatise attributed to one Najm al-Dīn 'Alī ibn Bakr al-Naysābūrī (d. ?) exhibits a new idealized audience.[97] It is not clear exactly who this Najm al-Dīn is, but his work, too, actively participates in an existing genre. Based on the rhetoric and style of the introduction, it is clear that Najm al-Dīn wrote this work when the genre of legal distinctions was already recognized and established. Najm al-Dīn wrote his treatise, he claims, in response to

93 Jamāl al-Dīn al-Asnawī, *Maṭāli' al-daqā'iq fī taḥrīr al-jawāmi' wa-l-fawāriq*, 2 vols., ed. Naṣr al-Dīn Farīd Muḥammad Wāṣil (Cairo: Dār al-Shurūq, 2007), 2:7.

94 Al-Asnawī, *Maṭāli' al-daqā'iq*, 2:9.

95 See al-Bāḥusayn, 146; Kızılkaya, 177–83; and Chapter Five, pp. 175.

96 Muḥammad ibn Ibrāhīm al-Baqqūrī, *Tartīb al-Furūq wa-khtiṣārihā*, 2 vols., ed. 'Umar ibn 'Abbād (Morocco: Wizārat al-Awqāf wa-l-Shu'ūn al-Islāmiyya, 1414/1994), 1:19.

97 This work has yet to be edited; I have found eight manuscripts of this work, see Appendix IV.

> a colleague [who] asked me to write a treatise on legal issues that agree in their structure but differ in their rulings, [a treatise] that is concise but effective in its presentation, easy to understand and hard to disagree with, a treatise that can be relied on in study circles (*yastadilluhu fī l-majālis*) and from which you can find guidance in schools (*yastaḍī' bihi min al-madāris*).[98]

Tellingly, the audience for this treatise is still students, both in study circles or salons, *majālis*, and formal contexts, law colleges. This treatise prepares them for conversations about Islamic law. One of the things that this demonstrates, however, is how the genre of legal distinctions could and did respond to a changing reading public. No longer was it only students who desired to read these treatises, but also interested non-jurists who sought access to highly specialized and erudite legal knowledge.[99]

Conclusion

This chapter has attempted to answer the question: what is a legal distinction? Through an examination of premodern definitions, we saw that legal distinctions were understood to be useful in two ways. First, legal distinctions were a particular tool to refine and harmonize a legal school's doctrine and were deemed to play a role in formal disputations. As will be seen in Chapter Three, the significance of disputations is likely understated in these discussions. We also observed widespread agreement about the nature of legal distinctions. The three premodern discussions analyzed are complementary and present similar pictures of legal distinctions. The lack of interest in defining legal distinctions, however, is perhaps stronger evidence of a shared understanding of legal distinctions in the premodern period.

The apologetic introductions to works of legal distinctions give us a different angle from which to answer the question of what a legal distinction is. In these discussions, we see these treatises as a result of the growing complexity of Islam-

98 See Najm al-Dīn al-Naysābūrī, *Kitāb al-Furūq*, MS Giresun Yazmalar 44, Suleymaniye Library, Istanbul, 1b. Other manuscripts of this work have a number of variants in this last line. Giresun Yazmalar 44 does not dot the consonantal skeleton of *yastadilluhu fī l-majālis*, such that it might also be read as *yusnad lahu fī l-majālis* (relied on in study circles), although this latter reading seems less probable. In Joseph Schacht's article, which includes a partial transcription of Leiden Or. 481, 3a, this passage reads: *yastahzi'u bihā fī l-majālis wa-yastaḍī'u bihā fī l-madāris*, and in Anon., *Kitāb al-Furūq*, MS Halet Efendi 780, Suleymaniye Library, Istanbul, 2b, *li-yantafi'a bihā fī l-majālis wa-yastaghnī 'an al-madāris*.

99 I discuss this issue at length in Chapter Five.

ic legal knowledge. Works of legal distinctions serve to shore up knowledge about the particularities of substantive doctrine among students. Presumably, then, a legal distinction is a tool for those studying Islamic law. The comparison found in a legal distinction is a review of two legal rulings, but also a review of how broad legal rules or precepts can and ought to be applied. Through the study of works of legal distinctions, students can review their knowledge of Islamic law.

More recently, scholars of Islamic law have understood legal distinctions primarily in relationship to the exercise of analogical reasoning. While this understanding is similar to premodern definitions, it shifts the relevance of legal distinctions from the domain of substantive law to that of legal theory. While premodern discussions focus on fact-patterns and rulings, modern definitions center of the correct application of a legal rationale (*ʿilla*). This subtle difference perhaps hints at the multiplicity of factors that led to the development of legal distinctions. Further, the importance of *furūq* in legal disputation is omitted by almost all modern discussion. As the next chapters will show, the earliest history of legal distinctions is complex. Several threads, such as a general scholarly interest in the concept of *furūq*, the increasing interest in legal disputation, and the development of substantive law, all came together to push forward the popularity of legal distinctions.

Chapter Two: A General History of Distinctions

Having discussed the rise of legal distinctions as a part of the systematization of Islamic law, this chapter looks at the use of distinctions in non-legal contexts. The most prominent books of distinctions outside of legal writings dealt primarily with philology (both grammar, *naḥw*, and lexicography, *lugha*) and medicine. Scholars have identified these fields as possible sources for the development of *al-furūq al-fiqhiyya*.[1] Muḥammad Abū l-Ajfān and Ḥamza Abū Fāris identify additional parallel phenomena, in other fields although these might be limited to specific books such as *al-Farq bayn al-naḥw wa-l-manṭiq* by Abū l-ʿAbbās Aḥmad ibn al-Ṭayyib al-Sarakhsī (d. 286/899)[2] and *Taṣarruf al-ʿibād wa-l-farq bayn al-khalq wa-l-iktisāb* by Abū Bakr Muḥammad al-Bāqillānī (d. 403/1013).[3] It is helpful to consider these last writings to be applied lexicographic distinctions, by which I mean works of lexicographic distinctions applied to the technical vocabulary of particular subfields. Each of these genres, medicine, language, and law, functions according to its own logic.

This chapter aspires to a thorough survey of the history and function of non-legal *furūq*.[4] My focus here lies primarily on philological works, since these make up the majority of the non-legal *furūq* writing. I shall briefly discuss the medical works addressing differential diagnostics (*al-furūq bayn al-amrāḍ*), although it is unclear whether these works form a literary tradition. Viewing these works as a whole shows that *al-furūq al-fiqhiyya* represent a transformation of linguistic

---

1 See Muḥammad Abū l-Ajfān and Ḥamza Abū Fāris, "*Dirāsa*," in Abū Faḍl Muslim ibn ʿAlī l-Dimashqī, *al-Furūq al-Fiqhiyya*, ed. Muḥammad Abū l-Ajfān and Ḥamza Abū Fāris (Beirut: Dār al-Gharb al-Islāmī, 1992), 26–43; and Wolfhart Heinrichs, "Structuring the Law: Remarks on the *Furūq* Literature," in *Studies in Honour of Clifford Edmund Bosworth Volume I: Hunter of the East; Arabic and Semitic Studies*, ed. Ian Richard Netton (Leiden: Brill, 2000), 1:332–44. Heinrichs's discussion relies heavily on Abū l-Ajfān and Abū Fāris.

2 They refer to him as Abū l-ʿAbbās Aḥmad ibn Muḥammad al-Sarakhsī. Abū l-Ajfān and Abū Fāris, "*Dirāsa*," 29.

3 Abū l-Ajfān and Abū Fāris, "*Dirāsa*," 29–30.

4 Two studies have mentioned non-*fiqh* precedents for the tradition of legal distinctions, but they only allude to potential connections. Abū l-Ajfān and Abū Fāris say that "*furūq* appeared in all scholarly disciplines to better distinguish, classify, and better explain" (Abū l-Ajfān and Abū Fāris, "*Dirāsa*," 28). They do not, however, provide an in-depth analysis of the connections between *furūq* in various fields. Heinrichs, meanwhile, is forthright in stating that his study "is no more than a preliminary characterisation of the notion and function of *furūq*..." (Heinrichs, "Structuring the Law," 340). Both studies, therefore, raise similar historical questions but do not attempt to answer them.

https://doi.org/10.1515/9783110605792-004

furūq.[5] Rather than a case of direct influence by which jurists can be said to definitively take form or function from lexicographical works, exploring these genres shows that the concept of distinctions was adapted by scholars for a variety of purposes in the fourth/tenth century, precisely when legal distinctions rose to prominence. Books of distinctions in these two disciplines, and in medicine, are, however, similar in terms of organization, presentation, and methodology.[6] It thus appears that the rise of lexicographic distinctions is related to the rise of legal distinctions. Perhaps legal distinctions drew on lexicographic distinctions, or perhaps the two genres arose simultaneously responding to similar intellectual and cultural trends.

Pursuing a historical epistemology of distinctions-thinking generally uncovers a shifting conceptualization of *farq* and *furūq* as modes of analysis across different disciplines.[7] Once established, the twin ideas of *farq* and *furūq* further inspired related works. Lexicographic distinctions focus on the subtle distinction in meaning or connotation between apparent synonyms. As works that seemingly reject synonymy and that serve as thesauruses, they operate on both a practical and theological level. As discussed in Chapter One, legal distinctions focus on the subtle distinctions between apparently similar legal cases and function for analysis of both substantive law and legal theory. Medical books on distinctions—handbooks to be used for differential diagnostics—analyze the ambigu-

---

5 For a full discussion of the concept of distinctions and what I refer to as distinctions-thinking, see the Excursus.

6 The similarities between these two genres are clear from an initial reading; further study, however, shows that the various *furūq* genres only share an organizational scheme: case A, case B, and a comparison. This similarity can be thought of as a further rule of distinctions writing. While the mode of comparison between them appears similar, a detailed comparison reveals these modes of comparison to be quite different.

7 Historical epistemology, as used in this chapter, refers to the "study of epistemological concepts as objects that evolve and mutate"; see Ian Hacking, *Historical Ontology* (Cambridge, MA: Harvard University Press, 2004), 9. Historical epistemology understands that "fundamental epistemic concepts and standards are subject to historical change"; see Uljana Feest and Thomas Sturm, "What (Good) is Historical Epistemology? Editors' Introduction," *Erkenntnis* 75 (2011): 290. In other words, it is a methodology that tries to understand the historical contingency of knowledge and knowledge standards. I take the drawing of distinctions—comparison—as an epistemic concept that helps to divide objects of knowledge and establish their identities. In part, this chapter attempts to show how the idea of a comparison "evolve[d] and mutate[d]" in response to various social and intellectual currents. Note that the seventy-fifth volume of *Erkenntnis*, in which the article by Feest and Sturm is published, is devoted to historical epistemology. For more on historical epistemology, see Arnold Davidson, *The Emergence of Sexuality: Historical Epistemology and the Formation of Concepts* (Cambridge, MA: Harvard University Press, 2002).

ously similar symptoms of different underlying diseases. Interestingly, these works of medical *furūq* lack discussion of medical treatment or theoretical analysis of maladies.[8]

Lexicographic works served as thesauruses, prominently demanded by chancery secretaries and other writers. They additionally made implicit theological claims about the cultural superiority of Arabs and the ontological superiority of Arabic. Thus, books of lexicographic distinctions provide examples to argue for the perfection of the Arabic language and its lack of redundancies (i. e., synonyms). Lexicographers thus showed that comparing two similar words can lead to the establishment of firm boundaries between them. In fields other than lexicography, scholars could use the technique of lexicographic distinctions productively, in order to coin new terms and cement definitions in disciplines as diverse as ethics, Sufism, philosophy, and law.

This chapter discusses the three major trends of distinctions literatures outside of legal distinctions. It begins with a brief discussion of the practical manuals of medical distinctions. It then discusses practical and theoretical distinctions in the domains of lexicography and phonology. Finally, I discuss the productive genre of applied lexicographic distinctions. Although the genre of applied lexicographic distinctions has not, to my knowledge, been named previously, works belonging to it are found in abundance in almost all premodern fields of Arabo-Islamic scholarship.

Furūq in Medicine

Medical authors may have been the first to produce books of *furūq*, which they did in order to foster differential diagnostics. Their books describe illnesses with similar symptoms and discuss the ways to distinguish between them to diagnose a patient correctly. The scant survival of these works may testify to their relative lack of prominence in the premodern period.[9]

---

8 It is possible that the texts of medical diagnosis implicitly argued for the possibility of induction as a tool of diagnosis. Understanding when induction was appropriate in medical reasoning was an important concern of Galen and later taken up by Ḥunayn ibn Isḥāq. See Richard Walzer, Introduction to *Galen on Medical Experience: First Edition of the Arabic Version with English Translation and Notes by R. Walzer*, ed. and trans. Richard Walzer (London: Oxford University Press, 1947).

9 Peter E. Pormann and Emilie Savage-Smith state that discussions of differential diagnostics was often included in works of medical ethics. See Peter E. Pormann and Emilie Savage-Smith, *Medieval Islamic Medicine* (Edinburgh: Edinburgh University Press, 2007), 86, 89.

Indeed, there seem to have only been four works of differential diagnostics composed in the premodern Arabic tradition, by Abū Bakr al-Rāzī (d. 313/925 or 323/935), Ibn al-Jazzār (d. 369/979), Aḥmad ibn Asʿad ibn Ḥalwān al-Dimashqī, also known as Ibn al-ʿĀlima (d. 652/1254), and Yūsuf ibn Ismāʿīl al-Kutubī (d. *ca* 754/1353).[10] One book on differential diagnostics has been published, in two editions, one attributing the work to Abū Bakr al-Rāzī and the other attributing the same work to Ibn al-Jazzār.[11] Ibn Ḥalwān's treatise and that of Ibn al-Kutubī survive in manuscript, although both are still unpublished.[12] Interestingly, the published text is identical to that attributed to Ibn Ḥalwān in MS Ayasofya 4838, Suleymaniye Library, Istanbul and also to the text attributed to Ibn al-Kutubī in MS Ahmet III 2120, also in the Suleymaniye.[13]

---

10 According to Ibn Abī Uṣaybiʿa, Ibn al-ʿĀlima was unrivalled in formal disputation (*lā yalḥiquhu fī l-jadal*). Ibn Abī Uṣaybiʿa mentions this work with the title *Kitāb al-Tadqīq fī l-jamʿ wa-l-tafrīq* (Ibn Abī Uṣaybiʿa, *ʿUyūn al-anbāʾ*, 266). On Ibn al-ʿĀlima, see Aḥmad ibn al-Qāsim Ibn Abī Uṣaybiʿa, *ʿUyūn al-anbāʾ fī ṭabaqāt al-aṭibbāʾ*, ed. Nizār Riḍā (Beirut: Dār Maktabat al-Ḥayāt, [1965]), 757–58; Shams al-Dīn Muḥammad ibn Aḥmad al-Dhahabī, *Taʾrīkh al-islām wa-wafayāt al-mashāhīr wa-l-aʿlām*, ed. ʿUmar ʿAbd al-Salām Tadmurī (Beirut: Dār al-Kitāb al-ʿArabī, 1419/1999), 48:115–16, 224. On Ibn al-Kutubī, see Khayr al-Dīn al-Ziriklī, *al-Aʿlām qāmūs tarājim li-ashhar al-rijāl wa-l-nisāʾ min al-ʿarab wa-l-mustaʿribīn wa-l-mustashriqīn*, 15th printing (Beirut: Dār al-ʿIlm li-l-Malāyīn, 2002), 8:217; and *GAL* S2:218. I discuss Ibn al-Jazzār and al-Rāzī below.

11 See Abū Bakr al-Rāzī, *Kitāb Mā l-fāriq aw al-Furūq aw Kalām fī l-furūq bayn al-amrāḍ*, ed. Salmān Qaṭāya (Aleppo: Jāmiʿat Ḥalab, Maʿhad al-Turāth al-ʿIlmī l-ʿArabī, 1398/1978) and Ibn al-Jazzār, *al-Furūq bayn ishtibāhāt al-ʿilal*, ed. Ramziyya l-Aṭraqjī (Baghdad: Wizārat al-Taʿlīm al-ʿĀlī wa-l-Baḥth al-ʿIlmī, Jāmiʿat Baghdād, Bayt al-Ḥikma, 1989).

12 Ibn al-ʿĀlima's manuscript appears to survive in a collection (*majmūʿa*) of medical texts. This manuscript is housed in the Suleymaniye Library in Istanbul, MS Ayasofya 4838, Suleymaniye Library, Istanbul; a microfilm of this manuscript can be found at the University of Utah, reel 190 of the Levey microfilm collection. Ibn al-Kutubī's work is also housed in the MS Ahmet III 2120, Suleymaniye Library, Istanbul and Levey reel 131, University of Utah Library. This work is not, however, the *Kitāb Mā lā yasaʿu l-ṭabīb jahluhu*, a treatise on pharmacology. See Ibn al-Kutubī, *Mā lā yasaʿu l-ṭabīb jahluhu*, MS Mansuri Collection R128.3.I127 1682, Library of Congress, Washington DC, available online http://lcweb2.loc.gov/service/amed/amed0001/2001/200149140/200149140.pdf, accessed January 27, 2019.

13 The main difference between the published texts and that found in the Ayasofya manuscript is that the text in MS Ayasofya 4838, Suleymaniye Library, Istanbul begins with a statement specifically attributing the book to "Abū l-ʿAbbās Aḥmad ibn Abī l-Faḍl Asʿad ibn Ḥalwān al-Ṭabīb" (MS Ayasofya 8438, 109b). Neither al-Rāzī nor Ibn al-Jazzār are identified as the author in their respective texts. Ibn Ḥalwān's manuscript is found in a collected volume (*majmūʿ*), the title page of which reads: "This is a collection (*majmūʿ*) of medical texts. The first book is *Tadbīr al-amrāḍ al-ḥādda* by Hippocrates, also containing the book *Asrār al-nisāʾ* by Galen and *al-Furūq* by Ibn Ḥalwān Ṭabīb." This is followed by a table of contents showing the nine books that make up this medical collection. It is striking that Ibn Ḥalwān is identified as the author three times in this

Examination of medical *furūq* suggests the precedence of these works to other writings on distinctions. More importantly, the earliest bio-bibliographic writings do not uniformly refer to the works of Ibn al-Jazzār and al-Rāzī by the title *Kitāb al-Furūq*, suggesting that *furūq* had not yet taken hold as a meaningful concept for medicine in the fourth/tenth century. That is, the word *furūq* had not yet emerged as a technical concept but rather continued to be a word used in its plain-sense meaning of "differences." While the term *furūq*, in the field of medicine, would eventually come to mean "differential diagnostics," the word by itself was not enough to convey this meaning during the time of al-Rāzī and Ibn al-Jazzār. Thus, early bio-bibliographical sources only inconsistently refer to al-Rāzī or Ibn al-Jazzār's books as *Kitāb al-Furūq*, employing a variety of other titles, such as *al-Furūq bayn al-ʿilal* or *al-ʿIlal al-mushkila*. The variety of possible titles indicate that the term *furūq* had not yet become a stable marker of a literary genre. Consequently, this points to the difficulty in understanding the content of works based on title alone, as the term *furūq* had not yet come to mean "differential diagnostics."

It appears that only one treatise of differential diagnostics has survived, although the manuscript tradition and the printed editions attribute this work to a variety of different authors. Salmān Qaṭāya was the first to edit and publish the work in question in 1978. In his edition, he attributes the text to al-Rāzī on the basis of in-text citations of al-Rāzī's works, the general style of the writing, bio-bibliographic sources, and the manuscript evidence.[14] Ramziyya l-Aṭraqjī, who edited this work in 1989, however, attributes it to Ibn al-Jazzār. In a preface to that edition, ʿĀdil al-Bakrī dismisses Qaṭāya's attribution, arguing that the writ-

manuscript, and that his book was prominent enough to be included in the sentence summarizing the collection. The manuscript is missing a few folios after the introduction. The first page of the distinctions text is 109b, which ends in the middle of the introduction, but page 110a is in the middle of chapter one, section one (*al-maqāla l-ūlā l-faṣl al-awwal*). Based on the available evidence, it is difficult to ascertain who the author of this work is. MS Ahmet III 2120 is largely identical to both the published texts MS Ayasofya 4838. The attribution to Ibn al-Kutubī is found only in a note on the title page of the manuscript, The note reads: "A book by the author of *Mā lā yasaʿu* on differential diagnosis (*min taṣnīfāt ṣāḥib* Mā lā yasaʿu *fī al-farq bayn al-amrāḍ al-mushtabiha*). I hope to address this question in a future study.

14 Qaṭāya bases his edition on the manuscript of this work found in the Wellcome Historical Medical Library. Interestingly, Ibn Sīnā is listed as the author of this manuscript on its title page. A.Z. Iskandar, who compiled the catalogue of Arabic works in the Wellcome collection, rejects this attribution and posits instead that this work was written by al-Rāzī. Qaṭāya does not mention Iskandar's attribution in his introduction. See A.Z. Iskandar, *A Catalogue of Arabic Manuscripts on Medicine in the Wellcome Historical Medical Library* (London: The Wellcome Historical Medical Library, 1967), 67.

ing style is not necessarily similar to that of al-Rāzī, but rather indicative of medical writing practices in the third/ninth and fourth/tenth centuries. He dismisses the three citations of al-Rāzī's other works as evidence of his authorship, asserting that the author "in these three places ... speaks of al-Rāzī in the third person, as a critic of al-Rāzī correcting al-Rāzī's views and opinions (*muṣaḥḥiḥan lahu ārāʾahu wa-mustadrikan ʿalayhi aqwālahu*)."[15] Al-Bakrī assumes that if al-Rāzī were citing himself, he would not take an oppositional approach to his earlier writings. Al-Bakrī continues, "This is not the language of someone speaking about himself; the author says, 'In his book, al-Rāzī says ... but I say' (*fa-huwa yaqūlu qāla l-Rāzī fī kitābihi kadhā ... wa-aqūlu kadhā*)."[16] Al-Bakrī is content that this argument disproves the attribution to al-Rāzī. He also rejects the possibility that the author of this work is Najm al-Dīn Aḥmad ibn Abī l-Faḍl ibn al-ʿĀlima, since he lived much later than the ninth century, and al-Bakrī understands this treatise to be an early work.

Al-Bakrī's claim of an early date for the work is based on the author's claim at the beginning that "my predecessors have not written a book like this one" (*lam yasbaq ilā mithlihi man taqaddama*).[17] Al-Bakrī concludes that, "based on this, what is most probable is that this work was written by Ibn al-Jazzār al-Qayrawānī."[18] Al-Bakrī credits the editor of this text, Ramziyya l-Aṭraqjī, with this attribution and appears quite convinced. He does not explain why he considers only these three names as possible authors, but it is likely due to the paucity of authors who are said in the biographical literature to have written works on differential diagnostics. This work appears to be the earliest book on differential diagnostics. Al-Rāzī and Ibn al-Jazzār are both remembered as having written a book on differential diagnostics. Since more sources point to al-Rāzī as the author of this text, I shall discuss in brief his importance to the history of Islamic medicine; many of the tropes found in biographies of al-Rāzī, however, appear in biographies of Ibn al-Jazzār as well.[19]

---

15 ʿĀdil al-Bakrī, "*Taqdīm al-kitāb*," in Ibn al-Jazzār, *al-Furūq*, ب.

16 Al-Bakrī, "*Taqdīm*," ب. Ellipsis in the original.

17 Al-Rāzī, *Mā l-fāriq*, 2; Ibn al-Jazzār, *al-Furūq*, 14.

18 Al-Bakrī, "*Taqdīm*," ب–ج.

19 The earliest biography about Ibn al-Jazzār comes from Ibn Juljul. Ibn Juljul's biographical entry does not cite any specific information on Ibn al-Jazzār's writings, although it does mention that Ibn al-Jazzār came from a family of physicians (*ṭabīb ibn ṭabīb wa-ʿammuhu ṭabīb*). As with al-Rāzī, Ibn al-Jazzār's biography reads like a hagiography. The sources tell us that Ibn al-Jazzār abstained from earthly pleasures and occupied himself with intellectual and religious pursuits. "He would participate in funerals and weddings, but would not eat at the receptions." Similarly, Ibn al-Jazzār, we are told, provided treatment to the nephew of al-Qāḍī l-Nuʿmān (d. 364/974) for an unspecified illness. Once he recuperated, al-Qāḍī l-Nuʿmān sent a messenger to Ibn al-Jazzār

Heinrichs uses this work to argue for the importance of medical *furūq* as a parallel genre to works on legal distinctions, writing:

> The medicinal parallel, embodied in such works as Abū Bakr al-Rāzī's (d. 313/925), seems much more convincing. Here the term *furūq* designates the element or elements which, in a syndrome of mostly similar symptoms, allow the differential diagnostics of the illness at hand. In the way in which two or more cases are similar in appearance but distinguishable by a crucial element of difference, the medicinal and the legal situation have much in common, and the differential diagnostics of the physician would yield a fitting metaphor for the work of the *faqīh* as a *mufarriq*.[20]

Heinrichs further claims that the parallel between medicine and law "seems much more convincing [than that between lexicography and law]." However, he fails to address the impact of this "medicinal parallel" on law, nor does the parallel as such tell us much about the history of these genres or the ways they may have impacted each other. One cannot disagree with Heinrichs that differential diagnostics—the topic of *furūq* in medicine—appears a "fitting metaphor" for *furūq* in law, but there is no evidence that the resemblance is more than superficial.[21]

Following Heinrichs lead, the analysis of this book of medical distinctions titled *al-Furūq* helps fill in these gaps. Qaṭāya emphasizes that this text should be used for diagnosis. "It is clear that [the author's] interest in this field (*hādhihi l-nāḥiya*)," he writes, "comes from the difficulty of practicing this craft [i.e., medicine,] daily and his confronting the difficulties and complications of differential diagnostics (*al-tashkhīṣ al-tafrīqī*)."[22] Since this work proclaims itself to be the first treatise written on the topic of differential diagnostics, Qaṭāya is satisfied with attributing this work to al-Rāzī.[23]

---

with "fine clothes and 300 gold coins." Ibn al-Jazzār thanked the messenger, but sent him back with the gifts. Although he was said to live a simple life, he left behind twenty-five *qinṭars* of books and 24,000 dinars. See Ibn Abī Uṣaybiʿa, *ʿUyūn al-anbāʾ*, 481 and Sulaymān ibn Ḥassān ibn Juljul, *Ṭabaqāt al-aṭibbāʾ wa-l-ḥukamāʾ*, ed. Fuʾād Sayyid (Cairo: Imprimerie de l'Insitut Français d'Archéologie Orientale, 1955), 88.

20 Heinrichs, "Structuring the Law," 334–35.

21 In other words, given that the tradition of differential diagnostics is unknown outside of one work with uncertain authorial attribution and therefore from an uncertain date, it is difficult to talk with any degree of confidence about influence.

22 Salmān Qaṭāya, "*Taṣdīr*" in Abū Bakr al-Rāzī, *Kitāb Mā l-fāriq aw al-Furūq aw Kalām fī l-furūq bayn al-amrāḍ*, ed. Salmān Qaṭāya (Aleppo: Jāmiʿat Ḥalab, Maʿhad al-Turāth al-ʿIlmī l-ʿArabī, 1398/1978), د.

23 Al-Rāzī, *Mā l-fāriq*, 2; Ibn al-Jazzār, *al-Furūq*, 14.

Abū Bakr Zakariyyā' al-Rāzī's work on differential diagnosis is remembered by at least three titles, *Kitāb Mā l-fāriq*, *al-Furūq*, and *Kalām fī l-furūq bayn al-amrāḍ*.[24] The biographical sources also tell us much about his vast bibliography. The earliest sources on al-Rāzī are Ibn al-Nadīm (d. 380/990) and Ibn Juljul (d. after 384/994–95), on which both the later Ibn al-Qifṭī (d. 646/1248) and Ibn Abī Uṣaybiʿa (d. 668/1270) rely.[25] Ibn Juljul gives a bibliography of the works written by al-Rāzī but does not mention the *Furūq* nor any work that could be construed as the *Furūq*. Ibn al-Nadīm, however, lists a book entitled *al-Risāla fī l-ʿilal al-mushkila*, which could very well refer to this book.[26] This is the only mention of a likely title that is roughly contemporaneous with al-Rāzī's life. Ibn Abī Uṣaybiʿa also attributes to al-Rāzī a work with a similar title, the *Risāla fī l-ʿilal al-mushkila wa-ʿudhr al-ṭabīb wa-ghayr dhālika*,[27] although he additionally ascribes a *Kalām fī l-furūq bayn al-amrāḍ* to him.[28] Finally, Ibn al-Qifṭī also lists the *Risāla fī l-ʿilal al-mushkila*.[29] It is also worth noting that al-Rāzī is credited with another work, on distinguishing ominous dreams from other kinds of dreams, the *Kitāb al-Farq bayn al-ru'yā l-mundhira wa-sā'ir ḍurūb al-ru'yā*, though it does not appear to have survived.[30]

None of these authors discusses the contents of these works, so only circumstantial evidence links the book under discussion to al-Rāzī. If the *Risāla fī l-ʿilal al-mushkila* does refer to the extant work on differential diagnostics, then it pre-

24 The printed edition of this work is based on three manuscripts. The first, entitled, *Mā l-fāriq*, is an undated copy found in the Wellcome collection in London likely from the eighteenth century according to Qaṭāya, the second is in the Malek National Library in Tehran apparently with no title and also dating from around the eighteenth century, and the third is a version from the Public Awqāf Library in Baghdad with the title *Kitāb al-Furūq bayn al-ishtibāhāt fī l-ʿilal*, which dates from Ramaḍān 1220/1805 (pp. ز–و).

25 Abū l-Rayḥān al-Bīrūnī (d. *ca.* 440/1048) also wrote a bio-bibliography of al-Rāzī, but he does not mention this work therein.

26 Ibn al-Nadīm, *al-Fihrist li-l-Nadīm*, 2 vols., ed. Ayman Fu'ād Sayyid (London: Mu'assasat al-Furqān li-l-Turāth al-ʿArabī, 1430/2009), 2.1:312. The title of this book can be translated as *A Treatise on Ambiguous Illnesses.*

27 Ibn Abī Uṣaybiʿa, *ʿUyūn al-anbā'*, 1:319. The title of this book can be translated as *A Treatise on Ambiguous Illnesses, an Excuse for the Physician, and More.*

28 Ibn Abī Uṣaybiʿa, *ʿUyūn al-anbā'*, 1:321. The title of this book can be translated as *A Work on the Distinctions between Illnesses.*

29 Ibn al-Qifṭī, *Ta'rīkh al-ḥukamā' wa-huwa Mukhtaṣar al-zūzanī al-musammā bi-l-Muntakhabāt al-multaqaṭāt min Kitāb Ikhbār al-ʿulamā' bi-akhbār al-ḥukamā'* (Baghdad: Maktabat al-Muthannā, 196[?]), 277.

30 Ibn Abī Uṣaybiʿa, *ʿUyūn al-anbā'*, 1:315–16; Ibn al-Nadīm, *al-Fihrist*, 2.1:308; Ibn al-Qifṭī, *Ta'rīkh*, 273. The title of this book can be translated as *The Difference between Dreams of Premonition and Other Kinds of Dreams.*

dates the *furūq* tradition in lexicography and law by approximately a century. Its later reception may perhaps explain why later authors referred to it as *Kitāb al-Furūq*, as these later authors were familiar with a formal *furūq* genre and potentially recognized this work as a part of it. Nevertheless, they included the alternate title *Risāla fī l-ʿilal al-mushkila* in their bibliographies, since it is attested in the earliest bibliographic works in this form.[31] It was thus only later scholars, familiar with *furūq* as a literary genre, who referred to it as *Kitāb al-Furūq*.

The genre of medical *furūq* is difficult to discuss in detail or with any certainty because of all the works listed in this genre by the bibliographical tradition only one has survived. The work under consideration here aims to provide a handbook for practicing physicians. The author claims explicitly that his book is to be used in this way, as a diagnostic manual. In describing his approach, he says:

> I have seen that the doctors of today only know about maladies what they can imagine on the basis of books, and the symptoms and causes (*bi-dalāʾilihi wa-asbābihi*) mentioned therein. These symptoms and causes, may, however, be shared between illnesses and illnesses can resemble one another. The aspirations of physicians fall short of comprehensive knowledge of how to engage in syllogistical and inferential thinking using the principles and rules of medicine (*bi-l-qiyās wa-l-istikhrāj min al-uṣūl wa-l-qawāʿid*). I have therefore seen a need to compose a book on causes, symptoms, and illnesses that are similar to each other. I gather here every two that resemble each other or are shared between illnesses, and then I distinguish (*ufarriqu*) between them.[32]

This work, as the author describes in the introduction, served as a practical handbook for diagnosis. It is organized as a series of questions and answers. The book itself has five chapters, each with several subsections consisting of numbered pairs of illnesses between which the author distinguishes.[33] Salmān Qaṭāya states that this work is split up "according to the organization followed at that time."[34] Each of the book's five chapters cover different parts of the body:[35] (1) the parts of the head (*ajzāʾ al-raʾs*);[36] (2) the respiratory system

31 A similar trend is seen with works of lexicographic distinction, see below.
32 Al-Rāzī, *Mā l-fāriq*, 1–2; Ibn al-Jazzār, *al-Furūq*, 14.
33 The manuscripts of this work were all copied much later than al-Rāzī's life. It is therefore unclear when the numbering system was introduced into this text. The numbering is added to the margins of the Ibn Ḥalwān manuscript in the same hand that copied the text. It is included in the main text of the two published editions.
34 Qaṭāya, "*Taṣdīr*," ج.
35 There is an interesting parallel with works of lexicographic distinction, which are also partially organized by parts of the body.
36 Al-Rāzī, *Mā l-fāriq*, 29–85; Ibn al-Jazzār, *al-Furūq*, 27–45.

(*ālāt al-tanaffus*);[37] (3) the stomach, the liver, the spleen, the kidneys, the bladder, and the reproductive system (*al-maʿida wa-l-kabd wa-l-ṭiḥāl wa-l-kulā wa-l-mathāna wa-ālāt al-tanāsul*);[38] (4) the whole body (*al-badan kulluhu*);[39] and (5) pulse and urine (*al-nabaḍ wa-l-bawl*).[40] Each pair of maladies is introduced with the phrase "What is the distinction between [X] and [Y] (*mā l-farq bayn* [*kadhā*] *wa-*[*kadhā*])?" The answer to the question, the elucidation of the distinction, is introduced with "The answer is (*wa-l-jawāb*) ..."

In contrast to lexicographical distinctions, which focus exclusively on the differences and take the similarities for granted, the author of the text discussed here undertakes to offer a complete comparison. He begins by explaining the similarities between the comparands and then explains the distinctions in detail. He often offers more than one distinction and, consonant with the work's stated purpose, his explanation of the distinction seeks to assist physicians in diagnosing illnesses. The distinctions that he highlights are limited to diagnosis, and the author does not elaborate in great length by explaining the treatments required for each illness or by describing how the symptoms in question came about.

The practical nature of the book helps elucidate resonances with the lexicographical and legal traditions. First, let us consider the author's definition of what a distinction is. "As for a distinction (*al-farq*)," he writes, "it is that through which things with similar characteristics can be distinguished, when a cause (*ḥukm*) has been affirmed in one thing and denied in the other, once it [the *farq*] merges with one particular thing."[41] A distinction occurs only through the process of comparison between two similar things that are in reality different. The distinction relies on the affirmation of one characteristic and the resulting denial of the other characteristic. He continues:

> Once you understand the realities of an issue, the question of distinction refers to differences in reality only in one regard, namely: with respect to the fact that there is something shared between the comparands. An example for this is the fact that animate and inani-

---

37 Al-Rāzī, *Mā l-fāriq*, 87–128; Ibn al-Jazzār, *al-Furūq*, 45–58.
38 Al-Rāzī, *Mā l-fāriq*, 129–231; Ibn al-Jazzār, *al-Furūq*, 59–90.
39 Al-Rāzī, *Mā l-fāriq*, 233–63; Ibn al-Jazzār, *al-Furūq*, 90–99.
40 Al-Rāzī, *Mā l-fāriq*, 265–99; Ibn al-Jazzār, *al-Furūq*, 99–108.
41 "*Ammā l-farq fa-huwa mā bihi l-tamyīz bayn al-dhawāt al-mushtabaha ʿind ilḥāq ḥukm wa-nafyihi ʿan al-ākhar baʿd ijtimāʿihi fī amr khāṣṣ*," al-Rāzī, *Mā l-fāriq*, 23. This passage is curtailed in the printed edition attributed to Ibn al-Jazzār: "As for distinction, it is what is used to distinguish between two things that resemble each other" (*ammā l-farq fa-huwa mā yumtāzu bihi aḥad al-shayʾayn al-mutashābihayn ʿan al-ākhar*), Ibn al-Jazzār, *al-Furūq*, 26. In both of these quotations, *farq* can be understood as distinction or as distinguishing characteristic, a term usually denoted as *fāriq*.

> mate bodies share the feature of being bodies, since both occupy three dimensions. No one asks about the distinction between animate and inanimate bodies unless one had no knowledge of what differentiates the one from the other.[42]

In bringing out the example of the animate and the inanimate, the author resorts to a principle of predication. Here, a body serves as the object of which anitemateness and inanitemateness can be predicated. Anitemateness and inanitemateness are two contradictory predicates and therefore cannot simultaneously exist in one body. Nevertheless, animate and inanimate bodies have in common that they are both bodies. The author compares these similarities to medical distinctions, evidently because the latter are not as evident or less widely known.

The main text of the work then follows the framework outlined above, presenting all of these distinctions in the form of a question. One such question is: "What is the distinction between a stroke occurring from matter blocking the interior of the brain (*al-mādda l-sādda li-buṭūn al-dimāgh*) and that occurring from a tumor (*waram*) therein?"[43] The author explains that while these two disorders are indeed alike in the way they "outwardly manifest themselves (*ishtarakā fī l-ḥaqīqa*)," their underlying "cause" (*sabab*) and "the manner in which the illness results from it" (*kayfiyyat wujūb al-ḥukm ʿanhu*) differ, both of which he expands upon in detail.[44] As for the difference in cause, he says: "It is evident. One is a blockage (*sadda*), while the other a tumor."[45] A stroke resulting from a blockage to the brain, he says, occurs as this blockage occurs, that is, the symptoms occur suddenly and severely, "in one moment" (*dafʿatan*). A stroke resulting from a tumor, however, happens "gradually." As the tumor grows, we are told, the vital spirit (*al-rūḥ al-nafsāniyya*) is slowly prevented from spreading through the body. It is the blockage of the vital spirit, which, presumably, is the direct cause of the stroke. Lastly, a stroke caused by a tumor is often accompanied by a fever, whereas a stroke resulting from sudden a blockage is not. The physi-

42 Al-Rāzī, *Mā l-fāriq*, 23; Ibn al-Jazzār, *al-Furūq*, 26. Once again, the Ibn al-Jazzār edition gives an abbreviated definition, "Once you understand the realities of an issue, the question of distinction does not refer to differences in reality." The language used by the author here is highly reminiscent of the technical terminology used in discussions of disputation. I reproduce the version attributed to al-Rāzī here to highlight these similarities: *wa-suʾāl al-farq lā yaruddu ʿalā l-mukhtalifāt bi-l-ḥaqīqa baʿd al-ʿilm bi-ḥaqāʾiqihā illa min wajh waqaʿa baynahumā fīhi min al-ishtirāk wa-dhālika ka-shtirāk al-ḥayawān aw al-jamād bi-tawassuṭ al-jism fī kawn kull wāḥid minhumā dhā abʿād thalātha fa-lā yusʾalu bi-mā l-farq bayn al-ḥayawān wa-l-jamād illā maʿ ʿadam al-ʿilm bi-l-mumayyiz li-kull wāḥid minhumā ʿan al-ākhar.*

43 Al-Rāzī, *Mā l-fāriq*, 37; Ibn al-Jazzār, *al-Furūq*, 30.

44 Al-Rāzī, *Mā l-fāriq*, 37; Ibn al-Jazzār, *al-Furūq*, 30.

45 Al-Rāzī, *Mā l-fāriq*, 37; Ibn al-Jazzār, *al-Furūq*, 30.

cian thus has the tools to diagnose these different kinds of strokes, looking at the onset of the stroke and the presence of fever. There is no discussion, however, of the different treatments necessitated by these distinct illnesses.

Medical works of distinctions are thus narrowly tailored, focused on the immediate phenomenon that presents itself, apparently lacking any broader theological import. On the other hand, lexicographic *furūq* books utilized discrete lexicographic problems to tackle theological debates about the nature of Arabic. Consider the way in which the author lays out his explanations in the following example, as well as the kind of information that he includes and what he leaves out.

> What is the distinction between the sediment found in urine that is the result of illnesses in the liver and that which is the result of illnesses of the kidneys?
>
> The answer: They are similar in reality (*ishtarakā fī l-ḥaqīqa*), but they differ in what they indicate (*iftaraqā fī madlūlihimā*) and how they are deduced. That sediment which comes from the liver is redder (*ashaddu ḥamratan*), while that which comes from the kidney leans more towards yellow. It is also possible that that from the kidneys is black. In the case of liver ailments, urine is never opaque (*al-bawl lā takūnu maʿ al-awwal naḍījan*), while kidney ailments can result in opaque urine.[46] The distinction is fully realized with the other symptoms of liver failure or the symptoms of pain in the kidneys.[47]

The author again gives detailed explanations of the illnesses to aid in diagnosis. His discussion focuses on the specific ways in which liver and kidney ailments manifest themselves in urine. He does not discuss how to treat liver or kidney ailments, but gives the information that is sufficient for a diagnosis.

The author's claim that his work should serve as a diagnostic manual is evident in the distinctions themselves; the claim is no mere trope with which the author begins his book. In general, however, the paucity of books on medical diagnosis generally precludes the conclusion that they had a significant impact on the genre of legal distinctions.

Furūq in Philology

Situating the rise of legal *furūq* within the context of the earlier development of distinctions-thinking in Arabic linguistic and lexicographic fields underscores

---

46 I am unsure of the precise meaning of *naḍīj* in this context; it appears to denote "opaque" or "turbid"; see Max Neuberger, "The Early History of Urology," trans. David Riesman, *Bulletin of the Medical Library Association* 25, no. 3 (1937): 156. I thank Dr. Paulina Giusti for this reference.
47 Al-Rāzī, *Mā l-fāriq*, 293; Ibn al-Jazzār, *al-Furūq*, 106.

the interconnectedness of law and grammar. Tracts of linguistic distinctions first developed from the study of obscure and rare Arabic words, and subsequently spilled over into other aspects of language, such as the semantic comparison (*farq*) of similar or synonymous words. Driven in part by theological concerns, semantic comparisons, in turn, led to more complex distinctions-thinking regarding the well-known question of synonyms in Arabic, a more robust way of explaining differences between words. Tracing the practical and polemical uses of lexicographical distinction literature from its earliest appearance to its apotheosis in the *Kitāb al-Furūq* by Abū Hilāl al-ʿAskarī (d. *ca.* 400/1009 – 10) uncovers a variety of tools, first found in this genre, that helped shape legally-inclined works of *furūq*.

Linguistic *farq* was a part of Arabic philological study from its earliest days. While the precise origins of Arabic linguistics remain uncertain, it is possible to outline a rough lineage of early books of distinction. These works are of two types: distinction in lexicography, and distinction between the letters of the Arabic alphabet. Lexicographic *farq* concern different words that appear to have the same meaning, i.e., synonyms. Lexicographers sought to uncover the nuances between these words, primarily by identifying different contexts in which each word may be employed. Unlike physicians, premodern Arabic philologists focus on analyzing words (signifiers) and their meanings (signifieds), rather than only on what underlies them (such as illnesses in the medical case). The distinctions they make are about the implicit connotations of known words, not the explicit manifestations of undiagnosed illnesses.

The earliest precursors to books on distinctions tackle *gharīb* and *nawādir*, words with obscure or rare usages. In essence, these lexical lists attempt to delineate the edges of the Arabic lexicon. These works, in turn, led to books that compare specialized vocabulary, e.g., for the body parts or for the life-cycles of animals and humans, often titled *Khalq al-insān*. Books on *Khalq al-insān* were also known by the title *Kitāb al-Farq*. These books are direct forerunners to lexical works with the word *furūq* in their titles. Not only is there a direct connection between their titles, in that the title *Kitāb al-Farq* uses the singular and *Kitab al-Furūq* the plural, but there is a further connection in terms of content. The logic of distinguishing, however, that operates in books of *farq* is quite different from that found in books of *furūq*.

A typical example of a linguistic *furūq* book is Abū Hilāl al-ʿAskarī's *al-Furūq al-lughawiyya*. This book consists of easily recognizable entries of linguistic *furūq* (i.e., two or more apparent synonyms and a discussion of their semantic difference), and evinces a well-developed scholarly tradition in lexicographical distinctions by the fourth/tenth century. This rhetorical style became so characteristic of the genre that much of the same organization, presentation, and content remains evident even as late as the seventeenth-century *furūq* work by İsmail Hakkı Bursevi (d. 1137/1725), which was composed with completely different goals, namely, to reinforce the knowledge of Arabic among non-Arab elites in the Anatolian peninsula.[48] The fact that al-ʿAskarī's *al-Furūq al-lughawiyya* constitutes a mature form of the genre indicates that, by the author's time, lexicographical *furūq* writing had evolved into a stable literary genre. Earlier works on distinction focused, by contrast, on the activity of distinguishing, as expressed by the title *Kitāb al-Farq*. Moreover, works in the genre of linguistic *furūq* began to function as a kind of thesaurus. By finding a word in a book of lexicographic distinctions, one could also find words with a similar, if not equivalent, meaning. Finally, early examples of *furūq* works were motivated in part by theological concerns about the nature of the Arabic language.

Adab al-kātib, a manual for chancery secretaries written by Ibn Qutayba (d. 276/889), already includes a section on *furūq* that functions as a thesaurus.[49] Ibn Qutayba understood the importance of distinctions between near-synonyms, suggesting that the ability to draw lexicographical distinctions was desired knowledge for secretaries writing for the state bureaucracy, whether for communicating with other secretaries or showcasing their profound erudition. In addition, the tradition of linguistic *furūq* was an extension of early lexicographical concern with the study of *aḍdād* (contronyms, i.e. words that can mean one thing and its opposite), *abdāl* (phonologically or semantically related letter pairs), and "obscure" and "rare" terms (*gharīb* and *nawādir*), treatises of which centered around synonym groupings (e.g., sections on distinct words for sword, camel, or horse).[50] It is likely that the practical aspect of linguistic *furūq* was the primary factor that led to its enduring use.

While thesauric works focus on semantic differences, *furūq* books also operate on a theological level. In this sense, these works participate in discussions about the relationship between God and Arabic as the language of God's revelation. As such, works of linguistic *furūq* can also function polemically. Thus, al-

---

48 There are many surviving manuscripts of this work. It is also available in a lithograph edition, İsmail Hakkı Bursevi, *al-Furūq*, no ed. (Dersaʿādet: Şirket-i Ṣaḥḥāfīye-'i ʿOsmanīye, 1308/1890–91); online at https://archive.org/details/furqbursal00smaiuoft, accessed May 2, 2019.

49 A section in this work is entitled "Chapters on Distinctions" (*abwāb al-furūq*). Ibn Qutayba, *Adab al-kātib*, ed. Muḥammad al-Dālī (Beirut: Muʾassasat al-Risāla, 1967), 144–62.

50 These two words, *gharīb* and *nawādir*, are often said to refer to different kinds of words, *gharīb* to obscure usages of known words and *nawādir* to rare words. In reality, however, there is a great deal of overlap in the use of these terms. For an example of this kind of work, see al-Ḥusayn ibn Aḥmad ibn Khālawayh, *Names of the Lion*, trans. David Larsen (Seattle: Wave Books, 2017).

ʿAskarī's *al-Furūq al-lughawiyya* seeks to demonstrate the differences between supposed synonyms in order to demonstrate the perfection of the Arabic language. The theological debate over the existence of synonyms in Arabic went to the heart of contentions about the nature of Arabic. In establishing subtle differences between similar words, the authors of these works seek to disprove the existence of complete synonymy in Arabic, and, by extension, superfluous elements in the language of God's revelation.

Since, in his view, Arabic contains no redundancies, it must be a perfect language. Abū Hilāl al-ʿAskarī makes this point explicitly:

> The proof that a difference in expressions and words requires a difference in meaning is the following. A noun is a word that refers to a concept denoted. When you indicate a concept once, it is understood. A second or third indication, therefore, does not convey additional meaning. He who established the Arabic language (*wāḍiʿ al-lugha*) is wise (*ḥakīm*) and did not include that which does not convey any meaning ... Any two words that are used for one concept or entity in one language (*kull ismayn yajriyāni ʿalā maʿnā min al-maʿānī aw ʿayn min al-aʿyān fī lugha wāḥida*)—each one of these words—requires a difference in meaning that the other does not require. Otherwise, the second word would be redundant and there would be no need for it.[51]

This theological claim constitutes the purpose of al-ʿAskarī's book. The theological and polemical concerns expressed in the lexicographical *furūq* genre suggests that a similar set of concerns can be found within the legal tradition. An interesting case here is the text *al-Furūq wa-manʿ al-tarāduf* ("Distinctions in Meaning and the Impossibility of Synonymy") by al-Ḥakīm al-Tirmidhī (d. *ca.* 298/910). While the title suggests a strong interest in the denial of synonymy, the work consists of a brief introduction and the presentation of lexicographic distinctions. Not all authors of works of lexicographic distinctions were primarily interested in denying synonymy. Yet even among authors who accepted Arabic synonymy, theological interests remained primary. The acceptance or rejection of synonymy was implicit in lexicographic distinctions as a literary enterprise.[52]

---

51 Abū Hilāl al-ʿAskarī, *al-Furūq al-lughawiyya*, ed. Muḥammad Ibrāhīm Salīm (Cairo: Dār al-ʿIlm wa-l-Thaqāfa, 1998), 22. While it is possible to interpret his statement as applying to all languages, in the context of a book on Arabic synonyms it is clear that he is interested in particular in the status of Arabic.

52 Al-Ḥakīm al-Tirmidhī, *al-Furūq wa-manʿ al-tarāduf*, ed. Muḥammad Ibrāhīm Juyūshī (Cairo: al-Nahār, 1998).

Early Lexicographical Activity

Arabic philology, a field that embraced grammar, phonology, and lexicography, was one of the first scholarly disciplines to develop in the early Muslim community. While each of these areas was to become a discrete discipline during the Abbasid era, they began as three "tracks" within a single discipline, known interchangeably as "*naḥw*" or "*lugha*." Practitioners of one field, therefore, could be referred by contemporaneous sources as engaging in either discipline.[53] As a result, later labels placed on earlier figures are frequently unhelpful in understanding earlier periods: an author called a "grammarian" (*naḥwī*) may not have been involved exclusively or even primarily with grammar, but may also have practiced lexicography. Given the breadth of study, factors driving development in one field must have influenced the other. It was only once these fields became separate disciplines that differences emerged between a *naḥwī* and a *lughawī*. Accordingly, the discussion here tries to focus on a broad range of philological activity.

Contemporary scholarship has disproportionately focused on early grammar instead of early lexicography. Moreover, even research on lexicography has tended to narrowly look at comprehensive dictionaries, such as the *Kitāb al-ʿAyn* by Khalīl ibn Aḥmad (d. *ca.* 170/786) or *Kitāb al-Jīm* by Abū ʿAmr al-Shaybānī (d. *ca.* 206/821), rather than at specialized dictionaries or lexica, such as dictionaries of plants, lists of arabicized words (*al-muʿarrab*), books of homonyms, and so on.[54] Recently, Ramzi Baalbaki has divided the history of Arabic lexicography into three different areas: (i) early lexicographical efforts, (ii) specialized lexica, and (iii) comprehensive lexica.[55]

Baalbaki shows that the early Arabic lexicographical tradition was concerned to gather the Arabic lexicon and organizing its words into a useable lin-

---

53 Monique Bernards, "Grammarians' Circle of Learning: A Social Network Analysis," in *ʿAbbasid Studies II: Occasional Papers of the School of ʿAbbasid Studies, Leuven, 28 June–1 July 2004*, ed. John Nawas (Leuven: Uitgeverij Peeters en Departement Oosterse Studies, 2010), 144 n. 2. See also Michael Carter, "Arabic Grammar," in *Cambridge History of Arabic Literature: Religion, Learning and Science in the ʿAbbāsid Period*, eds. M.J.L. Young et al. (Cambridge: Cambridge University Press, 1990), 118–38.

54 On comprehensive dictionaries, see especially John Haywood, *Arabic Lexicography: Its History and Its Place in the General History of Lexicography* (Leiden: Brill, 1965); Stefan Wild, *Das Kitāb al-ʿain und die arabische Lexicographie* (Wiesbaden: Harrassowitz, 1965); and Ḥusayn Naṣṣār, *al-Muʿjam al-ʿarabī: nashʾatuhu wa-taṭawwuruhu*, expanded ed., 2 vols. (Cairo: Dār Miṣr, 1408/1988). For further discussion, see Ramzi Baalbaki, *The Arabic Lexicographical Tradition: From the 2nd/8th to the 12th/18th Century* (Leiden: Brill, 2014), vii–x.

55 See Baalbaki, *Arabic Lexicographical Tradition.*

guistic resource.[56] As part of these efforts, lexicographers made explicit efforts to collect and explain obscure words and usages. Michael Carter views this activity as a "forerunner" of the comprehensive dictionaries of the fourth/tenth century and sees the earliest activity as consisting of "entirely secular word-lists, names of animals, meteorological features, near-homonyms, difficult genders and morphologies, etc."[57]

Despite Carter's claims that these word-lists were "entirely secular," leading to the lack of interest in this project on the part of those concerned with the Qur'an, many these works demonstrate certain theological tendencies.[58] In fact, the field of lexicography as a whole was hardly secular. Rather, it began, at least in part, as an attempt to understand the language of the Qur'an, thereby endowing it with a religious character that remained an enduring part of Arabic lexicography. While lexicography was not solely used to advance theological arguments, its religious underpinning cannot be ignored. The theological character of specialized word-lists encouraged a consideration of lexicographic *furūq* in their theological contexts, which played an important part in the emergence of *furūq*.

Some of the earliest scholarly lexicographical activity focused on "obscure words and rare usages" (*al-gharīb wa-l-nawādir*).[59] One impetus for collecting *gharīb* material was a concern with understanding and explaining the Arabic language of the Qur'an. This concern is particular evident among those scholars who used their scholarship to push for particular interpretations of the Qur'an. Not all philologists, however, agreed with the exegetical explorations of their colleagues.[60]

The point to note in this discussion is not whether or not any particular strain of lexicography was theological, but rather that lexicography could be used to serve a theological agenda or to demonstrate theological claims. Of course, not every lexicographer pursued lexicography out of piety or theological commitments to further the understanding of Islam's sacred text. It may be possible that Carter's analysis of the early activity as being overtly secular is correct, but those works nonetheless retained an importance for later and more theologically inclined lexicographers. In this sense, the theological motive was one of the primary factors that drove lexicography. The disagreement over the legitima-

---

56 Haywood, *Arabic Lexicography*, 12–19.

57 Michael Carter, "Lexicography, Medieval," in *Encyclopedia of Arabic Literature*, 2 vols., ed. Julie Scott Meisami and Paul Starkey (London: Ashgate, 1998), 2:467.

58 Carter, "Lexicography, Medieval," 467.

59 Baalbaki, *Arabic Lexicographical Tradition*, 63.

60 Baalbaki, *Arabic Lexicographical Tradition*, 41.

cy of lexicographers interpreting the Qur'an points to the fact that lexicographers were, in fact, involved in religious debates.[61]

Most of the lexical data found in works of distinctions was recorded by philologists performing "fieldwork," to use an anachronistic term. Lexicographers would go to the desert and collect linguistic data from nomadic Bedouins, who "provided much of the raw material for the early monographs that dealt with *ġarīb* and *nawādir* or with specific semantic fields."[62] Nomadic Bedouins were chosen because of their supposedly complete knowledge of Arabic since they were "pure Arabs," untainted by urban cosmopolitan life. Bedouins lived only among other Arabs, the thinking went, and would presumably speak an unadulterated form of Arabic. Indeed, the amount of linguistic data gathered by the lexicographers is remarkable.[63]

The collection of these words was done as a way of recording the scope of the Arabic language. It was not a guide to correct usage *per se*, a goal pursued by works of *furūq* proper. In fact, Thābit ibn Abī Thābit (*fl.* third/ninth c.), in his *Kitāb al-Farq*, says: "Occasionally, one of these words is used in place of another ... for reasons of poetic necessity."[64] This concession to poetic license, however, was exceptional, in Thābit's eyes, and only occurred under linguistic "duress" in order to fit poetic meter. As works of *gharīb* grew in the third/ninth century, authors sought new ways to organize them. The very category of *gharīb* already represents a certain level of sorting and classifying information. Only particular words are chosen as *gharīb*. Such collections were not attempting to capture the entire Arabic language, nor did they attempt, as other books do, to document solecisms (*laḥn*) or list contronyms (*aḍḍād*).

---

61 Baalbaki, *Arabic Lexicographical Tradition*, 41.

62 Baalbaki, *Arabic Lexicographical Tradition*, 20. Monique Bernards, however, has argued strongly against this view. While the Arabic sources are intent on informing us that both lexicographers and grammarians gathered their data through exhaustive travel, she notes that biographical sources do not provide any support for this idea. The idea of travelling for knowledge (*al-ṭalab fī l-ʿilm*), in her view, was primarily a literary trope, not a lived reality. See Monique Bernards, "*Ṭalab al-ʿIlm* amongst the Linguists of Arabic during the ʿAbbāsid Period," in *ʿAbbasid Studies: Occasional Papers of the School of ʿAbbasid Studies, Cambridge, 6–10 July 2002*, ed. J.E. Montgomery: (Leuven: Uitgeverij Peeters en Departement Oosterse Studies, 2004).

63 We learn from such informants, for example, that the word *shifa* refers to a human's lips, while *mishfar* to those of a camel, those of hoofed animals are called *jaḥfal* but for animals with cloven-hoofs the correct term is either *miqamma* or *miramma*. Some sources record this word as *marimma*, see Edward William Lane, *An Arabic-English Lexicon in Eight Parts*, 8 vols., reprint (Beirut: Librarie du Liban, 1968), s.v. "*marimma*," 1:1152. Thābit ibn Abī Thābit, *Kitāb al-Farq*, ed. Ḥātim Ṣaliḥ al-Ḍāmin (Beirut: Muʾassasat al-Risāla, 1408/1988), 18.

64 Thābit ibn Abī Thābit, *Kitāb al-Farq*, 20.

Words identified as *gharīb* and *nawādir* were organized thematically, alphabetically, or sometimes not at all; such organizational rubrics were similar to those employed in other specialized lexica. Books would be alphabetized in a variety of different ways: sometimes according to the first letter of the trilateral root of the term, sometimes according to the final letter within the root, sometimes according to the *abjadī* ordering of the Arabic alphabet, and sometimes according to the *alifbāʾī* sequence.[65] As Tilman Seidensticker writes: "Many books on *ʾaḍdād* did not order the words treated; [Abū Ṭayyib] al-Luġawī groups them according to the first radical; and aṣ-Ṣaġānī (d. 650/1252) uses a fully alphabetical arrangement. Books on homonyms were also composed from the beginning of the ninth century," though they do not have clear discernible ordering patterns.[66] Since it is the books of *farq* that are of primary interest to this study, their organizational patters will be examined in more detail.

Books of *Farq*

The thematic organization of linguistic books of *farq* is directly relevant to the *furūq* tradition. As *gharīb* works spread, their focus narrowed, often addressing particular areas of the Arabic language. Specifically, *gharīb* works began to draw from scriptural and related material, as in collections of *gharīb al-Qurʾān* (obscure words found in the Qur'an) and *gharīb al-ḥadīth* (obscure words found in the hadith). In addition, *gharīb* scholarship collected words related to less religious topics, such as plants (*nabāt*), horses (*khayl*), insects (*ḥasharāt*) or the physical constitution of humans (*khalq al-insān*). These topical *gharīb* books served as repositories of lexical data for particular subject areas.

Early books on *farq* are not direct comparisons of apparent synonyms. In this way, *farq* books are quite different from those of lexicographical *furūq*, and should be considered more of a sub-genre of works on the body parts and life-stages of animals. These *farq* works focus on explaining various technical terms for the body and life-cycle, not on clarifying distinctions between closely related words. As an example, the *Kitāb al-Farq fī l-lugha* written by Abū ʿAlī Muḥammad ibn al-Mustanīr (d. 206/821), better known as Quṭrub, is divided into the following sections, as given by Khalīl Ibrāhīm al-ʿAṭiyya and Ramaḍān ʿAbd al-Tawwāb, who edited the critical edition of this work. Their edition, from

---

65 For more on alphabetization, see *Encyclopedia of Arabic Language and Linguistics*, s.v. "Lexicography: Classical Arabic" (Tilman Seidensticker), 3:30–37.

66 *Encyclopedia of Arabic Language and Linguistics*, s.v. "Lexicography: Classical Arabic, 7. Specialized Lexica" (Tilman Seidensticker), 3:34.

1987, is based on a manuscript from the early fourth/tenth century manuscript housed in Vienna (a very early date for the manuscript of an Arabic book). While these division titles are not Quṭrub's, they provide insight into the way this work is indeed organized.[67]

1) Divisions of the Body
2) Birth, Pregnancy, and Terms for Offspring
3) Voices and Cries of Humans, Animals, and Birds
4) Sounds of Humans, Animals, and Birds
5) Groups of Humans and Animals
6) Death of Humans and Animals[68]

While the division of this work is relatively straightforward, the author nevertheless offers a deliberate structure, dividing the body from head to toe and tracing an individual from birth to death. Note that these lexicographic precursors to lexicographic *furūq* focus not on making a distinction, but take for granted that distinctions occur, i.e. that words are different. Within each broad category, Quṭrub assumes a diversity of distinct terms corresponding to different animals. The understanding that drives works of *farq* is the inherent similarity of synonyms. Later books on *furūq* understanding an inherent dissimilarity and seek to resolve potential confusion that may arise about the meaning of a term.

Curiously, interest in insects seems to have driven the earliest of the *farq* works. Ḥusayn Naṣṣār explains that this may be due to the Qur'an's mentions of insects (*ḥasharāt*), suggesting that the early lexicographers may have been driven by a hermeneutic need.[69] Naṣṣār points out that such works were at first standalone treatises, but later authors incorporated their own writing on this topic as chapters or sections of encyclopedic works like Ibn Qutayba's *Adab al-kātib* and *Fiqh al-lugha* by al-Thaʿālabī (d. 429/1039). Much of this *farq*

---

67 This work has been edited and published twice. The first publication, by Rudolf Geyer in 1888, was based on an incomplete manuscript, with the title *Mā khālafa fīhi l-insān al-bahīm fī asmāʾ al-wuḥūsh wa-ṣifātihi*. Abū ʿAlī Muḥammad ibn Mustanīr Quṭrub, *Das Kitāb al-wuḥūš von al-ʾAṣmaʿi mit einem Paralleltexts von Quṭrub*, ed. Rudolf Geyer (Vienna: F. Tempsky. 1888). More recently, Khalīl Ibrāhīm ʿAṭiyya and Ramaḍān ʿAbd al-Tawwāb have published a critical edition of this work. Abū ʿAlī Muḥammad ibn al-Mustanīr Quṭrub, *Kitāb al-Farq*, ed. Khalīl Ibrāhīm al-ʿAṭiyya and Ramaḍān ʿAbd al-Tawwāb (Maktabat al-Thaqāfa al-Dīniyya, 1987).
68 Quṭrub, *Kitāb al-Farq*, 28, see pp. 32–34 for a description of the Vienna manuscript.
69 Naṣṣār, *al-Muʿjam al-ʿarabī*, 100. In particular, Naṣṣār refers to the mentions of ants (Q al-Naml 27:18), bees (Q al-Nahl 16:68), flies (Q al-Ḥajj 22:73), scorpions (Q al-ʿAnkabūt 29:41), locusts (Q al-Aʿrāf 7:133, Q al-Qamar 54:7), and gnats (Q al-Baqara 2:26).

writing focuses on clarifying and distinguishing animal terms. They exhibit features that later writers adopted in lexicographic and legal works of *furūq*.

The lexicographer Abū Ziyād al-Kilābī (d. *ca.* 200/815–16) appears to have written the first work of lexicographic distinction (*al-farq*).[70] Shortly thereafter, Quṭrub wrote his *al-Farq fī l-lugha*, which is the earliest surviving work on linguistic distinction. The earliest examples of works on linguistic distinction (*al-farq*) are concerned to distinguish rare words used for the limbs, appendages, and actions of humans versus other animal and insect groups. Quṭrub's *al-Farq fī l-lugha* is quite similar to the other contemporaneous works titled *Kitāb al-Farq* of both al-Aṣmaʿī (d. *ca.* 213/828) and Thābit ibn Abī Thābit, both of which are alternatively titled *Khalq al-insān*.[71] The entries themselves are grouped around body parts so that, for instance, they all start with *bāb al-fam* (Chapter on Mouths), followed by *bāb al-anf* (Chapter on Noses), *bāb al-ẓufur* (Chapter on Nails), and so on.

Each chapter dismisses apparent synonyms by arguing that words with similar denotation actually refer to distinct kinds or classes of animal. Thābit ibn Abī Thābit states this explicitly in his introduction:

> This book covers those parts of the body for which there are different words when referring to humans, four-legged domestic animals, wild animals, and more. This is also a book that agrees with al-Aṣmaʿī, Ibn al-Aʿrābī, Abū ʿUbayd, Abū Naṣr and other scholars.[72]

The tradition of *farq* writing was passed down from teacher to student. Thābit ibn Abī Thābit's book is nearly identical to that of his teacher al-Aṣmaʿī. Thābit quotes al-Aṣmaʿī verbatim for long passages—usually with attribution. Quṭrub's book is arranged in largely the same way as al-Aṣmaʿī's. The organization of the *Kitāb al-Alfāẓ* by Ibn al-Sikkīt (d. 244/858), on the other hand, differs significantly, and its structure is hardly self-explanatory. While the arrangement of some sections is occasionally intuitive, connections between sections is frequently confounding. For instance, the first two chapters address wealth (*al-ghinā wa-l-khiṣb*) and poverty (*al-faqr wa-l-jadb*), while the next two treat groups (*jamāʿa*) and battalions (*katāʾib*). Both of these pairs are logically related—

---

70 Ramaḍān ʿAbd al-Tawwāb, "*Kitāb al-Farq li-Ibn Fāris wa-turāth al-farq fī l-ʿarabiyya,*" in *Kitāb al-Farq* by Ibn Fāris al-Lughawī, ed. Ramaḍān ʿAbd al-Tawwāb (Cairo: Maktabat al-Khātimī 1402/1982), 42. Ibn al-Nadīm also credits Abū Ziyād as the earliest philologist to write on distinctions, Ibn al-Nadīm, *al-Fihrist*, 1.1:118–90. The entry on Abū Ziyād is on 1.1:121.

71 ʿAbd al-Malik ibn Qurayb al-Aṣmaʿī, *Kitāb al-Farq*, ed. Ṣabīḥ al-Tamīmī (Beirut: Dār Usāmah, 1987).

72 Thābit ibn Abī Thābit, *Kitāb al-Farq*, 17.

wealth and poverty are antonyms; groups and battalions are near-synonyms—but the logic that puts wealth and poverty next to groups and battalions is not clear.

Unlike other authors, Ibn al-Sikkīt does accept synonymy in Arabic. For example, in the section *Bāb mā lā budda minhu* he lists synonyms for the phrase *lā budda minhu*, "there is no way out; one must do something." It begins on the authority of al-Aṣmaʿī: "There is no *ḥumma* from that nor a *rumma*. That is to say, there is no escape from this."[73] The author's putting the terms *ḥumma* and *rumma* in apposition (*badal*) suggests their semantic equivalence; Ibn al-Sikkīt uses one to stand for the other. Similarly, Quṭrub, author of the earliest surviving work on distinctions, does seem to believe in the existence of synonymy in the Arabic language. Jalal al-Dīn al-Suyūṭī (d. 911/1505) quotes him as asserting that "the Arabs used (*awqaʿat*) two words for one denotation to prove the breadth of their language (*kalāmihim*)."[74] This contrasts with the concern exhibited by many authors of works of linguistic distinctions to celebrate the perfection of the Arabic language.

Problems abound in the surviving manuscripts of these early works, precluding us from reaching general conclusions about their structure, contents, and objectives. Since the extant manuscripts are usually from centuries after the author's lifetime, we cannot know whether the original organization of these earliest works is preserved. "The preserved manuscripts may turn out to be half a millennium later than their originals and, though this may not be indicated in the manuscripts themselves, they may have undergone various recensions and redactions during this time."[75] Jaakko Hämeen-Anttila is correct in doubting the provenance of the organization. Not only can works be changed as they undergo copying and recopying, but there is still controversy over the nature of the earliest Arabic books as such. We do not know to what extent they were given a final redaction by the author, to what extent they could be considered authored

73 "*Lā ḥumma min dhālika wa-lā rumma, ayy lā budda minhu*," Yaʿqūb ibn Isḥāq ibn Sikkīt, *Kitāb al-Alfāẓ: Aqdam muʿjam fī l-maʿānī*, ed. Fakhr al-Dīn Qabbāwa (Beirut: Maktabat Lubnān Nāshirūn, 1998), 183.

74 Jalāl al-Dīn al-Suyūṭī, *al-Muzhir fī ʿulūm al-lugha wa-anwāʿihā*, 2 vols, ed. Muḥammad Aḥmad Jād al-Mawlā Bek, Muḥammad Abū l-Faḍl Ibrāhīm, and ʿAlī Muḥammad al-Bajāwī (Cairo: Maktabat Dār al-Turāth, n.d.), 1:400.

75 Jaakko Hämeen-Anttila, "al-Aṣmaʿī, Early Arabic Lexicography, and *Kutub al-Farq*," *Zeitschrift für Geschichte der arabisch-islamischen Wissenschaften* 16 (2005): 141.

works, and to what extent were they more open and receptive to further change and emendation.[76]

Kutub al-Furūq al-Lughawiyya

In the fourth/tenth century, the new concept of *furūq* emerges among lexicographers. Earlier books of *farq* focus on *nawādir* and *gharīb* (obscure and rare usages) limiting themselves, in the style of *Kitāb al-Alfāẓ*, to singular topics or themes. But by the time that al-Ḥakīm al-Tirmidhī composes his *Furūq waman' al-tarāduf* in the third/ninth century, the term *furūq* is no longer synonymous with rare or strange lexical usages, but is starting to be driven by concerns about synonymy. A change in terminology accompanied this increased focus on synonymy. These works of distinctions are, for the first time, given titles that include the term *furūq*. This is not the same as the title *Kitāb al-Farq fī l-lugha*, employed by Quṭrub, al-Aṣma'ī, and Thābit ibn Abī Thābit, among others, which only use the word in the singular. While these new treatises continued the various traditions within lexicographic scholarship, they develop a separate, more solidified concept of *furūq*, and evince stronger theological impulses. Abū Hilāl al-'Askarī's *Kitāb al-Furūq fī l-lugha* was among the earliest exemplars of this move, a work that highlights the theological stakes in this genre.[77]

Abū Hilāl al-'Askarī

Abū Hilāl al-Ḥasan ibn 'Abdallāh al-'Askarī was a prolific author, but was hardly prominent in his own time. According to George Kanazi, "our information about Abū Hilāl is very meagre, uninteresting and lacking in detail, because the early

76 See Gregor Schoeler, *The Genesis of Literature in Islam: From the Aural to the Read*, trans. Shawkat M. Toorawa (Edinburgh: Edinburgh University Press, 2009). The *Kitāb al-'Ayn* of Khalīl ibn Aḥmad is a pertinent example; many passages in this book seem to have been written by Ibn Durayd. See Ramzi Baalbaki, "*Kitāb al-'Ayn* and *Jamharat al-Lugha*," in *Early Medieval Arabic: Studies on al-Khalīl ibn Aḥmad*, ed. Karin C. Ryding (Washington D.C.: Georgetown University Press, 1998).

77 It is possible that the title *Kitāb al-Furūq* was a later addition to the text. The manuscript record and the bio-bibliographic tradition, however, all refer to it by either *Kitāb al-Furūq* or a slight variation on this title: *Kitāb al-Furūq al-lughawiyya* or *al-Furūq fī l-lugha*. Even if al-'Askarī himself did not title the text in this way, the tradition quickly recognized it as a work of distinctions and consistently referred to it as such.

sources mentioning him are very few."[78] In part, this obscurity can be ascribed to confusion with his similarly named teacher, Abū Aḥmad al-Ḥasan ibn ʿAbdallāh al-ʿAskarī (d. 382/993). Biographers often failed to distinguish between teacher and student, rendering any complicating the reconstruction of the student's biography. In order to understand the contribution of Abū Hilāl, a brief reconsideration of both two figures is worthwhile.

According to Kanazi, "[a]s early as the year 510 A.H.[/1116–17]), al-Silafī could point to a confusion between the two ʿAskarīs, Abū Aḥmad (293–382 A.H.) and Abū Hilāl (d. after 400 A.H.)."[79] Al-Silafī refers to Abū Ṭāhir Aḥmad ibn Muḥammad al-Silafī, a noted hadith scholar and grammarian.[80] He is quoted in Yāqūt's *Muʾjam al-udabāʾ* as blaming confusion between these figures on their similar names, stating that "it is likely that one was mentioned when the other was meant."[81] In fact, in order to resolve this misunderstanding, al-Silafī had to consult Abū l-Muẓaffar Muḥammad ibn Abī l-ʿAbbās al-Abīwardī (d. 507/1113), the foremost contemporary linguist (*al-raʾīs*) in Hamadan.[82] It is not clear that al-Silāfī was able to resolve his confusion, since "[t]he information provided by al-Silafī seems to be inaccurate in one place at least."[83] This means that even al-Silafī's account is already prone to uncertainty regarding the two al-ʿAskarīs.

Circumstantial evidence for the theological ideas of Abū Hilāl al-ʿAskarī does, however, point to his affiliation with Muʿtazilī theology. Kanazi, who be-

---

78 George Kanazi, *Studies in the Kitāb aṣ-Ṣināʿatayn of Abū Hilāl al-ʿAskarī* (Brill: Leiden, 1989), 1.

79 Kanazi, *Studies*, 2. See also their respective entries in the *Encyclopaedia of Islam*, Third Edition. Both entries are written by Beatrice Gruendler. While she devotes 1,158 words to Abū Aḥmad, Abū Hilāl received about half that number, 680 words. EI^3 s.v. "al-ʿAskarī, Abū Aḥmad" (Beatrice Gruendler) and EI^3 s.v. "al-ʿAskarī, Abū Hilāl" (Beatrice Gruendler).

80 Al-Silafī was born in Isfahan, travelled to Baghdad for his education, and then to Tyre and Alexandria where he settled. He was a well-known scholar and teacher. He was born in 472/1079–80 or 478/1085–86 and died on 5 Rabīʿ II, 576 / 8 August, 1180. Al-Silafī himself merits only a short biography in Ibn Khallikān's *Wafayāt al-Aʿyān*. See Shams al-Dīn Aḥmad ibn Muḥammad ibn Khallikān, *Wafayāt al-aʿyān wa-anbāʾ abnāʾ al-zamān*, ed. Iḥsān ʿAbbās (Beirut: Dār Ṣādir, 1398/1978), 1:105–107, no. 44; see also Mac-Guckin de Slane, trans., *Ibn Khallikan's Wafayat al-A'yan wa Anba' Abna' al-Zaman (M. de Slane's English Translation)*, vol. 1, ed. S. Moinul Haq (Karachi: Pakistan Historical Society, 1961), 152–56.

81 Yāqūt al-Ḥamawī l-Rūmī, *Muʿjam al-udabāʾ: Irshād al-arīb ilā maʿrifat al-adīb*, 7 vols., ed. Iḥsān ʿAbbās (Beirut: Dār al-Gharb al-Islāmī, 1993), 2:918.

82 On al-Abīwardī, see EI^3, s.v. "al-Abīwardī, Abū al-Muẓaffar Muḥammad" (Geert Jan van Gelder) and Yāqūt al-Ḥamawī, *Muʿjam al-udabāʾ*, 5:2360–76.

83 Kanazi, *Studies*, 2 n. 11.

lieves "that Abū Hilāl belonged to the Muʿtazilites,"[84] bases this conclusion primarily on three passages in Abū Hilāl's oeuvre. First, Abū Hilāl claims that Wāṣil ibn ʿAṭāʾ (d. 131/748–49) was the first Muslim to write on theology (*kalām*), offering a lengthy defense of his intellectual originality.[85] Second, Abū Hilāl hints at Muʿtazilī leanings in his *Kitāb al-Ṣināʿatayn*. In a discussion concerning the use of proofs (*al-baṣar bi-l-ḥujja*), he mentions the createdness of the Qur'an, one of the central tenets of the Muʿtazila. "Someone," he writes, "asked Abū ʿAlī Muḥammad ibn ʿAbd al-Wahhāb [d. 303/915–16], 'What proof is there that the Qur'an is created?' 'God could create something like it,' he answered."[86] Finally, in the introduction to that book, he further mentions his commitment to the principle of "the reward and punishment in the afterlife (*al-waʿd wa-l-waʿīd*)," another central tenet in Muʿtazilī theology.[87] In a study of his literary theory, Amal al-Mashāyikh also infers from Abū Hilāl's style of argumentation and his preference for *badīʿ* that he was a Muʿtazilī.[88]

The biographical dictionaries tell us the names of many of Abū Hilāl's teachers and students but provide no substantial information about them, perhaps, as Kanazi suggests, "due to their Shīʿite or Muʿtazilite sympathies."[89] This lack of information holds true for all of Abū Hilāl's teachers, save the aforementioned Abū Aḥmad al-ʿAskarī, about whom little is known with confidence. We do know, however, that "Abū Aḥmad al-Ḥasan b. ʿAbd Allāh b. Saʿīd al-ʿAskarī (293–382/906–93) was a prolific author and the leading scholar of his day in hadith, *lugha*, and *adab*."[90] Importantly, he was accused of being a Muʿtazilī.[91] We

---

84 Kanazi, *Studies*, 14.

85 Abū Hilāl al-ʿAskarī, *Kitāb al-Awāʾil*, ed. Muḥammad al-Miṣrī and Walīd Qaṣṣāb, 2 vols. (Damascus: Wizārat al-Thaqāfa wa-l-Irshād al-Qawmī, 1975), 2:134–38. Wāṣil ibn ʿAṭāʾ was the theologian credited with founding the Muʿtazila school of theology. See EI^2, s.v. "Wāṣil b. ʿAṭāʾ" (Josef van Ess).

86 Abū Hilāl al-ʿAskarī, *Kitāb al-Ṣināʿatayn al-kitāba wa-l-shiʿr*, ed. ʿAlī Muḥammad al-Bajāwī and Muḥammad Abū l-Faḍl Ibrāhīm ([Cairo:] Dār Iḥyāʾ al-Kutub al-ʿArabiyya, 1371/1952), 14.

87 Al-ʿAskarī, *al-Ṣināʿatayn*, 2. For more on the "promised good and the promised evil," see Richard M. Frank, *Beings and Their Attributes: The Teaching of the Basrian School of the Muʿtazila in the Classical Period* (Albany, NY: State University of New York Press, 1978).

88 Amal al-Mashāyikh, *Abū Hilāl al-ʿAskarī nāqidan* (Amman: Wizārat al-Thaqāfa, 2002), 72, 296. This claim is somewhat unclear. *Badīʿ* refers to the liberal use of figures of speech and paranomasia in writing. It was first espoused by "modern" (*muḥdath*) poets in the third/ninth and fourth/tenth centuries and later adopted by most Arabic writers. See EI^3, s.v. "*badīʿ*" (Geert Jan van Gelder) and Suzanne P. Stetkevych, *Abū Tammām and the Poetics of the ʿAbbāsid Age* (Leiden: Brill, 1991).

89 Kanazi, *Studies*, 9.

90 EI^3, s.v. "al-ʿAskarī, Abū Aḥmad" (Beatrice Gruendler).

also know that he and the Buyid Vizier al-Ṣāḥib ibn ʿAbbād (d. 385/995) were in close contact.[92] Ṣāḥib ibn ʿAbbād was "a tireless champion of [Basran] Muʿtazili rationalism."[93] Abū Aḥmad was one of Abū Hilāl's main teachers, if not his most important one.[94]

Abū Hilāl taught many students, although little is known about most of them. One of his students, Abū Saʿd Ismāʿīl ibn ʿAlī l-Rāzī l-Sammām, is mentioned as having been a prominent Muʿtazilī. We know from the *Siyar aʿlām al-nubalāʾ* of Shams al-Dīn al-Dhahabī (d. 748/1348) that he travelled widely in search of knowledge. "He was an authority on different readings of the Koran, on *ḥadīth* and *fiqh*. He had a deep knowledge of the Ḥanafite and Shafiʿite schools of law, and was at the same time one of the leading scholars of the Muʿtazila."[95] However circumstantial, this likewise points to Abū Hilāl al-ʿAskarī's inclination towards Muʿtazilī theology.[96]

Furthermore, later readers interpreted his works within a Muʿtazilite framework, a view that seems to gain support from the *Kitāb al-Furūq*. His discussion of the absence of complete synonymy in Arabic—a principle that he applies to language in general—resonates with a Muʿtazilī inclination to deny the existence of synonymy in the Arabic, as the language of God's revelation. Regarding the lack of synonymy in Arabic, he writes:

---

91 Ibn al-Jawzī, *al-Muntaẓam fī tawārīkh al-mulūk wa-l-umam*, ed. Sabīl Zakkār (Beirut: Dār al-Fikr, 1415/1995–96), 4265/9:43. Curiously, Ibn al-Jawzī includes al-Ḥasan's death notice in the chapter on the year 387/997, and mentions a story told by Abū Zakariyyāʾ Yaḥyā ibn ʿAlī l-Tabrīzī about an encounter al-Tabrīzī had with Abū l-Ḥasan. This story mentions that Abū l-Ḥasan passed away on 8 Dhū l-Ḥijja 379 / 9 March 990.

92 Kanazi, *Studies*, 5. See also Muḥsin al-Ḥusaynī l-ʿĀmilī, *Aʿyān al-Shīʿa*, 28 vols., ed. Ḥasan al-Amīn and Muḥsin al-Amīn (Beirut: Dār al-Taʿāruf li-l-Maṭbūʿāt, 1998) 8:216.

93 Encyclopaedia Iranica, s.v. "Ebn ʿAbbād, Esmāʿīl, al-Ṣāheb Kāfī al-Kofāt" (Maurice Pomerantz). According to the entry in EI^2, "[s]ome Shīʿīs like Ibn Bābūya ... claim [Ibn ʿAbbād] as one of them," and ʿAbd al-Jabbār accused him of being Shi'i as well. His Muʿtazilism, however, does not seem to have been in doubt; see EI^2, s.v. "Ibn ʿAbbād" (Claude Cahen and Charles Pellat). See also Maurice A. Pomerantz, *Licit Magic: The Life and Letters of al-Ṣāḥib ibn ʿAbbād (d. 385/995)*, (Leiden: Brill, 2017).

94 Kanazi, *Studies*, 7.

95 Kanazi, *Studies*, 9, citing Shams al-Dīn Muḥammad ibn Aḥmad al-Dhahabī, *Siyar aʿlām al-nubalāʾ*, 25 vols., ed. Shuʿayb al-Arnāʾūṭ and Muḥammad Taʿyīm al-ʿAraqsūsī (Beirut: Muʾassasat al-Risāla, 1317/1996), 18:55–60.

96 In addition, ʿAskar Mukram, Abū Hilāl's hometown, was the center of the "Jubbāʾī school" of Muʿtazilī theology, see EI^2, "Muʿtazila" (Daniel Gimaret). Josef van Ess claims that Abū Hilāl was "vermutlich Muʿtazilit." His only citation for this claim, however, is Kanazi's book cited here. Josef van Ess, *Theologie und Gesellschaft im 2. und 3. Jahrhundert Hidschra: Eine Geschichte des religiösen Denkens im frühen Islam*, 6 vols. (Berlin: De Gruyter, 1991–97), 4:246.

> The creator of the Arabic language is wise (*wāḍiʿ al-lugha ḥakīm*). He did not include in it that which does not convey meaning ... Every two words that are used for one concept or entity in one language, each one of these words requires a difference in meaning that the first does not entail. Otherwise, the second word would be redundant and there would be no need for it.[97]

Abū Hilāl argues that the creator of the Arabic language, presumably God, created a perfect language, which, in order to be perfect, cannot have two signifiers for one and the same signified.[98] Otherwise, one of these two signifiers would be redundant and could be removed from the language without any loss. Such redundancy would thus signify imperfection.

Other strong theological overtones run throughout Abū Hilāl's biography and works. While it seems likely that Abū Hilāl was a Muʿtazilī, he was not explicitly engaged in systematic theological debate, but rather invoked theological postulates in order to resolve linguistic questions and to further lexicographical analysis.[99] The implicit theological underpinnings of works like Abū Hilāl's constitute a nexus with, if not a direct influence on, the theological aspects of the *furūq* of the jurists. Indeed, Abū Hilāl himself says of his own work on *furūq:* "I turned my discussions in it [this work] towards (*wa-jaʿaltu kalāmī fīhi ʿalā*) what is found in God's scripture, what is common in the words of the jurists and theologians (*al-fuqahāʾ wa-l-mutakallimīn*), and the rest of the discussions of the learned (*wa-sāʾir miḥwārāt al-nās*)."[100]

Farq and the Arabic Alphabet

Grammarians and lexicographers undertook similar distinction-thinking regarding phonetic distinctions between individual letters, most notably between the letters *ḍād* and *ẓāʾ*. Distinctions between individual letters, like questions of synonym, often had theological implications. The correct spelling and pronunciation of the letters of the Qur'an had to be ensured for many purposes. Distinguishing between these two letters was more than just a lexicographical or

---

97 Abū Hilāl, *Furūq*, 22.

98 While Abū Hilāl is not explicit in identifying God as the creator of the Arabic language, his use of the singular in this passage is suggestive of this interpretation.

99 Many contemporary intellectual works made implicit theological or philosophical claims in the context of other discussions. See James E. Montgomery, "Speech and Nature: al-Jāḥiẓ, *Kitāb al-Bayān wa-l-tabyīn*, 2.175–207," Parts 1–4, *Middle Eastern Literatures* 11.2 (2008); 12.1 (2009); 12.2 (2009); 12.3 (2009).

100 Abū Hilāl, *Furūq*, 21.

phonological endeavor: the *ḍād* was imagined as pivotal to the self-understanding of Arabic as a unique language. As Jonathan Brown notes, "[w]ritings on the difference between *ḍād* and *ẓāʾ* or lists of [ḍ] – [ẓ] minimal pairs[101] constitute a long-lived genre in Arabic philology and belles-lettres."[102] These works, however, focused primarily on understanding the *ḍād*, not the *ẓāʾ*, due to the centrality of the letter *ḍād* in understandings of the Arabic language. Philologists believed that Arabic was the only language containing the letter *ḍād*. For this reason, Arabic was referred to as "the language of the *ḍād*" (*lughat al-ḍād*). In dictionaries, for instance, the main discussion of the letter *ḍād* centers on its place within the Arabic language. The *Tāj al-ʿarūs* says: "The *ḍād* is exclusive to the Arabs (*li-l-ʿarab khāṣṣatan*), i.e., it is exclusive to their language and it is not found in the languages of non-Arabs (*lughāt al-ʿajam*). This is the truth on which everyone agrees (*aṭbaqa ʿalayhi al-jamāhīr*)."[103]

In spite of this identification of the Arabic language with the letter *ḍād*, the pronunciation of this letter has always been a source of doubt and discomfort. Many Arabic letters, it seems, have no stable pronunciation, and the *ḍād* is in fact one of the most often confused letters in the Arabic alphabet. The many pronunciations of *ḍād* was not just a feature of spoken Arabic, but of other Semitic languages as well. Scholars of Old South Arabian, for instance, have stated that the *ḍād*/*ẓāʾ* distinction was already fading during the Late Antique period. This can be seen in inscriptions, where the two graphemes are somewhat interchangable.[104] This graphic merger suggests a phonological merging of the two letters in South Arabian, a phenomenon established with more certainty for spoken Arabic in the "classical" period.[105]

---

101 Minimal pairs are words that only differ in one letter. In this case, reference is to words that are spelled the same save that a *ḍād* is being replaced by a *ẓāʾ* or vice-versa.

102 Jonathan A. C. Brown, "New Data on the Delateralization of *Ḍād* and its Merger with *Ẓāʾ* in Classical Arabic: Contributions from Old South Arabic and the Earliest Islamic Texts on Ḍ / Ẓ Minimal Pairs," *Journal of Semitic Studies* 52.2 (2007): 345.

103 Muḥammad Murtaḍā l-Ḥusaynī l-Zabīdī, *Tāj al-ʿarūs min jawāhir al-Qāmūs*, ed. ʿAbd al-Sattār Aḥmad Farrāj et al., 40 vols. (Kuwait: Maṭbaʿat Ḥukūmat al-Kuwayt 1970), 8:315–16. See, however, Abū l-Fatḥ ʿUthmān ibn Jinnī, *Sirr ṣināʿat al-iʿrāb*, ed. Ḥasan Hindāwī (Damascus: Dār al-Qalam, 1985), 1:214–15, where he says that "the *ḍād* is found in non-Arabic languages in rare cases" (*lā tūjidu fī kalām al-ʿajam illā fī qalīl*).

104 Stefan Weninger, "More Sabaic minuscule texts from Munich," *Proceedings of the Seminar for Arabian Studies* 32 (2002), 218; Christian Julien Robin, "Les inscriptions de l'arabie antique et les études arabe" *Arabica* 68.4 (2001), 534.

105 David Cohen, "Koiné, langues communes et dialectes arabes," *Arabica* 9.2 (1962), 135. Ahmad Al-Jallad has also found evidence in Safaitic inscriptions in a shift in the pronunciation of this consonant in Old Aramaic and Safaitic in the Southern Levant. See Ahmad Al-Jallad,

Jonathan Brown, in a 2007 article, divides medieval writings on *ḍād* and *ẓāʾ* into four groups:

> (1) "Wordsmithing," that is, a written performance in which the author laments the current level of people's Arabic as a way of launching into a discussion of beautiful poetry.[106] This includes statements in treatises such as "Such a word is written with a *ḍād*, which can be seen from the following poem."
>
> (2) Philological writings, focusing on teasing out the precise distinction in signification between synonymous words like *ʿaḍḍa* and *ʿaẓẓa* ("to grab with the teeth, to bite"), which, while likely dialectic variants: "People say (*yuqāl*), 'A matter that distresses me has reached me, i.e., it torments me' (*warada ʿalayya amr ʿaẓẓanī yaʿnī ʿaḍḍanī*)."[107]
>
> (3) Phonological books that discuss the proper way to pronounce these letters when reciting the Qur'an.[108]
>
> (4) A category comprised of only one example, the book *al-Rawḥa fī l-ẓāʾ wa-l-ḍād* by by al-Jarbādhqānī (*fl.* 370/980), which covers all three of the preceding areas. "The work is exhaustive rather than practical or enjoyable," says Brown.[109] Brown considers it to form a separate group, although *al-Rawḥa* can also been seen as an anthology of the three previous categories.

Let us consider an example of this literature. Al-Ṣāhib ibn ʿAbbād's discussion of these two letters is about distinguishing *ḍād* from *ẓāʾ* both in speaking and spelling. According to Brown's categorization, this work is closest to a work of wordsmithing, wherein al-Ṣāḥib ibn ʿAbbād concerns himself with [ḍ] – [ẓ] minimal pairs as a prelude to citation of beautiful poetry. He claims, however, to envision something close to a full confusion between the letters, "because of the closeness of these letters for listeners (*taqārub ajnāsihima fī l-masāmiʿ*) ... and the confusion of the correct way to write them (*iltibās ḥaqīqat kitābatihimā*)."[110] In discussing the importance of elucidating and understanding the distinction between the two letters, al-Ṣāḥib ibn ʿAbbād says: "Do you not understand that if you said, '*qarraẓtu al-rajul wa-qarraḍtuhu*' ('I praised the man and denigrated him'), that *taqrīẓ* ('eulogizing') is your praise of him and

"New Evidence from a Safaitic Inscription for a Late Velar/Uvular Realization of *ṣ in Aramaic," *Semitica* 58 (2016): 257–70.

106 Brown, "New Data," 351–52.

107 Abū l-Qāsim Ismāʿīl al-Ṣāḥib ibn ʿAbbād, *al-Farq bayn al-ḍād wa-l-ẓāʾ*, ed. Muḥammad Ḥasan Āl Yā Sīn (Baghdad: Maktabat al-Nahḍa and al-Maktaba al-ʿIlmiyya, 1377/1958), 4.

108 Brown, "New Data," 352.

109 Brown, "New Data," 352.

110 Al-Ṣāḥib ibn ʿAbbād, *al-Farq bayn al-ḍād wa-l-ẓāʾ*, 3.

taqrīḍ ('denigration') is disparagement and faultfinding?"[111] It is curious that al-Ṣāḥib Ibn ʿAbbād chooses this distinction, since *qarraẓa* means "to praise" whereas *qarraḍa* can mean either "to denigrate" or "to praise."[112] That is to say that *qarraẓa* and *qarraḍa* can mean the same thing, thus rendering the distinction between the *ẓāʾ* and *ḍād* in these words negligible, depending on the speaker's intent.

The *ḍād* had a particular importance to early Muslim communities. What was it about this issue that drew the attention of Muslim scholars? Brown sees a strong theological component at work:

> Although philologists might have enjoyed such harmless dialectical curiosities, the actual phonological identity of a word was sacrosanct. In the language of God's revelation, each word and the root from which it was formed possessed a specific meaning inherently appropriate for the thing it indicated. As it became widely established in Arabic linguistic theory, 'the assumption in language is the absence of synonymy (*al-aṣl fī l-lugha ʿadam al-tarāduf*);' each root had a unique meaning. After all, for most great Muslim linguistic theorists, language was the result of divine inspiration and not human convention.[113]

Brown distinguishes between two different levels on which these texts are operating. On one level, he finds the medieval philologists "enjoy[ing] dialectical curiosities." Such writing seems to represent a large percentage of the writing on *ḍād-ẓāʾ* pairs. Al-Ṣāḥib ibn ʿAbbād's discussion of, for instance, *ʿaḍḍa* and *ʿaẓẓa* fits this description. Distinguishing between these two words provides scholars with an opportunity to attempt to control and delineate the parameters of Arabic—the second and third groups in Brown's list—and to engage in another reading of the poetic tradition.

Brown argues convincingly that this approach has theological objectives. Assigning particular meanings to individual words reaffirms the divine nature of the Arabic language as found in the Qur'an, God's speech. The claim is not that these scholars were motivated exclusively or even primarily by this theological impetus, but that such writing about the distinction between the *ḍād* and the *ẓāʾ* has a theological component. In particular, the divine nature of Arabic and the associated belief in the absence of synonymy motivates the exploration of distinction in words and letters alike. The search for an underlying consistency—here a direct one-to-one correspondance between signifier and signified—

---

111 Al-Ṣāḥib ibn ʿAbbād, *al-Farq bayn al-ḍād wa-l-ẓāʾ*, 3.
112 Lane, *Arabic-English Lexicon*, s.v. "*qarraḍa*."
113 Brown, "New Data," 365.

is a theme that runs throughout almost all of the literature examined in this study.

Farq and *Furūq* in Other Fields

Although medicine and linguistics were the primary fields that embraced distinctions-thinking, works on distinctions appear in a variety of other scholarly disciplines. Abū l-Ajfān and Abū Fāris mention that writings in *furūq* "flourished in all of the sciences."[114] In particular, their survey shows treatises in the fields of philology, medicine, logic, grammar, and theology.[115] Most of the works that they cite, however, are not extant or are of dubious attribution.[116] The paucity of information about many works of distinctions outside the fields of lexicography and law make it difficult to write a precise and detailed general history of this kind of writing. As evidence of the flourishing of *furūq* writing in medicine, Abū l-Ajfān and Abū Fāris cite Ibn al-Jazzār's *Farq bayn al-ʿilal*, a work also known as *al-Furūq*. As discussed above, the treatise published under this name is also attributed to other individuals in both manuscript and printed editions.[117] It remains, in my understanding, unclear whether one can say that Ibn al-Jazzār wrote a book of *furūq* or what this book looked like. The uncertainties surrounding this work may primarily indicate the occasional unreliability of the major bio-bibliographic sources used by Abū l-Ajfān and Abū Fāris, Ḥājjī Khalīfa's *Kashf al-ẓunūn* and al-Ziriklī's *al-Aʿlām*, rather than about *furūq* writing itself. There are, however, similar inconsistencies, in other scholarly traditions, such as

114 Abū l-Ajfān and Abū Fāris, "*Dirāsa*," 28.

115 Abū l-Ajfān and Abū Fāris, "*Dirāsa*," 29–30.

116 For instance, in a footnote to their discussion of *al-Farq bayn al-naḥw wa-l-manṭiq* by Abū l-ʿAbbās Aḥmad ibn Muḥammad al-Sarakhsī, they cite Ḥājjī Khalīfa (d. 1067/1657) and his *Kashf al-ẓunūn* (Abū l-Ajfān and Abū Fāris, "*Dirāsa*," 30n24). They also mention, however, that there is an entry for al-Sarakhsī in al-Ziriklī's *al-Aʿlām* which does not mention the existence of this work. Al-Ziriklī bases his entry on information in Ibn al-Qifṭī's *Akhbār al-ḥukamāʾ*, Yāqūt's *Muʿjam al-buldān*, and al-Dhahabī's *Siyar al-Nubalāʾ*. Neither al-Dhahabī nor Yāqūt lists any work by this al-Sarakhsī. Ibn al-Qifṭī notes several works by al-Sarakhsī, but not the *al-Farq bayn al-naḥw wa-l-manṭiq*. See Khayr al-Dīn al-Ziriklī, *al-Aʿlām*, 1:205; Shams al-Dīn al-Dhahabī, *Siyar aʿlām al-nubalāʾ*, 19:147–48; Shihāb al-Dīn Yāqūt ibn ʿAbdallāh al-Ḥamawī, *Muʿjam al-buldān*, 7 vols, no ed. (Beirut: Dār Ṣādir, 1397/1977), 3:209; and Ibn al-Qifṭī, *Akhbār al-ḥukamāʾ*, 77.

117 In this instance, Ziriklī bases his entry on Ibn al-Jazzār on Yāqūt's *Muʿjam al-udabāʾ* and al-Dhahabī's *Siyar al-aʿlām wa-l-nubalāʾ*. There is no mention of this work neither in either al-Dhahabī's *Siyar al-aʿlām* nor in Yāqūt's *Muʿjam al-udabāʾ*. See al-Ziriklī, *al-Aʿlām*, 1:85–86; al-Dhahabī, *Siyar*, 15:561–62; Yāqūt, *Muʿjam al-udabāʾ*, 1:187–88.

the putatively early proto-Sufi book on distinctions, the *Bayān al-farq bayn al-ṣadr wa-l-qalb wa-l-fuʾād wa-l-lubb*, attributed to al-Ḥakīm al-Tirmidhī. *Bayān al-farq* is clearly a work of applied lexicographic distinctions, but its date of composition remains unclear.[118]

Surveying *furūq* writing in these other fields shows that these writings do not represent new forms of distinctions-thinking, but should be considered discipline-specific versions of applied lexicographic *furūq*. That is to say, they apply the logic of lexicographic *furūq*—distinguishing between apparently synonymous words—for their own purposes. As such, these works do not represent new modalities of drawing distinctions or of making comparisons. The widespread use of the technique of drawing distinctions shows the impact of this lexicographic method in many others disciplines.

Farq in Philosophy

One early philosophical work of distinction belongs to the philosopher and polymath Qusṭā ibn Lūqā (d. *ca.* 300/912–13), namely, the *Risāla fī l-farq bayn al-rūḥ wa-l-nafs*.[119] As its title indicates, this work focuses on the distinction between spirit (*rūḥ*) and soul (*nafs*). Perhaps as a trope, Qusṭā ibn Lūqā states that he wrote this work is written in response to a query: "You, may God grant you honor, asked about the difference between the spirit and the soul, and

118 Yusūf Marʿī questions this attribution, although he does not expound on his reasons for doing so in Yūsuf Marʿī, ed., *Bayān al-farq bayn al-ṣadr wa-l-qalb wa-l-fuʾād wa-l-lubb al-mansūb li-Abī ʿAbdallāh Muḥammad ibn ʿAlī l-Ḥakīm al-Tirmidhī* (Amman: al-Markaz al-Malikī li-l-Buḥūth wa-l-Dirāsāt al-Islāmiyya, 2009).

119 There is some disagreement about the author of this text. According to ʿAlī Muḥammad Isbir, there is unanimity among the classical sources that Qusṭā ibn Lūqā is the author of this text (Isbir, ed. *Risāla fī l-farq*, 19–20). Louis Cheikho, on the other hand, attributes it to Ḥunayn ibn Isḥāq, because Cheikho's edition is a diplomatic transcription of the manuscript in the Khālidiyya Library in Jerusalem, which attributes this text, cautiously, to Ḥunayn ibn Isḥāq. Cheikho was the first to publish the Arabic of this text, but he mentions that it has been translated several times into Latin, always with the ascription to Qusṭā ibn Lūqā. The manuscript begins with the title, and then states "composed by Ḥunayn ibn Isḥāq al-ʿAbbādī for Muḥammad ibn Mūsā l-Munajjim. There has been disagreement regarding this. A group of scholars says that it is by Ḥunayn and another group that says it was written by Qusṭā ibn Lūqā for ʿĪsā ibn [Farrukhān Shāh]" (Cheikho, ed. *Risāla fī l-farq*, 245–46). See Ḥunayn ibn Isḥāq, *Risāla fī l-farq bayn al-nafs wa-l-rūḥ*, ed. Louis Cheikho, repr. in *Ḥunain ibn Isḥāq: Texts and Studies*, ed. Fuat Sezgin et al. (Frankfurt am Main: Institute for the History of Arabic-Islamic Science at the Johann Wolfgang Goethe University, 1999), and Qusṭā ibn Lūqā, *Risāla fī l-farq bayn al-rūḥ wa-l-nafs*, ed. ʿAlī Muḥammad Isbir (Damascus: Dār al-Yanābīʿ, 2006).

what the ancients had to say on this."[120] Qusṭā's method is rather straightforward: he discusses the concepts of the spirit and the soul, defines them, and finally explains them in detail to draw out their differences. He begins with the spirit, which he understands to be of two kinds, the animal spirit (*al-rūḥ al-ḥayawānī*) and the vital spirit (*al-rūḥ al-nafsānī*).[121] The first section of this epistle is on the animal spirit. He commences with a definition: "Know that the spirit is a subtle substance that spreads throughout the human body."[122] Qusṭā continues by elaborating on the definition, providing a clear description of the animal spirit and its functions. We learn that the animal spirit resides in the heart, and then in the next section, on the vital spirit, we learn that "it is emitted by the brain (*yanbūʿahu al-dimāgh*)."[123] He then continues to describe the vital spirit, its location and its functions. "What we have said is true, namely, that the spirit resides in the cavities of the brain (*tajwīfāt al-dimāgh*) and that it performs different actions."[124] Qusṭā follows with a short section on the soul, wherein he explains that it cannot really be defined: "Describing the soul according to its true nature is difficult, nearly impossible (*muʿtāṣ jiddan*). The proof of this is the disagreement among the generations of philosophers, i.e., Plato, Aristotle, Thales, and Chrysippus,[125] and likewise philosophers after them."[126] Qusṭā follows this with three sections on the soul, one on the definition of the soul according to Plato, another on how the soul moves the body and how this occurs (*al-kalām ʿalā taḥrīk al-nafs li-l-badan ʿalā ayy jiha huwa*), and finally one on the faculties of the soul (*quwā l-nafs*). These long discussions serve to establish the concepts being discussed and to explain the nuances behind the two concepts, soul and spirit.

Qusṭā's application of distinctions-thinking is entirely lexicographical. In comparing the two concepts, soul and spirit, Qusṭā emphasizes their technical definitions. From an understanding of these definitions, he believes, the distinction between soul and spirit becomes apparent. As seen above, this comparison based on definitions is the marker of lexicographic distinctions. This is why I propose to describe this style of distinction an applied lexicographic distinction.

120 Qusṭā ibn Lūqā, *Risāla*, 37; Cheikho, ed., 248.
121 Cheikho's introduction to this work says "With *rūḥ*, [the author] means that which the Greeks knew as πνεῦμα and the Byzantines as *spiritus*." Cheikho also defines *rūḥ ḥayawānī* as "*esprit vital*" and *rūḥ nafsānī* as "*esprit animal.*" See Cheikho, ed., 245.
122 Qusṭā ibn Lūqā, *Risāla*, 41; Cheikho, ed., 249.
123 Qusṭā ibn Lūqā, *Risāla*, 48; Cheikho, ed., 251.
124 Qusṭā ibn Lūqā, *Risāla*, 55; Cheikho, ed., 253.
125 In both editions, this name is rendered *Kharūstas*. ʿAlī Muḥammad Isbir explains that this is a mistake, and that the correct classical Arabic name for this philosopher is either *Kharusibus* or *Karsūbūs*. In modern Arabic, Chryssipus is normally given as *Kharīsībūs*.
126 Qusṭā ibn Lūqā, *Risāla*, 57; Cheikho, ed., 254.

Farq in Ethics

Applied lexicographic distinctions, as a style of analysis, also appear in the field of ethics in *al-Farq bayn al-naṣīḥa wa-l-taʿyīr* by Ibn Rajab al-Ḥanbalī (d. 795/1393). This work, too, exemplifies the approach of applied lexicographic distinctions as a style of analysis in Arabic letters. "This is a comprehensive yet abridged discussion on the difference between giving advice and reprimanding," writes Ibn Rajab. "They both share a meaning in that they both mean to say something to someone what that person does not want said (*kilā minhumā dhikr li-l-insān bimā yakrahu dhikrahu*)." [127] Both in giving advice and in reprimanding, one person tells someone else the correct course of action or behavior. This is their shared characteristic. Ibn Rajab continues: "The distinction between these concepts can be confusing for a lot of people." Ibn Rajab aims to dispel such confusion. The idea underpinning his work is that giving advice is a virtue, but that reprimanding others is a vice. In other words, the two concepts are similar in their outward appearance, but near opposites in their intention. For this reason, it is important to clarify the distinction between these two similar concepts, to ensure proper understanding of advice and reprimand.

Much as we see with Qusṭā ibn Lūqā, Ibn Rajab begins with definitions: "Know that saying something to someone that they do not want said is prohibited, if the intention behind it is only to disparage, blame, and fault (*al-dhamm wa-l-ʿayb wa-l-naqṣ*)."[128] Ibn Rajab does not explicitly tell the reader at the outset what he seeks to define, although it quickly becomes clear that he means to define reprimanding, *taʿyīr*. Ibn Rajab next adds another definition: "If, however, there was a benefit (*maṣlaḥa*) for the majority of Muslims, or even for just one of them (*li-ʿāmmat al-muslimīn aw khāṣṣa li-baʿḍihim*) and the intention behind talking to this person was to bring about this benefit, then it is not prohibited. Indeed, it is a recommended act."[129] Again, Ibn Rajab does not explicitly identify this statement with giving advice, but it is clear from context to what he refers. The reader thus knows that *naṣīḥa* is a virtue and *taʿyīr* a vice. From this beginning, Ibn Rajab makes his argument by showing various examples of others who have said or held that giving advice is a commendable act while reprimanding is not. He brings up the example of hadith transmitters inquiring about and making sure of the probity of other transmitters (*al-jarḥ wa-l-taʿdīl*), accepting the reports of worthy transmitters while disavowing reports of less trustworthy author-

---

127 Ibn Rajab al-Ḥanbalī, *al-Farq bayn al-naṣīḥa wa-l-taʿyīr*, ed. Najam ʿAbd al-Raḥmān (Damascus: Dār al-Maʾmūn li-l-Turāth, 1405[/1980]), 25.
128 Ibn Rajab, *al-Farq bayn al-naṣīḥa*, 25.
129 Ibn Rajab, *al-Farq bayn al-nasīḥa*, 25.

ities. He also cites examples from the hadith reinforcing the idea of giving advice and condemning reprimanding. He closes out his treatise with a warning that God will give everyone a just recompense.

As with Qusṭā ibn Lūqā, Ibn Rajab uses distinction-thinking as a way of investigating a particular discipline, in his case ethics. In so doing, both authors narrow their focus to a discussion of technical terms. Conversely, physicians, and jurists do not simply analyze words but uncover subtle differences between illnesses and legal rulings, respectively. Like the lexicographers, the analysis of Ibn Rajab and Qusṭā ibn Lūqā is based on definitions. The distinctions that they discuss help them explain fundamental differences between two concepts that outwardly resemble each other.

Farq in Law

Many legal works embrace the approach found in works of applied lexicographic distinctions. A late example is the work on legal principles called *Furūq al-uṣūl*, attributed to Kemalpaşazade (Ibn Kamāl Pāsha, d. 940/1534). Like the aforementioned works on philosophy and ethics, Kemalpaşazade compares a series of pairs of *uṣūl*, legal principles or precepts, all drawn between individual items of legal technical language. In this sense, they are all applied lexicographic distinctions. Among the *uṣūl* he compares, for instance, are the "necessary condition" (*al-sharṭ al-lāzim*) and the "optional condition" (*al-sharṭ al-ghayr al-lāzim*);[130] "restricting the reading of a revealed source" (*takhṣīṣ al-naṣṣ*) and "restricting the application of a legal cause" (*takhṣīṣ al-ʿilla*);[131] and "literal language" (*ḥaqīqa*) and "figurative language" (*majāz*).[132] In Kemalpaşazade's case, as in other works of applied lexiciographic distinctions, he transfers the strategy from lexicographic distinctions to technical legal terminology.

Kemalpaşazade introduces each pair of contrasting *uṣūl* with the phrase, "another distinction, between (*wa-farq ākhar bayn*)..." He then explains the relevant concepts, occasionally offering examples of how they are applied. For instance, he says:

> Another distinction, between restriction (*al-takhṣīṣ*) and exception (*al-istithnā'*): We say: The indication of restriction can either be coupled (*muqtarinan*) with a modified phrase or be

130 Kemalpaşazade, *Furūq al-uṣūl*, ed. Muḥammad ibn ʿAbd al-ʿAzīz al-Mubārak (Beirut: Dār Ibn Ḥazm, 2009), 65.

131 Kemalpaşazade, *Furūq al-uṣūl*, 72.

132 Kemalpaşazade, *Furūq al-uṣūl*, 91.

> postponed (*mutarākhiyan*) because restriction is understood on its own. Exception, however, is not understood on its own because it is the completion of a phrase. If you said, for instance, "I owe that person ten dinars minus one," they would be owed nine. If you said, however, "I owe that person ten dinars," and then paused, and later said "Minus one," you would owe him ten.[133]

Both *takhṣīṣ* and *istithnā'* limit the applicability of a revealed source, which may result in confusion. The distinction between them, he explains, is that a *takhṣīṣ* obtains when one clause establishes a fact or rule and then a second clause restricts the first, but *istithnā'* occurs when a single clause both establishes a fact or rule and restricts its scope at once. The distinction that Kemalpaşazade draws is between these two technical terms in legal theory. They are not laws or judgments themselves.

The phrases given in the above example demonstrate the fact that an exception needs to be directly connected to the clause it affects. The first phrase consists of one sentence. The exceptive clause "minus one" is connected to the clause "I owe that person ten dinars." The exceptive clause gains meaning through its connection to the rest of the sentence. The second phrase, with a pause between the two clauses, is an example of a failed exceptive phrase. The pause indicates the completion of a sentence, and the exceptive phrase "minus one" is therefore understood on its own, unconnected to the statement "I owe that person ten dinars." This phrase understood on its own bears no meaning, and, therefore, does not affect the previous clause.

The way in which Kemalpaşazade deals with the terms *al-naṣṣ al-mujmal* and *al-naṣṣ al-mufassar* will serve as a further example. Here he distinguishes between the epistemological status of laws that are established by consensus.[134] Specifically, he discusses the emergence of consensus about the meaning of Qur'anic passages. Certain passages require additional explanation, and the certainty of the rule that results from these passages, correspondingly, is of lower epistemological status. This is not the situation for a Qur'anic passage whose meaning is self-evident. When a consensus is reached on such verses, the resulting rule acquires the epistemological status of the Qur'an itself. In the case of self-evident verses, the consensus is then merely *pro forma*, since (in theory) there no interpretation is necessary in order to understand the divinely intended law. Since no interpretation is necessary, it is as if the law results directly from the Qur'an. In the case of verses needing explanation, however, any resulting legal interpretation emerges from the consensus on the explanation. For this rea-

133 Kemalpaşazade, *Furūq al-uṣūl*, 76.
134 Kemalpaşazade, *Furūq al-uṣūl*, 98.

son, it is attributed to the consensus. In this treatise, Kemalpaşazade uses only applied lexicographic distinctions. His analysis is centered purely on the correct understanding of technical legal terms; unlike works studied in upcoming chapters, he does not compare two legal problems and their outcomes—that is, he does not use the techniques of legal distinctions.

Conclusions

This chapter has surveyed the different genres in which distinctions literature flourished, as well as possible motivations and impulses for this kind of writing. Although physicians may have been writing about differential diagnostics from an early date, a genre called *furūq* first flourished in lexicography. In both disciplines, the structure and organization of writing is strikingly similar. The possible chronological priority of the medical distinctions literature may have paved the way for lexicographic works of this sort. Alternatively, their overlapping styles could be due to broader factors that led intellectuals in the Islamic world to seek to classify varieties of knowledge in the third/ninth and fourth/tenth centuries. These two genres also highlight potential uses for this kind of writing; medical works served as manuals for practitioners, and lexicographic works quickly moved from practical thesauruses to being fraught with theological concerns.

Medical distinctions involve a general symptom that has two potential causes, each being due to a different underlying disease. Lexicographic distinctions involve a general concept that is initially thought to be signified equally by two different words, upon which it is shown that the two words actually signify two different aspects of the concept in question. One difference between the medical and the lexicographic texts is that a symptom is visible whereas a concept thought to be signified equally by two words is an abstraction. Perhaps the more important difference is that the two differentiated diseases are different diseases whereas the two aspects of the concept in lexicography are conceptually related in some way. The way in which two illnesses are compared is not easily transferrable between fields of knowledge, as was the comparison between two words or technical terms.

As will made clear in the excursus, legal distinctions form yet a third kind of comparison. The style of reasoning used in works of legal distinctions is not simply a straightforward comparison, as it is in works distinguishing letters, words, or diseases. Rather, legal distinctions treat two specific legal problems and the legal reasoning that gives rise to the judgement applied in each of the two legal cases. Before discussing the *genre* of legal distinctions, however, we must turn towards the development of the *concept* of legal distinctions and the way that distinctions operated in formal legal disputations.

Chapter Three: *Jadal* as a Source for Legal Writings: The Cases of *Khilāf* and *Furūq*

The previous chapter explored the rise of a distinct mode of literary and intellectual production that self-consciously referred to itself as *furūq*, tracing the epistemological history of the concepts of *farq* and *furūq* to uncover the ways that distinctions-thinking operated in separate but related scholarly disciplines. This chapter follows a different thread in the early history of legal distinctions, turning more narrowly to look at the explicit legal background to the works on legal distinctions. As in Chapter Two, the discussion follows scholarly deployment of the distinct terms *farq* and *furūq* in the era before the genre of *furūq* emerged. These two terms arose in legal discourse as part of a theory of dialectics, known as disputation theory (*ʿilm al-jadal*), but were transformed in observable ways before the genre of *furūq* came into being as a self-conscious and distinct category of legal writing.

This chapter first examines the idea of distinction (*farq*) in early discussions of dialectics, noting that specialists in various disciplines used the term *farq* in handbooks of dialectics. The term *farq* was often placed besides or within the category of counter-objection (*muʿāraḍa*). A questioner would use the technique of *farq*-objection during a formal disputation in an attempt to show how the respondent's opinion on a given case is contradictory to another opinion he held in a closely related case. This technique was labelled *farq* because it asking a question: "What is the distinction between...?" (*mā l-farq bayn...*).

As Walter E. Young has demonstrated, dialectics were pervasive in early Muslim scholarly circles and constituted the arena in which legal thoughts and concepts were "forged."[1] In the course of such formalized disputations, many core concepts and ideas of law were developed and refined. The concept of distinction also played a prominent role in the early Islamic legal discourse about dialectics. After demonstrating the uses of the term distinction and etymologically related words – i.e. words derived from the same linguistic root (*f-r-q*) – I turn once more to ʿAbdallāh al-Juwaynī's *al-Jamʿ wa-l-farq*, which contains repeated and sustained dialectical argumentation. My analysis here demonstrates how al-Juwaynī envisioned and wrote his book as part of an existing tradition of juristic dialectic.

1 Walter E. Young, *The Dialectical Forge: Juridical Disputation and the Evolution of Islamic Law* (Cham: Springer, 2017).

https://doi.org/10.1515/9783110605792-005

Disputation and Distinction

Dialectics (*jadal*) in the Arabo-Islamic tradition were a rigorous and formalized "method for attaining truth" through adversarial inquisition.[2] Larry B. Miller has explained that dialectics was "synonymous with question and answer," and it could serve as a way to package and manipulate ideas and theories.[3] Young has recently labeled dialectics a "forge" in which both theoretical concepts and substantive law were formed. In Young's words, "[t]he exigencies of dialectical debate provided key motives, and forged key structures, elements, principles, and concepts for" many juristic disciplines.[4]

Disputation did not arise in the Islamic world in the field of law, however. Rather, as Miller shows, theology was the field in which formal Arabic dialectic began. Miller argues that this theological undertaking then quickly spread to philosophy and jurisprudence. Young takes issue with Miller's genealogical model, claiming that dialectics constituted a broad academic interest in its earliest stages.[5] Both Miller and Young agree about the importance of *ʿilm al-jadal* for Islamic knowledge in general and for Islamic law in particular.

A survey of theoretical writings on dialectics serves to trace the ways in which the term "distinction" was used therein. While the word "distinction" (*farq*) became a formalized concept in theoretical writings on legal dialectics, it is also worth considering the various occurrences of the word *farq* in theological dialectics as well as other words derived from the same root, i.e., *afraqa*, *iftaraqa*, *mufāriq*, etc.

Miller argues that dialectical theory emerged at the time of Ibn al-Rēwandī (*fl.* fourth/tenth c.).[6] Ibn al-Rēwandī's book, unfortunately, has not survived.

2 Larry B. Miller, "Islamic Disputation Theory: A Study of the Development of Dialectic in Islam From the Tenth Through Fourteenth Centuries" (Ph.D. Diss., Princeton University, 1984), 24.

3 Miller, "Islamic Disputation Theory," 15. The importance of Muslim dialectics for the *sic-et-non* method of Christian scholastics and the connections of Muslim dialectics to medieval European scholastic culture have been noted and discussed in George Makdisi, *The Rise of Colleges: Institutions of Learning in Islam and the West* (Edinburgh: Edinburgh University Press, 1981), 245–53.

4 Young, *Dialectical Forge*, 2.

5 Young, *Dialectical Forge*, 2–3, 27–32.

6 This scholar's name is given variously as Ibn al-Rāwandī, Ibn al-Rīwandī, or Ibn al-Rēwendī. Miller gives it consistently as Ibn al-Rīwandī, although al-Rāwandī appears to be the more common form. See EI^2, s.v. "Ibn al-Rāwandī or al-Rēwendī" (P. Kraus and G. Vajda), where he is referred to as Ibn al-Rāwandī throughout. I prefer al-Rēwandī, as in Josef van Ess, *Theologie und Gesellschaft im 2. und 3. Jahrhundert Hidschra: Eine Geschichte des religiösen Denkens im frühen Islam*, 6 vols. (Berlin: De Gruyter, 1991–97).

Miller calls attention to the earliest extant manuals of disputation as either continuous with or refutations of Ibn al-Rēwandī. Among these early scholars are the Jewish Qaraite Yaʿqūb al-Qirqisānī (*fl.* 4th/10th c), Muṭahhar ibn Ṭāhir al-Maqdisī (*fl. ca.* 355/965–66), and Ibn Ḥazm al-Ẓāhirī (d. 456/1064). While Miller believes that these texts reflect an exclusively theological mode of dialectic, Young has shown that many of these works could also be considered juristic. For example, Young says that al-Madqisī's *Bad' fī l-tārīkh* does not describe theological *jadal*, but *jadal* more generally, which encompasses theological and juridical dialectic.[7]

Miller claims that the earliest dialectical discussions were theological in nature. Young, however, argues that the earliest sources for dialectic can already be seen in some of the earliest books devoted to Islamic law. Young gives convincing arguments for correspondence between the dialectical techniques found in al-Shāfiʿī's *Ikhtilāf al-ʿirāqiyyīn* and those recorded in later handbooks. Much of his evidence is compelling, but it only shows that formalized conceptions of dialectical techniques existed before written handbooks of these techniques. Miller's argument that theological discourse was the original site of dialectical theory seems to me the most compelling. In addition to the evidence supplied by Miller, other scholars have also shown a robust tradition of theological disputation in the late antique eastern Mediterranean. Most notably, Michael Cook has called attention to Christian Syriac theological texts that contain blueprints for disputations with other religious groups that are highly reminiscent of Arabic theological texts.[8]

Young is correct to underscore that medieval Muslim scholars were "polymaths wearing 'many hats,'" thus showing the inherent cross-disciplinarity of these early scholars.[9] I nevertheless prefer the term "theological" to describe early writings on *jadal*, for two reasons. First, this category retains explanatory power for these books, even if the books do aim to cover more than theology. Miller convincingly shows the ways in which these scholars reacted against or were influenced by Ibn al-Rēwandī, a theologian. As responses to an argument from theology, these disputation handbooks served as sites of theological disa-

7 Walter E. Young, "The Dialectical Forge: Proto-System Juridical Disputation in the *Kitāb Ikhtilāf al-ʿIrāqiyyīn*." 2 vols. (PhD Diss., McGill University, 2012), 1:23–25.

8 The general framework is a blueprint structured by a back and forth presented with the terms "if they say ..., we reply ..." See Michael A. Cook, "The Origins of '*Kalām*,'" *Bulletin of the School of Oriental and African Studies* 43.1 (1980): 32–43. See also C. H. Becker, "Christliche Polemik und islamische Dogmenbildung," *Zeitschrift für Assyriologie und verwandte Gebiete* 26 (1912): 171–95.

9 Young, *Dialectical Forge*, 13.

greement. Second, these theoretical works on disputations were all written in roughly the same time period, in the early fourth/tenth century, before scholars began composing theoretical works on dialectic that were embedded within a juristic context. That is to say, the authors of these works were all in conversation with each other and involved in theology.

Farq in Theological Disputation

Based on the sources quoted by Miller, the theological tradition uses the term *farq* to designate a form of *muʿāraḍa*, counter-objection.[10] Abū Yūsuf Yaʿqūb al-Qirqisānī, a Qaraite scholar, discusses dialectical method in his book *Kitāb al-Anwār wa-l-marāqib.* Al-Qirqisānī repeatedly quotes a certain unnamed Muslim scholar as the authority on dialectical theory. Miller shows that this scholar is Ibn al-Rēwandī.[11] Al-Qirqisānī also includes a short discussion of the rules for dialectic, going through the kinds of questions one should ask and the correct ordering of the questions. Significantly, he most often uses the verb *faraqa* ("to distinguish," "to draw a distinction") to contrast two different positions. In describing how to refute someone else's position, al-Qirqisānī says one ought to say: "I concede that your rationale (*ʿillataka*) necessitates this opinion, but it also necessitates that you apply it to something that comes more quickly to mind ... Therefore, either show how the two cases are both true or both false, or explain how they differ (*wa-illā fa-fruq baynahumā*)."[12] Al-Qirqisānī does not give us a proper definition of the strategy of *farq*, suggesting that for him *farq* was not a formalized technique. Nevertheless, he describes a particular kind of objection in which the questioner attempts to catch the respondent in a contradiction. The questioner would finish by asking the respondent to explain the difference, or to distinguish, between two views held by the latter.

Al-Qirqisānī uses the word *farq* again in discussing the styles of objections (sg. *muʿāraḍa*) used by some theologians (*qawm min al-mutakallimīn*). Although al-Qirqisānī does not explicitly categorize distinction as a specific technique, he

---

10 Miller uses the term "counter-objection" to translate this word. Young renders this term as "counter-indication." I discuss the specific relationship between *farq* and *muʿāraḍa* below; note that some authors explicitly subsume *farq* under *muʿāraḍa*, while other authors use these two terms refer to separate categories.

11 Miller, "Islamic Disputation Theory," 24.

12 Yaʿqūb ibn Isḥāq al-Qirqisānī, *Kitāb al-Anwār wal-marāqib: Code of Karaite law*, ed. Leon Nemoy (New York: Alexander Kohut Memorial Foundation, 1939), 1:472; translation based on Miller, "Islamic Disputation Theory," 23.

nevertheless alludes to an idea strikingly similar to formal disputational *farq*. He offers the following counterfactual:

> If a Muslim were to say, "I affirm the prophecy (*nubuwwa*) of Moses based on the unanimous agreement (*iṭbāq*) of the Jews on the validity of his prophecy," then he must necessarily (*lazimahu*) affirm the prophecy of Aaron because of the Jews' unanimous agreement on his prophecy. If this person were then to deny Aaron's prophecy while still affirming that of Moses, he would be distinguishing (*qad faraqa*) between them [incorrectly], in affirming Moses while rejecting Aaron, in spite of the equivalent proofs for affirming their prophecies.[13]

In this example, al-Qirqisānī envisions a debate between a Muslim and a Jew. By accepting the agreement of the Jews as a valid indicator of Moses's prophecy, the imagined Muslim would also have to accept their agreement as a valid indicator of the prophecy of Aaron, since the Jews are also in agreement that Aaron was a prophet. Once the Muslim has accepted the unanimous agreement of the Jews as certain proof in one case, he must accept their unanimous agreement as certain proof in any case.[14] Here, however, the Muslim disputant accepts the opinion of the Jews for the prophecy of Moses, but not for that of Aaron. He has distinguished between them without any basis. In so doing, the Muslims has found himself in a contradiction.

13 Al-Qirqisānī, *al-Anwār wal-marāqib*, 1:475.

14 The passage seems to imply that Muslims do not generally accept the prophecy of Aaron. The actual status of Aaron in the Qur'an is not clear cut. The Qur'an names Aaron in its listing of prophets twice, once in Q al-Nisāʾ 4:163 and again in Q al-Anʿām 6:84. At the same time, the relationship between Moses and Aaron was likened to that between Muḥammad and ʿAlī, who was decidely not a prophet. In a hadith report, Muḥammad say, "ʿAlī, you are to me like Aaron to Moses, but there shall be no Prophet after me." The implication of this hadith is that ʿAlī's eloquence was helpful in spreading Muḥammad's message, just as Aaron's eloquence helped Moses communicate with Pharaoh. See EI^3, s.v. "Aaron" (Andrew Rippin). It may be the case, however, that al-Qirqisānī wants to make a point about counterfactuals, namely, that the rules of logic still obtain. In this case, the logical tool used is the *reductio ad absurdum* (*ilzām*). Lastly, Miller suggests that perhaps this passage is an argument that the counter-objection argument is a form of question and answer. The Ashʿarī theologian Ibn al-Fūrak (d. 406/1016) gives an equivalent discussion between two disputants about Muḥammad and Jesus. Miller, "Islamic Disputation Theory," 34–35; Muḥammad ibn al-Ḥusayn ibn Fūrak, *Maqālāt al-Shaykh Abī l-Ḥasan al-Ashʿarī Imām Ahl al-Sunna*, ed. Aḥmad ʿAbd al-Raḥīm al-Sāyiḥ (Cairo: Maktabat li-l-Thaqāfa l-Dīniyya, 1425/2005), 318. I thank Daniel Frank for help understanding this passage.

The use of the term *farq* in this passage is instructive.[15] The respondent, the Muslim, makes two statements that are at odds with each other. The first statement accepts something—the unanimous agreement of the Jews—as certain proof, the second statement rejects the certainty of that proof. It thus appears that the respondent has contradicted himself. The questioner can thus claim that the respondent has "distinguished incorrectly," that he has been inconsistent in his reasoning. The text employs the term *farq* in describing this inconsistency. *Farq* is not used precisely to refer to a particular kind of objection that has been lodged, but rather to the opportunity presented to the questioner to use the respondent's own reasoning to demonstrate that the rationale adduced by the respondent involves him in a contradiction.[16]

Based on al-Qirqisānī's discussion, it is clear that the term *farq* had not yet crystallized into a technical term, as he often uses *faṣl* and *farq* synonymously. Nevertheless, his theory of *farq* and *faṣl* is similar to the technique which is later found books of legal disputation called *farq*. Al-Qirqisānī's thirty-third chapter in his *al-Anwār wa-l-marāqib*, for example, is "On a question of distinction (*faṣl*) and that it requires that there be two answers."[17] This chapter explicates how questions that elicit distinctions (*faṣl*) work, and how, in order to be a valid disputational technique, such questions must be asked in regard to issues that have two different and contradictory answers. The author begins this chapter by saying, "Know that when you ask about the distinction between two things (*al-farq bayn shay'ayn*), that you have already distinguished between them (*faraqta*

15 Al-Qirqisānī uses this term two more times in this discussion with a similar meaning. He continues this discussion by stating, "One must also ask him (*wajaba ayḍan an yuqāl lahu*), 'What is the distinction (*mā l-farq*) between you and someone who affirms the prophecy of Aaron while denying that of Moses?'" (al-Qirqisānī, *al-Anwār wal-marāqib*, 1:475). This question aims to show the untenable position of the Muslim in attempting to affirm the prophecy of Moses while rejecting that of Aaron. In the example, the inverse opinions of the second scenario rest on the same faulty logic as that of the Muslim and are on their face absurd. Al-Qirqisānī uses the phrase *mā l-farq* ("What is the distinction?") throughout this paragraph. He also uses the term *mufāriq* ("distinction"), however, to denote the distinguishing trait that follows the verbs *farq* and *iftirāq*. He also makes mention of *tafriqa* (distinction) in a similar context: "Whoever rules (*ḥakama*) in disputed issues with a distinction must be asked for proof (*kull man ḥakama fī mawāḍiʿ al-ikhtilāf bi-l-jamʿ* [*wa-fī mawāḍiʿ al-jamʿ*] *bi-l-tafriqa fa-l-muṭālaba bi-l-burhān wājib ʿalayhi*)." See al-Qirqisānī, *al-Anwār wal-marāqib*, 1:478.

16 Miller discusses an equivalent example used by Muslim theologians, with Muḥammad and Jesus taking the place of Moses and Aaron. Although the end of this passage is not a question, "it could easily be turned into one." Some theologians even argued that such a statement is one that asks for a reply (*istikhbār*) and thus could be considered a question (*su'āl*). See Miller, "Islamic Disputation Theory," 34–35.

17 Al-Qirqisānī, *al-Anwār wal-marāqib*, 1:480.

baynahumā) as being either affirmed or denied."[18] The terms *faṣl* and *farq* are thus synonymous; the chapter on *faṣl* starts with the verb *faraqa*. For al-Qirqisānī, distinction is a dialectical maneuver that involves affirming one position while simultaneously invalidating another. He says, "When you distinguish between two things (*faraqta baynahumā*), you deny one of them and affirm the other."[19] This logic is demonstrated in the example of the prophecy of Aaron and Moses, when the questioner is poised to ask *farq*-based counterfactual questions that could only be answered through affirmation or denial: Does the Muslim believe in the unanimous agreement of the Jews as a valid proof or not? This same logic, however, does not carry over into later books of legal distinction, which are not aimed at denying one thing or the other, but instead aim at denying the very contradiction itself.

Farq in Legal Disputation

In handbooks of legal dialectics, discussions of *farq* become more formalized than in theological guides to disputation. Discussions of *farq* in legal dialectics echo, in large part, al-Qirqisānī's understanding of the concept of distinction, but the legal works give greater prominence to the word *farq* as a technical term. As a result, the term loses its plain-sense meaning of "distinguish" or "difference," as traced in the previous chapter, and instead comes to refer to a particular method of dialectical argumentation. The dialectical method of a *farq*-objection is a procedure of argumentation.

Farq, often understood as a subset of *muʿāraḍa* ("counter-objection"), refers to one kind question and answer procedure of argumentation, not only to one kind of comparison. A counter-objection can take issue with any aspect of the respondent's legal reasoning regarding the legal situation in question. A *farq* is a particular kind of counter-objection because it relates specifically to the legal rationale (*ʿilla*) under consideration. Young discusses why *farq* was seen to be a subset of the broader category of counter-objection: "[I]n establishing a charge of *farq*, [the questioner] claims an opposing *ʿilla* ... which he then links to a different *aṣl* ... in which [the questioner's] counter-*ʿilla* occasions the opposite to [the respondent's] *ḥukm*."[20] The *farq* is not a simply difference be-

18 Al-Qirqisānī, *al-Anwār wal-marāqib*, 1:480.
19 Al-Qirqisānī, *al-Anwār wal-marāqib*, 1:481.
20 Young, *Dialectical Forge*, 179.

tween two things, but rather the assertation of a fundamental distinction in rationale between two cases.

This process can be best understood through an example. A typical case is provided by the Andalusian Mālikī jurist, Abū l-Walīd al-Bājī (d. 474/1081), who explains *farq* in the context of a Mālikī scholar debating a Ḥanafī scholar:

> Mālikī: "Whoever kills someone with a blunt object shall be punished by retaliation. This is the case since the killer has unlawfully killed someone who is socially equal with an object that will likely kill him, and this deserves retaliatory punishment, just as if the killer had used a sharp object."
>
> Ḥanafī: "A sharp object is something that is used for the ritual slaughter of animals. It is because of this that we say that retaliation is required for a crime committed using such an object. The legal issue at hand, the blunt object, is not comparable, since animals cannot be slaughtered with a blunt object. This means that there is no punishment by retaliation for a murder committed with a blunt object, such as a small stick."[21]

In this example, the Mālikī jurist attempts to explain why the Mālikī *madhhab* imposes a retaliatory punishment on murder committed with both a blunt object and a sharp object. The Mālikī treats both killings as equal, as the type of weapon is of little consequence when considering intentional homicide, a tort warranting *qiṣāṣ*. The club, he argues, is a deadly weapon similar to a knife and thus its wielder deserves the same legal treatment as the knife-wielding killer. The Ḥanafī responds by drawing a distinction between these two weapons. For the Ḥanafī, murder with a knife is a more serious offense, presumably because the knife is prima facie a deadly weapon but a club is not. The use of knives to slaughter animals suggests that their primary purpose is killing. This default usage allows the jurist to distinguish between the presumed intent when they are used in cases of murder. For the Ḥanafī, a knife is evidence of clear intent for homicide and therefore leads to a charge of murder. A club, meanwhile, only allows for a charge of manslaughter, because the intent of the perpetrator cannot be clarified by recourse to the weapon. The everyday use of these objects provides insight into their legal functions; in formal terms, the *ʿilla* at work is the normal use of the object. Knives are used for killing living beings, while clubs are not normally used in this way.

At this point, the Ḥanafī seems to have made a more convincing argument than the Mālikī. In effect, the Mālikī claimed that these cases are equivalent be-

---

21 Sulaymān ibn Khalaf al-Bājī, *Kitāb al-Minhāj fī tartīb al-ḥijāj*, ed. ʿAbd al-Majīd Turkī (Beirut: Dār al-Gharb al-Islāmī, 1987), 203, ¶460. This section is also translated in Young, *Dialectical Forge*, 179–80.

cause striking someone with either a sharp or a blunt object will likely result in their death. In this sense, they are similar and the presumed intent of the killer is equivalent. The Ḥanafī, however, disagrees. According to him, the cases are distinct and not at all similar. The distinction, in his view, lies in the legal rationale that is used to determine intent. Due to the separate underlying rationales, the two kinds of killing are legally distinct, and therefore they occasion different punishments.

This brief back and forth is the exercise of a *farq*-objection. The Ḥanafī appears to have bested the Mālikī in this dispute. The Mālikī jurist presents a rational legal argument for retaliation. The Ḥanafī argues that the Mālikī is incorrect in his legal reasoning and posits a different consideration for the application of retaliation. The Ḥanafī seems to have the upper hand and to have gained an advantage through a more nuanced understanding of Islamic law. The Ḥanafī's response to the Mālikī is the *farq*-objection. Al-Bājī, himself a Mālikī, would not allow a Ḥanafī to win this dispute, and he continues by explaining how this objection is to be overcome. Al-Bājī's idealized response, of course, involves the Mālikī undermining the distinction drawn by the Ḥanafī.[22]

Al-Bājī's presentation of a *farq*-objection and the way to overcome this objection is characteristic of manuals of legal disputation. Many other jurists devote whole chapters to distinction in their dialectics handbooks. Imām al-Ḥaramayn al-Juwaynī (d. 478/1085), for instance, titles the twelfth chapter of his *al-Kāfiya fī l-jadal* "On Answering a Distinction" (*fī l-jawāb ʿan al-farq*). His discussion focuses on the use of *farq* as a disputational technique, however, not as a category of legal writing and analysis. A *farq*, in his mind, describes a particular objection to be overcome and the method for doing so. Al-Juwaynī writes:

> Know that to ask about the first term in an analogy, regarding its impossibility or inconsistency (*min al-manʿ wa-l-naqḍ*), invalid construction (*fasād al-waḍʿ*), lack of consistent applicability (*ʿadam al-taʾthīr*), inversion of the conclusion (*qalb*), and counter-objection (*muʿāraḍa*), is to ask about distinction (*al-farq*). This kind of objection can be responded to using any of the above rubrics.[23]

---

22 Al-Bājī, *Minhāj*, 203, ¶460.

23 Imām al-Ḥaramayn al-Juwaynī, *al-Kāfiya fī l-jadal*, ed. Fawqiyya Ḥusayn Maḥmūd (Cairo: Maṭbaʿat ʿĪsā l-Bābī l-Ḥalabī wa-Shurakāʾuhu, 1399/1979), 322. The translation of the technical terms is largely adapted from the terms used by Miller. He translates *ʿadam al-taʾthīr* as "ineffective *ratio legis*" (Miller, "Islamic Disputation Theory," 120–22) and *qalb* as "*methodos kata peritropēn*" (Miller, "Islamic Disputation Theory," 122–27). In his discussion of *manʿ*, he does not give a definitive translation of the term (Miller, "Islamic Disputation Theory," 113–18). On the terms, "*naqḍ*," "*fasād al-waḍʿ*," and "*muʿāraḍa*," see Miller, "Islamic Disputation Theory," 127–29, 118–20, and 133–34.

According to al-Juwaynī, if one's opponent draws attention to the non-transferability of a legal rationale, which amounts to a charge of *farq*, one may respond by referring to any one of the above-listed hermeneutic tools.

Abū l-Walīd al-Bājī states that a *farq* is "a counter-objection to the rationale (*ʿilla*) of the principal case" and that "it is the most legally specific (*afqah*) objection that can occur in a debate since the legal issue inherent in the problem becomes known in this way."[24] In other words, a *farq* is an objection based on a perceived incompatibility between the operative rationale in two legal cases. Lodging a *farq*-objection requires specific knowledge of legal rationales and how they operate. Likewise, overcoming a *farq*-objection requires a jurist to reinterpret the applicability of a particular legal rationale to multiple cases.

Because of the important role of the rationale in a *farq*-objection, al-Bājī categorizes all objections based on a legal rationale as *farq*. Al-Bājī's comprehensive account of distinction addresses two kinds of *farq* that may be employed in disputations. The first type claims that the two cases should be treated with reference to two different fact-patterns that result in two different outcomes due to two different legal rationales, a "clean break" between the two cases.[25] The second type of *farq* objects to the legal rationale at work in the case brought in the objection, but on different ground. Here, the questioner claims directly that the secondary case is a derived case while the original case is a principal case.[26] The questioner then states that the two primary cases are distinct. This means that there is a disagreement over the correct *ʿilla*s to apply to the case at hand. One party wishes to treat both cases with the same *ʿilla*, while the other part insists on the applicability of two different *ʿilla*s. The objection focuses on the correct rationale that applies to a particular case.[27] These two styles of *farq* operate with a related, but distinct, form of logic. In each of these, the contention of the questioner revolves around the precise relationships between similar cases with similar legal rationales.

24 Al-Bājī, *al-Minhāj*, 201, ¶456. Translation adapted from Miller, "Islamic Disputation Theory," 130.

25 Miller, "Islamic Disputation Theory," 132.

26 The ruling in a principal case (*aṣl*) is drawn directly from a revealed source. A legal rationale (*ʿilla*) may be deduced from the ruling in a principal case. The ruling of a derived case (*farʿ*), also called the instant case, is determined by the correct application of a legal rationale derived from a primary case. In the first type of *farq*, the questioner refers to two sets of primary cases, derived cases, and legal rationales. In the second type of *farq*, there is one principal case and one rationale that are contrasted to a principal case, a derived case, and a legal rationale.

27 Al-Bājī, *Minhāj*, 202, ¶457; see also Miller, "Islamic Disputation Theory,"132.

Farq thus became a formalized and highly elaborate technique in legal disputation. Whereas the term had been used informally in theological or philosophical disputation, it became a fully formed technique in handbooks of legal disputation. Understanding how to use *farq* offensively and how to overcome a *farq*-objection became a necessary part of successfully competing in a legal disputation. Attaining this knowledge required a thorough knowledge of substantive law, legal theory, and the connections between them. The formalization of *farq* thus relied upon an already elaborated system of legal thought and an established tradition of disputation. In this sense, it is not a surprise that the term *farq* appears in disputation manuals at the same time that doctrines of distinct Islamic legal schools were formalized.

Miller finds that authors incorporated this technique in the dialectical manuals of the fourth/tenth century. He notes, however, that *muʿāraḍa* was an "old technique" that predated the systematization of disputation theory.[28] Young confirms this finding, noting that dialectical strategies similar not only to *muʿāraḍa*, but also *farq*, and that other techniques appear in early works of Islamic substantive law as well. "[A]s a dialectical move employing verbs and nouns of root *f-r-q*, it [*farq*] is ubiquitous throughout the *Umm* ... Whatever the date we may consider *farq* to have crystallized as a uniform technical term, its practice and teaching as a dialectical move stretch back at least to the second century H."[29] Although Young does not find explicit discussions of *farq* in al-Shāfiʿī's *al-Umm*, he nevertheless finds instances of disputation within this text in which scholars employ questions and responses akin to later, formal techniques of *farq*.

The field of dialectics in Islamic intellectual culture, *jadal*, draws heavily on the Greek Aristotelian tradition.[30] While there seems to have been be a tradition of dialectics before the introduction of Aristotle into the Arabo-Islamic heritage, *jadal* quickly incorporated many of the formal features of the Aristotelian tradition once the Aristotelian corpus had become available in Arabic translation. Early juristic dialectics appear to be fairly free of Aristotelian influences, "[b]ut after jurisprudence had assimilated the techniques of theological dialectic, its own theory became influenced by logical terminology and techniques."[31]

---

28 Miller, "Islamic Disputation Theory," 33.

29 Young, *Dialectical Forge*, 180.

30 Young, *Dialectical Forge*, 188–213; Makdisi, *Rise of Colleges*, 107, 264–65; Miller, "Islamic Disputation Theory," 1–4, 52–77.

31 Miller, "Islamic Disputation Theory," iii. Miller's study carefully shows how the Arabo-Islamic tradition of disputation existed independently of Aristotle, adopted Aristotelian techniques and frameworks, and then transformed into a fully formalized system called "methods of inves-

Part of this pre-Aristotelian tradition involved some aspects of the counter-objection (*muʿāraḍa*), but Miller argues that there is a general category of *muʿāraḍa* that is part of the "native" pre-systematic techniques of disputation.[32] As the existing styles of disputation were formalized, *muʿāraḍa* needed to be incorporated into the formal system "the arguments brought forth cloud[ed] the difference between it and distinction (*faṣl*, *farq*)."[33] Distinction is often, but not always, presented as a a subcategory of *muʿāraḍa*, the latter being a notion that preceded Aristotelian influence. Miller seems to situate the concept of distinction as part of the dialectical tradition based on the work of Aristotle, although he does not elaborate on this point.

Young also seems to suggest a parallel between *farq* and one of the refutations offered by Aristotle in his *Sophistical Refutations*, specifically Aristotle's advice to "look for contradictions between the answerers' views and either his own statements or the views of those whose words and actions he admits to be right or those who are generally held to bear a like character and to resemble them."[34] Young draws parallels between these techniques and inconsistency (*naqḍ*), contradictions with the Qur'an, hadith, or scholarly consensus, and "with charges of contradicting the substantive law or method of one's own juristic *madhhab*."[35] While Young does not use the term *farq* in this discussion, the technique of evaluating Qur'an, hadith, and legal questions seems to be dialectical *farq*. This interpretation of Young's position only requires understanding Aristotle's statement "those whose works and actions [the questioner] admits to be right" as applying, in legal disputations, to the assumption that a disputant understands the doctrines of his particular legal school to be correct. Based on this statement, then, it seems possible that *farq* developed as a formal technique of disputation in connection with the reception of Aristotle's *Sophistical Refutations*. This supposition, however, follows naturally from the understanding that any participant in a legal disputation is an adherent to a particular legal school and defending the view of his school.

---

tigation (*ādāb al-baḥth*)." See also Mehmet Karabela, "The Development of Dialectic and Argumentation Theory in Post-Classical Islamic Intellectual History," (PhD Diss., McGill University, 2011).

32 Miller, "Islamic Disputation Theory," 38.

33 Miller, "Islamic Disputation Theory," 38; Young, "Dialectical Forge," 1:31n46.

34 Aristotle, *On Sophistical Refutations. On Coming-to-be and Passing Away. On the Cosmos*, trans. by E.S. Forster and D.J. Furley (Cambridge, MA: Harvard University Press, 1955), 85. See also Young, *Dialectical Forge*, 211–12.

35 Young, *Dialectical Forge*, 213.

Although *farq* is usually understood as a subcategory of *muʿāraḍa*, the question of the status of *farq* with regard to *muʿāraḍa* is not clear cut. Miller claims that while some of his primary sources portray *muʿāraḍa* as a broad category under which *farq* can be subsumed, other theorists see them as two distinct kinds of counter-objection.[36] Young understands *farq* as wholly subsumed under the concept of *muʿāraḍa* and rejects the possibility of them being distinct kinds of objections.[37] He argues, based on Abū Isḥāq al-Shīrāzī and al-Bājī, that a proper *muʿāraḍa* entails the construction of a new legal analogy. *Farq* involves invoking a new legal case that is seemingly related to the case at hand by way of the legal rationale. It is the applicability of this rationale that is at stake in a *farq*-objection. Since *farq* is one of the techniques through which a new analogy is constructed, it must be subsumed under *muʿāraḍa*, a broader category encompassing all techniques in which a counter-analogy is created.[38]

In other words, Young believes that the *muʿāraḍa* was a disputational technique that existed prior to the emergence of the technique of *farq*. He holds, however, that the process of *farq* itself is and only can be a subsection of *muʿāraḍa*. Certainly, the strategy of *farq* involves the comparison of a new set of facts with the legal discussion at hand. To take the above example, the Mālikī and the Ḥanafī argue about the legal status of murder using a blunt object and a sharp object. For the Mālikī, the two weapons are alike in their legal rationale (*ʿilla*), since weapons are immaterial for determining intent. They are also similar, in his view, in the legal ruling that results from the rationale, the imposition of retaliatory killing. The Ḥanafī scholar, who makes the case for a distinction (*farq*), produces a counter-analogy. For him, the two weapons are incompatible and disanalogous, the correct analogy hinges on the use of a sharp-weapon, not on the intent of the attacker. Therefore, there are two legal outcomes in the two cases, one being the imposition of *qiṣāṣ* for the sharp object and the other being the non-imposition of *qiṣāṣ* for the blunt object. This result is what Young calls the counter-*ḥukm*. Young claims, therefore, that this is simply one of the many kinds of counter-objection (*muʿāraḍa*), and that *farq* is subsumed within the category of counter-objections, which is both a broader category and an older one. While Young's argument that *farq* is exclusively a subsection of *muʿāraḍa* is convincing on the face of it, he fails to address those scholars who treat *farq* as a

36 Miller, "Islamic Disputation Theory," 130–31.

37 Both Miller and Young agree that *muʿāraḍa* was a particularly Arab, pre-*jadal* technique. Miller, "Islamic Disputation Theory," 37–38; Young "Dialectical Forge," 1:31n46; *idem*, *Dialectical Forge*, 180.

38 Young, *Dialectical Forge*, 176–82.

separate disputational category. Nevertheless, these two concepts, *muʿāraḍa* and *farq*, are clearly quite closely related.

Disputational Theory and Practice (*Khilāf*)

Furūq was not the only genre of legal writing that arose from the larger world of dialectics. Indeed, the relationship between these two disciplines, *furūq* and *jadal*, has gone relatively unnoticed.[39] The relationship between *khilāf*, comparisons of disputed legal points across (or within) *madhhab*s, and dialectics is much more widely understood. Young claims that disputation had a profound effect on the entirety of Islamic legal literature, arguing that every genre of pre-modern Islamic legal writing is influenced by the practice or theory of dialectics, but that of these genres, *khilāf*, has been impacted most clearly.[40] While Young shows that many Islamic legal concepts were elaborated within disputational contexts, the development of legal genres and their particular connections to *jadal* in legal contexts remain unclear. The legal genre most clearly related to disputation, however, is that of *khilāf*, also referred to as *ikhtilāf*.[41] In such contexts, *khilāf* does not refer to a particular technical term or style of disputation but to the act of disputation itself, especially when used in the context of a literary genre.

Joseph Schacht describes *ikhtilāf* "as a technical term, the differences of opinion amongst authorities of religious law, both between the several schools and within each of them."[42] Elsewhere, he describes the compilation of works of *ikhtilāf* as "comparative accounts of the doctrines of several schools (*ikhtilāf*, 'disagreement')."[43] The books reflecting discussions between schools relate to (real or imagined) discussions between schools on particular points of law. In part, their purpose was to show which school was superior. The books that Schacht refers to as "simple handbooks" are books that attempt to

---

39 There is a discussion of this connection in both Young, *Dialectical Forge* and Necmettin Kızılkaya, *İslâm hukukunda farklar: Furûk literatürü üzerine bir inceleme* (Istanbul: İz Yayıncılık, 2016). Aḥmad al-Ḥabīb hints at such a connection as well. Aḥmad ibn Ibrāhīm ibn ʿAbdallāh al-Ḥabīb, "*al-Muqadimma*," in ʿAbd al-Ḥaqq al-Ṣiqillī *al-Nukat wa-l-furūq li-masāʾil al-Mudawwana qism al-ʿibādāt*, ed. Aḥmad ibn Ibrāhīm ibn ʿAbdallāh al-Ḥabīb (PhD Diss., Jāmiʿat Umm al-Qura, 1416/1996), 79–81.

40 Young, "Dialectical Forge," 1:70.

41 These two terms seem to be used synonymously in the tradition to refer to contradictory legal opinions which cannot be harmonized.

42 EI^2 s.v. "Ikhtilāf" (Joseph Schacht).

43 Schacht, *Introduction to Islamic Law* (Oxford: Clarendon Press, 1964), 114.

establish a given opinion as prevalent within a particular school. Authors of these works also sought to catalog and resolve disagreements in order to "arrive at consensus on any doctrine of practice."[44] Paradoxically, however, by cataloging instances of disagreement, works of *khilāf* can also serve as permanent evidence of disagreement, or the lack of consensus, on particular issue. In this way, *khilāf* works serve to permanently upset the epistemological certainty that arises from consensus and lead only to probable certainty.[45]

In this respect, *furūq* and *khilāf* are almost opposite genres and concepts. Works of *khilāf* function offensively, seeking to establish the validity of one opinion at the expense of another. They achieve this through dialectical argumentation. *Furūq* works, on the other hand, function defensively, seeking to show how two seemingly contradictory opinions are in fact mutually consistent. *Furūq* works exist to harmonize laws, while works of *khilāf* exist to bring out legal dissonance. Although both of these genres emerged from the tradition of legal disputation, *khilāf* and *furūq* serve different goals. As such, these genres also discuss different sets of substantive doctrine. The doctrine discussed in works of *furūq* is, in reality, not contradictory; the doctrine discussed in works of *khilāf* is, in reality, contradictory.

Looking at this from a dialectical perspective, the "*farq*" of *furūq* constitutes a kind of counter-objection designed to overcome such objections. The questioner attempts to catch the proponent in a contradiction—upholding a certain *ʿilla* in one case, but unable to do so in another—by bringing up a separate legal problem and its ruling. The proponent responds by explaining the subtle distinction between both apparently "contradictory" cases. The connection between *farq* and *jadal* becomes evident upon only upon a close study of the dialectic tradition.

The connection between *khilāf* and *jadal*, however, is readily apparent: works of *khilāf* put disputational theory into practice.[46] Many of the treatises that make up al-Shāfiʿī's collected works, *Kitāb al-Umm*, are works that exemplify *khilāf*-dialectics. This includes the *Ikhtilāf al-ʿiraqiyyīn*, *Ikhtilāf Mālik wa-l-*

---

44 Makdisi, *Rise of College*, 107.

45 Joseph E. Lowry, "Is There Something Postmodern About *Uṣūl Al-Fiqh? Ijmāʿ*, Constraint, and Interpretive Communities," in *Islamic Law in Theory: Studies on Jurisprudence in Honor of Bernard Weiss*, ed. A. Kevin Reinhart and Robert Gleave (Leiden; Boston: Brill, 2014), 285–316.

46 Some works of legal disputation may reflect records of actual disputations. Other works, which only reflect theoretical records of disputation, can still be understood as a practical application of dialectical theory.

Shāfiʿī, and parts of his famed *Risāla*.[47] This genre seems to have been particularly prominent in early periods of Islamic law; Wael Hallaq attributes the abundance of contradictory opinions to the informal institutional context in which early jurists operated. The prevalence of too many individual jurists exercising their own opinion "explains the plurality of opinion in Islamic law, known as *khilāf* or *ikhtilāf*," which in turn explains the popularity of the *khilāf* genre.[48] In this early context, before affiliation with a legal school was the norm, a plurality of opinions arose and were reflected in writing.[49] When formulated in this manner, legal dialectics seem to be almost identical to the discipline of *khilāf*.[50]

One might then see the works of *khilāf* as records of formal disputation adhering to particular rules and strictures, and works about *ʿilm al-jadal*, the science of disputation, as the theoretical science describing the rules thereof. This seems to be Young's implicit understanding of the dialectical tradition. His criticism of Miller's dating of the tradition stems from his belief that *khilāf* works represent a well-developed and in-use theory of dialectics that is only later canonized by the books that Miller studies. This division between the works of disputation in practice (*khilāf*) and disputation in theory (*jadal*) also has a certain resonance with the distinction between legal compendia (*furūʿ*), which catalog substantive laws, and works of legal theory (*uṣūl al-fiqh*), which describe the procedures for deriving the substantive law found in legal compendia.

This brief survey of *khilāf* and its relationship with disputation shows an intimate connection between the sciences of *khilāf* and *jadal*. While most, if not all, genres of Islamic legal writing are indebted to an early and vigorous disputational environment, *khilāf* seems particularly tied to disputation. This debt has long been recognized and the two fields of inquiry, *khilāf* and *jadal*, have often been

---

47 The *Ikhtilāf al-ʿiraqiyyīn* is the disputational work studied by Young in his *Dialectical Forge*. The *Ikhtilāf Mālik wa-l-Shāfiʿī* addresses disputed points of doctrine between Mālik and al-Shāfiʿī. See Ahmed El Shamsy, "al-Shāfiʿī's Written Corpus: A Source-Critical Study" *Journal of the American Oriental Society* 132.2 (2012): 199–210. See also Muḥammad ibn Idrīs al-Shāfiʿī, *The Epistle on Legal Theory: A Translation of al-Shāfiʿī's* Risālah, trans. Joseph E. Lowry (New York: New York University Press, 2013), ¶¶133–34, ¶¶430–33, ¶¶510–21, and ¶¶634–49, among other examples.

48 Wael Hallaq, *Sharīʿa: Theory, Practice, Transformations* (Cambridge: Cambridge University Press, 2009), 82.

49 EI^2 s.v. "Ikhtilāf" (Schacht).

50 It also should be noted, as mentioned above, that the history of formalized disputation also tracks closely with the history of formalized theology, especially the defensive apologetic tradition of *kalām*. See Cook, "Origins of Kalām."

conflated.[51] Although *khilāf* and *jadal* do have an important connection, *khilāf* also served a purpose beyond that of dialectics—as a tool to impede the formation of consensus. As George Makdisi mentions, "Ijma', consensus, had its counterpart in khilaf, disagreement, difference of opinion. This situation gave rise, very early in Islam, to the need for codifying all opinion on which there was disagreement among the authoritative doctors."[52] Consensus, once formed, conferred a high epistemological status on a given result of legal interpretation. It was therefore important to catalog formal expressions of disagreement in order to prevent the erroneous formation of a consensus.

Aron Zysow explains the somewhat counterintuitive relationship between consensus and disputation:

> Consensus is a substitute for the infallible guidance of the Prophet. It is as close as one can come to the renewal of the Prophetic Mission which has come to an end with Muḥammad ... At the same time, however, the uniqueness of the Prophet must be preserved. Through consensus, ordinary Muslims must not gain prerogatives that surpass those of the Prophet.[53]

Both consensus and disputation generate correct legal doctrine. Voicing dissent helped halt the formation of consensus. *Khilāf* thus became a forum for structuring a clear and convincing dissent. Therefore, disputation can also serve to clarify which matters are known with certainty, since certainty should only be conferred in the presence of unanimity. Cases of *khilāf* thus engender only probabilistic knowledge instead of certain knowledge.

The connection between these two disciplines, *khilāf* and *jadal* has long been noted. George Makdisi mentions this connection in *Rise of Colleges* and quotes Ḥājjī Khalīfa (d. 1068/1657) making exactly this point. "Hajji Khalifa identified *'ilm al-khilaf*, the science of differences of opinion, of controversy, with jadal, dialectic, which was itself a part of *mantiq*, logic, adding: 'except that this science (jadal) is applied particularly to religious matters', —religious, as distinct from 'foreign sciences.'"[54] Indeed, Ḥājjī Khalīfa's discussion of *'ilm al-khilāf* reads like a discussion of dialectic itself. He explicitly equates the two,

---

51 This conflation perhaps signals a need to differentiate legal dialectic from philosophical and theological dialectic.

52 Makdisi, *Rise of Colleges*, 106.

53 Aron Zysow, *The Economy of Certainty: An Introduction to the Typology of Islamic Legal Theory* (Atlanta: Lockwood Press, 2013), 236.

54 Makdisi, *Rise of Colleges*, 110, quoting Ḥājjī Khalīfa, *Kashf al-ẓunūn 'an asāmī l-kutub wa-l-funūn*, ed. Şerefettin Yaltkaya and Kilisli Rifat Bilge (Istanbul: Milli Eğitim Basımevi, 1971), 1:721: "*'ilm al-khilāf ... wa-huwa l-jadal alladhī huwa qism min al-manṭiq illā annahu khuṣṣa bi-l-maqāyīs al-dīniyya.*"

"*ʿIlm al-khilāf* ... is dialectics (*wa-huwa al-jadal*)."[55] He also mentions that the people involved in *khilāf* are either "the respondent" (*al-mujīb)* or questioner (*al-sāʾil*)," the two protagonists found in works of disputation.[56] For Ḥājjī Khalīfa, there seems to be no substantial difference between these two fields.

Much of Ḥājjī Khalīfa's information regarding the scholarly disciplines comes from the *Miftāḥ al-saʿāda wa-miṣbāḥ al-siyāda* by ʿIṣām al-Dīn Ṭaşköprüzāde (d. 968/1561), a work that, in turn, owes a debt of gratitude to the *Irshād al-qāṣid ilā asnā l-maqāṣid* by Ibn al-Akfānī (d. 749/1348). Jan Just Witkam points to this connection when he says that Ḥājjī Khalīfa "probably did not use the *Iršād al-Qāṣid* (although he was familiar with the text and knew Ṭaşköprüzāde's debt to it), but he was highly dependent on, among other works, Ṭaşköprüzāde's encyclopedia, which he quotes on numerous occasions."[57] This flow of bibliographic knowledge, from the relatively unknown Ibn al-Akfānī to the monumental work by Ḥājjī Khalīfa deserves greater study,[58] given that "[f]rom Kātib Čelebī [i.e. Ḥājjī Khalīfa] the line [of knowledge transmission] goes straight to the great bibliographical surveys which are the product of Arabic studies in Western Europe in the 19th and 20th centuries: Ahlwardt's catalogue of the Berlin manuscript collection and Brockelmann's *History of Arabic Literature.*"[59] These three works—Ibn al-Akfānī, Ṭaşköprüzāde, and Ḥājjī Khalīfa—should be seen as a cohesive tradition, a multigenerational current in Islamicate bibliographical writing.

The discussion of *khilāf* in this bibliographic tradition shows that these authors disagree about what exactly the discipline of *khilāf* entails. As mentioned, Ḥājjī Khalīfa identifies this science with disputation. In his *Miftāḥ al-saʿāda*, Ṭaşköprüzāde includes two separate discussions of both *jadal* and *khilāf*. The first discussions occurs in a section on the "Sciences that protect one from error in debate and learning."[60] The second mention *jadal* and *khilāf* occurs in

55 Ḥājjī Khalīfa, *Kashf al-ẓunūn*, 1:721.

56 Ḥājjī Khalīfa, *Kashf al-ẓunūn*, 1:721.

57 Januarius Justus Witkam, "Ibn al-Akfānī (d. 749/1348) and his bibliography of the sciences," *Manuscripts of the Middle East* 2 (1987), 40.

58 In particular, Witkam's study shows how Ibn al-Akfānī's *Irshād al-qāṣid* served as the node of transmission for some of the earlier classifications of the sciences, including works by Ibn Sīnā, al-Farābī, Ibn al-Nadīm and al-Shahrastānī. See Witkam, "Ibn al-Akfānī," 39.

59 Witkam, "Ibn al-Akfānī," 40.

60 Aḥmad ibn Muṣṭafā Ṭaşköprüzāde, *Miftāḥ al-saʿāda wa-miṣbāḥ al-siyāda fī mawḍūʿāt al-ʿulūm*, no ed. (Beirut: Dār al-Kutub al-ʿIlmiyya, 1405/1985), 1:283. The other disciplines that he lists alongside *khilāf* and *jadal* in this section are "rules for studying" (*ʿilm ādāb al-dars*) and the "science of speculation" (*ʿilm al-naẓar*).

his section on the "Sciences of legal theory."[61] His understandings and discussions of both *jadal* and *khilāf* are almost indistinguishable. In the first discussion, he states that "the principles (*mabādi'*) of *khilāf* are derived from the science of *jadal*; *jadal* acts as the substance and *khilāf* as the form it takes."[62] Ṭaşköprüzāde however, maintains a strict distinction between these two sciences, although he laments the ignorance of scholars of his time, in which this has been largely forgotten, "to the point," he says, "that students of our time do not comprehend the difference between *khilāf*, *jadal*, and *munāẓara*."[63]

In categorizing *khilāf* alongside *jadal*, Ṭaşköprüzāde likewise suggests that these two disciplines be treated as separate fields. Of disputation, he says:

> It is the science that investigates the ways through which one confirms any situation he so wishes (*ibrām ayy waḍ' urīda*) or attacks any situation that may arise (*hadm ayy waḍ' kāna*). This is one of the branches of speculation and the foundation of this science is disagreement (*wa-mabnī l-'ilm al-khilāf*). *Khilāf* is based on disputation, which is one part of the investigations of logic, although it is specific to the religious sciences.[64]

This section on disputation is similar in many ways to Ḥājjī Khalīfa's discussion of *khilāf*, even though it treats a different discipline. Both authors mention the close connection of *khilāf* to the religious sciences as well as to the field of logic.

What, then, is the science of *khilāf* according to Ṭaşköprüzāde? Ṭaşköprüzāde provides two definitions. First, he says, "it is the science that investigates the different ways of applying deductive reasoning from particular and general indicants."[65] *Khilāf* is, therefore, unconcerned with defending or attacking particular opinions or viewpoints, but directly tied to differing interpretations of legal indicants. In other words, *khilāf* here is inseparable from its specific legal context. This point is reaffirmed in the second definition, from his

---

61 Ṭaşköprüzāde, *Miftāḥ al-sa'āda*, 2:556. The other disciplines that he lists alongside *khilāf* and *jadal* in this section are the "science of speculation" (*'ilm al-naẓar*) and the "science of debate" (*'ilm al-munāẓara*).

62 Ṭaşköprüzāde, *Miftāḥ al-sa'āda*, 1:283. In the previous discussion of *jadal* and *khilāf*, he says, "the distinction between *khilāf* and *jadal* is in the form and substance. *Jadal* investigates the substance of the disputational proofs (*mawādd al-adilla l-khilāfiyya*) while *khilāf* investigates their forms (*ṣuwarihā*)" (Ṭaşköprüzāde, *Miftāḥ al-sa'āda*, 2:556).

63 Ṭaşköprüzāde, *Miftāḥ al-sa'āda*, 1:283.

64 Ṭaşköprüzāde, *Miftāḥ al-sa'āda*, 1:281. The discussion of *jadal* in legal theory is almost identical. "It is the confirmation of any situation that may arise (*ithbāt ayy waḍ' kāna*) or an attack against any situation that may arise (*hadm ayy waḍ' kāna*). It is one of the rational sciences (*al-'ulūm al-'aqliyya*) although it is also a branch of the science of legal theory" (Ṭaşköprüzāde, *Miftāḥ al-sa'āda*, 2:555).

65 Ṭaşköprüzāde, *Miftāḥ al-sa'āda*, 1:283.

chapter on *uṣūl al-fiqh.* "It is the disputation that occurs between the adherents of the legal schools (*bayn aṣḥāb al-madhāhib al-far'iyya*), such as Abū Ḥanīfa, al-Shāfi'ī and their peers."[66] Not only is *khilāf* intrinsically legal, but it is the disputation that is exclusively based on the extrapolated reasoning of the founders of the legal schools.

Ṭaşköprüzāde closes his discussion by stating that "it is possible to place the science of disputation and *khilāf* within the branches of the discipline of legal theory."[67] Ṭaşköprüzāde categorizes *khilāf* as falling under the rubric of legal theory, while Ḥājjī Khalīfa considers *khilāf* to be part of substantive law or law in general. The latter does not mention that it is part of *uṣūl al-fiqh*, instead referring to the necessity of "knowing the *qawā'id* by means of which one understands the derivation of positive laws" and "memorizing those disputed laws."[68] While *khilāf* requires the knowledge of substantive doctrine and of the relationships between substantive doctrine and first-order principles, Ṭaşköprüzāde clearly notes that it does not require understanding how to deduce positive laws; that is the work of a *mujtahid.* Someone involved in *khilāf* need only be able to understand the work, teachings, and writings of a *mujtahid.*

Ibn al-Akfānī, the third author of this bibliographic group, offers another approach. Ibn al-Akfānī does not consider *khilāf* to be an independent science and thus has no entry for *khilāf.* Rather, he sees *khilāf* as a subdiscipline of *jadal* and mentions *khilāf* in his entry on disputational theory. Of *'ilm al-jadal*, he says:

> The Science of Disputation. A science through which the following is known: how to present legal proofs, refute doubt, impugn legal proofs (*qawādiḥ al-adilla*), and structure points in a *khilāf* debate. The science of disputation came about from *jadal* which is a part of logic, but it is restricted to religious investigations. There are many methods of disputation, but the best of them (*ashbahuhā*) is al-'Amīdī's method.[69]

---

66 Ṭaşköprüzāde, *Miftāḥ al-sa'āda*, 2:556. *Amthāl* refers to the eponyms of the legal schools.
67 Ṭaşköprüzāde, *Miftāḥ al-sa'āda*, 1:284.
68 Ḥājjī Khalīfa, *Kashf al-ẓunūn*, 1:721.
69 Muḥammad ibn Ibrāhīm ibn Sā'id al-Anṣārī, Ibn al-Akfānī l-Ḥakīm al-Mutaṭayyib, *Irshād al-qāṣid ilā asnā l-maqāṣid fī anwā' al-'ulūm*, ed. 'Abd al-Mun'im Muḥammad 'Umar and Aḥmad Ḥilmī 'Abd al-Raḥmān (Cairo: Dār al-Fikr al-'Arabī, [1990]), 163; Januarius Justus Witkam, ed., *De egyptische arts Ibn al-Akfānī (gest. 749/1348) en zijn indeling van de wetenschappen* (Leiden: Ter Lugt Pers, 1989), 44, ll.580–83. This final statement is a reference to the work of Rukn al-Dīn Muḥammad ibn Muḥammad al-'Amīdī (d. 615/1218), a Central Asian scholar who wrote two works on legal disputation, *al-Ṭarīqa l-'amīdiyyah fī-l-khilāf wa-l-jadal* and *Irshād al-ṭarīqa.* See also the praise for al-'Amīdī and his method in Ibn Khaldūn, *Ta'rīkh Ibn Khaldūn al-musammā Dīwān al-mubtada' wa-l-khabar fī ta'rīkh al-'arab wa-l-barbar wa-man 'āṣarahum min dhawī l-sha'n al-akbar*, 8 vols, ed. Khalīl Shaḥāda and Suhayl Zakkār (Beirut: Dār al-Fikr,

For Ibn al-Akfānī, not only is *khilāf* a religious science, but so is the science of disputation itself. He makes this point explicit in his entry, and this categorization is reaffirmed through his categorization. Ibn al-Akfānī presents a clear hierarchy of the sciences: for him, *jadal* belongs to the science of norms (*ʿilm al-nawāmīs*) or the legal sciences (*al-ʿulūm al-sharʿiyya*). These sciences, in turn, fall under what he calls the "the highest order of the religious sciences (*ʿilm aʿlā; al-ʿilm al-ilāhī*)," which itself is a part of "the speculative philosophical sciences (*al-ʿulūm al-ḥikmiyya al-naẓariyya*)." The speculative philosophical sciences themselves are a part of "philosophical sciences, or what is studied for its own sake (*al-ʿulūm al-ḥikmiyya; mā yakūnu maqṣūdan li-dhātihi*)," as opposed to the ancillary sciences.

These three bibliographers present different conceptions of disputation and *khilāf*. They also present quite different histories, uses, and identities of these sciences. For Ḥājjī Khalīfa, the technical term *khilāf* is of great importance. He devotes an entry to this discipline, but view this discipline as interchangeable with disputation.[70] For Ḥājjī Khalīfa, the legal takes precedence over the philosophical or the speculative. Disputation is purely a branch of legal studies. For Ṭaşköprüzāde, *khilāf* and disputation are distinct sciences, although they are both concerned with discovering truth. In this sense, they correspond to what both Miller and Young find to be the chief aim of early dialectical theory, attaining and refining knowledge. Ṭaşköprüzāde would certainly not approve of Ḥājjī Khalīfa's definition, as he laments those who conflate *khilāf* and *jadal*. As for Ibn al-Akfānī, he presents *jadal* as important, but subsumes *khilāf* entirely under *jadal*. For him, it is only *jadal* that matters, and it matters because of its relationship to both law and philosophy.

Modern scholars draw connections between the three bibliographical works in large part because of shared themes. Witkam says, "Ṭaşköprüzāde devised his own division of the sciences, but he incorporated much of Ibn al-Akfānī's text within the framework of his [*Miftāḥ*]."[71] This statement is paralleled in Gerhard Endress's study of encyclopedias in the Arabic tradition. Endress says that Ibn al-Akfānī's work "became the model" for Ṭaşköprüzāde because they "both present the 'highest aim', *al-maqṣad al-asnā*, attained by Muslim scholarship in the

---

1981), 1:579; *idem*, *The Muqaddimah: An Introduction to History*, 3 vols., trans. Franz Rosenthal (New York: Pantheon Books, 1958), 3:33–34.

70 This may result from his work's vision of scholarship and scholarly life as entirely book-centered. *Kashf al-ẓunūn* focuses almost exclusively on texts as the primary form of intellectual capital, although such a focus is not necessarily indicative of Ottoman views of knowledge more broadly.

71 Witkam, "Ibn al-Akfānī," 40.

later Middle Ages in uniting both traditions, the Islamic and the Hellenistic."[72] Ḥājjī Khalīfa later used Ṭaşköprüzāde as a model for his own work. This borrowing is detectable even in their discussions of *khilāf* and *jadal*; in spite of the distinct approaches taken by each of the three authors, there are verbatim passages shared between all three works.

The most straightforward example of this borrowing is in Ḥājjī Khalīfa's discussion of *jadal*, which entry begins with a long quotation from Ṭaşköprüzāde's *Miftāh al-saʿāda* and ends with the phrase "as in (*kadhā fī*) the *Miftāḥ al-saʿāda*."[73] Ḥājjī Khalīfa adds, however, that it is not farfetched to say that *ʿilm al-jadal* is the same thing as *ʿilm al-munāẓara*, the very statement lamented by Ṭaşköprüzāde as ignorance. Another obvious borrowing by Ḥājjī Khalīfa is the claim that disputation is a part of logic, although devoted primarily for religious sciences.[74]

The connection drawn by these bibliographers between *khilāf* and *jadal* is largely framed in terms of debating difference between the Sunni legal schools, although later *khilāf* treatises sometimes focus on rulings disputed within schools. *Al-Inṣāf fī maʿrifat al-rājiḥ min al-khilāf ʿalā madhhab al-imām al-mubajjal Aḥmad ibn Ḥanbal* by ʿAlāʾ al-Dīn Abū l-Ḥasan ʿAlī ibn Sulaymān al-Mardāwī (d. 885/1480 – 81) is a well-known example of a work of *khilāf* written within a legal school. The author is concerned to explain and clarify the *khilāf* found in the *Muqniʿ* of Muwaffaq al-Dīn ibn Qudāma (d. 620/1223). Al-Mardāwī's interest lies in illustrating some of the conflicting opinions given by Ibn Qudāma and explaining which ones are more reliable. He praises the *Muqniʿ* as one of the "most useful and greatest" books in the Ḥanbalī school, "however," he writes "[Ibn Qudāma] gives conflicting opinions on some issues without giving preference to either (*aṭlaqa fī baʿḍ al-masāʾil al-khilāf min ghayr al-tarjīḥ*). Weak and sound opinions thus appear alike to those who contemplate this book (*fa-*

72 Gerhard Endress, "The Cycle of Knowledge: Intellectual Traditions and Encyclopaedias of the Rational Sciences in Arabic Islamic Hellenism," in *Organizing Knowledge: Encyclopaedic Activities in the Pre-Eighteenth Century Islamic World*, ed. Gerhard Endress (Leiden; Boston: Brill, 2006), 133.

73 Ḥājjī Khalīfa, *Kashf al-ẓunūn*, 1:579 – 80.

74 The phrase is found in all three texts, but not with identical wording. Ibn al-Akfānī says, "*al-jadal alladhī huwa aḥad ajẓāʾ al-manṭiq lakinnahu khuṣṣiṣa bi-l-mabāḥith al-dīniyya*" (Ibn al-Akfānī, *Irshād al-qāṣid*, 163). In Ṭaşköprüzāde, the phrase is "*al-jadal alladhī huwa aḥad ajzāʾ mabāḥith al-manṭiq lakinnahu khuṣṣa bi-l-ʿulūm al-dīniyya*" (Ṭaşköprüzāde, *Miftāḥ al-saʿāda*, 1:281). Ḥājjī Khalīfa quotes this phrase in his entry on *jadal*, on 1:579. In his entry on *khilāf*, he says, "*wa-huwa l-jadal alladhī huwa qism min al-manṭiq illā annahu khuṣṣa bi-l-maqāṣid al-dīniyya*" (Ḥājjī Khalīfa, *Kashf al-ẓunūn*, 1:721).

shtabaha ʿalā l-nāẓir fīhi l-ḍaʿīf min al-ṣaḥīḥ)."[75] Al-Mardāwī seeks to determine which opinions are dependable (*muʿtamad, madhhab*) and which are not. Interestingly, in his introduction he gives a detailed explanation of the formulations that Ibn Qudāma uses that lead to confusion over the correct doctrine.[76] *Khilāf* could thus be a way of voicing and, perhaps, resolving disagreements—in keeping with its historical connection with dialectics.

Although *khilāf* and *jadal* evolved alongside of and by means of interactions with each other, *furūq* seems to leave most of its argumentative history behind, in so far as the genre of *furūq* operates with primarily implicit links to the history of *farq* as a formal disputational maneuver. Nevertheless, the disputational background of *farq* can be understood to be present, even if normally latent, throughout works of legal distinctions.

Disputation in *Furūq*

In Chapter One, we mentioned the connection between legal disputation and the contents of *al-Jamʿ wa-l-farq* by Abū Muḥammad ʿAbdallāh ibn Yūsuf al-Juwaynī (d. 438/1047). Here, we shall look in more detail at the ways that al-Juwaynī presents disputations in this work. This analysis explores not only the moments of disputation, but how the discussion in *al-Jamʿ wa-l-farq* maps on to the theoretical discussions of *farq* that are included in manuals of legal disputation. Although al-Juwaynī himself did not write a manual of legal disputation, he was certainly familiar with disputational theory and practice.[77]

In some explanation of the distinctions between seemingly contradictory laws in this work, al-Juwaynī follows his explanation of the distinction with a blueprint for a disputation. For example, in he writes in the chapter on purity that "Some of the scholars in our school distinguished (*faṣala*) between mineral salt (*al-milḥ al-jabalī*) and sea salt (*al-milḥ al-māʾī*) dissolving in water. They hold that it is permissible to perform ablutions with water that has sea salt dissolved in it, but it is not permissible with water that has mineral salt."[78] Al-Juwaynī explains that the distinction rests on the underlying substance of the salt: sea salt is coagulated water and is thus equivalent to water (*māʾ fī l-aṣl*), and, therefore,

---

75 Alāʾ al-Dīn Abū l-Ḥasan ʿAlī ibn Sulaymān al-Mardāwī, *al-Inṣāf fī maʿrifat al-rājiḥ min al-khilāf ʿalā madhhab al-imām al-mubajjal Aḥmad ibn Ḥanbal*, 12 vols., ed. Muḥammad Ḥāmid al-Faqī (Cairo: Maṭbūʿat al-Sunna l-Muḥammadiyyah, 1374/1955), 1:3.

76 Mardāwī, *al-Inṣāf*, 1:4–13.

77 Ṭaşköprüzāde, *Miftāh al-saʿāda*, 1:282.

78 ʿAbdallāh al-Juwaynī, *al-Jamʿ wa-l-farq*, 1:56–57.

pure. Mineral salt, however, is not made of water and is thus a polluting substance.[79]

After giving a detailed explanation of this idea and the legal distinction arising from the difference between these kinds of salt, al-Juwaynī includes a brief example of dialectic. "If someone says," he writes, "'But even mineral salt is coagulated water (*mā' inʿaqada*). All salt is just water in its essence (*mā min milḥ illā wa-l-mā' aṣluhu*).' We respond, 'The matter is not all the same, as you have described it (*laysa l-amr ʿalā hādhihi l-jumla*).'"[80] Al-Juwaynī thus inscribes dialectical argumentation into his discussion of a distinction. This is a simple argument, with only one objection and one counterobjection, but it nevertheless brings to the fore the disputational framework in which works of legal distinctions could be used. These "mini-disputations" regularly feature in al-Juwaynī's book. In al-Juwaynī's chapter on ritual purity, we find them in twenty-two of the 172 distinctions in this work.[81] This short model disputation, as the others, tracks closely with the *farq*-objection of the *jadal*-theorists.

A *farq*-objection is a dialectical technique focused on the correct application of a legal rationale through analogical reasoning. In the above discussion, the first term in the analogy would be the salt water. In terms of building a legal *qiyās*, the fact-pattern can be thought of as follows: the precedent (*aṣl*) is sea salt. The ruling (*ḥukm*) is that it is ritually pure. The legal rationale (*ʿilla*) for this ruling is that the sea salt is nothing more than water in a different physical state and that water is pure in its essence. In this comparison, then, the instant case (*farʿ*) is that of mountain salt. When one tries to apply the legal rationale (*ʿilla*) of the precedent to the instant case, it turns out to be inappropriate. Salt found in a cave is simply not water in a different physical state; legally speaking it is an entirely different substance. Therefore, the rationale is not found in the second case, the precedent ruling cannot apply to it, and the ruling for mountain salt becomes that it is not ritually pure. It is not coagulated water; it is something else.

As discussed above, Imām al-Ḥaramayn al-Juwaynī insisted that "asking about the first term in an analogy ... is asking about a distinction."[82] His father, ʿAbdallāh al-Juwaynī, likewise distinguishes between these two cases by implicitly appealing to a lack of applicability, what al-Ḥaramayn al-Juwaynī refers to as "ʿ*adam al-ta'thīr*" (lack of consistent applicability) in his manual of disputation.

79 ʿAbdallāh al-Juwaynī, *al-Jamʿ wa-l-farq*, 1:57.

80 ʿAbdallāh al-Juwaynī, *al-Jamʿ wa-l-farq*, 1:57.

81 My count of the distinctions follows the enumeration done by the editor ʿAbd al-Raḥmān al-Mazīnī.

82 Imām al-Ḥaramayn al-Juwaynī, *al-Kāfiya*, 322, see also above p. 89.

When al-Bājī calls *farq*, "the most legally specific kind of objection," he does this because it deals exclusively with the legal rationale (*ʿilla*) underlying legal rulings.[83] All of these discussions explicitly connect *farq*, legal analogies, and correctly connecting a precedent case with an instant case through the application of a legal rationale. A disagreement and ensuing disputation about the lack of applicability of the legal rationale in one ruling to another is exactly what is described in al-Juwaynī's text.

One more example illustrates the connection between *furūq* and dialectic. In this same chapter on purity, al-Juwaynī says:

> If a person defecates, performs an ablution with sand, then wipes himself, his ablution is not valid. Were, however, a person to defecate, perform an ablution with water, and then wipe themselves without touching the anus or vagina, their ablution is valid. Al-Shāfiʿī took an explicit position in favor of both rulings (*al-masʾalatān manṣūṣatān*) in the recension of al-Rabīʿ ibn Sulaymān [(d. 270/883)].[84]

In this situation, the al-Juwaynī draws a distinction between normal ablutions, *wuḍūʾ*, and special dispensation made for an ablution with sand, *tayammum*. The latter is only allowed when there is not enough pure water available to perform the normal ablution, and, as a special dispensation, does not purify in the same way as *wuḍūʾ*. This, claims al-Juwaynī, is the "clearest of the distinctions between them." Al-Juwaynī starts with a general statement about *wuḍūʾ* and *tayammum*. In a way, he is using the definition of these two terms to create an initial distinction between these two scenarios. He then explains the implication of these definitions: "*Wuḍūʾ* is more purifying (*aqwā*) and *tayammum* is less purifying (*aḍʿaf*)."[85] This distinction is clear, ritual purification with water is more purifying than a ritual purification with sand.

There is, however, another distinction between these two situations. *Tayammum* is only permissible where water cannot be found, and searching for water after the *tayammum* renders it ineffective. *Tayammum* can only be done when there is no water to be found, not as a substitute for finding water. Searching for water after the *tayammum* "voids his ablution, whether he finds water or not."[86] Searching for water does not void an ablution in cases of *wuḍūʾ*, since an ablution with water is routine and a lack of water was not an issue. This issue, however, is not necessarily so simple, and al-Juwaynī men-

83 Al-Bājī, *Minhāj*, 201, ¶456.
84 ʿAbdallāh al-Juwaynī, *al-Jamʿ wa-l-farq*, 1:118.
85 ʿAbdallāh al-Juwaynī, *al-Jamʿ wa-l-farq*, 1:118.
86 ʿAbdallāh al-Juwaynī, *al-Jamʿ wa-l-farq*, 1:118.

tions a disagreement in this regard and provides the following example of a disputation.

> If, however, someone says, "Is it not sufficient to use rocks for wiping [i.e., and not have recourse to water]?"
>
> We say, "Yes, but there are two kinds of required duties: an actual, required duty (*wājib mutaʿayyan*) and a substitute duty (*wājib mutamaththil*). A required duty, for example, is a rich person freeing a slave as a penance for a *ẓihār* divorce.[87] An example of a substitute duty is a rich person freeing a slave as a penance for breaking an oath. Both of these actions are characterized as required. Similarly, when a man defecates, the required duty is that he wipe himself with water, and the substitute duty is to do so with stones. If someone who has performed *tayammum* is then required to search for water because of an external impurity, his *tayammum* becomes void."
>
> If someone then says, "Is it not the case that, were he to have completed his *tayammum* with an impurity on his backside, you would consider his *tayammum* void because of his having to search for water to clean this impurity?"
>
> We reply, "This impurity is different than impurity from excrement, because the impurity from excrement is the one that originally necessitated the ablution, either *wuḍūʾ* or *tayammum*. Any impurity which necessitates an ablution is assigned a particular set of legal rules and is unlike any other. Do you not agree that when he completes his *tayammum*, it is not permissible for him to begin his prayer as long as he does not wipe himself, and that he should begin his prayer with an impurity which was on his backside? This is the case, although usually we would prefer he perform the prayer again at a later time."[88]

This second distinction between *wuḍūʾ* and *tayammum* is much more detailed. Because it rests on a fine point of law, there is greater ground for disagreement between the two cases distinguished by al-Juwaynī. Indeed, the speaker's disagreement does not lie on any distinction between *wuḍūʾ* and *tayammum*, but rather on the ancillary issue of the impurities related to defecation and wiping the anus. The first objection reported by al-Juwaynī focuses on the requirements for wiping the anus after defecation. Al-Juwaynī's discussion of the distinction implies that water is required for this, and the objection is that water is not required, as using clean rocks can be sufficient. This would make al-Juwaynī's distinction meaningless, since wiping does not necessarily require searching for

---

87 *Ẓihār* refers to a legally valid, but detestable, form of divorce. The husband repudiates his wife by comparing her to his mother by uttering the formula "You are to me like my mother's back (*anti ʿalayya ka-ẓahr ummī*)." With this formula, the husband causes an immediate divorce. Since this is a valid formula, the divorce takes hold, but, since according to the jurists it is immoral, the husband is required to make penance.

88 ʿAbdallāh al-Juwaynī, *al-Jamʿ wa-l-farq*, 1:118–20.

water. Al-Juwaynī counters, however, by creating a hierarchy of distinctions. He thus introduces the concept of *wājib mutamaththil*, a stand-in or substitute duty. Yes, one can sometimes wipe with rocks instead of water, but that is only when water is not available. This situation still calls for searching for water, which renders the *tayammum* void.

A final objection continues in a similar vein. The imagined questioner notes that if someone performs *tayammum* with an impurity on his body, he would still have to search for water to clean this impurity, but the *tayammum* is nevertheless valid. Implicit in this charge is that al-Juwaynī contradicts himself in the way he treats *tayammum* and the search for water, as the questioner has found an example in which the person who performs a valid *tayammum* was and still is in search of water, but does not have a problematic initial ablution. Al-Juwaynī responds to this by making a further distinction between these impurities. The impurity on one's backside can be ignored for purposes of prayer if the affected person performs a *tayammum*. In other words, for the purposes at hand, he is considered legally pure in spite of the presence of actual impurity on his person. Therefore, the need to search for water is not urgent and this does not render his *tayammum* void. After defecation, however, the impurity that arises is directly a result of the defecation. It is the same act that both engenders the need for water for purification and, separately, the need for water for wiping. Since one act brings about both circumstances, and both require water, an impure individual cannot perform *tayammum* first and search for water later. One should perhaps search for water, use rocks for wiping, and then perform *tayammum*.

Again, this disputation connects to descriptions of *farq* found in manuals of disputation in a straightforward manner. The questioner doubts the situation (*fasād al-waḍʿ*)[89] set up by ʿAbdallāh al-Juwaynī. Al-Juwaynī counters this using the first distinction, explaining why the situation is, in fact, as he describes. The second objection is an attempt to draw out a contradiction (*naqḍ*) in al-Juwaynī's reasoning, another strategy found in the manuals of disputation discussed above. The questioner then mentions what he finds to be an equivalent situation with a divergent ruling, to show al-Juwaynī why he is wrong. Al-Juwaynī then distinguishes these two situations and overcomes this objection by showing the coherence in his thought and the lack of commensurability between these two kinds of impurity. This typical case shows *jadal* at work in a book of legal distinctions.

Al-Juwaynī's *al-Jamʿ wa-l-farq* does not clarify the relationship between actual legal disputations, the theory of legal disputation, and the list of particular

89 Imām al-Ḥaramayn al-Juwaynī, *al-Kāfiya*, 322.

counter-objection *furūq* compiled by Imām al-Ḥaramayn al-Juwaynī. Nevertheless, al-Juwaynī sees his book as contributing to an advanced, and highly specialized, legal debate, one in which jurists defend all positions of their legal school. Al-Juwaynī even alludes to such a scenario at the beginning of his book, when he states, "Legal issues may have similar appearances but different rulings because of legal rationales (*ʿilal*) that require different rulings."[90]

He also comments that his predecessors wrote some works "on this topic" (*fī hādha l-bāb*) but that it was restricted to a "very limited number of cases."[91] This is to say, al-Juwaynī was not the first jurist to write on the subtle distinctions between apparently contradictory legal rulings. From this terse statement, it is unclear whether al-Juwaynī is referencing standalone treatises of legal distinctions —similar works which have not survived—or to passages within substantive legal treatises that discuss these subtle differences. It was al-Juwaynī's goal, however, to be exhaustive, and in this he was certainly successful when one considers the legacy and popularity of his work.

Conclusion

The dialectical context in which Islamic law arose as a scholastic activity was instrumental in the rise of legal distinctions as a form of legal writing. As dialectic became both formalized and institutionalized, new forms and rules of argumentation developed. One such form of argumentation was the objection by way of distinction (*farq*, *faṣl*). In disputation, positing a distinction was one of several procedures for objecting to an opponent's statement. It constituted a particular way of locating and utilizing a potential contradiction in an opponent's reasoning, based on their reliance on specific rationales (*ʿilal*) in particular cases. It went right to the heart of the legal matter, and, therefore, must have been a powerful tool in disputation. Books of legal distinctions thus incorporated much of the logic that went into the disputational *farq*-objection.

There are two key differences between these understandings of *farq*, however. First, disputational-*farq* was a particular procedure in a disputation, to be introduced and countered in predetermined ways. In a disputation, *farq* referred to a challenging question: What is the distinction between this case and that case? In this way, *farq* challenged someone to prove they did not hold contradictory opinions. Works of *furūq*, however, understand *farq* as a kind of comparison fo-

90 ʿAbdallāh al-Juwaynī, *al-Jamʿ wa-l-farq*, 1:37.
91 ʿAbdallāh al-Juwaynī, *al-Jamʿ wa-l-farq*, 1:37.

cused solely on distinguishing between two apparently contradictory laws. In other words, works of *furūq* contain correct answers to the questions of a *farq*-objection. Second, disputational *farq* was a strategy for showing contradiction—a method to show an inconsistency—but books of legal *furūq* assume that a school's doctrine is internally consistent. In almost perfect opposition to disputational *farq*, books of *furūq* prove that there is no contradiction in the law, or, more specifically, in the rulings discussed in these works. Thus, it appears that legal *furūq* arose first as a blueprint for defending against *farq* in disputation, but quickly took on a literary and aesthetic life of its own.

This impetus for writing works of legal *furūq* stands in stark contrast to the impetus behind *khilāf*. *Khilāf* continues the argumentative style of disputation and the genre of *khilāf* is motivated by the idea that the law, as developed within and between the legal schools, will inevitably lead to disagreement and contradiction. Authors of *khilāf* works might have particular understandings of what is correct, and thus privilege one ruling or understanding over others, but those authors also lay bare the potential inconsistences and disagreements found at the deeper level of legal justifications found in *fiqh*. These inconsistencies are exactly what legal *furūq* seeks to remedy.

Excursus: The Logic of Legal Distinctions

We have already discussed the rise of distinctions as a concept in the Arabic intellectual tradition and seen that distinctions arose as a concept based on, but distinct from, that of distinction. The Arabic plural term *furūq* signals a different kind of reasoning from that of the singular *farq*. The change from *farq* to *furūq* can be seen by looking at the titles of books in various fields, particularly lexicography. Books titled *farq* and *furūq* both dealt with synonyms, but each word gestured toward a different conceptual approach. *Farq* books are organized around broad conceptual groupings—such as the parts of the body or the stages of the life-cycle. Synonyms in books of *farq* are therefore distinguished based on their applicability to the conceptual grouping. *Furūq* books, on the other hand, compare apparent synonyms to tease out (or, create) minute differences between them. The organization of these two types of books is thus radically different. A different logic for discussing synonymy or the lack thereof results in a different organization of information.

Chapter Two explored the difference between these two approaches and the correlation between the use of *farq* or *furūq* in the title and the organization of a book. Here, I detail logic particular to works of lexicographical and legal distinctions in order to highlight the conceptual difference between these two applications of "distinctions-thinking." This excursus also interrogates the logic at work in each of these disciplines to show how these distinctions are fundamentally different. While similar motives may have fostered the emergence *furūq* treatises and *farq* treatises, the two genres involved different intellectual activities.

This difference between the singular and plural use of "distinction" is particularly relevant for legal distinctions, where the singular *farq* is used to denote an applied linguistic distinction, while the plural *furūq* is used, almost exclusively, to denote legal distinctions. Chapter Two discussed works that address distinction based on the lexicographic model, such as *al-Farq bayn al-naṣīḥa wa-l-taʿyīr* by Ibn Rajab al-Ḥanbalī (d. 795/1393) or *al-Farq bayn al-ḥadd wa-l-taʿzīr* by Ibn Taymiyya (d. 728/1328). These kinds of works do not address laws, but legal concepts.[1] Therefore, they explain the meaning of each of specific terms or concepts in its plain-sense or normal usage (*fī l-lugha, lughatan*) and in its technical legal meaning. They also discuss references in the Qur'an and the ha-

1 Among the many kinds of treatises devoted to one particular distinction, there are many on the distinction between bribes and gifts. See, for instance, ʿAbd al-Ghanī l-Nābulusī, *Taḥqīq al-qaḍiyya fī l-farq bayn al-rishwa wa-l-hadiya*, ed. ʿAlī Muḥammad Muʿawwaḍ and ʿĀdil Aḥmad ʿAbd al-Mawjūd (Cairo: Maktabat al-Zahrāʾ, 1412/1991).

https://doi.org/10.1515/9783110605792-006

dith that inform the legal meaning the concept under consideration, and when these meanings apply. Through these layers of meaning, the distinction between two concepts is established.

Works of applied lexicographical distinctions do not explain the difference(s) between two laws (*far*ʿs or *ḥukm*s). Instead, these works distinguish between technical terms within Islamic law. Legal distinctions, however, operate with a unique logic, distinct from distinctions in lexicography. The difference between *farq* and *furūq*, as will be seen, is similar to the difference between legal theory (*uṣūl al-fiqh*) in general and a discussion a specific tool of legal reasoning (*aṣl*).[2] These two Arabic terms are related both conceptually and etymologically, of course, but this is only a surface similarity. The simple relationship between the names masks a complex conceptual relationship between both terms.

Books on legal *furūq* do not adopt a lexical framework, but instead employ a framework whereby laws take the place that words would in linguistic works. In so doing, they also transform the concept of "distinction" itself. In a linguistic distinction, authors juxtapose two words in order to offer their "true" meaning. This explanation provides the distinction between the two signifiers. The role of minute distinctions could be easily integrated into theological presumptions about the language of God's revelation. Lexicographic distinctions enabled the establishment of differentiations in language, so that supposed synonyms came to complement and expand the semantic scope of Arabic. But, in this conception, Arabic was not God's *only* perfect creation, the rejection of synonymity could easily be transferable to Islamic law. Arabic grammar and Islamic law are the two matrices which God instituted and therefore, jurists implicitly argued grammar and law could be comparable in this manner.

A legal distinction does not contrast two signifiers, but two fact-patterns and two legal rulings. The legal rulings themselves must be carefully detailed, and the particularities of the fact-patterns to which they refer, explained. In this way, the discussion of the fact-pattern, its legal ruling, and the rationale that connects that fact-pattern to that ruling clarifies the distinction between the two rulings. The reasoning used produces differences between the legal rationales that undergird the two different legal problems. These rationales are not always readily apparent in the ruling itself, but are a product of the jurist's trained mind. This is how the jurists transformed concept of distinction. They moved from simply comparing of two linguistic definitions to comparing underlying legal rationales. In lexicography, the distinction involves the relationship be-

2 See Devin Stewart, "Muḥammad b. Dāʾūd al-Ẓāhirī's Manual of Jurisprudence, *al-Wuṣūl ilā maʿrifat al-uṣūl*," in *Studies in Islamic Legal Theory*, ed. Bernard Weiss (Leiden: Brill, 2002).

tween signifier and signified, while in law, the distinction involves the relationship between a fact-pattern, a ruling, and a legal rationale that binds them together.[3]

Understanding Lexicographic Distinctions

Clarifying the components of any lexicographic comparison will enable a better understanding of how a lexicographic distinction works. A straightforward example of a linguistic distinction comes from *Adab al-kātib* by Ibn Qutayba (d. 276/889), a manual for chancery secretaries. This work covers all the material considered necessary for being a competent secretary, and much of this work is focused on proper writing. As part of this effort, Ibn Qutayba includes a section on lexicographic distinctions (*abwāb al-furūq*) in his work. Ibn Qutayba does not explicitly discuss most elements of this comparison, but they are crucial for understanding the intellectual work that he undertook. In this example, Ibn Qutayba discusses two words that are, apparently, thought to be synonyms for the word "skin" (*jild*): *adama* and *bashara*. "The visible side of a person's skin —from his head and the rest of his body—is called *bashara* and the interior side is called *adama*."[4] This distinction compares two signifiers, *bashara* and *adama*. The general signified of both words is skin (*jild*). Although Ibn Qutayba attempts to show that these two words are not synonymous, their comparison obviously depends on a pre-existing idea of synonymity. This assumption of equivalence is what suggests comparison. The first component of this analysis rests on the supposed conflation of the terms, that is, as referring to the same referent.

In addition to the general concept being discussed, linguistic distinctions also present two near-synonyms that refer to different varieties subsumed under a general concept. The author of a work on lexicographic distinctions

3 It is worth explaining, in brief, the logic of a distinction in medicine. In medicine, the surface similarity between the two comparands (symptoms) invites a comparison. The comparison reveals that the underlying causes of the comparands (illnesses) are radically different. Once fully understood, the two symptoms are understood to be caused by different illnesses and share no more than a mere surface coherence. In this regard, they may be seen as similar to legal distinctions. Our analysis of distinctions in medicine, differential diagnostics, relies entirely on one book with dubious attribution. While intriguing, more evidence of the spread and chronology of differential diagnostics is needed before drawing strong conclusions about its role in the history of legal distinctions.

4 Abū Muḥammad ʿAbdallāh ibn Muslim ibn Qutayba, *Adab al-kātib*, ed. Muḥammad al-Dālī (Beirut: Muʾassasat al-Risāla, 1981), 144.

then clears up the confusion of the referents through exposition. In this case, Ibn Qutayba resolves the confusion between the two words *adama* and *bashara*. He explains exactly what each one means so that the reader understands that each word, in fact, has a different referent.

The same analysis can be applied to the lexicographic pairs discussed in *al-Furūq al-lughawiyya* by Abū Hilāl al-ʿAskarī (d. *ca.* 400/1009–10). He says:

> The distinction between *mithl* and *naẓīr:* Two *mithl*s are fully complementary in their essence (*takāfaʾā fī l-dhāt*), as mentioned above.[5] A *naẓīr*, meanwhile, is that which corresponds to another in regard to similar actions of which they are capable. For example, a grammarian (*al-naḥwī*) is the *naẓīr* of another grammarian, even if what they say or write about grammar is different. It is not correct to say (*lā yuqāl*), "a grammarian is a *mithl* of another grammarian," because equivalence (*tamāthul*) refers, in reality, to the most characteristic attributes which are the essence.[6]

In this example, the words *mithl* and *naẓīr* appear as the two specific signifiers. These two words both refer to equivalence or interchangeability. The distinction between them is not as straightforward as that between *adama* and *bashara*. Nevertheless, Abū Hilāl says, they are indeed different. *Mithl*, which he describes briefly, refers to equivalence in the very essence of a thing. A *naẓīr*, however, is a resemblance between two things, one of which can fulfill the function of the other; *naẓīr* refers to a superficial or functional equivalence, not an essential equivalence.

In Abū Hilāl's example, a grammarian is a *naẓīr* of another grammarian since they have equivalent training and qualifications. One can perform the function of the other as they are functionally equivalent even if their ideas or output differ. They are not *mithl*, however, since each grammarian is a different person, so their essences are not interchangeable. Thus, *naẓīr* and *mithl* are different words. Even if they convey similar meanings, these two words are not really synonyms.

Linguistic distinctions function through the combination of three signifieds, one general and two specific. The two specific signifieds are stated explicitly in the comparison—*adama* and *bashara* or *mithl* and *naẓīr*. The general signified is never explicitly stated. Instead, it is implied through the very act of comparison. Ibn Qutayba's comparison functions when the reader understands that the implied signifier is skin; Abū Hilāl's when the reader understands the implied sig-

5 Here, al-ʿAskarī is referring to his first discussion of the meaning of the word, on page 154, in which he says: "Two *mithl*s are two things that are equivalent in their essence" (*al-mithlayn mā takāfaʾa fī l-dhāt*).

6 Al-ʿAskarī, *al-Furūq*, 155.

nifier is equivalence. With these three elements in place, the author then explains each of the specific signifiers so that the relationship between the three signifiers is made clear. Both specific signifieds are related to the general signified, but different from each other. The close relationship between the three signifieds is real; while they are not identical, the difference between them is subtle.

The resonances of a framework in which linguistic and legal relations are seen to be highly congruent, can also be found in works of *uṣūl al-fiqh*. Éric Chaumont argues that this is one of the foundations upon which Abū Isḥāq al-Shīrāzī bases his *al-Lumaʿ fī uṣūl al-fiqh*, writing "the language of legal discourse is formally *identical* to the language of the Arabs."[7] Legal *furūq* provide a different perspective about how jurists relate the fields of grammar and Islamic law. While Chaumont's comparison involves discursive similarities between law and grammar, the example of comparative *furūq* allows for a one-to-one comparison of the structure of legal and grammatical tools of reasoning. I showed in Chapter Three that the genre of legal distinctions arises as an extension and continuation of the disputational technique of distinction. Distinction as a method for objecting in formal disputations was specific to the field of legal disputation, with al-Bājī going as far as to call it "the most legal of objections."[8] This statement might help us understand the intellectual background behind legal distinctions, but it also raises the question of the relationship between legal disputation and distinctions writing in disciplines other than law. Writing about subtle but important distinctions between related elements arose slightly earlier in lexicography than in law. The documented interrelations between law and lexicography suggest that there were relationships and exchange between these disciplines beyond what appears in the historical record.

Understanding Legal Distinctions

The relationships that exist between the signifiers in a lexicographic distinction are not similar to the relationships found in the comparisons known as legal distinctions. Legal distinctions function rather in a different manner. Legal distinctions compare two fact-patterns that seem similar, but are actually distinct, if not incomparable. The potential contradiction inherent in legal distinctions is re-

7 Éric Chaumont, "Préface" in *Kitāb al-Lumaʿ fī uṣūl al-fiqh; le Livre des Rais illuminant les fondements de la compréhsion de la Loi; Traité de théorie légale musulmane,* trans. Éric Chaumont (Berkeley, Robbins Collection, 1999), 23.
8 Al-Bājī, *al-Minhāj,* 201 ¶456.

solved by explaining that two rulings are not contradictory, but rather apply to completely different fact-patterns. Any potential confusion between the two fact-patterns results from a failure to understand the reasoning behind the ruling, which is what the distinction explains. An example from the *Kitāb al-Furūq* of As'ad al-Karābīsī (d. 570/1174–75) helps to illustrate this point.

> Abū Ḥanīfa [(d. 150/767)] says, "If a worm exits the body through one of the two excretory passages, the anus or the urethra (*aḥad al-sabīlayn*), it nullifies a minor ablution. If it exits through a wound, however, it does not."
>
> The distinction is that the worm is always somewhat moist and this moisture is slightly impure. Slight impurity, if it exits the body through one of the two excretory passages, nullifies a minor ablution. As for a worm exiting through a wound, it is also always somewhat moist. This moisture, too, is slightly impure. Slight impurity, if it exits the body through somewhere other than one of two passages, does not nullify impurity. In addition, the worm is an animal and is therefore assumed to be pure. A pure thing, such as air, if it exits through one of the two passages, necessarily nullifies a minor ablution. If, however, it exits through somewhere other than one of the two passages, it does not nullify a minor ablution, such as with tears and sweat.
>
> Muḥammad ibn Shujā' [Ibn al-Thaljī, (d. 266/880)] distinguished between these cases in another way. The worm that exits through a wound is generated from flesh. Therefore, it is akin to a piece of flesh separating from the body without bleeding and not through the two passages. If such a thing were to happen, it would not nullify a minor ablution. The worm exiting through a wound is equivalent to a piece of skin detaching from the body without bleeding. As for a worm that exits from one of the two passages, however, it is generated from impurity. If only this impurity exited the body, it would invalidate a minor ablution. The same holds for whatever is generated from this impurity whenever it exits the body.[9]

A legal distinction is composed of two (or more) fact-patterns and their associated ruling. These can be labelled Fact-Pattern 1, Fact-Pattern 2, Ruling 1, Ruling 2, etc., for each fact-pattern and ruling. In this example, the two laws treat instances of a worm exiting the human body. Fact-Pattern 1 deals with a worm exiting the body through the urethra or the anus; Fact-Pattern 2 deals with a worm exiting the body through a wound. These situations resemble each other; in Arabic the resemblance is referred to as *al-tashābuh fī l-ṣūra* (similarity in form). The apparent contradiction lies in the ruling. In Ruling 1, a minor ablution is nullified, but in Ruling 2, a minor ablution is not nullified. If Fact-Pattern 1 and Fact-Pattern 2 are indeed similar, then confusion arises about their opposing rulings. The author offers a distinction that rests on the fact that a worm that exits through the urethra or anus is, legally, not comparable to a worm that exits

9 As'ad al-Karābīsī, *al-Furūq*, 1:34–35.

through a wound. The reasoning behind the substantive law resolves the apparent contradiction.

Asʿad al-Karābīsī's comparison is unlike the comparisons in lexicographical distinctions, in which the compared words are ultimately similar. Asʿad al-Karābīsī offers two ways to distinguish between these two cases. In both, however, the upshot is that these cases are not analogous. In some way, the confusion that leads these cases to look the same results from a lack of knowledge of the underlying rationale of the two rulings. In order to resolve the confusion, the reader must better understand the reasoning that generates the rules.

Lexicographic distinctions are grouped together based on a shared general signification between two signifiers. The difference lies in the specific signification between the two. In a sense, however, it is correct to group the two signifiers together. Book of legal distinctions explain why it is wrong to group two such situations together.

A further example displays the kind of reasoning at work in legal distinctions. Asʿad al-Karābīsī writes:

> Someone makes a gift of a female slave, and then wants her to be returned. The recipient says, "You gifted her to me when she was a minor, but now she has come of age and increased in value." If the donor accuses him of lying (*kadhdhabahu*), the presumption is in favor of the donor (*al-qawl qawl al-wāhib*).
>
> Had the gift been land, however, the situation would be different. The recipient says, "You gifted it to me and it was barren and empty, but I planted in it and built some structures on it." If the donor contradicts him, the presumption is in favor of the recipient.

The common fact-pattern in both instances is a gift that the donor wishes to have returned. Fact-Pattern A involves the court proceeding in which testimony is elicited concerning return of the gift of a female slave, while Fact-Pattern B is a proceeding eliciting testimony about the return of a gift of land.[10] It appears that the two situations are identical, since they both involve testimony concerning the return of a gift. Ruling A, however, results in the testimony of the donor of the girl being accepted over that of the recipient, while Ruling B results in is the testimony of the recipient of the land being accepted over that of the donor. As with the previous example, each ruling is the mirror opposite of the other.

The discussion of the distinction sheds light on why this seeming contradiction exists. Al-Karābīsī continues:

---

10 It seems likely that there is a missing fact here, namely that the recipient in each case wants compensation for the return of the gift since he claims that what he is returning is more than what he received.

> The distinction is that, in the case of the female slave, the capital asset (*al-ʿayn*) is a single thing. This is demonstrated by the fact that it is invalid to designate a price for the gift (*ifrād al-thaman bi-l-hiba*). The donor did not claim it was a gift of two things, but rather he claimed that he gifted one thing. He also claimed the right to take back his gift. The standard ruling grants him the right of return. Therefore, if the recipient wants to nullify this right, he should not be believed.
>
> Land is not like this. Because it consists of two capital assets, it is permissible to designate each of these as the gift. The recipient is then able to claim that the gift was both things, while the donor insists that it was only one. There is no obvious fact to contradict the recipient's designation of the gift as two. He could have both built and planted during this period. Therefore, the presumption is in favor of the recipient. It is as if the recipient had said, "You have gifted me (*wahabta minnī*) both of these slaves," but the donor replies, "No, I have gifted you only one of them." In this situation, the presumption goes to the recipient. This situation with the two slaves is like the situation with the gift of land.

Here, the gift contract differs in each situation. There is not one law that applies to all gifts, rather, the particular assets gifted impact how the gift contract is construed, even if this contract exists only implicitly. The gift contract for a slave woman entails the person herself. Therefore, the intended asset of the gift was clear, even if it was left underspecified. The fact that the slave is a single asset leaves no room for doubt as to this intention. In the case of land, however, the gift is not quite so simple. A gift of land consists of both the use of the land to build structures and the use of the land for agriculture. The fact that land is composed of two separate assets opens room for doubt as to the exact asset intended to be gifted: the use of land for building, the use of the land for agriculture, or farm. There is, therefore, a clear distinction between both fact-patterns, thus settling the apparent contradiction. Resolving seeming incongruities within a school's doctrine was the methodology common to all works of legal distinctions.

Concluding Thoughts

How should we understand the genre of legal distinctions? As seen in Chapter Two, there seem to be strong parallels between the genre of legal distinctions and the genre of lexicographic distinctions. The two can be thought of as parallel genres and both share a similar method of organizing information. Indeed, at a surface level, it can appear that legal distinctions simply borrow an organizational style from the already existing genre of lexicographic distinctions. Yet we have seen here that the logic which undergirds both genres is actually quite distinct, despite these surface similarities. Given the chronological precedence of *furūq* works in lexicography, it seems that jurists chose to borrow generic conventions from lexicographers. In adapting this genre, however, the necessities of legal reasoning altered its inherent logic.

As discussed in Chapter Three, the reasoning of legal distinctions conforms well with the theoretical explanations of *farq*-objections in handbooks of legal disputation. The logic of legal distinctions can be understood neatly within the context of a disputation and disputation theory. Even without the formal analysis of disputation theory, the comparisons in works of legal distinctions are clear and dialectic. It may seem that we can understood books of legal distinction exclusively as operating within the field of legal disputation. This assumption, however, forces us to revisit the relationship between the genres of lexicographic and legal distinctions. If legal distinctions are the logical result of a kind of disputation, then it might be said that lexicographic distinctions borrowed this genre from Islamic law, or perhaps from Islamic legal thinking. This second explanation seem textually satisfying, yet is chronologically inconsistent with the evidence available to us.

Chapter Four: Riddles and Entertainment

In the previous chapters, this book examined three strands of legal thinking that contributed to the rise in distinctions writing. We saw that the use of the term *furūq* to describe legal treatises served to signal the existence of the genre of legal distinctions. We also saw that the structure and organization of treatises in this genre set it apart from other kinds of legal writing. There are, however, also books in the Arabo-Islamic heritage that read nearly identically to the legal distinctions treatises examined in earlier chapters but self-identify as belonging to genres other than legal distinctions. Many of these works fall under the ambit of what is termed legal riddles (*al-alghāz al-fiqhiyya*). The existence of these books underscores the elasticity of legal distinctions as a genre, and challenges our understanding of the consistency of legal genres. This elasticity is also present in some of the other "secondary" genres of Islamic law, that is, all genres except for legal theory, legal compendia, and legal digests, including, among other genres: legal maxims (*al-qawāʿid al-fiqhiyya*), purposes of the law (*maqāṣid al-sharīʿa*), and cognate and similar legal cases (*al-ashbāh wa-l-naẓāʾir*). This chapter explores the porous boundary between legal *furūq* and legal riddles, showing the importance of social practice to the development, and partial convergence, between between these modes of thinking. In particular, the performance of legal knowledge in literary salons (*majālis*) fostered a demand for a particular packaging of this information, and books of riddles and distinctions converged, in part, as a way to satisfy this particular demand. This trend begins early in the history of legal distinctions, in the fifth/eleventh century, but seems to become a dominant paradigm in Mamluk Cairo.

The modern academic study of the Arabo-Islamic heritage has essentially overlooked the study of riddles as a form of scholarly rhetoric both in Islamic law and in a variety of other scholarly disciplines. As a rhetorical field, the practice of riddles in Arabic encompasses activities described by the term *alghāz*, in addition to various other terms that refer to riddles including: *muʿammayāt*, *aḥājī*, and *imtiḥān*. These terms may indicate slightly different activities and different kinds of texts, but there does appear to be a discursive commitment to differentiating between these genres. There are important relationships between riddles and dialectical question and answer.

One of the assumptions made throughout this study is that unified groups, which I refer to as call "genres," exist within Islamic legal literature, and that the term "genre" can be applied to works of legal distinctions. This study has differentiated between the concept of legal distinctions, a way of legal reasoning, and the genre of legal distinctions, a way of organizing legal information into books.

https://doi.org/10.1515/9783110605792-007

In the previous chapters, I described legal distinctions as a concept, with a distinct genealogy, epistemology, and logic. I have also shown how closely the concept of legal distinctions tracks with the genre of legal distinctions. This chapter demonstrates, however, that the genre of legal distinctions impinged on and was impinged on by other closely related kind of legal writing. It attempts, in part, to understand this genre in the broader context of Islamic legal literature.

The discussion of the histories of legal distinctions in the previous chapters was, to a certain extent, tautological. I assumed an outline of the history of legal distinctions and that there exist prehistories for legal distinctions, that is, various trends that contributed to the development of the concept of a legal distinction. Allowing for a multiplicity of origins for this concept has granted us insight into the complex intellectual world from which distinctions emerged. There are clear intertextual relationships between books of lexicographic, medical, and legal distinctions, which highlight the shared intellectual world of these scholarly pursuits. At the same time, I clarified the connections between legal disputation and the development of legal distinctions, both in terms of legal reasoning and in terms of the content of books of distinction.

Books of legal distinctions represent a certain stage of development and refinement in the history of Islamic legal writing and in the science of Islamic law. Nevertheless, the previous chapters focused on books of legal distinctions as an ending point. While this focus is useful for an analysis of legal distinctions, it is nevertheless convenient to claim that the concept I term "legal distinctions" achieves its full realization in the genre of legal distinctions and that the genre represents the maturation of the concept, but this is not necessarily the case. In fact, one of the claims I have made is that the concept of legal distinctions can be found outside of the context of books of legal distinctions, for instance in texts of disputation or in works that are only partially devoted to legal distinctions. What makes a book of legal distinctions unique is that it consists almost entirely of these distinctions; a fact which has been seen repeatedly in the works examined in previous chapters. What, however, of works that seemingly fit this criterion in their contents but do not announce themselves as works of legal distinctions?

This chapter will answer this question through an analysis of works of legal riddles. The coming together of writing on legal distinctions and legal riddles is a noteworthy development in the history of Islamic legal literature. In fact, riddles increasingly take on the form of legal distinctions and legal distinctions take on the presentation style of riddles. This trend, which can be seen almost from the beginning of the writing of distinctions, reaches its height during the Mamluk period, especially in Cairo. While both genres overlapped, they did not converge completely. Nevertheless, it is sometimes difficult to ascertain whether certain legal books belong to the genre of distinctions or to that of riddles or how this difference is indeed meaningful. A case in point is manuscript Esad Efendi 884 in the Suleymaniye Library, which is a collection (*majmūʿ*) of works on legal riddles. The table of contents on the first page states, "The following books of Ḥanafī legal riddles (*alghāz*) are included in this codex…"[1] Yet, two of the three works in this collection are works of legal distinctions entitled *Kitāb al-Furūq*.[2]

In this chapter, I first trace the tradition of literary and intellectual salons in Arabo-Islamic culture, with a particular focus on their style and popularity in Mamluk Cairo, as the spread of riddles accompanies the spread of salons. Then, I introduce the art of legal riddles and the practice of solving legal riddles. Due to the paucity of scholarship on legal riddles, this chapter offers a preliminary exploration of this style of writing and an initial analysis of its underlying logic. Next, I highlight the convergence between works of riddles and distinctions, a trend that peaked in Mamluk Cairo, and discuss the implications of this for our understanding of genre. In this chapter, I focus on the history of *majālis*—literary salons, study circles, and more—in Arabo-Islamic culture, then follow the tradition of legal riddles, focusing on the way in which legal riddles package the information of Islamic law. I conclude with a look the coming together of riddles and distinctions of and some of the implications of this convergence.

Literary Salons, Learning, and Culture

Examining the social context in which legal knowledge was performed is crucial to understanding the motivations for changes in legal literary aesthetics.[3] Almost all of this knowledge performance, however, took place in venues referred to as

---

1 MS Esad Efendi 884, Suleymaniye Library, Istanbul, 1a.

2 MS Esad Efendi 884, 1a. The two works, according to this table of contents, are *Kitāb al-Furūq li-l-Imām al-Farghānī* and *Kitāb al-Furūq*. The first work in this collection is simply entitled *Kitāb al-Tahdhīb*.

3 Links between social realities and the writing of books of Islamic law can yield interesting conclusions in most areas of Islamic law. For instance, David Vishanoff argues that al-Shāfiʿī's *Risāla* can be best understood as a composite work made up of three separate treatises combined into one work. The second and third treatises, according to Vishanoff, represent actual dialogues between al-Shāfiʿī and his critical contemporaries. Importantly, Vishanoff understands from this that the *Risāla* was therefore composed and disseminated over time and in parts. See David R. Vishanoff, "A Reader's Guide to al-Shāfiʿī's *Epistle on Legal Theory* (*al-Risāla*)," *Islam and Christian-Muslim Relations* 28.3, 245–69.

majālis. Majālis (sg. *majlis*; teaching sessions, literary gatherings, salons) were a widespread phenomenon in the premodern Islamic world, which undoubtedly took on different forms and functions over a broad geographic and chronological scope. George Makdisi suggests that the term *majlis* was used by scholars to refer to all sorts of scholastic gatherings. He thus speaks of "literary clubs" for the "institutionalized learning" of medicine, philosphy, and philosophical theology;[4] "humanist circles" for the study of belles-lettres (*adab*);[5] and "academies" attended by grammarians.[6]

In the *Encyclopaedia of Islam*, *majālis* are described as places "where political and judicial decisions were adopted, plaintiffs, panegyrists and other visitors gathered, and questions of literature or law were debated."[7] Of particular interest for this study are the sessions in which "questions of literature or law were debated." In order to see why books of legal riddles were produced and the reasons for their merging with books of legal distinctions, it is necessary to analyze the contexts in which Islamic law was discussed publicly. "In these public audiences, plaintiffs and petitioners were present, but poets and scholars ... also participated."[8] The term *majlis* thus could refer to almost any gathering of people, the court of a sovereign, a teaching-session, a poetry reading, or even a gathering of friends. *Majlis* was the most popular term for scholastic gatherings outside of the madrasa context.[9] The following discussions, however, focus only on scholarly and literary gatherings.[10]

Although *majālis* differed across time and space, several constants should be kept in mind. The first is that *majālis* were held both at the court of the ruler, for example the sultan or caliph, and in non-courtly contexts. The difference between these two kinds of *majālis* is not necessarily in the activities con-

---

4 George Makdisi, *The Rise of Humanism in Classical Islam and the Christian West: With Special Reference to Scholasticism* (Edinburgh: Edinburgh University Press, 1990), 60 – 61.

5 Makdisi, *Rise of Humanism*, 61.

6 Makdisi, *Rise of Humanism*, 61.

7 EI^2 s. v. "*madjlis*" (ed.), citing R. Brunschvig, *La Berbérie orientale sous les Ḥafṣides des origines à la fin du XV siècle* (Paris: Adrien-Maisonneuve, 1940 – 47), 2:37.

8 EI^2 s. v. "*madjlis*" (ed.).

9 It is possible that teaching hospitals as well should be exempted along with madrasas, but the precise terminology associated with the teaching of medicine falls outside the scope of the present study. See as well the detailed discussion of the semantic range of the premodern term *majlis* in George Makdisi, *Rise of Colleges: Institutions of Learning in Islam and the West* (Edinburgh: Edinburgh University Press, 1982), 10 – 12; *idem*, *Rise of Humanism*, 60 – 64.

10 It should not be missed that the disputations discussed in Chapter Three also happened in venues referred to as *majālis*. In this chapter, however, I refer primarily to gatherings that were not venues for formal disputation.

ducted therein, but in the stakes of the performance. As will be seen, courtly *majālis* were moments to compete for patronage, either direct patronage to compose works or indirect patronage through lucrative governmental appointments. Non-courtly *majālis* were important settings for the discussion, evaluation, and spread of books, ideas, and scholarly reputations. As literary and intellectual salons, participants in the *majālis* sought to display the depth and scope of their knowledge and impress and entertain other participants.[11]

The convergence of riddles and distinctions began in Abbasid times and peaked during the Mamluk and Ottoman periods. There has been research conducted on the literary salons of the Abbasid period and scholarly salons in Ottoman urban centers, yet much less is known about the *majālis* of the Mamluk era. This section will look first at Abbasid-era *majālis*, and then turn towards early Ottoman *majālis* in Egypt and the Eastern Mediterranean. We shall then investigate the *majālis* of Mamluk Egypt, assuming certain continuities with both Abbasid and Ottoman practice.[12]

According to Samer Ali, literary salons "proliferated in the [third/]ninth century, enabling more littérateurs to cultivate the *adab* skills needed to participate, socialize, and gain personal influence."[13] For him, literary salons, referred to as *mujālasa* rather than *majālis* during this period, were occasions for scholars to embed themselves within literary communities and learn the skills necessary to garner patronage.[14] Régis Blachère likewise characterizes the salon in this period as having "a high standing, no one could hope for public admiration if he were not a man of the world, an agreeable conversationalist, having a sharp mind and quick with wordplay, skilled in creating situations which he could

11 I use the term literary salon to refer to gatherings of intellectuals to discuss intellectual matters, including but not limited to literature (*adab*).

12 This assumption of continuity is, for now, provisional. We shall see that these is some evidence of this continuity. This study takes this position based on the idea that non-courtly *majālis* were organized and primarily attended by local participants. The transition from Mamluk to Ottoman rule did not involve mass movement of people. Those who participated in *majālis* in Egypt in the time immediately before and immediately after the Ottoman conquest were the same people.

13 Samer Ali, *Arabic Literary Salons in the Islamic Middle Ages* (South Bend, IN: Notre Dame University Press, 2010), 192.

14 Ali also argues that literary salons were sites in which a shared historical memory was created and cemented. I do not address this aspect of salons directly in this chapter, but it reaffirms the importance of literary salons as sites of knowledge production, not just sites for the display of knowledge.

turn to his advantage."[15] The skills cultivated by attending and performing in such salons allowed scholars "to impress one's audience, in fidelity to shared standards of competence," impacting how much "*adab*-type speaking" was structured.[16]

These skills helped communicate knowledge beyond the immediate setting, as there was a continuity in the patterns of knowledge production in most types of intellectual salons.[17] Connections between courtly and private salons suggest the existence of a broad intellectual community, which maintained certain standards and expectations for what constituted knowledge or artistic production and for the forms in which it ought to be expressed.

Literary salons focused on topics beyond language and literature. L.E. Goodman finds that recognizing the debates occurring between Muḥammad ibn Zakariyyāʾ al-Rāzī (d. *ca.* 312/925 or 323/925) and Abū Ḥātim Aḥmad al-Rāzī (d. *ca.* 322/934) is crucial to understand how these philosophers presented their ideas, both in person and in their works. The contours of philosophical debates and philosophical writing do not necessarily align in all respects with literary debates. For instance, Goodman finds philosophical *majālis* to be "informal gatherings ... not public performances of a formal nature."[18] The literary salons discussed by Samer Ali have a much more formal context, particularly those *majālis* that involved the recitation of poetry. Even so, both literary and philosophical sessions were high-level scholarly exchanges between socially significant members of society.

---

15 Régis Blachère, *Un poète arabe du IVe siècle de l'Hégire (Xe siècle de J.-C.): Abou ṭ-Ṭayyib al-Motanabbî* (Paris: Adrien-Maissonneuve, 1935), 130. Translation based on citation in EI² s.v. "*madjlis*" (ed.).

16 Ali, *Arabic Literary Salons*, 192. The impact that live performance had on the composition and content of *adab* and poetry should not be understated. Performance mattered a great deal in Arabic literature and also, as Dominic P. Brookshaw has shown, for Persian poetry in medieval Iran as well. Joel Blecher has found references to scenes from *majālis* in Ibn Ḥajar al-ʿAsqalānī's hadith commentary *al-Fatḥ al-bārī fī Ṣaḥīḥ al-Bukhārī*. See Dominic P. Brookshaw, "Palaces, Pavilions, and Pleasure-Gardens: The Context and Setting of the Medieval *Majlis*," *Middle Eastern Literatures* 6.3 (2003): 199–223; and Joel Blecher, "*Ḥadīth* Commentary in the Presence of Students, Patrons, and Rivals: Ibn Ḥajar and *Ṣaḥīḥ al-Bukhārī* in Mamluk Cairo," *Oriens* 41 (2013): 261–87.

17 The continuities between different kinds of salons, point to shared societal standards of knowledge and knowledge presentation, in spite of potential differences between salons held in various contexts.

18 Their informal nature sets this debates apart from the formal disputations discussed in Chapter Three. L.E. Goodmann, "Rāzī vs Rāzī – Philosophy in the *Majlis*," in *The* Majlis: *Interreligious Encounters in Medieval Islam*, ed. Hava Lazarus-Yafeh, Mark R. Cohen, Sasson Somekh, and Sidney Griffith (Harrasowitz Verlag: 1999), 101.

The most important observation in these two discussions is the parallel between the intellectual activity of the *majlis* and the written intellectual record.[19] Cultural context affects literary production and intellectual production is related to a certain kind of social life. Indeed, there are parallels here with the tradition of formal disputation discussed in Chapter Three that was enshrined in a variety of text, most notably in the genre of *khilāf*. Further, the existence of intellectual *majālis* among various social strata signals the potential relevance of intellectual production to different social groups, including merchants, scholars, and political elites. This is particularly important for intellectual trends in the Mamluk Sultanate. These trends include (i) the role of imported Mamluks—primarily from Northwest Asia—and their children in seeking education, (ii) the expansion of *majālis* to include a wider spectrum of socioeconomic classes, and (iii) the rising interest in solving riddles in these *majālis*.

The role of the Mamluks themselves was crucial for the cultural history of the Mamluk Sultanate. Mamluks were enslaved young boys, primarily Qipchaks and Circassians, brought to Cairo to be trained as part of the ruling military class. As imported youths striving for a career in the military or government bureaucracy, the Mamluks and their children represented a new bloc of people for whom education and learning became an important social goal. Since the children of the Mamluks could not follow in the footsteps of their fathers into the military, the Mamluks sought to educate their children, focusing primarily on "Arabic, calligraphy, and the fundamentals of religious sciences."[20] These fields comprised the basis for the education and the cultural lives that they developed as adults. Ulrich Haarman emphasizes the importance of "the cultural life [found] in the houses of the lowly Mamluk private soldiers (*jundī*) who often quite understandably sought and found comfort for a disappointing military and public career in the bliss of piety, poetry, and scholarship."[21] While many of them may have found only "bliss" in pursuing intellectual activities, others were able to use this to achieve renown. Intellectual and literary interests, of course, were

---

19 Goodman says that "[t]he language ... of the debate is rapid fire and conversational." A "rapid fire and conversational" tone is not indicative of most philosophical writing, suggesting certain discontinuities between the presentation of philosophical activity in in-person interactions and writing. Goodman, "Rāzī vs Rāzī," 101.

20 Ulrich Haarman, "Arabic in Speech, Turkish in Lineage: Mamluks and Their Sons in the Intellectual Life of Fourteenth-Century Egypt and Syria," *Journal of Semitic Studies* 33.1 (1988), 86–87.

21 Haarman, "Arabic in Speech," 85–86.

found among more than just the professional scholars, with some Mamluks being known "as authors of good verse and as literary entertainers."[22]

As other intellectuals of the time, certain Mamluks and their children attended *majālis* and were known for "sponsor[ing] salons that included both Turkish and Arabic entertainment."[23] At the same time, the breadth of learning at salons served the professional lives of the non-military elite. Carl Petry reminds us that "[t]he literary skills [a member of the civilian elite] acquired qualified him for a wide range of careers, and one of the characteristic features of the man of learning was his multicompetence—his ability to hold positions in diverse occupational fields at the same time."[24] These factors led to an expansion of the ways in which socially diverse groups interacted with and consumed knowledge.[25] This can be seen, in part, in the participation of a non-scholarly, middle class artisans at the public reading of books. Konrad Hirschler has documented their presence at the readings of *Taʾrīkh madinat Dimashq* by Ibn ʿAsākir (d. 571/1176). In his study of the reading notes on manuscripts of this work, he finds that "[c]onsiderable numbers of craftsmen, traders and other non-scholars not only interacted ... in these readings with the scholarly world, but the various sources show that their participation started to be taken seriously."[26] The social life of Mamluk Cairo and Damascus thus valued learning and knowledge.[27]

Helen Pfeifer has shown the recurrence of *majālis* in accounts of scholarly networks in the sixteenth century, especially in exchanges between scholars from the Mamluk Sultanate and the Ottoman Empire. "In general," she writes "these particular *majālis* can be thought of as by-invitation-only gatherings attended by well-to-do Muslim men for the purpose of social and intellectual exchange."[28] Because of the importance of Mamluk Cairo and Damascus as centers

---

22 Haarman, "Arabic in Speech," 95.

23 Margaret Larkin, "Popular Poetry in the Post-Classical Period," in *Cambridge History of Arabic Literature: Arabic Literature in the Post-Classical Period*, ed. Roger Allen and D.S. Richards (Cambridge: Cambridge University Press, 2006), 221.

24 Carl F. Petry, *The Civilian Elite of Cairo in the Later Middle Ages* (Princeton: Princeton University Press, 1981), 312.

25 It is possible that a similar trend could be found earlier, but it is documented clearly for the first time in the Mamluk Empire. This is due, in part, to the mass-movement of scholars resulting from the Mongol invasions and the rise of Cairo as the major center of Arabic learning.

26 Konrad Hirschler, *The Written Word in the Medieval Arabic Lands: A Social and Cultural History of Reading Practices* (Edinburgh: Edinburgh University Press, 2012), 69.

27 The accessibility of learning and the exposure to knowledge production and performance in non-urban areas remains unclear.

28 Helen Pfeifer, "Encounter after the Conquest: Scholarly Gatherings in 16th-Century Ottoman Damascus," *International Journal of Middle East Studies* 47 (2015), 221.

of learning in the period before the sixteenth century, knowledge of Arabic and the Arabic tradition was foundational to these gatherings, all the more so in light of the prevalence of non-Arab elites among the Mamluks and the Ottomans.[29] These salons "were an integral part of elite travel ... and functioned as key venues in which men from different parts of the empire encountered one another."[30] They served as meeting points for travelling elites, and were also opportunities for local scholarly communities to interact with outside communities in the form of travelling scholars.[31] The social place of these *majālis* in the Ottoman period is reminiscent of that in the Abbasid-period *majālis:* in both cases *majālis* served as venues for the movement of scholars and ideas.

Pfeifer also shows that in late sixteenth and early seventeenth centuries, literary salons were venues for book circulation and served as a way for books to acquire positive reviews.[32] Salons became an initial venue for book publication, a semi-public way of introducing a book to a scholarly audience who could judge its merit. In this way, the stakes of the salon were high, and scholars needed to impress audiences. Poets similarly used literary salons to circulate their poetry. In this way, "[t]he *majlis* also played a vital role in the dissemination of poems: scholars commented on them, musicians were inspired by them and listeners spread their renown."[33]

Due to their high social standing, salons also cultivated friendships and social networks. As Pfeifer tells us, the scholar and biographer al-Ḥasan al-Būrīnī (d. 1024/1615) "was widely appreciated for his ability to captivate salon audiences: 'he was never at a scholarly *majlis* without being its nightingale.'"[34] More importantly, authors of biographical dictionaries relied on literary salons for information about contemporaries.[35] However, it is hard to know exactly what transpired, even at elite salons. While primary sources occasionally describe salons, full transcripts or lengthy detailed recounting of the exchanges or conversations are rare.

---

29 Pfeifer, "Encounter," 221.
30 Pfeifer, "Encounter," 221
31 Pfeifer, "Encounter," 223.
32 Pfeifer, "Encounter," 229.
33 Brookshaw, "Palaces," 200.
34 Pfeifer, "Encounter," 230, quoting Najm al-Dīn al-Ghazzī, *Luṭf al-samar wa-qaṭf al-thamar min tarājim aʿyān al-ṭabaqāt al-ūlā min al-qarn al-ḥādī ʿashr*, ed. Maḥmūd al-Shaykh (Damascus: Wizārat al-Thaqāfa wa-l-Irshād al-Qawmī, 1981), 359. Ḥasan al-Būrīnī was a Shāfiʿī jurist, biographer, and poet and studied with Abū l-Barakāt Badr al-Dīn al-Ghazzī (d. 984/1577) in Cairo.
35 Pfeifer, "Encounter," 230–31.

An important facet of *majālis* is their often-contentious nature. Inasmuch as salons were venues for the public display of knowledge, they were also opportunities to prove the superiority of one's own knowledge. Pfeifer stresses "the competitive nature of salons," a spirit of competition sharply distinguishes literary salons from other venues for knowledge-performance, such as a study circle.[36] The *Fatḥ al-bārī*, the commentary by Ibn Ḥajar al-ʿAsqalānī (d. 852/1449) on the *Ṣaḥīḥ* of al-Bukhārī (d. 256/870), provides an example of the importance of social settings for the production and display of knowledge in ninth/fifteenth century Mamluk Cairo.

Al-Fatḥ al-bārī was a text that took form in study circles and subsequently used by the author in salons. The *Fatḥ* in particular shows this history of contention and demonstrates how important *majālis* were to the study of hadith. In the words of Joel Blecher, this book "emerged amidst the discussion of the *Ṣaḥīḥ* in the live presence of his [Ibn Ḥajar's] students."[37] Coming from this background, *al-Fatḥ* was formed through al-ʿAsqalānī's exchanges with his students. Once parts of this book emerged as a written commentary, these discussions move from oral to written, from the *majlis* to the text. The text, however, was also used in later *majālis*, when the information moved from text back to *majlis*.

Blecher has located a particularly compelling case of this interchange, from *majlis* to text and back, in a series of exchanges between Ibn Ḥajar al-ʿAsqalānī and Shams al-Dīn al-Harawī (d. 829/1426), a rival for a Shāfiʿī judgeship who had recently arrived at the Cairo court. At a gathering in the Sultan's garden, Ibn Ḥajar challenged al-Harawī to determine who had greater mastery of hadith. Ibn Ḥajar solved a vexing question related to the nature of the "everlasting shade in heaven" in Q Raʿd 13:35. With this superior knowledge and understanding of the Qur'an, Ibn Ḥajar bested al-Harawī, thus guaranteeing himself a judgeship, a moment he later recounted in *al-Fatḥ al-Bārī*.[38] This episode demonstrates the way in which knowledge moved from book and forth between then *majlis* and written book, creating a reciprocal relationship between written knowledge and performed knowledge.[39]

---

36 Pfeifer, "Encounter," 233.

37 Blecher, "Ḥadīth Commentary," 266, see also 265–68.

38 This session is remembered in Ibn Ḥajar al-ʿAsqalānī, *Fatḥ al-bārī*, 18 vols., ed. ʿAbd al-ʿAzīz ibn Bāz (Beirut: Dār al-Maʿrifa, 1970), 2:143–44, citation from Blecher, "Ḥadīth Commentary," 278–80, where he translates the relevant passage.

39 The process through which this book has been described in detail by Joel Blecher. He describes how Ibn Ḥajar would first compose this work in private, but "continued to contemplate and shape his understanding of *Ṣaḥīḥ al-Bukhārī* in the presence of students during his ongoing

The encounter between Ibn Ḥajar and Shams al-Dīn al-Ḥarawī involved interpretation of the Qur'an and hadith. Similar episodes relating to Islamic law are less commonly found. Surviving transcripts of Maluk-era salons are carefully edited and only indirectly represent the discussions that took place. Nevertheless, they provide an interesting glimpse into how knowledge was performed at the court of the Sultan. Salons of the Sultan al-Qanṣūh Ghawrī (r. 1501–16), for example, discussed Islamic law, using riddles as a vehicle for legal discussions.[40] This record of the *majālis* at the court of al-Ghawrī are one of the few records we have of a courtly *majālis* and one of the few direct transcripts of any *majālis* involved in legal discussions. Although there are many primary sources that recount *majālis* or summarize their proceedings, they do not provide a detailed description of the goings-on in any one *majlis*.

In two articles on Mamluk prose, Muhsin al-Musawi has similarly shown a connection between the active intellectual culture and the composition of books during the Mamluk Sultanate. "The sheer variety of prose-writing," he writes, "attests to the existence of a dynamic culture characterized by the active involvement of littérateurs, widespread networks and a magnanimous devotion to the world of writing."[41] The importance of both littérateurs and social networks to the production and consumption of knowledge also explains, according to al-Musawi, the prevalence of encyclopedic writing during this period: "Islamic medievalists usually focused on the compendium as a treasury of knowledge; the compiler is thus a producer who aims to provide readers with a reservoir which would otherwise by inaccessible in its original form, found in scattered books."[42] Al-Musawi places the author acting as compiler as the driving force behind book composition; however, it is just as likely that competing demands from readers shaped texts. Given the prominence of *majālis* in Mamluk culture, the role of social networks in the spread and dissemination of books, and the importance of *majālis* towards opinion shaping, the possibility that authors shaped books with the public in mind cannot be overlooked. Market forces were, of course, not the only elements of scholarly production, but they can

---

meetings with them," that is, in a teaching-*majlis*. Joel Blecher, *Said the Prophet of God: Hadith Commentary Across a Millenium* (Oakland: University of California Press, 2018), 52.

40 Ḥusayn ibn Muḥammad al-Sharīf, *Nafā'is majālis al-sulṭāniyya fī ḥaqā'iq asrār al-Qur'āniyya*, MS Ahmet III 2680, Topkapı Sarayı Müzesi Kütüphanesi, Istanbul, 60.

41 Muhsin al-Musawi, "Pre-Modern Belletristic Prose," in *Cambridge History of Arabic Literature: Arabic Literature in the Post-Clasical Period*, ed. Roger Allen and D.S. Richards (Cambridge: Cambridge University Press, 2006), 132.

42 Muhsin al-Musawi, "The Medieval Islamic Literary World-System: The Lexicographic Turn," *Mamluk Studies Review*, 17 (2013), 52.

be seen in how books of legal distinction respond to public demand in a particular kind of legal knowledge.

Literary salons in Mamluk Egypt were so commonplace that al-Khalīl ibn Aybak al-Ṣafadī (d. 764/1363) composed a parodistic commentary set in a fictional literary gathering. This commentary, *Ikhtirāʿ al-khurāʿ*, is a commentary on two nonsense verses of Arabic poetry.[43] The frame of the story in which the *Ikhtirāʿ* takes places demonstrates an idealized *majlis*. "Abū Khurāfah [the protagonist of the story] narrates that he was at a party one night with a number of other people—an evening of the literary folk ... They are sitting around chatting about literature, reciting lines for each other."[44] When the guests hear Abu Khurāfah's nonsense lines, they struggle to understand the beauty he sees in this poetry, so they propose finding a commentary. The scene invented by al-Ṣafadī, though a caricature, represents a possible example of the literary salons. We see a group of educated elites (*ẓurafāʾ*) gathered together discussing poetry. These figures are not presented as scholars, but nevertheless enjoy intellectual and literary activities. They vie to impress each other through their knowledge of beautiful poetry, and seek the aesthetic pleasure of hearing and understanding it.[45]

The *majlis* remained a site for knowledge-performance after the end of Mamluk power. As we learn from Nelly Hanna's work on Ottoman Cairo, salons continued to be an important part of life from the sixteenth to eighteenth centuries. Hanna focuses on the salon as part of middle-class and elite intellectual exchange, noting that it included, "the diverse forms existing for the transmission of learning and knowledge such as the spread of a book culture, the coffeehouse, the literary salon—and their significance for our understanding of the way that the middle-class culture was shaped during [this] period."[46] By this period, the *majlis* was one of several significant social venues for knowledge-performance.[47] *Majālis* continued to cover a wide variety of topics, including *dhikr* (Sufi recitation sessions), literary salons, arenas for music, chess, and other scholarly endeavors that discussed *fiqh* or *tafsīr*.[48]

---

43 Kelly Tuttle has studied this work in her dissertation, see Kelly Tuttle, "Expansion and Digression: A Study in Mamlūk Literary Commentary" (PhD Diss., University of Pennsylvania, 2013), 79–108.

44 Tuttle, "Expansion and Disgression," 85–86.

45 Khalīl ibn Aybak al-Ṣafadī, *Ikhtirāʿ al-khurāʿ*, ed. Fārūq Asalīm (Damacus: Ittiḥād al-Kuttāb al-ʿArab[, 2000]).

46 Nelly Hanna, *In Praise of Books: A Cultural History of Cairo's Middle Class, Sixteenth to Eighteenth Century* (Cairo: The American University in Cairo Press, 2004), 14.

47 Hanna, *In Praise of Books*, 73.

48 Hanna, *In Praise of Books*, 73.

These middle-class *majālis* constituted extensions of the "popular poetry" salons in Mamluk Cairo attended by "patrons and consumers who hail, if not from the lower classes, at least from what might be considered a kind of petite bourgeoisie."[49] In speaking of "popular" scholarly culture, I refer to activities in which the participants were not only observers but had opportunities to be performers as well. It is this potential for participation that offered attendees an opportunity to demonstrate their knowledge.[50]

Modern discussions of "middle-class salons" and "the rise of popular poetry" involving some members of the "merchant class" remain vague due to a lack of information about what exactly occurred during these meetings. For instance, it seems likely that someone who could be described as a "middle class merchant" possessed less familiarity with religious sciences than professional scholars, merchants could have been familiar with relevant areas of laws, such as contract and commercial law. In other words, any discussion of a specialized intellectual topic such as *fiqh* or hadith criticism at a salon probably did not carry the same level of sophistication as a *majlis* at the court of the Sultan. This does not mean, however, that such topics were not discussed in non-elite or non-courtly salons, in addition to various kinds of poetry and literature.

Other evidence circumstantial points to a transference between oral and written exchanges in *majālis*. As mentioned in Chapter One, the distinctions book attributed to Najm al-Dīn al-Naysābūrī states that it is was meant to be used in *majālis*. In one manuscript of this work, the author says: "A colleague (*baʿḍ ikhwānī*) asked me to write a book ... that you can consult during discussions in *majālis* (*yastadilluhu fī l-majālis*) and from which you can find guidance in schools (*yustaḍīʾa bihi min al-madāris*)."[51] This is a strange passage, and it seems to have given copyists trouble as well, as no two manuscript witnesses provide the same reading.[52] The juxtaposition of *majālis* and *madāris* in this context, in addition to providing a rhyme, perhaps indicates that the *majālis* are not

49 Larkin, "Popular Poetry," 193–94.

50 These broad phenomena have been studied in some detail, but there is still need for study of more specific contexts, see Jonathan P. Berkey, "Popular Culture under the Mamluks: A Historiographical Survey," *Mamluk Studies Review* 9.2 (2005): 133–46; and Boaz Shoshan, *Popular Culture in Medieval Cairo* (Cambridge: Cambridge University Press, 1993).

51 MS Giresun Yazmalar 44, Suleymaniye Library, Istanbul, 1b.

52 The Giresun Yazmalar manuscript, in general, is written in an exceptionally clear hand with full diacritical marks, i.e. with both dots and vowels markers (*al-ḥarakāt*). The phrase *yastadilluhu fī l-majālis*, however, has only the consonantal skeleton without any diacritical marks. The other reading of this phrase could be *yasnadu lahu fī l-majālis*, depended upon in *majālis*.

study sessions, and that the interest in works of distinctions came from non-scholastic contexts.

Of the seven witnesses to this text, four omit this introduction entirely, despite the remarkable similarities between these seven texts otherwise.[53] The other three manuscripts of this text with an introduction are MS Halet Efendi 780, Suleymaniye Library, Istanbul; MS Yazma Bağışlar 1187, Suleymaniye Library, Istanbul; and MS Or. 481, Leiden University Libraries, Leiden. Here, MS Halet Efendi 780 and MS Yazma Bağışlar 1187 read "to benefit from during *majālis* while doing without school training (*li-yantfiʿa bihā fī l-majālis wa-yastaghnā ʿan al-madāris*)."[54] The Leiden manuscript has a third reading for this text. This text reads "to entertain with in *majālis* and to learn from in schools (*yastahziʾu bihā fī l-majālis wa-yastaḍīʿu bihā fī l-madāris*)."[55] In all three of these texts, the text and the meaning of this phrase are different. The second variant presents law colleges as unimportant; instead of offering the book as a sort of cheat-sheet for Islamic law, it obviates the requirement of a complete formal legal education. The Leiden manuscript sees itself as a source of entertainment and a supplement to this education. In all of these readings, however, *majālis* and *madāris* are paralleled, suggesting that they each refer to different venues for the learning and performance of legal knowledge.

Literature and Practice of Legal Riddles

Legal distinctions were always closely related to legal riddles. The tradition of posing and solving legal riddles serves largely as play and entertainment, and authors in this tradition justify their works as worthwhile diversions. In one book of legal riddles, the Mālikī jurist Ibn Farḥūn (d. 799/1397) cites a proverb by ʿAlī ibn Abī Ṭālib (d. 40/661) as an apology for the practice of posing riddles: "Divert the soul on occasion, for it rusts just as metal does."[56] A diversion, in this case, creating riddles, serves to refresh and enliven the soul. Ibn Farḥūn continues his defense of posing riddles by discussing a prophetic hadith found in al-

---

53 I discuss this text in Chapter Five, pp. 188–90.

54 MS Halet Efendi 780, Suleymaniye Library, Istanbul, 1b; MS Yazma Bağışlar 1187, Suleymaniye Library, Istanbul, 84b. MS YB1187 has a slight variant in the second clause, reading: "*yantafiʿu bihā fī l-majālis wa-yastaghnā bihā ʿan al-madāris*," "to benefit from this book in salons and not need school training because of it."

55 MS Or. 481, Leiden University Libraries, Leiden, 3a.

56 Ibrāhīm ibn ʿAlī ibn Farḥūn, *Durrat al-ghawāṣṣ fī muḥāḍarat al-khawāṣṣ*, ed. Muḥammad Abū l-Ajfān and ʿUthmān Baṭīkh (Cairo: Dār al-Turāth[, 1980]), 62–63.

Bukhārī's *al-Ṣaḥīḥ* and in the *Muwaṭṭa'* of Mālik ibn Anas (d. 179/795), among other hadith collections:

> Ismā'īl [ibn Abī Uways (d. 226/840 – 41)] said: Mālik [ibn Anas] related to me, on the authority of 'Abdallāh ibn 'Umar [(d. 73/693)], the following:
>
> The Messenger of God, may God's prayers and peace be upon him, said, "There is a tree whose leaves never fall. It is, indeed, like a Muslim (*wa-hiya mathal al-muslim*). Tell me, what is it?"
>
> People's thoughts turned to the desert trees, but it occurred to me that it was the date-palm (*al-nakhla*), nevertheless I shied away from responding.
>
> "O, Messenger of God, will you tell us what it is?" we asked.
>
> "It's the date-palm," he replied.
>
> I talked to my father ['Umar ibn al-Khaṭṭāb (d. 24/644)] about what I had thought and he said, "I would have liked nothing better than for you to have said that to him (*la-an takūna qultahā aḥabbu ilayya min an takūna lī kadhā wa-kadhā*)."[57]

In this example, Muḥammad himself participates in the act of creating riddles, posing a question to a crowd gathered before him. If Muḥammad sanctions this activity, then it must be meritorious. At the same time, this story ends with a father's gentle chiding of his son for not having hazarded a guess, a confirmation that riddles are a meritorious activity in which to engage. While this aspect of the story does not involve Muḥammad directly, this tradition approved legal riddles as an edifying activity. 'Umar ibn al-Khaṭṭāb, one of the Sunni 'rightly-guided caliphs,' longed for his son to answer correctly because he saw it as an opportunity to impress Muḥammad and demonstrate his son's wit. Asking and answering questions no longer functions only as a tool for scholars to hone their skills, but as an activity for people to partake in entertainment. Drawing on the examples of the Prophet and 'Alī ibn Abī Ṭālib, Ibn Farḥūn legitimates scholarly entertainment. In starting his book in this fashion, Ibn Farḥūn draws on earlier models of legal riddles in order to establish a precent, which he can then follow.

One general contemporary account of riddles explains that riddles are exercises in wordplay, punning, or the use of metaphors and imagery. "Typically, an intentionally misleading question presents an enigma that can be resolved only by a clever 'right' answer."[58] In the question that Muḥammad poses in the above

57 Muḥammad ibn Ismā'īl al-Bukhārī, *Saḥīḥ al-Bukhārī*, "*Kitāb al-'Ilm*," s.v. "Bāb al-ḥayā' fī l-'ilm."

58 *Princeton Encyclopedia of Poetry and Poetics*, s.v. "Riddles" (Andrew Welsh and Eric J. Rettberg).

account, the comparison between believers and trees supplies the misleading question, and the answer of the palm-tree, the clever solution. This template holds true for linguistic riddles as well as for legal riddles. Riddles are seemingly simple questions with elusive answers or opaque statements, which invite the participation of the reader or listener. Books of riddles seek to provoke curiosity and intellectual engagement on the part of readers or an audience. Discerning the answer becomes a test of skill, but falling short still allows readers to contemplate the answer and enjoy the play in the relationship between the riddle and the correct response.

Posing riddles is an inherently social activity involving at least one person to pose the question and someone else to attempt an answer. Riddles obtain their value by exploiting a knowledge disparity between the one posing the riddle and the audience, enabling status-enhancement on the part of the figure in power and those who know the correct solution. Riddles thrived as a textual genre in which a book's narrator assumes the role of questioner or riddler. Ḥājjī Khalīfa (d. 1067/1657), for example, sees *alghāz* as primarily a textual genre, writing, "It is the science from which the precise and more or less unknown meaning of words are known."[59] For him, *alghāz* is a science, i.e., a textual tradition. Indeed, the very inclusion of *alghāz* as a written genre in its own right in the bibliographic work written by Ḥājjī Khalīfa signals the importance of riddles as a mode of writing in the classical tradition.[60]

In spite of this importance, scholars have only recently begun to analyze riddles as a serious form of Arabo-Islamic literature.[61] This lacuna leaves many underexplored problems, such as the major works or authors within this field, or

59 Ḥājjī Khalīfa, *Kashf al-ẓunūn*, 1:149.

60 Interestingly, riddles do not seem to have been a popular genre within Persian writing. In fact, Seyed-Gohrab says that there are "no such collections [of riddles], and riddles are scattered throughout poetic *dīvāns*, " A. A. Seyed-Gohrab, "The Art of Riddling in Classical Persian Poetry," *Edebiyat* 12 (2001), 15. In his study, he finds that riddles as a literary technique were quite important in Persian literature, particularly within the *qaṣīda* form and that it "may, in fact, be regarded as a legacy of Middle Persian literature" (Seyed-Gohrab, "Art of Riddling," 31). It is peculiar that books of riddles were very popular in Arabic but found no real currency in Persian.

61 See, for instance, Thomas Bauer's entry in EI[3] on Khālid ibn ʿAbdallāh al-Azharī, a grammarian from fifteenth century Egypt. In this entry, Bauer discusses al-Azharī's writings, but the *al-Alghāz al-naḥwiyya* (*The Grammatical Riddles*) is mentioned only in passing. "Several works of al-Azharī were published in early prints that are hardly accessible today or are still in manuscript, among them *al-Alghāz al-naḥwiyya* ("Grammatical riddles"), probably printed in Cairo 1281/1864." In part, the lack of study of riddles is due to the lack of printed editions. EI[3] s.v. "al-Azharī, Khālid ibn ʿAbdallāh" (Thomas Bauer).

the relationship between riddles and other forms of knowledge and entertainment. As implied by Ḥājjī Khalīfa, riddles encompass legal topics as well as linguistic or lexicographic issues. Muḥammad Sālimān's recent study of Arabic riddles focuses exclusively on linguistic riddles, both grammatical and lexicographic.[62] There are, however, also books of riddles in other scholarly disciplines, including law.[63] Indeed, the history of legal riddles in the Arabic tradition ought to also include literary (*adab*) works that recount the figure of the Jurist of the Arabs (*faqīh al-ʿarab*).[64] Nevertheless, the specific motives for telling and recording legal riddles remains to be discovered.

Muḥammad Abū l-Ajfān and ʿUthmān Baṭīkh, the editors of Ibn Farḥūn's work on legal riddles, *Durrat al-ghawāṣṣ fī muḥāḍarat al-khawāṣṣ*, suggest that riddles helped jurists develop a more complete understandings of substantive law and are helpful for memorizing obscure points of law.[65] More than merely producing knowledge, riddles were also a social practice in which professionals and cultural elites enhanced their own status. Against Abū l-Ajfān and Baṭīkh, it

---

62 Muḥammad Sālimān, *Fann al-alghāz ʿind al-ʿarab wa-maʿhu l-Lafẓ al-lāʾiq wa-l-maʿnā l-rāʾiq; al-Alghāz al-naḥwiyya; al-Ṭāʾir al-maymūn fī ḥall lughz al-Kanz al-madfūn*, ed. Muḥammad Sālimān (Cairo: al-Hayʾa al-Miṣriyya al-ʿĀmma li-l-Kitāb, 2012).

63 See EI^2 s.v. "Lug̲h̲z" (Mohamed Bencheneb).

64 The *faqīh al-ʿarab* seems to be a trickster figure prominent in early Islamic writings. He makes appearances in the *maqāma* collection of al-Harīrī, particularly the thirty-second *maqāma*, *al-maqāma l-ṭibiyya*, but also in such works as *Futyā faqīh al-ʿarab* by the lexicographer Aḥmad ibn Fāris (d. 395/1004). Ibn al-Jawzī includes a refutation of fatwas issued by the *faqīh al-ʿarab* in his *Tablīs Iblīs*. The existence of this figure signals us towards intersections of intellectual play and Islamic law that seem to prefigure a more formalized genre of riddles within the textual world of Islamic law. This history remains to be written. The existence of a jurist-figure in works of *adab* and the collections of his fatwas may grant us insight into contestations over legal authority and the status required to interpret the Qur'an and hadith, in a manner similar that discussed in to Joseph E. Lowry, "The First Islamic Legal Theory: Ibn al-Muqaffaʿ on Interpretation, Authority, and the Structure of the Law," *Journal of the American Oriental Society* 128 (2008): 25–40 and *idem*, "The Legal Hermeneutics of al-Shāfiʿī and Ibn Qutayba: A Reconsideration," *Islamic Law and Society* 11 (2004): 1–41. See also, Jaakko Hämeen-Anttila, *Maqama: A History of a Genre* (Weisbaden: Harrassowitz, 2002), 157–58, 269–70, 344. I thank Matthew L. Keegan for alerting me to the importance of the *faqīh al-ʿarab* for the history of legal riddles and for these references. Abū l-Faraj ʿAbd al-Raḥmān ibn ʿAlī ibn al-Jawzī, *Talbīs Iblīs*, no ed. (Beirut: Dār al-Qalam, 1403[/1983]), 123; Abū Muḥammad al-Qāsim ibn ʿAlī l-Ḥarīrī, *Maqāmāt al-Ḥarīrī* (Beirut: Maktabat al-Maʿārif, 1873), 325–48; Abū l-Ḥusayn Aḥmad ibn Fāris al-Lughawī, *Kitāb Futya faqīh al-ʿarab*, ed. Ḥusayn ʿAlī Maḥfūẓ in *Majallat al-Majmaʿ al-ʿIlmī l-ʿArabī* 33.3 (1377/1958): 441–66; 33.4 (1377/1958): 633–56.

65 Muḥammad Abū l-Ajfān and ʿUthmān Baṭīkh, "*Dirāsa tamhīdiyya*," in Burhān al-Dīn Ibrāhīm ibn Farḥūn al-Mālikī, *Durrat al-ghawāṣṣ fī muḥāḍarat al-khawāṣṣ*, ed. Muḥammad Abū l-Ajfān and ʿUthmān Baṭīkh (Cairo: Dār al-Turāth; Tunis: al-Maktaba al-ʿAtīqa[, 1980]), 37.

seems likely that social practices led to the composition of these books, rather than the composition of a genre of books altering existing social practices.

While the word *lughz (pl. alghāz)* seems to be the most commonly used word to describe the act of asking and solving riddles, it also competes with other terms such as *uḥjiya* (pl. *aḥājī*), *muʿammā* (pl. *muʿammayāt*), *muʿāyat* (pl. *muʿāyāt*), *imtiḥān* (pl. *imtiḥānāt*) and even *al-asʾila wa-l-ajwiba*. Some authors argued for strong distinctions between these terms. Ibn Farḥūn, for example, relates each term to a different branch of learning. According to the Algerian scholar Mohamed Bencheneb, the *lughz* and *uḥjiya* are both riddles in the style of question and answer, while the *muʿammā* is a riddle without the question and answer. [66] The word *muʿāmmā*, however, can also be used to mean a code or secret writing.[67] The works discussed by Bencheneb on riddles and puzzles are primarily lexicographical or linguistic. "The enigma [(*lughz*)] is generally in verse, and characteristically is in an interrogative form."[68] A riddle demands to be solved, the answer almost certainly involving a play on words or a double-entendre. All three styles of riddles are generally, but not always, in verse.

These three terms for riddles do not seem to have a particular relevance in the legal realm. Ibrāhīm ibn Nāṣir ibn Ibrāhīm al-Bashar finds no difference between the various terms for riddles: *alghāz, muʿammā, uḥjiya*, in al-Jurjānī's work of legal riddles. Al-Jurjānī's book, al-Bashar says, "is not a book of *alghāz* in the technical meaning of the word (*al-maʿnā l-muṣṭalaḥ ʿalayhi*), even though it is counted among these works and considered one of them. The author, may God have mercy on him, had a different goal with this book."[69] Further, al-Bashar discounts the idea of riddles as a genre: "It did not become an independent branch of legal studies at all," he explained, "even if some scholars dedicated books to this topic."[70] Despite this claim, there are many extant books of legal riddles.

The riddles in such books are generally presented in dialogue form. Ibn Farḥūn's book forms a series of consecutive simulated dialogs. Each riddle is introduced with a conditional protasis, the phrase, "If you were to ask... (*fa-in qulta*)," and the answer provides the apodosis, "I would reply... (*wa-qultu*)." The dialogues are blueprints, similar to the inclusion of disputations in some books

66 EI² s.v. "Lughz" (Mohamed Bencheneb).
67 See EI² s.v. "Muʿammā" (Clifford E. Bosworth).
68 EI² s.v. "Lughz" (Mohamed Bencheneb).
69 Ibrāhīm ibn Nāṣir ibn Ibrāhīm al-Bashar "*al-Muqaddima*," in Abū l-ʿAbbās Aḥmad ibn Muḥammad al-Jurjānī, "*Kitāb al-Muʿāyāt fī l-fiqh ʿalā madhhab al-Imām al-Shāfiʿī*," ed. Ibrāhīm ibn Nāṣir ibn Ibrāhīm al-Bashar (PhD Diss., Jāmiʿat Umm al-Qurā, 1415[/1994]), 37.
70 Al-Bashar, "*al-Muqaddima*," 37.

of legal distinctions.[71] Given the importance of riddles at *majālis*, the dialogic presentation in these works was likely a blueprint for or perhaps representation of performance. Arriving at the solution to a legal riddle involves a high degree of sophisticated legal and linguistic education. Fortunately for the reader, these books also provide solutions. In this way, a book of riddles prepares one for participation in a *majlis* and simulates an actual *majlis*. The book poses questions for the reader to answer. The reader can attempt to solve the riddle and then verify their answer with the one provided in the text. The possibility for enjoyment comes through attempting and, perhaps, succeeding to solve the puzzle, or failing to solve it, through understanding the solution to the puzzle on reading it.

The Ḥanafī jurist Ibn al-Shiḥna (d. 882/1515–16) wrote a typical work of this genre, *al-Dhakhā'ir al-ashrafiyya fī alghāz al-ḥanafiyya*. Most of the riddles he posed begin with the conditional, "If someone were to say..." (*in qīla...*) and the solution to the riddle is introduced with the formula "the reply is... (*wa-l-jawāb...*)."[72] He seems to have come up with the majority of these riddles, though he also includes riddles from a book titled *al-Tahdhīb fī dhihn al-labīb* by a certain Ibn al-ʿIzz.[73] The daunting riddles from *al-Tahdhīb* have different phrasing than those in *al-Dhakhā'ir* and are also followed by their solutions.[74] Generally, solving the riddles involves either thorough mastery of substantive law, a mastery of the Arabic language and linguistic interpretation, or both. For instance, Ibn al-Shiḥna asks:

> Question (*fa-in qīla*): Which wells cannot be used for ablutions until one bucketful of water has been poured out from it?
>
> Answer (*fa-l-jawāb*): Any well containing a bucket that has previously been used to draw water from a well has sufficiently impure water that it may not be used for ablutions. Performing ablutions with the water from such a well is only permitted once one bucketful of water has been poured out from it. This ruling is applied in a proportionally consistent

---

71 See Chapter Three.

72 See ʿAbd al-Barr ibn Muḥammad ibn al-Shiḥna, *Alghāz al-ḥanafiyya li-Ibn al-Shiḥna l-musammā al-Dhakhā'ir al-ashrafiyya fī alghāz al-ḥanafiyya*, ed. Fāṭima Shihāb (Cairo: al-Maktaba al-Azhariyya li-l-Turāth, 2014).

73 I believe this refers to Abū l-Maḥāsin ʿAlī ibn ʿAlī ibn Muḥammad ibn Abī l-ʿIzz (d. 792/1389). See Mu'assasat Āl al-Bayt, *al-Fihris al-shāmil li-l-turāth al-ʿarabī l-islāmī l-makhṭūṭ*, 2nd ed. (Amman: Mu'assasat Āl al-Bayt, n.d.), 41:29. See also Markaz al-Malik al-Fayṣal li-l-Buḥūth wa-l-Dirāsāt al-Islāmiyyah, *Khizānat al-turāth: Fihris shāmil li-ʿanāwīn al-makhṭūṭāt wa-amākinihā wa-arqām ḥifẓihā fī maktabāt al-ʿālam*, no. 5919, CD-ROM. The *Khizānat al-turāth* catalog is also available online at al-Maktaba al-Shāmila, http://shamela.ws/browse.php/book-5678, accessed December 1, 2018.

74 He discusses his use of Ibn al-ʿIzz's work on page 3. For an example, see below.

> manner; the number of buckets of water poured out should be equivalent to the number of times the impure bucket was used.[75]

This riddle consists of a difficult legal question, the solution to which rests on knowing the details of purity law. Water in a well is pure but can be tainted by the addition of impurities. This riddle asks why or how a well may be purified by extracting exactly one bucket of water. In order to solve the riddle, one has to know purity law, the status of water in a well, its potential pollutants, and the remedies for the pollution, detailed intricacies of substantive law.

Other riddles require an exercise in linguistic interpretation, as in one riddle cited from Ibn al-ʿIzz, whose answer is provided by Abū Ḥanīfa himself: "It is said that someone asked Abū Ḥanīfa, 'What do you think about someone who says to his wife, 'I do not wish for Heaven, nor do I fear Hell. I eat carrion and blood. I take the word of (*uṣaddiqu*) Jews and Christians and I loathe God (*abghuḍu l-ḥaqq*)..."[76] The man continues in this way making statement after statement, all of which appear to repudiate his Muslim faith. Instead of answering the question, however, Abū Ḥanīfa gauges the opinions of his companions. "They all respond," the story continues, "'the one who says this is an infidel!' Upon hearing this, Abū Ḥanīfa smiled and said, 'No, he is a true believer (*mu'min*)!'"[77] How can this be?

The answer, supplied by Abū Ḥanīfa, involves a prodigious act of linguistic interpretation. His solution reinterprets every one of the speaker's statements in order to show how each aligns with proper behavior and belief. Further, not only is this person shown to be a Muslim in good standing, but Abū Ḥanīfa demonstrates that this speaker has attained a high level of religious knowledge and piety. Abū Ḥanīfa explains each one of the speaker's sentences as having a pious meaning, thus, "I do not wish for Heaven, nor do I fear Hell" means that he wishes for and fears their Creator, "I eat carrion and blood" means that he eats fish and locusts and liver and spleen.[78] After reading Abū Ḥanīfa's explanations, the reader is compelled to agree with Abū Ḥanīfa's assessment that the speaker is indeed a true believer.[79]

In this explanation, Abū Ḥanīfa interprets the phrase "'I do not wish for Heaven..." as implying an elided phrase (*al-ḥadhf*). The speaker's full meaning, according to this interpretation, is "I do not wish for Heaven, I wish for God," but

75 Ibn al-Shiḥna, *Dhakhā'ir al-ashrafiyya*, 8.
76 Ibn al-Shiḥna, *Dhakhā'ir al-ashrafiyya*, 199.
77 Ibn al-Shiḥna, *Dhakhā'ir al-ashrafiyya*, 199.
78 Ibn al-Shiḥna, *Dhakhā'ir al-ashrafiyya*, 190.
79 Ibn al-Shihna, *Dhakhā'ir al-ashrafiyya*, 199–200.

the speaker elides the second clause. In interpreting the second statement in this manner, Abū Ḥanīfa reads it favorably, with a presumption of legality. His reading of the second clause is similarly receptive. Only animals that have been ritually slaughtered are permissible for eating; the consumption of blood is never acceptable. In spite of this, Abū Ḥanīfa understands that this statement is not about eating carrion and blood, but rather an allusion to a statement a made by the Prophet Muḥammad. "There are two kinds of carrion and two kinds of blood that have been made licit for us. The carrion is fish and locust, the blood, liver and spleen."[80] The statement is therefore to be understood as a specific reference to this prophetic hadith and not as a general statement about dietary practice. In making this allusion, the speaker is demonstrating his own knowledge of the Prophetic tradition. His words not only echo those of the Prophet, but this hadith is also used as an authoritative prooftext in legal discussions of what is permissible to eat.[81] He is quoting Muḥammad, and quoting him in a correct context. All of the speaker's statements are interpreted in this fashion by Abū Ḥanīfa and the deep religious learning of the speaker is brought to the fore.

These are two examples of the kind of reasoning and presentation found in works of legal riddles, showing that the legal content of riddles makes books of riddles serious legal works and that the reader must have a strong grounding in substantive doctrine, legal theory, and the Arabic language in order to solve many of the riddles presented in these books. A reader lacking the knowledge to answer a riddle can also learn about the law by reading these works. These examples also highlight the degree to which jurists could indulge in intellectual play. These books witness moments of sustained pleasure in the intricacies of Islamic law and legal theory. At the same time, they remain serious works of Islamic law. By citing the example of Abū Ḥanīfa, the eponym of a legal school, Ibn Shiḥna argues for the legitimacy of riddles, but also demonstrates the posing and solving riddles is activity in which the eponymous founder of the legal school participated.

80 See ʿAlāʾ al-Dīn al-Kāsānī, *Badāʾiʿ al-ṣanāʾiʿ fī tartīb al-sharāʾiʿ* (Beirut: Dār al-Kutub al-ʿIlmiyya, 1406/1998), 5:58. This hadith appears in Ibn Mājah in his chapter on *ṣayd*, and his chapter on Foods (*aṭʿima*), in *Sunan Abī Dāwūd* in the chapter on Foods (*aṭʿima*), in Mālik's *Muwaṭṭaʾ* on the Description of the Prophet (*ṣifat al-nabī*), and in the *Musnad* of Aḥmad ibn Ḥanbal, see Arent Jan Wensinck, *Concordance et indices de la tradition musulmane: les six livres, le Musnad d'al-Dārimī, le Muwatta' de Mālik, le Musnad de Aḥmad ibn Ḥanbal* (Leiden: Brill, 1933), 1:226.
81 See al-Kāsānī, *Badāʾiʿ al-ṣanāʾiʿ*, 5:58; al-Ḥasan ibn Manṣūr al-Uzjandī Qāḍīkhān, *Sharḥ al-Ziyādāt* (Beirut: Dār Iḥyāʾ al-Turāth al-ʿArabī, 2005/1426), 5:2117.

My understanding of play in the context of Islamic law is inspired by the work of Norman Calder, particularly his *Islamic Jurisprudence in the Classical Era.*[82] Calder's discussion of play develops from his understanding of Islamic law as a stable set of rules and relationships, which jurists constantly attempt to reinvent and redescribe. For him, "play" is in many ways the primary literary feature of Islamic law: "the most characteristic features of development through time are those that reflect, not an interest in new rules, but a self-reflective interest in the tradition itself and in the modes of expressing inherited rules."[83] Accordingly, any development in Islamic law might occur as a literary or rhetorical innovation, as a legal innovation, or both. In this legal context, play can involve two activities, a rich linguistic analysis and the pursuit of stylistic refinement and organizational clarity. Calder has emphasized the importance of the development of rhetorical features of Islamic legal writing. "Real measurable development, implying a process that is more or less continuous through time and in a definable direction, can be distinguished only in relation to organisational technique, linguistic presentation, and syntactical virtuosity."[84] In Calder's telling, this aspect of legal thinking made the study of law "a joy and delight" for premodern jurists.[85] Calder's emphasis on the aesthetic dimensions of legal literature reminds us that classical Islamic juriprudence (*fiqh*) was both a project to understand the theory and doctrine of Islamic law, a divinely inspired set of norms, and the variety of literary representations of this law.[86]

---

82 See also, however, the discussion of Calder's earlier ideas about play in Islamic law in the "Alta Discussion" in *Studies in Islamic Legal Theory*, ed. Bernard Weiss (Leiden: Brill, 2006), 413–14.

83 Norman Calder, *Islamic Jurisprudence in the Classical Era*, ed. Colin Imber (Cambridge: Cambridge University Press, 2010), 71.

84 Calder, *Islamic Jurisprudence*, 35.

85 Calder, *Islamic Jurisprudence*, 86.

86 Calder is convincing in his analysis in terms of the genres that he studies, the *mabsūṭ* and the *mukhtaṣar.* Other scholars, however, have shown doctrinal development in other genres of Islamic legal writing. In particular, Baber Johansen has demonstrated how Ottoman legal commentaries showed important changes in substantive law. Other studies have also shown development occurring in fatwa literature. Wael Hallaq discusses development from a theoretical standpoint and David S. Powers and Yosef Rappaport have demonstrated this from a social historical perspective. These important studies do not undermine Calder's conclusions for the two genres he studies nor his general approach to Islamic legal texts. See Baber Johansen, "Legal Literature and the Problem of Change," in *Islam and Public Law: Classical and Contemporary Studies*, ed. Chibli Mallat, 29–47 (London: Graham and Trotman); *idem*, *The Islamic Law on Land Tax and Rent: The Peasants' Loss of Property Rights under the Hanafite Doctrine* (London: Croom Helm, 1988); Wael Hallaq "From *Fatwās* to *Furūʿ*: Growth and Change in Islamic Substantive Law," *Islamic Law and Society* 1 (1994): 29–65; David S. Powers, *Law, Society, and Culture in*

This kind of intellectual play is witnessed in both books of legal riddles and books of legal distinctions. For Calder, play facilitates the improvement of legal information. He discusses how play is used to increase the precision of legal language and clarify the relationship between laws and ideas. In riddles, of course, the play works differently, rendering the law at first ambiguous or obscure, only clarifying it through the answer. Both steps demand a high degree of linguistic play and the creative exploration of linguistic and legal issues. The intellectual dexterity involved in solving a riddle make this activity an enjoyable way to hone a legal mind. Ibn Farḥūn even makes a statement to this effect in the introduction to his book on legal riddles: "[I]t is necessary for a scholar to test his colleagues by asking them the most obscure questions possible (*al-masāʾil al-ʿawīṣāt*) to test their minds' ability to clarify difficult questions (*muʿaḍḍalāt*) and decipher obscure questions (*al-mushkilāt*)."[87] Ibn Farḥūn thus implies that some of the most obscure questions possible are to be found in the form of legal riddles, and that solving legal riddles helps maintain a sharp mind.

It was not only legal riddles, however, where some of these obscure questions were to be found. Many works of legal distinctions packaged law as riddles or quasi-riddles, comparing laws in ways that seem at first confusing or even unintelligible, but which through prolonged comparison actually reveals a straightforward distinction, much like riddles present a straightforward situation in an intentionally obscure or complex fashion. The relationship between riddles and distinctions as legal concepts was hardly a one-way affair, as the reasoning of legal distinctions showed became a compelling way of presenting legal riddles.

Legal Distinctions as Play

The style of presentation of legal riddles proved useful to authors of works of legal distinctions. In addition, the form and logic of legal distinctions were equally useful for the presentation of legal riddles. Many works of legal distinctions, particularly those written in Mamluk Cairo, adopt the rhetorical style of the riddle-form, and vice-versa.

The influence of riddles on legal distinctions can be seen clearly in the chapter on legal distinctions in Ibn Nujaym's *al-Ashbāh wa-l-naẓāʾir*. The first section

---

the Maghrib, 1300–1500 (Cambridge: Cambridge University Press, 2002); and Yossef Rapoport, *Marriage, Money, and Divorce in Medieval Islamic Society* (Cambridge: Cambridge University Press, 2005).

87 Ibn Farḥūn, *Durrat al-ghawāṣṣ*, 64.

of this chapter focuses on his discussion of ritual purity.[88] The first distinction in this section reads, "If one piece of animal dung (*buʿra*) falls into a well, it does not render the water impure. However, if half a piece of animal dung (*naṣfuhā*) falls into a well, it does render the water impure."[89] This distinction seems to challenge the most basic laws of logic: how can a greater amount of an impure substance be less impure than a lesser amount? Like a riddle, this logical affront prods the reader to reflect, to understand how these two situations can result.

The next distinction is just as confusing: "It is not incumbent on a man to help his sick wife perform her minor ablutions, but it incumbent on him to help his sick slaves, male or female, perform their minor ablutions."[90] Again, this situation seems to defy common sense, as privileging the religious duties of one's slaves over one's wife contravenes the expected social order. Not only would this devalue marriage relative to slavery and concubinage, but this distinction also seems to place the religious needs of an enslaved person above those of a free person. Again, this distinction stokes a sense of curiosity in the reader, highlighting what is to come. Because the distinction seems so absurd, the reader expects the author to resolve this discomfort. Ibn Nujaym must resolve both the contradiction between the laws compared and the seeming incongruity between these substantive laws and common sense. The anticipation established by the comparison and the resolution thereof through the discussion of the distinction borrows from the presentation style of riddles, which aims to entertain the reader or audience.

In the case of animal dung falling into a well, Ibn Nujaym explains that a lesser quantity is more polluting than a greater quantity because when "one piece of animal dung falls into the well, it is covered by an outer crust, which prevents the pollutants from spreading, whereas this is not the case with half of a piece."[91] This explanation functions on two separate levels. First, on stylistic

---

88 Ibn Nujaym claims that all of his distinctions come from the "the legal distinction work written by Imām al-Karābīsī titled *Talqīḥ al-Maḥbūbī*." The reference to al-Karābīsī likely refers to Asʿad ibn Muḥammad al-Karābīsī's book, *al-Furūq*. The *Talqīḥ al-Maḥbūbī*, however, refers to a work by a different author, the *Talqīḥ al-ʿuqūl fī l-furūq* by Aḥmad ibn ʿUbayd Allāh al-Maḥbūbī (d. 630/1232–33), also known as Ṣadr al-Sharīʿa al-Awwal. It is unclear how or why Ibn Nujaym conflates these two works. His discussion in fact follows the *Talqīḥ* of al-Maḥbūbī, as is also confirmed by the commentary tradition. Modern sources agree on the date of al-Maḥbūbī's death, but I am unable to find a premodern source attesting to this date.

89 Zayn al-ʿĀbidīn Ibrāhīm ibn Nujaym al-Miṣrī, *Kitāb al-Ashbāh wa-l-naẓāʾir* with Aḥmad ibn Muḥammad al-Ḥamawī, *Ghamz ʿuyūn al-baṣāʾir sharḥ Kitāb al-Ashbāh wa-l-naẓāʾir*, no ed. (Beirut: Dār al-Kutub al-ʿIlmiyya, 1985/1405), 4:285.

90 Ibn Nujaym, *al-Ashbāh wa-l-naẓāʾir*, 4:286.

91 Ibn Nujaym, *al-Ashbāh wa-l-naẓāʾir*, 4:285.

grounds, it accounts for the absurdity involved in the phrasing of the compared fact patterns. Contrary to the presentation, Ibn Nujaym does not say that less volume of pollutant pollutes more, but that the two different volumes operate in dissimilar fashions. Second, this proposal draws on rules regarding ritual purity, where a pollutant can impact a pure substance by penetrating it. The lesser volume of a pollutant thus seeps more easily into the well water, whereas the greater quantity is imagined to be more controlled, and, therefore, less able to dissipate.

The case of performing ablutions for another turns on similar logic. Ibn Nujaym explains, "The distinction is that the slave is his property and the slave's upkeep is incumbent upon him, whereas his wife is not his property."[92] The requirement for helping a slave with their ablution, then, forms part of the requirement for the upkeep (*iṣlāḥ*) of one's property. Since the slave in this example is Muslim, part of the owner's responsibility is to assist her to perform religious duties. There is no such responsibility regarding a man's wife, since she is not his property. The initial formulation of the proposed contradiction indicates that a man has a greater religious duty to a slave than to his wife, in effect, a form of linguistic play on the part of the author. The resolution of the distinction resolves the apparent contradiction by turning to duties arising as a result of property ownership.

While the explanations that Ibn Nujaym offers in his comparisons are provocative, his explanation of the distinction between the compared laws places them within the standard doctrinal parameters of Islamic law. Further, the reasoning that he proposes makes the seeming incongruity clear and shows the outcomes to be logical. With the rationale presented, the strange case of the conflicting laws no longer appears absurd, but rather as an anomaly, which results from normal processes of legal reasoning. Indeed, these comparisons are only surprising because of the way each fact-pattern was written by Ibn Nujaym.

Ibn Nujaym's writing was both playful and didactic, appearing within a work that served as a comprehensive survey of Ḥanafī law in the sixteenth century. In many ways, his book offers a snapshot of contemporary *fiqh*. The chapters in his book treat: (i) general principles (*al-qawāʿid al-kulliya*), (ii) useful remarks on points of law (*al-fawāʾid*), (iii) harmonization and distinction (*al-jamʿ wa-l-farq*),[93] (iv) riddles (*al-alghāz*), (v) legal stratagems (*ḥiyal*), (vi) distinctions (*al-*

92 Ibn Nujaym, *al-Ashbāh wa-l-naẓāʾir*, 4:286.

93 This section is not on legal distinctions, even though its title suggests it may be so. It instead consists of comparisons of different legal ideas or concepts, rather than specific comparisons of laws and their outcomes. For instance, topics treated include "The Differences between the Minor and Major Ablutions," "The Differences between Wiping over a Shoe (*masḥ al-khuff*)

furūq), and (vii) stories and correspondence (*al-ḥikāyāt wa-l-murāsalāt*). Taken together, they bespeak the widespread sense of intellectual play among elite jurists. In fact, only the second chapter, on *fawā'id*, corresponds to a traditional, straightforward topics of Islamic law.

The Merging of *Alghāz* and *Furūq*

Ibn Nujaym's legal distinctions are clearly reminiscent of legal riddles. This generic influence, however, went in both directions. In many works of legal riddles, jurists wrote books whose content reflects the genre of legal distinctions, but titles whose indicate that they are works of legal riddles.

Abū l-ʿAbbās Aḥmad al-Jurjānī's *al-Muʿāyāt fī l-fiqh* is a clear example of this convergence. Ostensibly a book about legal riddles, it has almost always been received by readers as a book of legal distinctions. The term *al-muʿāyāt* in the title denotes a particular kind of riddle, but should probably be understood here as a synonym for *alghāz*.[94] Nevertheless, the majority of this work does not consist of riddles, but of legal distinctions. One manuscript even titles this work *Kitāb al-Furūq li-l-Jurjānī* (*al-Jurjānī's Distinctions Treatise*).[95]

Al-Jurjānī writes in the introduction to this work:

> The following are questions fit to be asked as riddles or to test someone's knowledge. I present them organized by legal topic to increase the usefulness of this book and to make consulting it easier.[96]

The majority of the legal puzzles in this work juxtapose pairs of seemingly contradictory legal rulings. Ibrāhīm al-Bashar, who edited this work, summarizes its contents as follows: "(i) legal distinctions, (ii) legal maxims and precepts (*al-*

---

and Washing the Foot," and "The Differences between Menstruation and Childbirth (*al-nifās*)." It is more reminiscent of a work of applied lexicographic distinctions. See Ibn Nujaym, *al-Ashbāh wa-l-naẓā'ir*, 3:287–479, 4:5–286.

94 Further research into riddles need to be conducted before this statement can be made with confidence.

95 This manuscript is catalogued under *Fiqh Shāfiʿī* 915, I thank Noha Abou Khatwa with helping me identify the accession number of this manuscript. It is also the manuscript used in the Dār al-Kutub al-ʿIlmiyya edition of this work, see Abū l-ʿAbbās Aḥmad ibn Muḥammad al-Jurjānī, *al-Muʿāyāt fī l-ʿaql aw al-Furūq*, ed. Muḥammad Fāris (Beirut: Dār al-Kutub al-ʿIlmiyya, 1993), 14–15.

96 Al-Jurjānī, al-*Muʿāyāt*, 144.

qawāʿid wa-l-ḍawābiṭ),[97] and (iii) legal riddles, but the primary topic of the book is [legal distinctions]."[98] In fact, one could understand that all three categories are, in this text, actually types of riddles.

Al-Jurjānī's use of distinctions introduces yet another function for legal distinctions, as a vehicle for asking hard questions. Previously, we have seen distinctions function as specific objections within formalized disputation, as a method for highlighting the relationship between substantive law, and a genre through which to organize Islamic legal knowledge. Other Shāfiʿī scholars accepted, to a degree, al-Jurjānī's statement and read this work as primarily addressing riddles through the form of distinctions; for examples, Ibn Qāḍī Shuhba says that the *Kitāb al-Muʿāyāt* "included different kinds of ways to test someone's knowledge (*al-imtiḥān*), such as riddles, distinctions, and exceptions from legal precepts."[99]

The distinctions that al-Jurjānī provides are largely indistinguishable from those in other books of legal distinctions, and would not be out of place in them. For example, one legal distinction from his chapter on prayer is typical of the distinctions genre.

> If, while praying, someone decides to stop his prayer, the prayer is nullified, even if he does not actually stop it.
>
> If, however, while reciting the Qur'an, someone decides to stop his recitation, it is not nullified as long as he does not stop reciting.
>
> The distinction between these two is that prayer requires an intention to pray and becomes void by any action that negates this intention. Thus, a prayer is nullified by the mere intention of stopping it. Reciting the Qur'an, however, does not require such intention, thus it is not nullified by the intention of stopping.
>
> The hajj is not treated according to this principle, for it is not nullified by an action that negates the intention to perform it. Because of this, a hajj is not voided by an intention of stopping.[100]

This passage compares the role of intention in two ritual acts, prayer and Qur'an recitation. The distinction between these two acts lies in their connection to the

97 These two terms comprise one category.

98 Al-Bashar, "*Muqaddima*," 91.

99 Ibn Qadi Shuhba, *Ṭabaqāt al-shāfiʿiyya*, 4 vols., ed. al-Ḥāfiẓ ʿAbd al-ʿAlīm Khān (Beirut: Dār al-Kutub al-ʿIlmiyya, 1407[/1986), 1:260.

100 Al-Jurjānī, *al-Muʿāyāt*, 191. Compare also with the discussion of ʿAbdallāh al-Juwaynī, see above, Ch. 1, pp. 26–27. See also Abū Muḥammad ʿAbdallāh ibn Yūsuf al-Juwaynī, *al-Jamʿ wa-l-farq*, 3 vols., ed. ʿAbd al-Raḥmān ibn Salāmah ibn ʿAbdallāh al-Mazīnī (Beirut: Dār al-Jīl, 1424/2004), 1:39.

required intentionality. Prayer is completely invalid without intention, yet a recitation from the Qur'an is still ritually valid even without prior intention. Al-Jurjānī then introduces a third ritual act, the hajj pilgrimmage. The status of the hajj pilgrimage is perplexing, as it seems to fit with both camps. It requires intention to begin, but it does not require a continuous intention throughout.

But how did the use of distinctions work in a book of legal riddles? In part, al-Jurjānī is less interested the kind of presentation and logic followed by distinctions, but, instead, formulates his claims in a more interactive manner, as a riddle to be solved or a question to be answered. The primary difference here is its potential for performance in a *majlis*; its packaging emphasizes the paradoxical nature of ritual. Since the book primes the reader to look for moments of contemplation, the riddle inherent in this distinction is readily apparent. Al-Jurjānī asks the reader to provide the distinguishing characteristic.

The use of legal maxims and precepts (*al-qawāʿid wa-l-ḍawābiṭ*) in al-Jurjānī's book should be understood similarly. Al-Jurjānī's use of maxims and precepts follows a set pattern. He first states a broad precept or maxim, then lists the exceptions to it. One example, from the chapter on ritual purity, starts by stating a puzzle through a legal maxim, "Water can never remain pure inside of an impure container." This maxim expresses a general truth about Shāfiʿī legal doctrine: pure water becomes contaminated in an impure container. As happens with general truths, "there, however, are two exceptions."[101] Knowing these exceptions serve as the solution to the puzzle.

> The first exception is a container made from the skin of carrion. When a lot of water (*māʾ kathīr*) is poured into it, the water does not become impure. The second is a pure vessel from which a dog has drunk. When a lot of water (*māʾ kathīr*) has been poured into it, the water does not become impure. The water in these cases is pure, but the vessel is impure.[102]

The underlying rationale for both exceptions is that pouring a large quantity of water into these vessels renders the water pure. In these two situations, although the vessel is impure, this impurity is not legally relevant given enough pure water within it. It is as though the vessel becomes purified when a lot of water is poured into it because of the purifying nature of water. As a result, water in such a vessel can be pure and remain so, even though the impurity inherent to the container remains.

---

101 Al-Jurjānī, *al-Muʿāyāt*, 151.
102 Al-Jurjānī, *al-Muʿāyāt*, 151.

Finally, al-Jurjānī includes a small number of more typical riddles (*alghāz*) in this work. A straightforward riddle presents a complex scenario, sometimes in question-and-answer form, such as one regarding inheritance: "A deceased person leaves behind a group of heirs that includes men and women. He leaves them 600 gold coins. One of his heirs receives exactly one gold coin."[103] The solution to this riddle is to describe the make-up of the heirs such that this situation could take place. The solution demands knowledge of the makeup of the heirs, such that the Qur'anically prescribed inheritance laws grant one of them exactly one coin, one six-hundredth of the inheritance. This math problem requires a full understanding of the shares owed to each heir. Al-Jurjānī provides the solution: "The solution is that he leaves behind a wife, a mother, two daughters, twelve brothers, and one sister. His sister gets one gold coin. The remainder, after the required shares to his mother, sister, and daughters, is twenty-five gold coins. His brothers get twenty-four gold coins, and the sister is left with one."[104] This solution creates a precise group of heirs such that one of them is entitled to exactly one gold coin. This question can also be understood as asking that one devise a situation in which an heir is entitled to receive one six-hundredth of the estate.[105]

We can see how al-Jurjānī manipulates these legal forms—distinctions, maxims, precepts, and riddles—to highlight both the enigmatic nature of particular legal doctrines and the overall coherence of the law. The riddles (*alghāz*) in this work operate in similarly ways as the distinctions and exceptions to maxims and adages. Of course, the different forms of riddles that he uses allow him to present the information in different ways. In the context of his book, which aims to provoke the reader into contemplating the intricacies of Islamic law, the general maxim serves no purpose without enumerating the exceptions to it. The exceptions, as seen above, are the specific situations that simultaneously serve to prove the validity of the rule and establish its limits. In contrast, the riddle is the statement of a highly specific situation, both a set of actions and a set

---

103 Al-Jurjānī tells us that "[t]his question is known as the 'Question of the Gold Coins (*al-dīnāriyyah*).'" Al-Jurjānī, *al-Mu'āyāt*, 560.

104 Al-Jurjānī, *al-Mu'āyāt*, 560.

105 See Noel J. Coulson, *Succession in the Muslim Family* (Cambridge: Cambridge University Press, 1971), 35–39. The division of shares is as follows. Since the deceased has children, his wife gets one eighth. His mother receives one sixth. His daughters each receive one third, since there are multiple daughters and the man had no sons. The sum of the inheritance given to his vertical relations is 23/24 of his wealth, or 575 dinars. The rest of his heirs should then split one twenty-fourth of his inheritance, 25 dinars, with the sister receiving half of a brother's share. The brothers each receive two gold coins, leaving one gold coin for the sister.

of outcomes. The riddle's formulation attracts the attention of the reader, who attempts to understand how it is that the situation described can come about. The legal problem in a *lughz* provides the necessary information to solve a legal puzzle, but leaves unstated the particularities that make the outcomes match the situation. The specificity of the situation in the above riddle is a sharp contrast to his statement of a general rule, "water can never remain pure inside of an impure container." The latter provides an underdetermined statement that could be used as part of an argument in support of a particular legal ruling. In this sense, distinctions and riddles both serve to elucidate specific situations while the exceptions to general rules reinforce broader legal frameworks. In al-Jurjānī's *al-Muʿāyāt*, the difference between distinctions and riddles is minimized.

Separating Riddles and Distinctions: The Case of Jamāl al-Dīn al-Asnawī

There is a clear convergence between riddles and distinctions writing in the Mamluk period. This convergence was, of course, neither complete nor ubiquitous, as not all books of legal distinctions adopted the logic and style of riddles and not all books of riddles adopted the logic and style legal distinctions. Jamāl al-Dīn al-Asnawī (d. 772/1370), a Shāfiʿī jurist who lived in Cairo, was one figure who only partially embraced the coming together of riddles and distinctions. He studied religious sciences, including law, grammar, and the rational sciences, which earned him the post of lector and recitation in 727/1327. He taught at various law colleges around Cairo and *tafsīr* at the Ibn Ṭūlūn Mosque. Eventually, he began working with the Treasury as a market inspector, though he withdrew from this job to dedicate himself to teaching and writing. His scholarly fame in Cairo grew and he became "one of the primary religious authorities."[106]

The biographical tradition tells us that al-Asnawī was an influential scholar. Reports refer to him as the leader of the Shāfiʿī scholars of his time (*shaykh al-Shāfiʿiyya*) and the author important books.[107] Ibn Qāḍī Shuhba says that "[m]any people studied closely with him; the majority of the scholars from all of Egypt were his students (*akthar ʿulamāʾ al-diyār al-miṣriyya ṭalabatuhu*)."[108]

---

106 Ibn Qāḍī Shuhba, *Ṭabaqāt al-shāfiʿiyya*, 3:98–99.
107 Ibn Qāḍī Shuhba, *Ṭabaqāt al-shāfiʿiyya*, 3:100.
108 Ibn Qāḍī Shuhba, *Ṭabaqāt al-shāfiʿiyya*, 3:100.

While these claims should be taken with a grain of salt, they paint a picture of al-Asnawī as a leading intellectual figure. Among his many works, al-Asnawī wrote a book of legal distinctions, *Maṭāliʿ al-daqāʾiq fī taḥrīr al-jawāmiʿ wa-l-fawāriq*, and a book of legal riddles, *Ṭirāz al-maḥāfil fī alghāz al-masāʾil.* [109]

Due to his prominent status as a Shāfiʿī and his involvement in shaping the intellectual outlook of scholars in Mamluk Cairo, his views on riddles and distinction are of particular interest. His participation in both genres shows that they had become vehicles for literary and pedagogical expression, at least for the Shāfiʿī school.[110] His book on legal distinctions follows the model of ʿAbdallāh al-Juwaynī.[111] Unsurprisingly, al-Asnawī mentions al-Juwaynī's work and situates his book within a Shāfiʿī legal tradition. Al-Asnawī's book continues the traditional presentation of seemingly contradictory laws and reflects the disputational origins of legal distinctions by including extended discussions designed to counter potential objections. Even so, his disputations are much more elaborate than those included by al-Juwaynī, as can be seen from the following passage on fasting, which concerns, at least initially, the use of the *siwāk*, a particular kind of twig used to clean one's teeth for ritual purification:

> The common ruling in our school is that it is reprehensible for someone fasting to use a *siwāk* in the afternoon (*baʿd al-zawāl*). This is due to the hadith in which Muḥammad says "The scent (*al-khulūf*) of someone's breath is sweeter to God than the scent of the *siwāk*." This is told on the authority of Abū Hurayra and is in both the *Saḥīḥ* of Muslim and of al-Bukhārī.[112] *Khulūf*, with a *ḍamma* on the *khāʾ*, means change or alteration. The legally salient issue (*wajh al-dalāla*), as al-Rāfiʿī said,[113] is that the evidence of worship is affirmed by the scent.[114] Because of this, getting rid of the scent is reprehensible.

109 See Naṣr al-Dīn Farīd Muḥammad Wāṣil's introductory volume to Jamāl al-Dīn al-Asnawī, *Maṭāliʿ al-daqāʾiq fī taḥrīr al-jawāmiʿ wa-l-fawāriq*, 2 vols., ed. Naṣr al-Dīn Farīd Muḥammad Wāṣil (Cairo: Dār al-Shurūq, 2007), esp. 1:161–94.

110 Being the head of the Shāfiʿī school in the capital of the sultanate undoubtedly gave al-Asnawī's views special importance. The legal system in Mamluk Cairo was complex, but the Mamluk Sultanate privileged the Shāfiʿī school over the other legal schools. See Joseph H. Escovitz, *The Office of Qāḍī al-Quḍāt in Cairo under the Baḥrī Mamlūks* (Berlin: Klaus Schwarz Verlag, 1984).

111 See the discussion of this work on Chapter One.

112 The hadith is in al-Bukhārī's *Ṣaḥīḥ* in two chapters, Fasting (*ṣawm*) and Clothing (*libās*). The hadith is in the *Ṣaḥīḥ* of Muslim in his chapter on Fasting (*ṣiyām*). It is also found in Tirmidhī's *Jāmiʿ*, Nisāʾī's *Sunan*, Ibn Mājah *Sunan*, Dārimī's *Sunan*, Mālik's *Muwaṭṭaʾ*, and the *Musnad* of Aḥmad ibn Ḥanbal. See Wensinck, *Handbook*, 2:69.

113 This refers to the famous Shāfiʿī jurist, ʿAbd al-Karīm ibn Muḥammad al-Rāfiʿī (d. 623/1226). Along with Abū Zakariyyāʾ al-Nawawī (d. 676/1277), al-Rāfiʿī was one of the two most important Shāfiʿī jurists in the Mamlūk period. See El Shamsy, "The *Ḥāshiya* in Islamic Law: A Sketch of Shāfiʿī Literature," *Oriens* 41 (2013); 292–93.

Moreover, we also avoid the *siwāk* before the afternoon, because the change in breath most often occurs because of food, not because of fasting, as al-Rāfiʿī says. This necessitates the distinction between someone who has a meal before daybreak and someone who does not, as well as a distinction between someone who eats something at night and someone who, because of a malady or an illness, does not. Due to this, al-Ṭabarī,[115] who wrote a commentary on *al-Tanbīh*, says if the scent of his mouth is altered in the afternoon because of some other reason, such as sleeping and the like, his use of the *siwāk* is not reprehensible.

It is said, however, that a *siwāk* is not reprehensible for someone who is fasting until after the afternoon prayer, as the above-mentioned al-Ṭabarī related.

Others, however, hold that it is never reprehensible (*lā yukrahu muṭlaqan*). This was mentioned in al-Nawawī's *Rawḍa*,[116] and it is mentioned in his commentery on the *Muhadhdhab*.

Yet others hold that using a *siwāk* in this fashion is not reprehensible for superogatory prayers but reprehensible for required prayers, to guard against ostentation (*al-riyāʾ*). Al-Rāfiʿī mentioned this in his chapter on fasting on the authority of al-Qāḍī l-Ḥusayn.[117] You will learn, in the Chapter on Funerals that cleansing the blood of a martyr is forbidden by the rules laid out therein. The purpose of this is what the Prophet alluded to: "On the Day of Resurrection, they will come and their jugular veins will spurt liquid the color of blood but with the scent of musk."[118]

Here, one might ask, "What is the distinction between the prohibition here, in the case of martyrdom, even though the scent of breath is like the scent of musk, and its only being reprehensible there, in the case of prayer, even though it is better smelling than it (*aṭyab minhu*), i.e. better than the scent of musk?"

---

114 The citation is likely from al-Rāfiʿī's *al-Sharḥ al-kabīr*, although there is a verbatim passage found in Abū Isḥāq al-Shīrāzī's *al-Muhadhdhab* as well as al-Nawawī's commentary *al-Majmūʿ sharḥ al-muhadhdhab* and the *Nihāyat al-muḥtāj* by Shams al-Dīn al-Ramlī (d. 1004/1595). Abū Isḥāq al-Shīrāzī, *al-Muhadhdhab fī fiqh al-Imām al-Shāfiʿī*, ed. Muḥammad al-Zuḥaylī (Damascus: Dār al-Qalam, 1416/1996), 1:67; Abū Zakariyyāʾ Muḥyī l-Dīn ibn Sharaf al-Nawawī, *Kitāb al-Majmūʿ sharḥ al-Muhadhdhab li-l-Shīrāzī*, ed. Muḥammad Najīb al-Muṭīʿī (Jedda: Maktabat al-Irshād, 1992) 1:330–31; Shams al-Dīn Muḥammad ibn Aḥmad al-Ramlī, *Nihāyat al-muḥtāj ilā sharḥ al-Minhāj fī l-fiqh ʿalā madhhab al-Imām al-Shāfiʿī wa-maʿahu Ḥashiyat Abī l-Ḍiyāʾ Nūr al-Dīn ʿAlī l-Shabrāmallisī l-Qāhirī l-mutawaffī 1087 H [wa-] Ḥāshiyat Aḥmad ibn ʿAbd al-Razzāq ibn Muḥammad ibn Aḥmad al-maʿrūf bi-l-Maghribī l-Rashīdī*, no ed. (Beirut: Dār al-Kutub al-ʿIlmiyya, 1424/2003), 1:182.

115 Abū l-ʿAbbās Aḥmad ibn ʿAbdallāh al-Ṭabarī (d. 694/1295).

116 See n. 113, above. For more on al-Nawawī, see Fachrizal A. Halim, *Legal Authority in Premodern Islam: Yaḥyā ibn Sharaf al-Nawawī in the Shāfiʿī School of Law* (Abingdon, Oxon: Routledge, 2015).

117 Al-Ḥusayn ibn Muḥammad ibn Aḥmad al-Marwazī (d. 462/1069).

118 This hadith can be found in the *Sunan* of al-Nisāʾī, in his chapter on *Taḥrīm* and *Qasāma*, in al-Tirmidhī's *Jāmiʿ* on his *Tafsīr* of Q al-Nisāʾ 4, and in the *Musnad* of Aḥmad ibn Ḥanbal. See Wensinck, *Handbook*, 3:73.

> Perhaps the distinction is the certainty regarding that topic [i.e. martyrdom] and its heightened importance, since it involves them exposing their souls to death because of their glorification of the religion. Therefore, a prohibition on the removal of all traces of martyrdom serves to help proclaim the wondrousness of his fate. The blood's remaining on his body is like a banner that demonstrates his true nature for anyone who is unaware or unmindful of it.[119]

As this excerpt demonstrates, al-Asnawī's work contains straightforward comparison of substantive laws together with their legal rationales, not a presentation of a curious or unexpected circumstance requiring a clever interpretation. In other words, this is not a riddle. This is a straightforward legal distinction, which even includes a long defense in the style of those used in legal disputation.

Similarly, al-Asnawī's work on legal riddles does not reflect the convergance of riddles with distinctions. His *Ṭirāz al-maḥāfil* contains set of legal riddles the tradition of question and answer writing (*al-as'ila wa-l-ajwiba*). One question it asks about the permissibility of fact-patterns that are seemingly impermissible or the identity of a seemingly impossible legal entity clarifies the obstacles given in the question:

> Riddle (*mas'ala*): A prayer that must be performed, but cannot be made up. Indeed, making it up is not permissible.
>
> Solution (*ṣūratuhu*): The Friday prayer, which is not made up if it is missed. Rather, you make up the noon prayer. The noon prayer is a different prayer, not a replacement for the Friday prayer.
>
> Someone may then say: "Why can it not be made up on a different Friday?" Neither travel nor another legitimate reason require this (*li-qā'il an yaqūla limā lā yaṣiḥḥu qadạā'ahu fī jumʿa ukhrā ghayr wājiba bi-sabab safar wa-naḥwihi*).[120]

This riddle hinges on the peculiar status of the *jumʿa* prayer. It is required at the same time as the noon prayer (*al-ẓuhr*), but has an additional requirement that it be performed in a communal mosque with others. Since a communal prayer must be performed in a communal mosque (*jāmiʿ*) at the required time, a missed communal prayer cannot be made up.[121] There is only one opportunity for communal prayer each week. However, this riddle assumes that communal prayer is

119 Al-Asnawī, *Maṭāliʿ al-daqā'iq*, 2:22–23.

120 Jamāl al-Dīn al-Asnawī, *al-Alghāz al-fiqhiyya wa-huwa l-kitāb al-musammā Ṭirāz al-mahāfil fī alghāz al-masā'il*, ed. Muḥammad ʿUthmān and Ṭaha ʿAbd al-Ru'ūf Saʿd (Cairo: al-Maktaba al-Azhariyya li-l-Turāth, 1433/2012), 109.

121 For more on the history of communal mosques, see Baber Johansen, "The All-Embracing Town and Its Mosques," *Revue de l'Occident musulman et de la Mediterranée* 32 (1981): 139–61.

an additional requirement added to the Friday noon prayer, so that while missing the communal prayer cannot be rectified, the noon prayer can. Presumably, the audience is aware that missing a *jumʿa* prayer does not excuse a Muslim from performing the noon prayer, but solving the riddle requires knowledge of the difference between the *jumʿa* and the *ẓuhr* prayers. As a mark of the play involved in this text, this riddle ends with a follow-up question that attempts to undermine the solution and the answer to this question. While posed as a riddle, this is again a style similar to that of legal disputation.

In terms of content, al-Asnawī does not—indeed, refuses—to bring together riddles and distinctions in these two works. Yet, the activities of solving riddles and distinctions writing intersect, as distinctions by definition rest on initially confusing details and riddles demand differentiating among confusing legal minutiae. Nevertheless, al-Asnawī did not present his distinctions as intractable problems nor his riddles in the form of distinctions. As a result, his works remind us that not all works of this type come together in this period. Rather, the convergence of distinctions and riddles signals the beginning of new possibilities within these two legal genres, as this chapter has shown.

Comparison of the introductions to these two works does reveal that al-Asnawī understood them to belong to almost identical traditions of legal writing, in spite of the way he composed these works. Al-Asnawī begins by situating each book in a well-known written tradition in order to provide readers a framework for each book. In his *Maṭāliʿ al-daqāʾiq*, he claims that there are two kinds of works in the Shāfiʿī school that deal with legal distinctions. The first deals directly with the topic, such as his own *Maṭāliʿ al-daqāʾiq*, the *al-Farq wa-l-jamʿ* by ʿAbdallāh al-Juwaynī, and *al-Wasāʾil fī furūq al-masāʾil* by Abū l-Khayr Salāma ibn Ismāʿīl ibn Jamāʿa l-Maqdisī (d. 480/1087–88) as his predecessors. These are the only two books that directly tackle the subject of legal distinctions in the Shāfiʿī *madhhab*, according to al-Asnawī.[122] A second strand of writing deals with legal distinctions indirectly, encompassing "something broader than legal distinctions *per se* (*mā huwa aʿamm minhu*)."[123] In this second tradition, he cites *al-Muṭāraḥāt* by Abū ʿAbdallāh ibn al-Qaṭṭān (d. 359/970), *al-Muskit* by Abū ʿAbdallāh al-Zubayrī (d. 317/929–30), and *al-Muʿāyāt* by Abū l-ʿAbbās al-Jurjānī (d. 482/1089–90).[124] Al-Asnawī both affirms the idea of *furūq* as a distinct genre and highlights that this genre held for him and his readers, working within

122 Jamāl al-Dīn al-Asnawī, *Maṭāliʿ al-daqāʾiq fī taḥrīr al-jawāmiʿ wa-l-fawāriq*, 2 vols., ed. Naṣr al-Dīn Farīd Muḥammad Wāṣil (Cairo: Dār al-Shurūq, 2007), 2:8.

123 Al-Asnawī, *Maṭāliʿ al-daqāʾiq*, 2:7.

124 Al-Asnawī, *Maṭāliʿ al-daqāʾiq*, 2:8–9.

the expectations towards a particular discipline. This discussion also shows how permeable the genres of distinctions and riddles could be.

Al-Asnawī introduces *Ṭirāz al-maḥāfil*, similarly, naming books that deal directly with legal riddles as well as those that tackle the subject only indirectly. He places this work of legal riddles within a tradition that includes *al-Muṭāraḥāt* by Abū ʿAbdallāh ibn al-Qaṭṭān, *al-Muskit* by Abū ʿAbdallāh al-Zubayrī, *al-Ḥiyal* by Abū Ḥātim al-Qazwīnī (d. *ca.* 440/1048–49), *al-Muʿāyāt* by Abū l-ʿAbbās al-Jurjānī, *al-Iʿjāz fī l-alghāz* by ʿAbd al-ʿAzīz al-Mufīd al-Jīlī (*fl.* 629/1231–34), and *Simṭ al-farāʾid wa-ghurar al-fawāʾid* by Muḥibb al-Dīn al-Ṭabarī (d. 694/1295).[125] Ironically, this list includes all of the works listed in *Maṭāliʿ al-daqāʾiq*. l-Asnawī further conflates these genres by adding "works of distinctions, stratagems (*ḥiyal*), and difficult to answer questions (*al-asʾila dhāt al-ajwiba al-ʿawīṣa*)."[126] In each of these lists, he brings these two traditions together, though he does not equate them.

As mentioned above, one method of thinking about the classification of genres in the Arabo-Islamic tradition depends on the titles of works.[127] Al-Asnawī, however, operates with a different approach, assuming that genres are porous and that books can belong to multiple traditions. He therefore mentions several of the same works as belonging to both genres and alludes to the permeability of genre by saying that some books fall in "this genre exclusively" (*li-hādhā l-nawʿ bi-khuṣūṣihi*) while others "cover something broader (*yashtamilu ʿalā mā huwa aʿamm minhu*)."[128]

Ibn Farḥūn, al-Asnawī's approximate contemporary who also lived in Egypt, also uses the word *nawʿ* to refer to "genre" in his book of legal riddles, *Durrat al-ghawāṣṣ fī muḥāḍarat al-khawāṣṣ*. "I have not found a book of this genre," he writes "within the writings of the Mālikī school (*lam aqif li-l-mālikiyya ʿalā taʾālīf min hādhā l-nawʿ*)."[129] His use of the term *nawʿ* to describe his *Durrat al-ghawāṣṣ* suggests an awareness of various modalities of writing, much like al-Asnawī. Their use of the same term to describe something akin to literary

125 Al-Asnawī, *Ṭirāz al-maḥāfil*, 32–36.
126 Al-Asnawī, *Ṭirāz al-maḥāfil*, 32.
127 Bio-bibliographical sources use criteria similar to this as a shorthand when discussing written works. Thus, in the *ṭabaqāt* tradition, the distinctions work by ʿAbdallāh al-Juwaynī is known as *al-Furūq*, while in the manuscript record it is known as *al-Jamʿ wa-l-farq*. Further evidence of the important of titles can be found in the existence of rhyming titles, both those that create a rhyme with the contents of the work (as in Qarāfī's *Anwār al-burūq fī anwāʾ al-furūq*) and commentaries rhyming with the title of the work on which they are commenting (as in the commentary on al-Qarāfī's text, *Idrār al-shurūq ʿalā Anwāʾ al-furūq*).
128 Al-Asnawī, *Maṭāliʿ al-daqāʾiq*, 2:7.
129 Ibn Farḥūn, *Durrat al-ghawāṣṣ*, 65.

genre, however, points to a shared understanding of genres and legal genres between these two authors.

Conclusion

This chapter explored interactions between styles of legal writing and the social consumption of knowledge from the late Abbasid period until the beginnings of Ottoman control in Egypt, identifying the Mamluk period as when interests in riddles as an art form and the proliferation of intellectual *majālis* collided to serve as venues for the performance of knowledge. The spread of literary salons and the attendant growth in a market for riddles as a form of social capital became characteristic of cultural life. The effect of such developments on intellectual production can easily be seen in the changes undergone by legal distinctions in this period. These trends affected the writing of works of legal distinctions by promoting their integration with riddles and pushed books of riddles towards greater popularity. These two trends were not confined to legal writings, nor to the composition of original works.

Everett Rowson has addressed some of the conjunctions between *majālis* and the consumption and production of knowledge during this period. He stresses that commentaries on the works of Ibn Zaydūn written in Mamluk Cairo aimed, in part, to be encyclopedic. Of their two authors, he says:

> [B]oth Ibn Nubātah and al-Ṣafadī were addressing several audiences, and accomplishing several intentions, at once. Their commentaries offered students a panorama of the world of literary learning ... At the same time, peers ... were expected to congratulate themselves on recognizing, and even anticipating, the information and allusions as they were presented ... A broader audience was offered a smorgasbord of "*fawā'id*," "useful bits," which they could savor and incorporate into their dinner conversation.[130]

Rowson highlights some of the themes discussed in this chapter, namely the important links between social practices relating to the production and manipulation of legal knowledge and the composition of scholarly literature. His work also underscores the reciprocal interactions between socio-cultural developments and writing, underlining the relationship of a reading public to legal riddles. The rhetorical style of riddles, both adapted and adopted by books of legal distinctions, offers various levels of engagement. Riddles can be enjoyed by

130 Everett Rowson, "An Alexandrian Age in Fourteenth-Century Damascus: Twin Commentaries on Two Celebrated Arabic Epistles," *Mamluk Studies Review* 8 (2003), 109–10.

"peers ... recognizing, and even anticipating, the information and allusions" contained in the riddles and their solutions.[131] Riddles can also offer enjoyment for a reader when looking at the answer and working backwards to understand its connection to the riddle. While some *majlis* participants may have recognized the content of these commentaries and solutions to riddles, others were exposed to and entertained by new information, which they could later deploy.

The later history of legal distinctions shows how social factors could lead to changes in the aesthetics of scholarly writing. The convergence of riddles and distinctions was a minor development in this genre but is indicative of a larger change in the history of legal writing. The changes that brought about increased interest in riddles were not limited to a narrow corpus. Instead, the integration of this corpus of riddle-distinctions into the *fiqh* tradition made the rhetoric of riddles a new style of legal writing. In other words, the reification of this tradition, as seen in Ibn Nujaym's *al-Ashbāh wa-l-naẓāʾir*, denudes the aesthetics of riddles from the context of performances and makes this another rhetorical mode of legal writing.

We saw the beginnings of this trend at work in al-Jurjānī's *al-Muʿāyāt*. This work deploys legal distinctions in a novel manner, to perplex and to provoke the reader into a deeper contemplation. The use of three different legal forms—*furūq*, *qawāʿid* and *ḍawābiṭ*, and questions—to convey riddles underscores the creative potential of the Islamic legal tradition as different concepts are employed for the sake of intellectual play. Al-Jurjānī's legal play in centered on repackaging legal distinctions, maxims, and precepts as legal riddles for dual purposes of pedagogy and entertainment.

While these trends impacted legal writing, they did not dominate the production of written legal scholarship during the Mamluk period. Indeed, much of the legal-literary output of this period was driven by the institutional needs of the *madhhab*s, madrasa educational practices, and even the personal interests and concerns of individual scholars.[132] At the same time, the personal needs and interests of individual jurists and perceived institutional needs of the *madhhab* shaped the conditions for texts that sought to rewrite the tradition according to a new aesthetic.[133] This chapter shows that the social uses of legal knowledge and its various forms contribute to a convergence between legal riddles and legal

---

131 Rowson, "Alexandrian Age," 109–10.

132 On the institutional background, see El Shamsy, "*Ḥāshiya*" for a discussion of the importance of commentaries for Islamic law.

133 See, for instance, Norman Calder, *Islamic Jurisprudence*, especially Chapter 2 and Éric Chaumont "L'autorité des textes au sein du šāfiʿisme ancien" (paper presented at the conference "Rethinking Islamic Law: Can *Fiqh* be Applied Law?," Rabat, Morocco, 13–15 November, 2013).

distinctions, and how a variety of social and institutional settings contributed to the production of Islamic legal knowledge.

Chapter Five: A Bibliographic Survey of the Distinctions Genre

This chapter presents a critical narrative bibliography of the genre of legal distinctions and their known manuscripts.[1] This bibliography takes a three-pronged approach to its discussion of the legal distinctions genre: It considers printed editions of *furūq* works, extant manuscripts and manuscript catalogs, and discussions of specific works within the Arabo-Islamic heritage. A printed or manuscript edition of a work of legal distinctions is the best evidence of a work of legal distinctions, since it can be read and analyzed, and indeed, printed works of legal distinctions were the starting point for this bibliography.

An analysis of extant manuscripts and manuscript catalogs, that is, of the material history of legal distinctions writing, adds two facets to our understanding of this tradition.[2] First, as material history, these manuscripts give evidence of the widespread interest in works of legal distinctions. Manuscripts of legal distinctions were made throughout the classical Muslim world: from North Africa to the Eastern Mediterranean through Central Asia into the Indian subcontinent. Manuscripts were produced into the eighteenth century, well after new works of legal distinctions stopped being written. The factors that go into manuscript production are many and vary across time and space, although it was universally costly and time-intensive. Given the resources that went into the production of a manuscript, each manuscript of a *furūq* treatise should be understood as an endorsement of the intellectual project of *furūq*.[3]

In addition, a close look at the manuscript evidence reveals a tradition of at least two semi-anonymous, untitled works of legal distinctions that circulated alongside the better-known works discussed in the previous chapters. The classical Arabic bio-bibliographical tradition is concerned primarily with original works written by known authors. The bio-bibliographies are much less interested in the copying and spread of manuscripts, let alone of texts with unknown au-

---

1 See Appendix I and Appendix II.

2 I use the term material history broadly, as defined by Ian Woodward: "objects are the material things that people encounter, interact with and use. Objects are commonly spoken of as material culture … The field of material culture studies … incorporates a range of scholarly inquiry into the uses and meanings of objects." Ian Woodward, *Understanding Material Culture* (London: Sage, 2007), 3.

3 While the manuscript record does not necessarily tell us the role that these manuscripts had in the societies or specific social or curricular contexts in which they were produced, the continuous production of these works indicates steady interest in these works.

https://doi.org/10.1515/9783110605792-008

thors. It is not, therefore, surprising that the classical tradition does not discuss these two anonymous texts. Their existence in numerous manuscript copies, however, shows that we cannot rely solely on the bio-bliographical works to reconstruct the history of genres of legal (and probably other kinds of) writing.[4] These works may also elude us when using manuscript catalogs, which operate under similar assumptions to bio-bibliographies. Equally important, these two works sound a note of caution in regard to assumptions about authorship and Islamic legal culture.

Finally, this catalog also considers mentions and discussions of works of legal distinctions within the Arabo-Islamic heritage.[5] The interest in this heritage is first focused on locating works which do not appear to be extant. Most works of legal distinctions have not survived, so references to these works or citations from them in other books from the Arabo-Islamic heritage provide a valuable resource for better cataloging the totality of *furūq* works produced. There are, of course, issues with providing the generic identity of works based only on a brief discussion or a title, since we do not have access to the entirety or even the majority of the actual text. These issues make this task more difficult, but do not render it fruitless.

The below analysis builds on earlier, partial, accounts of the literary history of legal distinctions, in particular on the work of ʿUmar al-Sabīl, Yaʿqūb al-Bāḥusayn, Wolfhart Heinrichs, and Necmettin Kızılkaya.[6] These four lists complement

4 The bio-bibliographical tradition, in particular works of legal *ṭabaqāt*, is concerned with recording the names of those who wrote novel works of legal distinctions, but largely unconcerned with the copying of already existing works. *Ṭabaqāt* works have been discussed in various studies, see, for instance, Stephen Humphreys, *Islamic History: A Framework for Inquiry*, rev. ed. (Princeton: Princeton University Press, 2001), 187–209; R. Kevin Jaques *Authority, Conflict, and the Transmission of Diversity* (Leiden: Brill, 2006), 1–23; and Chase F. Robinson, *Islamic Historiography* (Cambridge: Cambridge University Press, 2003), 55–82.

5 My search through the classical tradition relied on close reading of shorter bio-bibliographical texts, citations in secondary scholarship, and full-text searches on the Windows version of the text database *al-Maktaba l-Shāmila*, available at http://www.shamela.ws, accessed May 2, 2019.

6 In addition, almost every modern edition of a book of legal distinctions includes a partial bibliography of *furūq* texts. Most of these lists are not comprehensive, but they nevertheless help point to how the works have been received in Arabophone scholarship. Yaʿqūb al-Bāḥusayn, *al-Furūq al-fiqhiyya wa-l-uṣūliyya: muqawwamātuhā, shurūṭuhā, nashʾatuhā, taṭawwuruhā; dirāsa naẓariyya waṣfiyya tārīkhiyya* (Riyadh: Maktabat al-Rushd, 1419/1998), 83–105; Heinrichs, "Structuring the Law," 341–44; Necmettin Kızılkaya, *İslâm hukukunda farklar: Furûk literatürü üzerine bir inceleme* (Istanbul: İz Yayıncılık, 2016), 89–208; ʿUmar ibn Muḥammad ibn ʿAbdallāh al-Sabīl, "*al-Muqaddima*," in ʿAbd al-Raḥīm ibn ʿAbdallāh Zarīrānī, *Īḍāḥ al-dalāʾil fī l-farq bayn al-masāʾil*, ed. ʿUmar ibn Muḥammad ibn ʿAbdallāh al-Sabīl (Mecca: Wizārat al-

each other and each is worth consulting. Al-Sabīl's list of works is extensive, although he lists several books that are not really works of legal distinctions.[7] Al-Bāḥusayn's bibliography includes brief discussions of the contents of each work, when known, either through his own inspection or through secondary reports from contemporary and post-classical authors. Heinrich's list is the most preliminary and is in part derived from that provided in the introduction to Muslim al-Dimashqī's *Kitāb al-Furūq*.[8] Finally, Kızılkaya's discussion builds on the previous works and provides insightful analysis into most of these works and their authors.

All of the above-mentioned catalogs build on the work of the Ottoman bibliographer Ḥājjī Khalīfa (d. 1068/1657) and his comprehensive *Kashf al-ẓunūn*. His bibliography is indispensable, although not without some errata. *Kashf al-ẓunūn* aimed to provide a complete bibliographical survey, organized alphabetically by title, of the entirety of Islamicate scholarship up to the author's lifetime. It contains a mention of all of the manuscripts inspected by Ḥājjī Khalīfa, as he tells us, "the names of many thousands of volumes in the libraries that I personally examined."[9] He also includes works to which he has seen reference to, but which may not have been extant. *Kashf al-ẓunūn*, however, presents a skewed picture of the field of distinctions literature. For instance, judging only by Ḥājjī Khalīfa's work it would seem that both the Mālikī and Ḥanbalī did not participate in composing works of legal distinctions as "Distinctions in the Shāfiʿī School" (*al-Furūq fī furūʿ al-shāfiʿiyya*) and "Distinctions in the Ḥanafī School" (*al-Furūq fī*

Taʿlīm al-ʿĀlī, Jāmiʿat Umm al-Qurā, Maʿhad al-Buḥūth al-ʿIlmiyya wa-Iḥyāʾ al-Turāth al-Islāmī, 1414/1993), 1:28 – 41.

7 He cites, for example, *al-Istighnāʾ fī l-farq wa-l-istithnāʾ*, also known as *al-Iʿtināʾ fī l-farq wa-l-istithnāʾ*, by Muḥammad ibn Abī Bakr ibn Sulaymān al-Bakrī (d. ninth/fifteenth c.), a work on legal maxims, and *Qurrat al-ʿayn wa-l-samʿ fī bayān al-farq wa-l-jamʿ* by Badr al-Dīn ibn ʿUmar ibn Aḥmad ibn Muḥammad al-ʿĀdilī l-ʿAbbāsī l-Shāfiʿī (d. *ca.* 970/1562 – 63), a work on Sufism, not Islamic law.

8 See Muḥammad Abū l-Ajfān and Ḥamza Abū Fāris "*Dirāsa*" in Abū l-Faḍl Muslim al-Dimashqī, *al-Furūq al-fiqhiyya*, ed. Muḥammad Abū l-Ajfān and Ḥamza Abū Fāris (Beirut: Dār al-Gharb al-Islāmī, 1992), 37 – 43. Heinrichs also builds on the list provided in Joseph Schacht, "Aus zwei arabischen *Furūq*-Büchern," *Islamica* 2 (1926), 508 – 10.

9 Ḥājjī Khalīfa, *Mīzān al-ḥaqq fī khtiyār al-aḥaqq*, (Istanbul: Maṭbaʿat Abū l-Ḍiyāʾ, 1306/1889), 142. This translation comes from Eleazar Birnbaum, "Kātib Chelebi (1609 – 1657) and Alphabetization: A Methodological Investigation of the Autographs of his *Kashf al-Ẓunūn* and *Sullam al-Wuṣūl*," in *Scribes et manuscrits du Moyen-Orient*, ed. François Déroche and Francis Richard (Paris: Bibliothèque nationale de France, 1997), 241.

furūʿ al-ḥanafiyya) are the only two *madhhab*-specific titles he includes.[10] More problematic, however, are the several errors and misattributions in his work.[11]

I list here one representative problem with the *Kashf* as it relates to the study of distinctions writing. One error in Ḥājjī Khalīfa's text is his listing of *Talqīḥ al-Maḥbūbī* as an alternate title for Asʿad al-Karābīsī's book. He says, "*Furūq al-Karābīsī*, also called *Talqīh al-Maḥbūbī*; the author of the *Ashbāh* [i.e. Ibn Nujaym (d. 970/1563)] mentions this at the beginning of his section on *furūq*."[12] This information comes from Ibn Nujaym's *al-Ashbāh wa-l-naẓāʾir*, the sixth chapter of which is devoted to legal distinctions. In introducing that chapter, Ibn Nujaym says, "This is the chapter on *furūq*, and I discuss here something from every legal topic. I selected and compiled this chapter from *al-Furūq* of [Asʿad?] al-Karābīsī, which is called *Talqīḥ al-Maḥbūbī*."[13] The identification of al-Karābīsī's *Furūq* by Ibn Nujaym as the *Talqīḥ al-Maḥbūbī* is erroneous on two levels. First, as mentioned above, al-Karābīsī's book is entitled *Kitāb al-Furūq*, and this seems to be the only name this book has in the historical record up to the time of Ibn Nujaym. The alternate title that he gives, however, "*Talqīḥ al-Maḥbūbī*," is the title of a different work of legal distinctions. The *Talqīḥ* is a *furūq* work entitled *Talqīḥ al-ʿuqūl fī furūq al-manqūl*, which is written by Aḥmad ibn ʿUbayd Allāh al-Maḥbūbī (d. 630/1232–33), also known as Ṣadr al-Sharīʿa al-Awwal.[14]

---

10 Ḥājjī Khalīfa, *Kashf al-ẓunūn ʿan asāmī l-kutub wa-l-funūn*, 2 vols., ed. Şerefettin Yaltkaya and Kilisi Rifat Bilge (Istanbul: Milli Eğitim Basımevi, 1971), 2:1257–58. He does mention, however, al-Qarāfī's *Furūq* under the title *Anwār al-burūq fī anwāʿ al-furūq* (Ḥājjī Khalīfa, *Kashf al-ẓunūn*, 1:186).

11 Other authors have noticed specific errata in the *Kashf al-ẓunūn*, but there has not been much scholarship that has explored the limits of this work. Frank Griffel, for instance, notices a "confusion of names" in an entry for a book on arithmetic, but does not extend his observation, see Frank Griffel, "On the Character, Content, and Authorship of *Itmām Tatimmat Ṣiwān al-ḥikma* and the Identity of the Author of *Muntakhab Ṣiwān al-ḥikma*," *Journal of the American Oriental Society* 133.1 (2013), 11n53. Similarly, Jan Just Witkam has noted that "[a] number of doubtful readings and dubious bibliographical references in the *Kashf al-Ẓunūn* ... can only be explained and corrected by comparison with Ibn al-Akfānī's [*Irshād al-Qāṣid*]." Jan Just Witkam, "Ibn al-Akfānī (d. 749/1348) and His Bibliography of the Sciences," *Manuscripts of the Middle East* 2 (1987), 40. The best study of the reliability of this work is Birnbaum, "Kātib Chelebi (1609–1657) and Alphabetization."

12 Ḥājjī Khalīfa, *Kashf al-ẓunūn*, s.v. "*Furūq al-Karābīsī*," 2:1258.

13 Ibrahīm Ibn Nujaym al-Miṣrī, *al-Ashbāh wa-l-Naẓāʾir* printed with Aḥmad ibn Muḥammad al-Ḥamawī, *Ghamz ʿuyūn al-baṣāʾir Sharḥ Kitāb al-Ashbāh wa-l-nazāʾir*, no ed. (Beirut: Dār al-Kutub al-ʿIlmiyya, 1985/1405), 4:284.

14 There are many alternate titles given as well for this book, see Appendix I.

This error is repeated in the various editions of Ibn Nujaym's *al-Ashbāh* that I consulted. It seems, indeed, to be an error made by Ibn al-Nujaym himself, faithfully transmitted across manuscripts. Aḥmad ibn Muḥammad al-Ḥamawī (d. 1099/1687–88) makes a note of this error in his commentary on this work, *Ghamz ʿuyūn al-baṣāʾir.*

> The correct thing to say would be al-Maḥbūbī's book on *furūq*, which is called *Talqīḥ al-Maḥbūbī*. These are two separate books, not one book. The claim that he was confused about these two books is unlikely to be correct, owing to the contents of this chapter. What probably occurred is that there was a slip of the pen of the original scribe (*al-nāsikh al-awwal*).[15]

Still, the error has been enshrined into the text by later copyists, inscribed into the bibliographical tradition by Ḥājjī Khalīfa, and normalized by Ismail Bāshā l-Baghdādī (d. 1922) in *Hadiyat al-ʿārifīn*, where, under Asʿad ibn Muḥammad al-Karābīsī, his work of legal distinctions is cited as "*Talqīḥ al-ʿuqūd fī l-furūq min al-furūʿ al-ḥanafiyya*."[16]

It is unclear how exactly this confusion came about. The origin of the error was perhaps an unwitting mistake from Ibn Nujaym or from the original scribe of this work. It is also possible that Ibn Nujaym and his circle were confused about the identity of these two works. In either case, it is worth nothing that later copyists refused to correct this error and that the tradition came to accept this erroneous identification.

Earlier attempts to list all works of *furūq* have been led astray by the inclusion of works whose titles seemingly indicate their membership in this genre, but actually are not part of the genre. Some of the works that have been erroneously included have not survived, yet external evidence suggests that they were in fact works of law in related genres, such as riddles, question and answer, and legal maxims.[17] Some catalogers have erred by including works of applied lexicographical distinctions, some regarding Arabic lexicography in general and others

---

15 Aḥmad ibn Muḥammad al-Ḥamawī, *Ghamz ʿuyūn al-baṣāʾir: Sharḥ Kitāb al-Ashbāh wa-l-naẓāʾir* printed with Ibrahīm ibn Nujaym al-Miṣrī, *al-Ashbāh wa-l-Naẓāʾir*, 4 vols. no ed. (Beirut: Dār al-Kutub al-ʿIlmiyya, 1985/1405), 4:284.

16 Ismāʿīl Bāshā l-Baghdādī, *Hadiyat al-ʿārifīn: Asmāʾ al-muʾallifīn wa-āthār al-muṣannifīn*, 2 vols. (Beirut: Dār Iḥyāʾ al-Turāth al-ʿArabī, n.d.), 1:204.

17 These works include *al-Muskit* by al-Zubayrī, which is perhaps a work of legal riddles, *al-Muṭāraḥāt* by Ibn al-Qaṭṭān (d. 359/970), which is likely a work in the genre of question-and-answer, and *al-Naẓāʾir al-fiqhiyya* by Abū ʿImrān al-Qayrawānī (d. ?), a work of legal maxims.

dealing with technical vocabulary in Sufism or Islamic law.[18] In addition, several books have been published recently that attempt to extract legal distinctions from discussions in early works of Islamic law. These books can appear to be part of the genre of legal distinctions, but are not since they are modern constructions of the *furūq* books certain authors could have written.[19] This category includes books such as *al-Furūq al-fiqhiyya li-l-Imām Mālik* edited by Ibrāhīm Ismāʿīl Jalāl, the legal distinctions of al-Shāfiʿī's *Kitāb al-Umm*, and the legal distinctions of Ibn Qayyim al-Jawziyya (d. 751/1350).[20]

While most works of legal distinctions were authored by Sunni jurists, I have identified two works, neither extant, that appear to be Shiʿi works of legal distinctions. The first is in Ibn al-Nadīm's (d. 380/990) entry for al-Ḥasan ibn Maḥmūd al-Sarrād (or al-Zarrād, *fl.* mid second/eighth c.), where Ibn al-Nadīm attributes a *Kitāb al-Furūq* to Aḥmad ibn Muḥammad al-Barqī (d. third/ninth c.).[21] The work's early date, however, renders this identification as a work of legal distinctions implausible.[22]

---

18 For instance, *al-Furūq* by al-Ḥakīm al-Tirmidhī, a work of lexicographic distinctions, not legal distinctions; *Qurrat al-ʿayn wa-l-samʿ fī bayān al-farq wa-l-jamʿ* by Badr al-Dīn ibn ʿUmar al-Ḥuraythī (d. *ca.* 970/1562–63), a work of applied lexicographic distinctions about Sufism, *Furūq al-uṣūl* attributed to Kemalpaşazade (d. 940/1534), a work of applied lexicographic distinctions about legal theory, and *al-Furūq* by ʿUmar ibn Raslān al-Bulqīnī (d. 805/1403), likely a work of applied lexicographic distinctions about Islamic law. The authorship of *Furūq al-uṣūl* is unclear. Most manuscripts do not attribute the book to any author, although some attribute it to Kemalpaşazade, as does the printed edition. Kemalpaşazade, *Furūq al-uṣūl*, ed. Muḥammad ibn ʿAbd al-ʿAzīz Mubārak (Beirut: Dār Ibn Ḥazm, 2009). *Al-Furūq* by al-Bulqīnī most likely refers to his *al-Farq bayn al-ḥukm bi-ṣiḥḥa wa-l-ḥukm bi-l-mūjib*, see al-Bāḥusayn, *al-Furūq al-fiqhiyya*, 160.

19 It is likely, however, that detailed and careful work such as this on the specific doctrine of individual jurists can give us a better understanding of the changes and dynamism inherent in legal compendia.

20 Ibrāhīm Ismāʿīl Jalāl, *al-Furūq al-fiqhiyya li-l-Imām Mālik* (Beirut: Dār al-Kutub al-ʿIlmiyya, 2007); Sāmī Muḥammad Ṣubḥ, *al-Furūq al-fiqhiyya ʿind al-Imām al-Shāfiʿī fī Kitāb al-Umm* (Beirut: Dār al-Muqtabas, 2018). I thank David Vishanoff for alerting me to this last book. Ibn Qayyim al-Jawziyya's legal distinctions have been collected and published twice, Yūsuf al-Ṣāliḥ, *al-Furūq al-fiqhiyya li-Ibn Qayyim al-Jawziyya muntazaʿ min aghlab kutub Ibn Qayyim raḥimahu llāh taʿālā* (Riyadh: Yūsuf al-Ṣāliḥ, 2009) and Abū ʿUmar Sayyid Ḥabīb ibn Aḥmad al-Madanī l-Afghānī, *al-Furūq al-fiqhiyya ʿind Imām Ibn Qayyim al-Jawziyya jamʿan wa-l-dirāsa*, 3 vols (Riyadh: Maktabat al-Rushd Nāshirūn, 2009).

21 Ibn al-Nadīm, *al-Fihrist li-l-Nadīm*, 2 vols., ed. Ayman Fuʾād Sayyid (London: Muʾassasat al-Furqān li-l-Turāth al-ʿArabī, 1430/2009), 2.1:73.

22 Unfortunately, the published edition of *al-Maḥāsin* that I consulted did not have a section entitled *Kitāb al-Furūq*, see Aḥmad ibn Muḥammad ibn Khālid al-Barqī, *al-Maḥāsin*, 2 vols., ed. al-Sayyid Jalāl al-Dīn al-Ḥusaynī (Tehran: Dār al-Kutub al-Islāmiyya 1370/1951). While

The other possible Shi'i work of legal distinctions is *al-Jamʿ wa-l-farq* by ʿAlī ibn Yaḥyā ibn Rāshid al-Washlī l-Zaydī l-Yamanī (d. 777/1375 – 76). As his *nisba* al-Zaydī indicates, ʿAlī ibn Yaḥyā was almost certainly a Zaydī Shi'i. Al-Sabīl, however, in his bibliography of legal distinctions, includes ʿAlī ibn Yaḥyā as a Shāfiʿī scholar and omits "al-Zaydī" from ʿAlī ibn Yaḥyā's name. Al-Sabīl does not cite a death date for ʿAlī ibn Yaḥya, only noting that he was born in 662/1264 – 65.[23] Very little information is recorded about this work. Writing in the middle of the twentieth century, Muḥammad ibn Zabāra mentions this work in his appendix to Muḥammad al-Shawkānī's *al-Badr al-ṭāliʿ*. He includes it as one of ʿAlī ibn Yaḥyā's works and says, "In his *al-Jamʿ wa-l-farq*, he wrote things that no one previously has written."[24] ʿAlī ibn Yaḥyā does not seem to be particularly prominent in the historical record but appears primarily as a hadith transmitter.[25] Since I cannot rule out the possibility that either of these two works belongs to the genre of distinctions writing, I include them in my survey. At the same time, the existence of only two works that may be part of the genre may prove the rule that there is, generally speaking, no Shi'i tradition of writing books of legal distinctions.

The critical bibliography I present below represents a marked advance over previous efforts, partly because it draws heavily on them and partly due to recent technological advancements. The digitization of manuscript catalogs has made it possible to search a greater number of catalogs more efficiently than ever before.[26] Any bibliography is always preliminary, and I look forward to seeing this list improved as further collections are digitized. Nevertheless, as will be seen below, I have "discovered" many manuscripts unattested in other pub-

there are other editions of this text, which I have not been able to consult, it seems unlikely that *al-Maḥāsin*, a work of hadith, would include a section on legal distinctions.

23 Aḥmad ibn ʿAbdallāh al-Jandārī, *Tarājim al-rijāl al-madhkūra fī sharḥ al-azhār* (n.p.: Maṭbaʿat al-Tamaddun, 1332/1913), 25. A birth date of 662 makes a death date of 777 unlikely, though by no means impossible.

24 Muḥammad ibn Muḥammad ibn Zabāra al-Ḥasanī l-Yamanī, *Mulḥiq al-badr al-ṭāliʿ bi-maḥāsin man baʿd al-qarn al-sābiʿ* (Beirut: Dār al-Maʿrifa, n.d.), 1:183 – 84.

25 See, for instance, the citations in Muḥammad ibn Ibrāhīm ibn al-Wazīr, *al-ʿAwāṣim wa-l-qawāṣim fī l-dhabb ʿan sunnat Abī Qāsim*, ed. Shuʿayb al-Arnāʾūṭ (Beirut: Muʾassasat al-Risāla, 1415/1994).

26 This is particularly true for most manuscript libraries in the United States, Europe, and Turkey. As of the writing of this chapter, however, the already digitized catalog of the Suleymaniye Library is not available online, but only accessible in the reading room at the Suleymaniye library. The catalogs of the other public libraries in Turkey, however, are all available via http://www.yazmalar.gov.tr, accessed May 2, 2019.

lished bibliographies, identified manuscripts of works considered to be no longer extant, and erased some doubts about the identity of several manuscripts.[27]

Important works that were frequently copied constitute a problem for any bibliographer. The abundance of copies of Ibn Nujaym's *al-Ashbāh wa-l-naẓā'ir* (Turkey's digital portal alone contains 127 copies!) would overshadow all of the other works here.[28] Similarly, the *Anwār al-burūq fī anwā' al-furūq* by Shihāb al-Dīn al-Qarāfī (d. 684/1285) also survives in seemingly infinite copies throughout the world. Despite the popularity of these works, it does not appear that they are central to the *furūq* tradition.[29] These two works were, however, the subject of many commentaries complicating the matter further. These two works, together with their commentaries, have nearly become genres unto themselves and deserve a separate study. Additionally, neither of these two works fits squarely within the genre of legal distinctions. This survey acknowledges the existence of these two works, but does not treat them as comprehensively as the other works of legal distinctions.[30]

---

27 It should go without saying, but the works of catalogers and librarians is invaluable for projects such as this.

28 Indeed, this would be sufficient material for a study devoted only to the manuscripts of this work, and is beyond the brief critical bibliography presented here.

29 In fact, al-Qarāfī's work is likely not a work of legal distinctions at all, as discussed below.

30 A brief mention should be made here regarding *al-Ashbāh wa-l-naẓā'ir* by Jalāl al-Dīn al-Suyūṭī (d. 911/1505). Although al-Suyūṭī's text seems to serve as a model for Ibn Nujaym's text, the two works differ in notable ways. One such way is the lack of a section on legal distinctions in al-Suyūṭī's text. The sixth chapter of his work is titled "On Similar Legal Topics and What Distinguishes Them" (*fī abwāb mutashābiha wa-mā ftaraqa fīhi*). This seems to correspond to the third chapter in Ibn Nujaym's text, "Assimilation and Distinction" (*al-jam' wa-l-farq*). Despite not discussing legal distinctions, al-Suyūṭī nevertheless seems to understand his *al-Ashbāh wa-l-naẓā'ir* as related to legal distinctions. Towards the end of the introduction of this work, al-Suyūṭī states that "sometimes a case opposes its similar cases in regards to their ruling because of a particular discernable attribute (*min al-naẓā'ir mā yukhālifu naẓā'irahu fī l-ḥukm li-mudrak khāṣṣ*). This is the discipline (*al-fann*) known as *furūq*, which distinguishes between similar cases which are united (*mutaḥḥida*) because of their fact-patterns and general implication, but differ in their ruling and legal rationale"; Jalāl al-Dīn al-Suyūṭī, *al-Ashbāh wa-l-naẓā'ir fī qawā'id wa furū' al-shāfi'iyyah*, ed. 'Abd al-Karīm al-Faḍīlī (Beirut: Dār al-Kutub al-'Ilmiyya, 1411/1990), 7. This statement seems to indicate a close connection between *al-ashbāh wa-l-naẓā'ir* and the discipline of *furūq*. Ibn Nujaym makes a similar claim in his introduction, when he calls his sixth chapter, the chapter on *furūq*, "the sixth chapter: *al-ashbāh wa-l-naẓā'ir.*" (Ibn Nujaym, *al-Ashbāh wa-l-naẓā'ir*, 1:38). In spite of the close connections that may have existed between *al-ashbāh wa-l-naẓā'ir* and *furūq*, al-Suyūṭī's text should not be considered a work of distinctions. This issue is discussed further in the Conclusion.

Narrative Listing of Furūq Works

In this bibliography, I identify thirty-six works of legal distinctions. The spread of these works among the legal schools is somewhat uneven, thirteen for the Shāfiʿī school, nine for the Ḥanafīs, eight for the Mālikīs, and four for the Ḥanbalīs, and two works, which may or may not belong to the genre, authored by Shi'is. Organizing these works chronologically uncovers two periods of intense writing of books of *furūq:* the fifth/eleventh century and the late seventh/thirteenth through mid-eighth/fourteenth centuries. It is important to keep in mind that the data is vague; the lifetime of the author serves as a rough estimate of the date of composition when precise dates of the composition of a *furūq* work is missing.[31] Because of this imprecision, the bibliography is organized by chronologically by century. This organization is somewhat arbitrary, but seems to be the most logical for later reference.

The permeability of the genre of legal distinctions is one of the most important observations of this study and therefore the classification of later well-attested, and even published works, can be difficult. In general, I have chosen to be overly inclusive regarding such difficult-to-classify works. I chose to include two types of suspect works: works no longer extant about which little is known, and works seemingly at the boundaries of the genre of legal distinctions. For instance, I include both *al-Furūq* by Ibn Surayj and al-Jurjānī's *al-Muʿāyāt* in my bibliography, even though I believe it is unlikely that Ibn Surayj wrote such a book and that al-Jurjānī's *al-Muʿāyāt* fits in the genre.[32]

This chapter presents a narrative version of the critical bibliography, including a brief discussion of each *furūq* work and its author. The critical bibliography, however, is also presented in two alternate formats in Appendix I and Appendix II. Appendix I organizes *furūq* works chronologically by legal school (*madhhab*), and includes a final section on works incorrectly said to be works of legal distinctions. Appendix I also preserves all of the bibliographic and reference information contained in this narrative. Appendix II arranges these works chronologically, but excludes all references.

31 The precise date of composition is unknown for the vast majority of *furūq* treatises.
32 See below and Chapter Four, pp. 144–48.

The Fourth/Tenth Century

Identifying the first work of legal distinctions is not easy. There are several candidates that could have written the first work of legal distinctions: Ibn Surayj (d. 306/918),[33] al-Zubayr ibn Aḥmad al-Zubayrī (d. 317/929–30),[34] al-Ḥakīm al-Tirmidhī (d. *ca.* 298/910),[35] Abū l-Ḥasan ʿAlī ibn Aḥmad al-Nasawī (d. *ca* 320/932),[36] and Muḥammad ibn Ṣāliḥ al-Karābīsī (d. 322/933–34).[37] This early period is further complicated by later inter-*madhhab* polemics. Did Shāfiʿīs first discover the usefulness of thinking through distinctions and therefore write the earliest works in this genre? Or was it Ḥanafī scholars who have pride of place in developing this new style?

None of these works can be easily categorized as an early work of legal distinctions. In spite of its title, *Kitāb al-furūq*, Ibn Surayj's book seems only to be a commentary on al-Muzanī's *Mukhtaṣar.*[38] The surviving selections of al-Zubayrī's book do not talk about legal distinctions.[39] Al-Nasawī is mentioned only in the *al-Fihrist* and not remembered by any other premodern author.[40] Al-Tirmidhī's book of distinctions is about lexicography.[41] The book attributed to al-Karābīsī's survives, but this attribution is almost certainly spurious and the text itself is highly corrupt and riddled with lacunae.[42] Finally, the lack of discussion of these works in the earliest extant sources also throw their veracity in doubt.

---

33 Heinrichs, "Structuring the Law," 342; al-Bāḥusayn, *al-Furūq al-fiqhiyya*, 68, 72–73, 84; al-Sabīl, "*al-Muqaddima*," 1:34.

34 Al-Bāḥusayn *al-Furūq al-fiqhiyya*, 68, 73–74; Kızılkaya, *İslâm hukukunda farklar*, 142–43; al-Sabīl, "*al-Muqaddima*," 1:35.

35 Al-Bāḥusayn *al-Furūq al-fiqhiyya*, 69–70.

36 Heinrichs, "Structuring the Law," 342; Kızılkaya, *İslâm hukukunda farklar*, 143; Schacht, "*Furūq*-Büchern," 509; Ibn al-Nadīm, *al-Fihrist*, 2.1:55.

37 Heinrichs, "Structuring the Law," 341; al-Bāḥusayn, *al-Furūq al-fiqhiyya*, 69, 74, 84; Kızılkaya, *İslâm hukukunda farklar*, 143–45; al-Sabīl, "*al-Muqaddima*," 1:28.

38 Ḥājjī Khalīfa, *Kashf al-ẓunūn*, s.v. "*al-Furūq fī furūʿ al-shāfiʿiyya*," 2:1257–58.

39 Tāj al-Dīn al-Subkī, *Ṭabaqāt al-shāfiʿiyya al-kubrā*, 3:296.

40 Ibn al-Nadīm, *al-Fihrist*, 2.1:55.

41 Muḥammad ibn ʿAlī l-Ḥakīm al-Tirmidhī, *al-Furūq wa-manʿ al-tarāduf*, ed. Muḥammad Ibrāhīm al-Juyūshī (Cairo: al-Nahār, 1998).

42 Throughout the text, ʿAbd al-Muḥsin al-Zahrānī, the editor, finds himself forced to insert whole clauses and sentences in order for this text to convey correct meaning. These are all moments where al-Zahrānī has added one or more sentences, with a footnote that reads: "This is not found in any of the manuscripts (*laysat fī jamīʿ al-nusakh*)." The additions, he reasons, are required by (1) the context (*al-siyāq*), (2) Ḥanafī tradition (*al-marājiʿ; lā yastaqīmu al-ḥukm illā bihi*), (3) the comparison made in the distinction (*al-farq*). The problems with the text discussed in this section are problems with the text as it is in the manuscript. Al-Zahrānī's

A more critical evaluation of the evidence suggests that the origins of this genre should be interrogated as a construction of self-justifying narratives about the past. Why did it become important to claim in the Mamluk and early Ottoman periods that so many fourth/tenth-century jurists were the first to have written these works? These claims often also reflected competition among the different Sunni legal schools, with a desire to claim primacy in different areas of legal development. Indeed, it is only in the ninth/sixteenth century that Muḥammad ibn Ṣāliḥ al-Karābīsī becomes credited with his book, an attribution that not only appears suddenly in several bibliographic sources, but also on several manuscripts.[43]

The Fifth/Eleventh Century

The fifth/eleventh century was momentous for the history of legal distinctions; during this century the genre of legal distinctions became established and widespread. The Shāfiʿī *madhhab* produced five works of legal distinctions during this century: *al-Kifāya fī l-furūq wa-l-laṭāʾif* by Abū ʿAbdallāh al-Ḥusayn ibn ʿAbdallāh al-Ṭabarī (d. *ca* fifth/eleventh c.);[44] *al-Jamʿ wa-l-farq* by Abū Muḥammad

editorial editions are indeed essential for this text to be readable in any sensible fashion. See Muḥammad ibn Ṣāliḥ al-Karābīsī, *Kitāb al-Furūq*, ed. ʿAbd al-Muḥsin Saʿīd Aḥmad al-Zahrānī (Ph.D Diss., Jāmiʿat Umm al-Qurā, 1418/1997), 191, 202, 331, 365, among other examples.

43 See ʿAbd al-Muḥsin Saʿīd Aḥmad al-Zahrānī, "*Dirāsa*," in *Kitāb al-Furūq* by Muḥammad ibn Ṣāliḥ al-Karābīsī, ed. ʿAbd al-Muḥsin Saʿīd Aḥmad al-Zahrānī, (Ph.D Diss., Jāmiʿat Umm al-Qurā, 1418/1997), 47–53.

44 The author of this work is Abū ʿAbdallāh al-Ḥusayn ibn ʿAbdallāh al-Ṭabarī. This is confirmed by all of the biographies of al-Ḥusayn ibn ʿAbdallāh, with the exception of that written by Abū Isḥāq al-Shīrāzī, who does not mention this work. See al-Bāḥusayn, *al-Furūq al-fiqhiyya*, 90–91; Ibn Qāḍī Shuhba, *Ṭabaqāt al-shāfiʿiyya*, 4 vols., ed. al-Ḥāfiẓ ʿAbd al-ʿAlīm Khān (Beirut: Dār al-Kutub al-ʿIlmiyya, 1407[/1986]), 1:181, no. 142; Jamāl al-Dīn al-Asnawī, *Ṭabaqāt al-shāfiʿiyya*, 2 vols., ed. Kamāl Yūsuf al-Ḥūt (Beirut: Dār al-Kutub al-ʿIlmiyya, 1407/1987), 2:61–62, no. 767; Abū Isḥāq al-Shīrāzī, *Ṭabaqāt al-fuqahāʾ*, ed. Iḥsān ʿAbbās (Beirut: Dār al-Rāʾid al-ʿArabī, 1970), 126. Other sources, however, attribute this work to Abū ʿAbdallāh al-Ḥusayn ibn Muḥammad ibn al-Ḥasan al-Ḥannāṭī l-Ṭabarī (d. *ca* 495/1101–02), see al-Sabīl, "*al-Muqaddima*," 1:37; ʿUmar Riḍā Kaḥḥāla, *Muʿjam al-muʾallifīn: Tarājim muṣannifī l-kutub al-ʿarabiyya*, 4 vols. (Damascus: Muʾassasat al-Risāla, 1376/1957), 1:636, no. 4795; Ḥājjī Khalīfa, *Kashf al-ẓunūn*, s.v. "*al-Furūq fī furūʿ al-shāfiʿiyya*," 2:1499; Ismāʿīl Bāshā l-Baghdādī, *Hadiyat al-ʿārifīn*, 1:311. These sources, however, are all late. Earlier biographies of al-Ḥannāṭī do not attribute this work to him, see Ibn Qāḍī Shuhba, *Ṭabaqāt*, 1:179–81, no. 141; Tāj al-Dīn al-Subkī, *Ṭabaqāt al-shāfiʿiyya l-kubrā*, 10 vols, ed. ʿAbd al-Fattāḥ Muḥammad Ḥulw and Maḥmūd

ʿAbdallāh ibn Yūsuf al-Juwaynī l-Shāfiʿī (d. 438/1047);[45] *al-Wasāʾil fī furūq al-masāʾil* by Salāma ibn Ismāʿīl ibn Jamāʿa l-Maqdisī l-Shāfiʿī (d. 480/1087–88);[46] *al-Muʿāyāt* by Abū l-ʿAbbās al-Jurjānī;[47] and *al-Furūq* by Abū l-Maḥāsin ʿAbd al-Wāḥid ibn Ismāʿīl al-Rūyānī l-Ṭabarī (d. 501/1107 or 502/1108).[48]

ʿAbdallāh al-Juwaynī's book is by far the most important work of legal distinctions in the history of the Shāfiʿī school. Al-Juwaynī's claim that it was one of the first works written on legal distinctions within the Shāfiʿī school is further evidence that Ibn Surayj's book was not in fact in this genre. Al-Zarkashī (d. 794/1392), in his *al-Manthūr fī l-qawāʿid*, lists the works of al-Juwaynī and Salāma ibn Ismāʿīl ibn Jamāʿa as the two exemplars of this style of writing.[49] Unfortunately, it seems that this latter work has not survived, so it is difficult to ascertain anything about its form or content. The evidence from the Arabo-Islamic bibliographical tradition, however, points toward it being a work of legal distinctions.[50] Similarly, *al-Kifāya fī l-furūq* by Abū ʿAbdallāh al-Ḥusayn ibn ʿAbdallāh al-Ṭabarī and the *Kitāb al-Furūq* by al-Rūyānī do not appear to be extant, so their place in the *furūq* genre remains uncertain.[51] Abū l-ʿAbbās Aḥmad ibn Muḥammad al-Jurjānī also wrote his *al-Muʿāyāt* in the fifth/eleventh century. While I argue that al-Jurjānī's work is perhaps best understood as a work of legal riddles, it nevertheless consists overwhelmingly of legal distinctions and has

---

Muḥammad al-Tannāḥī (Cairo: Dār Iḥyāʾ ʿUlūm al-ʿArabiyya, 1994), 4:367–71, no. 397; al-Asnawī, *Ṭabaqāt*, 1:193–94, no. 362; al-Shīrāzī, *Ṭabaqāt al-fuqahāʾ*, 118.

45 Heinrichs, "Structuring the Law," 342; al-Bāḥusayn, *al-Furūq al-fiqhiyya*, 87; Kızılkaya, *İslâm hukukunda farklar*, 151–54; al-Sabīl, "*al-Muqaddima*," 1:35–36.

46 Al-Bāḥusayn, *al-Furūq al-fiqhiyya*, 88–89; Kızılkaya, *İslâm hukukunda farklar*, 161–63; al-Sabīl, "*al-Muqaddima*,"1:36.

47 Heinrichs, "Structuring the Law," 342; al-Bāḥusayn, *al-Furūq al-Fiqhiyya*, 89–90; Kızılkaya, *İslâm hukukunda farklar*, 163–65; al-Sabīl, "*al-Muqaddima*," 1:36–37.

48 Al-Bāḥusayn, *al-Furūq al-fiqhiyya*, 92; al-Sabīl, "*al-Muqaddima*," 1:37.

49 Badr al-Dīn al-Zarkashī, *al-Manthūr fī l-qawāʿid*, 3 vols., ed. Taysīr Fāʾiq Aḥmad Maḥmūd and ʿAbd al-Sattār Abū Ghudda (Kuwait: Wizārat al-Awqāf wa-l-Shuʾūn al-Islāmiyya, 1402/1982), 1:69.

50 Ḥājjī Khalīfa, *Kashf al-ẓunūn*, s.v. "*al-Jamʿ wa-l-farq*," 1:601 and "*al-Furūq fī furūʿ al-shāfiʿiyya*," 2:1258; *GAL* 1:385–86, S1:667; Kaḥḥāla, *Muʿjam*, 2:307, no. 8443; Shihāb al-Dīn ʿAbd al-Ḥayy ibn Aḥmad ibn al-ʿImād, *Shadharāt al-dhahab fī akhbār man dhahab*, 10 vols., ed. ʿAbd al-Qādir al-Arnāʾūṭ and Maḥmūd al-Arnāʾūṭ (Damascus: Dār Ibn Kathīr, 1406/1986–1414/1993), 5:176–77; al-Asnawī, *Ṭabaqāt*, 1:165–66, no. 305; Ibn al-Subkī, *Ṭabaqāt*, 5:73–94, no. 439; Ibn Qāḍī Shuhba, *Ṭabaqāt*, 1:209–11, no. 171.

51 For al-Ḥusayn al-Ṭabarī, see references in note 44 above. For al-Rūyānī, see Ibn al-Subkī, *Ṭabaqāt*, 7:193–204, no. 901; al-Asnawī, *Ṭabaqāt*, 1:272, no. 518; Kaḥḥāla, *Muʿjam*, 2:332, no. 8626. Ibn al-ʿImād, *Shadharāt al-dhahab*, 6:8; Ziriklī, *al-Aʿlām* 4:175; Ibn Qāḍī Shuhba, *Ṭabaqāt*, 1:287, no. 256.

been considered part of the genre. For example, it is identified as such on the cover of a manuscript of this work catalogued as 915 *fiqh shāfiʿī* in the Dār al-Kutub al-Miṣriyya in Cairo.[52]

There was only one Ḥanafī work of distinctions written in this century: *al-Ajnās wa-l-furūq* by Abū ʿAbbās Aḥmad ibn Muḥammad al-Nāṭifī l-Ṭabarī l-Ḥanafī (d. 446/1054–55).[53] This work exists in at least two copies at the Süleymaniye Library in Istanbul.[54] It is also mentioned in most of the biographical literature, although no information is given as to its contents. Ḥājjī Khalīfa records the alternate title *al-Ajnās fī l-furūʿ*.[55] ʿUmar Riḍā l-Kaḥḥāla's *Muʿjam al-muʾallifīn* seems to suggest that *al-Ajnās* and *al-Furūq* are two separate works, even though most other sources consider this the title of one book.[56] While the title indicates a work of legal distinctions, the phrase *al-ajnās wa-l-furūq* could also mean something like "[Legal] Types and the Differences between Them," in which case the book might have explained different ways to group and categorize substantive doctrine or legal-theoretical principles. While *furūq* can have a very specific technical legal meaning, it also retained its general meaning of "differences."

The Mālikī *madhhab* produced four works of legal distinctions in this century: *Furūq masāʾil mushtabiha fī l-madhhab* by Abū l-Qāsim ʿAbd al-Raḥmān ibn Muḥammad ibn al-Kātib (d. 408/1017),[57] *al-Jumūʿ wa-l-furūq* by al-Qāḍī ʿAbd al-Wahhāb al-Baghdādī (d. 422/1031),[58] *al-Furūq al-fiqhiyya* by Abū l-Faḍl Muslim

---

52 In addition, Carl Brockelmann referred to this work as a "*furūq* work in the strictest sense" (*GAL* S1:505). I discuss this book in Chapter Four, pp. 144–48.

53 Heinrichs, "Structuring the Law," 341; al-Bāḥusayn, *al-Furūq al-fiqhiyya*, 88; Kızılkaya, *İslâm hukukunda farklar*, 157–59; al-Sabīl, "*al-Muqaddima*," 1:28. See also *GAL* 1:372, S1:636; Zayn al-Dīn Qāsim ibn Quṭlūbughā, *Tāj al-tarājim fī ṭabaqāt al-ḥanafiyya: Die Krone der Lebensbescheibungen enthaltend die Classen der Hanefiten*, ed. Gustav Flügel (Leipzig: In Commision bei F. A. Brockhaus, 1862), 6–7, no. 16; Muḥyī l-Dīn Abū Muḥammad ʿAbd al-Qādir ibn Muḥammad al-Qurashī, *al-Jawāhir al-muḍiyya fī ṭabaqāt al-ḥanafiyya*, 5 vols., ed. ʿAbd al-Fattāḥ Muḥammad al-Ḥulw (Giza: Hajr, 1413/1993), 1:297–98, no. 221; al-Ziriklī, *al-Aʿlām*, 1:213; Taqī l-Dīn ibn ʿAbd al-Qādir al-Tamīmī l-Dārī, *al-Ṭabaqāt al-saniyya fī ṭabaqāt al-ḥanafiyya*, 4 vols., ed. ʿAbd al-Fattāḥ Muḥammad Ḥulw (Riyadh: Dār al-Rifāʿī, 1983), 2:71–72, no. 343.

54 See al-Sabīl, "*al-Muqaddima*," 1:28; MS Nuruosmaniye 1371, Suleymaniye Library, Istanbul; MS Esad Efendi 542, Suleymaniye Library, Istanbul.

55 Ḥājjī Khalīfa, *Kashf al-ẓunūn*, s.v. "*al-Ajnās fī l-furūʿ*," 1:11.

56 Kaḥḥāla, *Muʿjam*, 1:287, no. 2086.

57 Heinrichs, "Structuring the Law," 341; al-Bāḥusayn, *al-Furūq al-fiqhiyya*, 84–85.

58 Heinrichs, "Structuring the Law," 341; al-Bāḥusayn, *al-Furūq al-fiqhiyya*, 85–86; Kızılkaya, *İslâm hukukunda farklar*, 148–51; al-Sabīl, "*al-Muqaddima*," 1:31.

ibn ʿAlī al-Dimashqī (d. fifth/eleventh c.),[59] and *al-Nukat wa-l-furūq li-masāʾil al-Mudawwana* by ʿAbd al-Ḥaqq al-Ṣiqillī (d. 466/1073–74).[60] All of these works, save the earliest by Ibn al-Kātib are extant. Al-Qāḍī ʿIyāḍ (d. 544/1149) describes Ibn al-Kātib's work as a work of distinctions, and writes that he has heard from Abū l-Qāsim al-Ṭābithī (d. ?) that this book contains forty-one distinctions.[61]

Al-Qāḍī ʿAbd al-Wahhāb al-Baghdādī and one of his students, Abū l-Faḍl Muslim al-Dimashqī, also wrote works of legal distinctions. Muslim's book is virtually identical to that of al-Qāḍī ʿAbd al-Wahhāb. Although al-Baghdādī's text was once presumed lost, Jalāl al-Jihānī has shown that MS 588 at the Markaz Dirāsāt al-Mujāhidīn al-Lībiyīn in Tripoli, Libya, is actually a copy of al-Qāḍī ʿAbd al-Wahhāb's work.[62] Abū l-Ajfān and Abū Fāris had considered the manuscript in question to be a copy of al-Dimashqī's *Kitāb al-Furūq* and used it in their edition of al-Dimashqī's *Kitāb al-Furūq.*[63] This manuscript, MS 588, even preserves the attribution to al-Qāḍī ʿAbd al-Wahhāb.[64] Al-Jihānī presents compelling evidence that this is indeed a copy of al-Qāḍī ʿAbd al-Wahhāb's work of distinctions, including the fact that al-Mawwāq (d. 897/1492) includes a verbatim quotation from al-Qāḍī ʿAbd al-Wahhāb's *Furūq* in his *al-Tāj wa-l-iklīl.* The passage cited by al-Mawwāq is found in the manuscript bearing al-Qāḍī ʿAbd al-Wahhāb's name, but not in the copies attributed to Muslim al-Dimashqī.[65] Maḥmūd al-Ghiryānī, who discusses the relationships between these two texts in more detail, also concludes that the Libyan manuscript in question should be attributed to al-Qāḍī ʿAbd al-Wahhāb.[66]

---

59 Heinrichs, "Structuring the Law," 341; al-Bāḥusayn, *al-Furūq al-fiqhiyya*, 86–87; Kızılkaya, *İslâm hukukunda farklar*, 155–57; al-Sabīl, "*al-Muqaddima*," 1:31.

60 Heinrichs, "Structuring the Law," 341; al-Bāḥusayn, *al-Furūq al-fiqhiyya*, 88; Kızılkaya, *İslâm hukukunda farklar*, 159–61.

61 See al-Qāḍī ʿIyāḍ, *Tartīb al-madārik wa-taqrīb al-masālik li-maʿrifat aʿlām madhhab Mālik*, 8 vols., ed. Saʿīd Aḥmad Aʿrāb ([Rabat?:] Wizārat al-Awqāf wa-l-Shuʾūn al-Islāmiyya, 1402/1982), 7:253. Other editions, however, refer to Abū l-Qāsim al-Ṭābithī as Abū l-Qāsim al-Ṭāʾī. Heinrich's claim that al-Qāḍī ʿIyāḍ knew this "by autopsy" may be a misreading (Heinrichs, "Structuring the Law," 341).

62 It is unclear to me whether the manuscript is now at the Markaz al-Lībī li-l-Maḥfūẓāt wa-l-Dirāsāt al-Tārīkhiyya or al-Hayʾat al-ʿĀmma li-l-Awqāf wa-l-Shuʾūn al-Islamiyya.

63 Jalāl al-Jihānī, "*Muqaddima*," in Abū Muḥammad ʿAbd al-Wahhāb al-Baghdādī ibn ʿAlī l-Qāḍī, *al-Furūq al-Fiqhiyya*, ed. Jalāl ʿAlī l-Qadhdhāfī l-Jihānī (Dubai: Dār al-Buʿūth li-l-Dirāsāt al-Islāmiyya wa-Ihyāʾ al-Turāth, 1424/2003), 17–21.

64 Al-Jihānī, "*Muqaddima*," 18. See also MS 588, Markaz Dirāsāt al-Mujāhidīn al-Lībiyīn, Tripoli.

65 Al-Jihānī, "*Muqaddima*," 35.

66 See Maḥmūd Salāmah al-Ghiryānī, "*al-Qism al-dirāsī*," in ʿAbd al-Wahhāb al-Baghdādī, *al-Furūq al-fiqhiyya li-l-Qāḍī ʿAbd al-Wahhāb al-Baghdādī wa-ʿalāqatuhā bi-Furūq al-Dimashqī*,

The final Mālikī work of legal distinctions is *al-Nukat wa-l-furūq li-masāʾil al-Mudawwana wa-l-Mukhtalaṭa* by ʿAbd al-Ḥaqq al-Ṣiqillī. ʿAbd al-Ḥaqq was a jurist from Sicily, who studied Mālikī jurisprudence with "the scholars of Qarawiyīn" in North Africa.[67] ʿAbd al-Ḥaqq travelled twice to Mecca for the *ḥajj*. In these travels, he met various scholars including al-Qāḍī ʿAbd al-Wahhāb al-Baghdādi and Imām al-Ḥaramayn al-Juwaynī. *Al-Nukat wa-l-furūq* is a straightforward work of legal distinctions drawn from the substantive doctrine of the foundational schools of the Mālikī *madhhab*, the *Mudawwana* and the *Mukhtalaṭa.*[68]

The literary record thus shows that the genre of legal distinctions had fully emerged by the end of the fifth/eleventh century, while the fourth/tenth century was a time when this genre was underdeveloped or perhaps not yet underway. The only surviving work from the fourth/tenth century is the *Kitāb al-Furūq* by Muḥammad ibn Ṣāliḥ al-Karābīsī, although the attribution of this work is problematic. The fifth/eleventh century, however, saw a tremendous burst of activity in the composition of works of legal distinctions, primarily by Shāfiʿī and Mālikī jurists, and by one Ḥanafī. The Ḥanbalī *madhhab* would only adopt distinctions later. *Furūq* works of this period display the organization and presentation that comes to define the genre, that is, they are mostly organized in a traditional legal style (*al-tabwīb al-fiqhī*), with chapters dedicated to particular areas of the law, starting with ritual matters (*ʿibādāt*) and moving to transactions (*muʿāmalāt*). The characteristic rhetoric of books of legal distinctions involves comparing and contrasting two (or more) laws that appear to, but do not actually, contradict each other.

The Sixth/Twelfth Century

Only one book of legal distinctions, the *Kitāb al-Furūq* by Abū l-Muẓaffar Asʿad ibn Muḥammad ibn al-Ḥusayn al-Naysābūrī l-Karābīsī l-Ḥanafī was written in

---

ed. Maḥmūd Salāmah al-Ghiryānī (Dubai: Dār al-Buḥūth li-l-Dirāsāt al-Islāmiyya wa-Ihyāʾ al-Turāth, 1424/2003).

67 Ibrāhīm ibn ʿAlīibn Farḥūn, *al-Dībāj al-mudhahhab fī maʿrifat aʿyān ʿulamāʾ al-madhhab,* 2 vols., no ed. (Beirut: Dār al-Kutub al-ʿIlmiyya, 2004), 2:56.

68 On these texts, see above, Ch. 1, 37 n. 84. Ibn Farḥūn, *al-Dībāj*, 2:56; Muḥammad ibn Muḥammad Makhlūf, *Shajarat al-nūr al-zakiyya fī ṭabaqāt al-mālikiyya*, 2 vols. (Cairo: al-Maṭbaʿat al-Salafiyya wa-Maktabatihā, 1349[/1930 – 31]), 1:116.

the sixth/twelfth century.[69] This work is the first extant *furūq* work from the Ḥanafī *madhhab* that can be both securely attributed to its author and is undoubtedly part of the legal distinctions tradition. In his introduction, al-Karābīsī mentions that he came across the distinctions contained in his book through his studies with Abū l-ʿAlāʾ Ṣāʿid ibn Muḥammad (d. 502/1109): "These legal cases I gleaned from books ... I heard the imam and judge Abū l-ʿAlāʾ ... bring out the distinguishing factor (*iẓhār al-furqān*) between them."[70] Al-Karābīsī does not mention, however, his knowledge of this writing style as a genre nor any precedents for distinctions writing within the Ḥanafī school. It is curious that he would be unaware of the book by Muḥammad ibn Ṣāliḥ since Muḥammad ibn Ṣāliḥ was a Ḥanafī scholar who lived in Samarqand, where Asʿad al-Karābīsī also lived. Asʿad's silence on this matter is one piece of evidence that calls into question the authenticity of the attribution of a book of legal distinctions to Muḥammad ibn Ṣāliḥ al-Karābīsī. Asʿad al-Karābīsī's book became quite important as a work of Ḥanafī distinctions. Ḥanafī authors used it as a model when writing later works of legal distinctions, and it is the main book for which Asʿad al-Karābīsī is remembered. It is frequently mentioned in the classical sources, and there exist many manuscript witnesses of this work.[71] It has been edited and published three times in the late twentieth century, while other important Ḥanafī works of legal distinctions continue to exist only in manuscript form, signalling its continued importance.

The Seventh/Thirteenth Century

The seventh/thirteenth century inaugurated a second flurry of activity in the composition of works on legal distinctions. Two Shāfiʿī books were written in this period, *al-Fuṣūl wa-l-furūq* by Abū l-ʿAbbās Najm al-Dīn Aḥmad ibn Muḥam-

---

69 Heinrichs, "Structuring the Law," 341; al-Bāḥusayn, *al-Furūq al-fiqhiyya*, 91–92; Kızılkaya, *İslâm hukukunda farklar*, 166–67; al-Sabīl, "*al-Muqaddima*," 1:28–29.

70 Asʿad ibn Muḥammad al-Karābīsī, *al-Furūq li-l-Karābīsī*, 2 vols., ed. Muḥammad Ṭumūm and ʿAbd al-Sattār Abū Ghudda (Kuwait: Wizārat al-Awqāf wa-l-Shuʾūn al-Islāmiyya, 1402/1982), 1:33.

71 Ḥājjī Khalīfa, *Kashf al-ẓunūn*, s.v. "*al-Furūq fī furūʿ al-ḥanafiyya*," 2:1257; *GAL* 1:375, S1:642; Kaḥḥāla, *Muʿjam*, 1:351, no. 2603; Schacht, "*Furūq*-Büchern," 508; al-Qurashī, *al-Jawāhir al-muḍiyya*, 1:386, no. 314; Ibn al-ʿImād, *Shadharāt al-dhahab*, 4:4; al-Tamīmī l-Dārī, *al-Ṭabaqāt al-saniyya*, 2:171, no. 473; al-Baghdādī, *Hadiyat al-ʿārifīn*, 1:204; Ibn Quṭlūbughā, *Tāj al-tarājim*, 12, no. 44.

mad ibn Khalaf ibn Rājiḥ al-Maqdisī l-Ḥanbalī l-Shāfiʿī (d. 638/1241)[72] and *al-Furūq* by Abū l-ʿAbbās Kamāl al-Dīn Aḥmad ibn Kashāsib al-Shāfiʿī l-Dizmārī (d. 643/1245).[73] Neither of these two works survives, but both authors are mentioned frequently in the biographical literature.

Ibn Kashāsib was a jurist in Damascus known for his piety and virtue. Significantly, he was also an avid traveler, and the biographical sources quote Abū Shāma's statement that Ibn Kashāsib "goes on the pilgrimage often and performs many good deeds."[74] Ibn Kashāsib's many pilgrimages likely brought him into contact with scholars and ideas from throughout the Islamic world, potentially providing both inspiration for his book on legal distinctions and opportunity to promote his book.

Najm al-Dīn al-Ḥanbalī was a Ḥanbalī jurist who lived in Damascus, Baghdad, Hamadan, and Bukhara. The sources indicate that it was in Bukhara, after a thorough education in the Ḥanbalī school, that Najm al-Dīn al-Ḥanbalī transferred allegiance to the Shāfiʿī school. He returned to Damascus after this "conversion," enjoying a successful career as a jurist and teacher. In this period, he wrote his *al-Fuṣūl fī l-furūq*. Al-Asnawī notes that he remained known by his *nisba* al-Ḥanbalī in spite of his later adherence to the Shāfiʿī school.[75]

Only one Ḥanafī book of legal distinctions was written in the seventh century, *Talqīḥ al-ʿuqūl fī furūq al-manqūl* by Aḥmad ibn ʿUbayd Allāh al-Maḥbūbī l-Ḥanafī, Ṣadr al-Sharīʿa al-Awwal (d. 630/1232–33).[76] This should be considered the most important work of Ḥanafī distinctions before the twentieth century. A

---

72 Heinrichs, "Structuring the Law," 343; al-Bāḥusayn, *al-Furūq al-fiqhiyya*, 95; Kızılkaya, *İslâm hukukunda farklar*, 167–68; Ibn al-ʿImād, *Shadharāt al-dhahab*, 7:331; al-Sabīl, "*al-Muqaddima*," 1:37.

73 Al-Bāḥusayn, *al-Furūq al-fiqhiyya*, 95–96; al-Sabīl, "*al-Muqaddima*," 1:37.

74 See Shihāb al-Dīn Abū Shāma ʿAbd al-Raḥmān al-Maqdisī, *Tarājim rijāl al-qarnayn al-sādis wa-l-sābiʿ al-maʿrūf bi-l-Dhayl ʿalā l-Rawḍatayn*, ed. Ibrāhīm Shams al-Dīn (Dār al-Kutub al-ʿIlmiyya 1422/2002), 5:270, although in this edition his name is erroneously listed as "Aḥmad ibn Kātib al-Zumārī." For citations of this phrase, see Ibn al-Subkī, *Ṭabaqāt*, 8:30, no. 1054; al-Asnawī, *Ṭabaqāt*, 1:152, no. 289; Ibn Qāḍī Shuhba, *Ṭabaqāt*, 2:100, no. 401. See also Kaḥḥāla, *Muʿjam*, 1:232, no. 1695; and al-Baghdādī, *Hadiyat al-ʿārifīn*, 1:94.

75 It is perhaps the repeated references to him as "al-Ḥanbalī" that led Heinrichs to include Najm al-Dīn as a Ḥanbalī scholar in his bibliography. See, however, al-Asnawī, *Ṭabaqāt*, 1:211–12, no. 404; Ibn Qādī Shuhba, *Ṭabaqāt* 2:71, no. 371; and Kaḥḥāla, *Muʿjam*, 1:262–63, no. 1896. For references to this work, see Badr al-Dīn Muḥammad ibn Bahādur al-Zarkashī, *al-Baḥr al-muḥīṭ fī uṣūl al-fiqh*, no ed. (Cairo: Dār al-Kutubī, 1414/1994), 7:220; 7:245; 7:394; and 8:38.

76 Heinrichs, "Structuring the Law," 341; al-Bāḥusayn, *al-Furūq al-fiqhiyya*, 94; Kızılkaya, *İslâm hukukunda farklar*, 172–73; al-Sabīl, "*al-Muqaddima*," 1:29. These sources all agree on this date, although I am unable to locate a premodern source for this datum.

large number of manuscript witnesses for this work are preserved, and this work is mentioned frequently in the secondary literature, although it remains unpublished.[77] The lack of a readily-available published edition of *al-Talqīḥ*, however, has made As'ad al-Karābīsī's text the most popular Ḥanafī work of legal distinctions today.[78]

Though his work was important, al-Maḥbūbī seems to have been a relatively obscure figure. Ibn Quṭlūbughā in his *Tāj al-tarājim* tells us that "'Ubayd Allāh ibn Mas'ūd ibn Maḥmūd ibn 'Ubayd Allāh ibn Maḥmūd, Ṣadr al-Sharī'a l-Maḥbūbī was a critical and meticulous scholar."[79] This is likely a reference to Aḥmad ibn 'Ubayd Allah's father, although here the father is referred to as Ṣadr al-Sharī'a. This is odd since scholars make a point of referring to Aḥmad al-Maḥbūbī as Ṣadr al-Sharī'a al-Awwal, that is, "the first," in contrast to 'Ubayd Allāh ibn Mas'ūd ibn Aḥmad al-Maḥbūbī l-Bukhārī (*fl.* 747/1346–47), his descendent, who is known as Ṣadr al-Sharī'a l-Thānī, "the second," or al-Aṣghar, "the younger." Ibn Quṭlūbughā also mentions a book titled *Talqīḥ al-'uqūl fī l-furūq*, the title of which bears very close resemblance to that by Aḥmad al-Maḥbūbī. However, this title is attributed by Ibn Quṭlūbughā to Aḥmad ibn Ḥubb Allāh ibn Ibrāhīm and no further information is given about the author.[80] Similarly, al-Tamīmī l-Dārī's *al-Ṭabaqāt al-saniyya* has two listings that seem to refer to this author. The first is for "Aḥmad ibn 'Abdallāh ibn Ibrāhīm Shihāb al-Dīn al-Ḥanafī" who wrote *Tanqīḥ al-'uqūl fī furūq al-manqūl*.[81] A different entry also exists for "Aḥmad ibn 'Ubayd Allāh ibn Ibrāhīm ibn Aḥmad ... al-Maḥbūbī" to whom is attributed a book entitled "*Tanqīḥ al-'uqūl*

77 Ḥājjī Khalīfa, *Kashf al-ẓunūn*, s.v.v. "*Talqīḥ al-'uqūl fī furūq al-manqūl*," 1:481, "*Furūq fī furū' al-ḥanafiyya*," 2:1257; *GAL* 1:380; Kaḥḥāla, *Mu'jam*, 1:191, no. 1415; al-Bāḥusayn, *al-Furūq al-fiqhiyya*, 94; al-Sabīl, "*al-Muqaddima*," 1:29. Al-Sabīl and al-Bāḥusayn state that this work was edited as part of an MA thesis at al-Azhar University by 'Abd al-Hādī Shīr al-Afghānī, but online resources suggest that this edition was completed as an MA thesis at Ain Shams University. See http://research.asu.edu.eg/handle/987654321/9953, accessed April 29, 2019. The edition, however, has not been published.

78 It is difficult to understand the causality in this situation. Was al-Karābīsī's work printed so many times because of its contemporary importance to Ḥanafī scholars? Or, is al-Karābīsī so well-known among Ḥanafī scholars because this work is readily available in a printed edition? A study of this issue would shed much light into the processes by which the classical tradition has been and continues to be received by contemporary scholarship.

79 Ibn Quṭlūbughā, *Tāj al-tarājim*, 29–30, no. 118.

80 Ibn Quṭlūbughā, *Tāj al-tarājim*, 9, no. 29.

81 Al-Tamīmī l-Dārī, *al-Ṭabaqat al-saniyya*, 1:364, no. 208.

fī furūq al-manqūl."[82] Unfortunately, al-Tamīmī l-Dārī does not give death dates for either scholar.

The noted Egyptian jurist Shihāb al-Dīn Aḥmad ibn Idrīs al-Qarāfī also wrote his *Anwār al-burūq fī anwāʾ al-furūq*, sometimes referred to as *Kitāb al-Furūq*, in the seventh/thirteenth century.[83] This is perhaps the best-known work titled *al-Furūq*, as more manuscripts and printed editions of this work exist than for almost every other work of legal distinctions combined. Yet it is a very peculiar work, leading to disagreement among scholars as to whether it is really a work of *furūq*.[84] This is likely because al-Qarāfī's work does not fit neatly into the genre of legal distinctions, but is more similar to a work of legal maxims (*al-qawāʿid al-fiqhiyya*). The author himself states that he "made the beginnings of research into legal maxims (*qawāʿid*) by discussing distinctions and asking, in a disputation, for the distinction between two derived cases (*al-furūq wa-l-suʾāl ʿanhā bayn farʿayn*) or two legal maxims."[85] His work is as concerned with maxims and general principles as it is with minute distinctions between rules of positive law. Indeed, al-Qarāfī's use of the term *furūq* seems more aligned to the usage of lexicographical distinctions than legal ones.[86]

---

82 Al-Tamīmī l-Dārī, *al-Ṭabaqat al-saniyya*, 1:376, no. 220.

83 Heinrichs, "Structuring the Law," 341–42; al-Bāḥusayn, *al-Furūq al-fiqhiyya*, 152–54; Kızılkaya, *İslâm hukukunda farklar*, 173–90; al-Sabīl, "*al-Muqaddima*," 1:32–33.

84 While Heinrichs includes this work in his bibliography, along with a brief list of commentaries on it, al-Bāḥusayn omits it from his own survey of works of legal distinctions, considering it instead a work of "*al-furūq al-uṣūliyya*." With this term, al-Bāḥusayn means something quite similar to the notion of "applied linguistic distinction" developed in the Excursus. Kızılkaya does include this work in his list, along with many of commentaries and supercommentaries, but acknowledges that this work is not like other works of legal distinctions. Heinrichs, "Structuring the Law," 341–42; al-Bāḥusayn, *al-Furūq al-fiqhiyya*, 152–154; Kızılkaya, *İslâm hukukunda farklar*, 173–90.

85 Abū l-ʿAbbās Aḥmad ibn Idrīs al-Qarāfī, *al-Furūq aw Anwār al-burūq fī anwāʾ al-furūq*, printed with *Idrār al-shurūq ʿalā anwāʾ al-furūq* by Ibn al-Shāṭṭ, *Tahdhīb al-Furūq* and *al-Qawāʿid al-sanniyya fī l-asrār al-fiqhiyya* by Muḥammad ʿAlī ibn Ḥusayn al-Makki, 4 vols., ed. Khalīl Mansūr (Beirut: Dār al-Kutub al-ʿIlmiyya, 1418/1998), 1:9.

86 See the discussion of applied lexicographic distinctions above, Excursus, pp. 110–12. Al-Qarāfī is sometimes credited with a second work on legal distinctions, *al-Iḥkām fī tamyīz al-fatāwā ʿan al-aḥkām wa-taṣarrufāt al-qāḍī wa-l-imām*, Kızılkaya, *İslâm hukukunda farklar*, 175–77. This work, however, is not a work of legal distinctions, but rather, as its title indicates, a work on judges, muftis, and their procedures and rulings. Muhammad Khalid Masud, Brinkley Messick, and David S. Powers, "Muftis, Fatwas, and Islamic Legal Interpretation," in *Islamic Legal Interpretation: Muftis and Their Fatwas*, ed. Muhammad Khalid Masud, Brinkley Messick, and David S. Powers (Cambridge, MA; London: Harvard University Press, 1996), 18–19. See also the recent translation of this work, Shihāb al-Dīn al-Qarāfī, *The Criterion for Distinguishing Legal*

In this century, members of the Ḥanbalī school also began writing works of legal distinctions. I have identified three such Ḥanbalī works: *al-Furūq fī l-masāʾil al-fiqhiyya* by Ibrāhīm ibn ʿAbd al-Wāḥid ibn ʿAlī ibn Surūr al-Maqdisī l-Ḥanbalī (d. 614/1218);[87] *al-Furūq* by Abū ʿAbdallāh Muḥammad ibn ʿAbdallāh al-Sāmarrī l-Ḥanbalī, also known as Ibn Sunayna (d. 616/1219);[88] and *al-Furūq* by Abū ʿAbdallāh Muḥammad ibn ʿAbd al-Qawī ibn Badrān al-Maqdisī l-Ḥanbalī (d. 699/1299 – 1300).[89] The first of these works is no longer extant. Its author, a prominent Ḥanbalī jurist, was born in a small village called Jammāʿīl on the West Bank of the Jordan River.[90] He lived most of his life in Damascus, though he traveled widely. The title of his work, *al-Furūq fī masāʾil al-fiqhiyya*, indicates that his work was indeed on legal distinctions.[91]

The history of Ibn Sunayna's work is more complicated. According to Schacht, this work was written by Muʿaẓẓam al-Dīn Abū l-Fatḥ ʿAbdallāh ibn Hibat Allāh al-Sāmarrī (d. 545/1150).[92] But this work was in fact written by Abū ʿAbdallāh Muḥammad ibn ʿAbdallāh al-Sāmarrī,[93] as evidenced by the manuscript of al-Sāmarrī's *Kitāb al-Furūq* in the Ẓāhiriyya Collection in the Asadiyya Library in Damascus, together with the biographical tradition, which attributes a work of legal distinctions to Abū ʿAbdallāh Muḥammad al-Sāmarrī, but not to Abū l-Fatḥ ʿAbdallāh al-Sāmarrī.[94]

Opinions from Judicial Rulings and the Administrative Acts of Judges and Rulers, trans. Mohammad Fadel (New Haven: Yale University Press, 2017).

87 Al-Bāḥusayn, *al-Furūq al-fiqhiyya*, 93; al-Sabīl, "*al-Muqaddima*," 1:40.

88 Heinrichs, "Structuring the Law," 343; al-Bāḥusayn, *al-Furūq al-fiqhiyya*, 93 – 94; Kızılkaya, *İslâm hukukunda farklar*, 168 – 71; al-Sabīl, "*al-Muqaddima*," 1:40.

89 Al-Bāḥusayn, *al-Furūq al-fiqhiyya*, 96; al-Sabīl, "*al-Muqaddima*," 1:40.

90 At present, this village is called Jamma'in.

91 ʿAbd al-Raḥmān Muḥammad ibn Aḥmad ibn Rajab, *al-Dhayl ʿalā Ṭabaqāt al-ḥanābila*, 5 vols., ed. ʿAbd al-Raḥmān Muḥammad ibn Sulaymān al-ʿUthaymīn (Mecca: Maktabat al-ʿUbaykān, 1425/2005), 3:198 – 220, the book itself is mentioned on 3:200; Kaḥḥāla, *Muʿjam*, 1:42, no. 312; Mujīr al-Dīn ʿAbd al-Raḥmān ibn Muḥammad al-ʿUlaymī, *al-Durr al-Munaḍḍad fī dhikr asḥāb al-imām Aḥmad*, 2 vols., ed. ʿAbd al-Raḥmān ibn Sulaymān al-ʿUthaymīn ([Riyadh(?)]: Maktabat al-Tawba, 1412/1992), 1:339, no. 969; Ibn al-ʿImād, *Shadharāt al-dhahab*, 7:105 – 108.

92 Schacht, "*Furūq*-Büchern," 507 – 508. Heinrichs accepts this attribution in Heinrichs, "Structuring the Law," 343.

93 Al-Bāḥusayn, *al-Furūq al-fiqhiyya*, 93 – 94; al-Sabīl, "*al-Muqaddima*," 1:40.

94 Heinrichs lists this work as being written by Abū l-Fatḥ in his bibliography, even though in a footnote he admits that it is more likely that it is by Ibn Sunayna. Heinrichs, "Structuring the Law," 343. For Abū l-Fatḥ, see Ibn al-ʿImād, *Shadharāt al-dhahab* 7:126 – 27; Dhayl, *Ṭabaqāt al-ḥanābila*, 3:249 – 51. Muʿaẓẓam al-Dīn's name is written on the cover page of the manuscript in Damascus; this can be seen on the reproduction printed in al-Yaḥyā's edition of this text, see

The Eighth/Fourteenth Century

The eighth/fourteenth century continued to see the production of many works of legal distinctions. The Shāfiʿī *madhhab* witnessed three works of legal distinctions in this century: *al-Jamʿ wa-l-farq* by Sirāj al-Dīn Yūnus ibn ʿAbd al-Majīd ibn ʿAlī l-Hudhalī l-Armantī l-Shāfiʿī (d. 725/1325);[95] *al-Furūq* by Abū Umāma Shams al-Dīn Muḥammad ibn ʿAlī ibn ʿAbd al-Wāḥid ibn Yaḥyā l-Dukkālī l-Maghribī l-Miṣrī l-Shāfiʿī, also known as Ibn al-Naqqāsh (d. 763/1361);[96] and *Maṭāliʿ al-daqāʾiq fī taḥrīr al-jawāmiʿ wa-l-fawāriq* by Jamāl al-Dīn ʿAbd al-Raḥīm ibn al-Ḥasan al-Asnawī l-Shāfiʿī (d. 772/1370).[97] Of these, only Jamāl al-Dīn al-Asnawī's is extant. Al-Asnawī was the head of the Shāfiʿī school in Cairo and wrote works in nearly all areas of Islamic law.[98] Al-Asnawī's book on distinctions is particularly interesting since it opens with a brief history of legal distinctions writing. The author does not include mention of the other two Shāfiʿī works from the eighth century, even though his book was likely the last of the three to be written.[99]

Sirāj al-Dīn al-Armantī was a Shāfiʿī who held judicial posts throughout Egypt, specifically in Qus (Qūṣ), Cairo, Ikhmīm, al-Bakhnasā,[100] and Bilbeis. His *nisba*, Armantī, refers to the village of Armant in Upper Egypt where he was born. Al-Armantī's work is remembered in the bibliographical tradition and appears to be a work of legal distinctions but is no longer extant.[101]

Muḥammad ibn Ibrāhīm ibn Muḥammad al-Yaḥyā, "*Muqaddima*," in *Kitāb al-Furūq ʿalā madhhab al-imām Aḥmad ibn Ḥanbal* by Muʿaẓẓam al-Dīn Abū ʿAbdallāh al-Sāmarrī, ed. Muḥammad ibn Ibrāhīm ibn Muḥammad al-Yaḥyā (Riyad: Dār al-Ṣumayʿī, 1997), 112. This work has been edited in two parts. The first, edited by al-Yaḥyā contains only the section on ritual duties (*al-ʿibādāt*), al-Sāmarrī, *Furūq*, ed. Yaḥya. The rest of the book was edited by Anas ibn ʿUmar ibn Muḥammad al-Subayyil as a master's thesis for Jāmiʿat Umm al-Qurā in Mecca in 1435/2014, Muʿaẓẓam al-Dīn Abū ʿAbdallāh ibn Sunayna al-Sāmarrī, *al-Furūq min awwal kitāb al-jināyāt ilā nihāyat al-kitāb dirāsatan wa-taḥqīqan*, ed. Anas ibn ʿUmar ibn Muḥammad al-Subayyil (MA Thesis, Jāmiʿat Umm al-Qurā1, 1435/2014). Joseph Schacht also edited and published short selections from this text, Schacht, "*Furūq*-Büchern," 525–37.

95 Al-Bāḥusayn, *al-Furūq al-fiqhiyya*, 96–97; al-Sabīl, "*al-Muqaddima*," 1:37.

96 Al-Bāḥusayn, *al-Furūq al-fiqhiyya*, 96–97; al-Sabīl, "*al-Muqaddima*," 1:37.

97 Heinrichs, "Structuring the Law," 343; al-Bāḥusayn, *al-Furūq al-fiqhiyya*, 100; Kızılkaya, *İslâm hukukunda farklar*, 191–94; al-Sabīl, "*al-Muqaddima*," 1:38.

98 I discuss him and his works in more detail above, in Chapter Four, pp. 148–54.

99 The *Maṭāliʿ* appears to have been written late in al-Asnawī's life, by which time al-Armantī had already passed. It is less clear that he wrote this work before that by Ibn al-Naqqāsh.

100 Known also today as Bahnasa and by its ancient name, Oxyrhynchus.

101 See Ibn al-Subkī, *Ṭabaqāt*, 10:430–33, no. 1419; al-Asnawī, *Ṭabaqāt*, 1:85–86, no. 149; Ibn al-ʿImād, *Shadharāt al-dhahab*, 8:125–26; Kaḥḥāla, *Muʿjam*, 2:193, no. 18608; Ḥājjī Khalīfa, *Kashf*

The nature of Ibn al-Naqqāsh's work is less clear. Ibn al-Naqqāsh was also a Cairene Shāfiʿī who travelled throughout the Levant, with stays in Damascus and Hama. His work is mentioned often in the bibliographical tradition, but is given several names: *al-Furūq*,[102] *al-Farq*,[103] *al-Naẓāʾir wa-l-furūq*, and *al-Naẓāʾir fī l-furūq*.[104] It seems likely that *al-Naẓāʾir fī l-furūq* was the first title of his book, since the earliest sources mention it as the name of this treatise.[105] By this late date, legal distinctions had become a fully formed and widely recognized genre. I therefore understand that Ibn al-Naqqāsh titled his book *al-furūq* as a way of signaling that it belonged to this genre.[106] A similar assumption, based on the word *furūq* in the title, may have led Ḥājjī Khalīfa to give *al-Furūq* as the title for this book and drop the word "*al-Naẓāʾir*."[107]

As in the previous century, only one Ḥanafī work of legal distinctions was written in the eighth/fourteenth century, *al-Furūq* by Tāj al-Dīn Aḥmad ibn ʿUthmān ibn Ibrāhīm ibn Muṣṭafā l-Turkumānī l-Mārdīnī l-Ḥanafī, known as Ibn al-Turkumānī (d. *ca.* 744/1343–44).[108] This work is likely not extant, although a manuscript on legal distinctions in the Ẓāhiriyya collection in the Asadiyya library in Damascus is attributed to him.[109] Little is known about Ibn al-Turkumānī. The sources relate only that he was a notable Ḥanafī from a scholarly family who lived in Cairo.[110]

---

al-ẓunūn, s.v. "*al-Furūq fī furūʿ al-shāfiʿiyya*," 1:601; Ibn Qāḍī Shuhba, *Ṭabaqāt*, 2:301–302, no. 574.

102 Ḥājjī Khalīfa, *Kashf al-ẓunūn*, s.v. "*al-Furūq fī furūʿ al-shāfiʿiyya*," 2:1258.

103 Baghdādī, *Hadiyat al-ʿārifīn*, 2:162.

104 Ibn al-ʿImād, *Shadharāt al-dhahab*, 8:339; Ibn Qāḍī Shuhba, *Ṭabaqāt*, 3:132; Kaḥḥāla, *Muʿjam*, 3:521.

105 Shihāb al-Dīn Aḥmad ibn ʿAlī ibn Muḥammad ibn Ḥajar al-ʿAsqalānī, *al-Durar al-kāmina fī aʿyān al-miʾa l-thāmina*, 4 vols., no ed. (Beirut: Dār Iḥyāʾ al-Turāth al-ʿArabī, [197–]), 4:71–74. Al-ʿAsqalānī says it is "a book about distinctions (*ṣannafa ... kitāban fī l-furūq*)."

106 It is also possible that given this assumption, later authors, in particular Ḥājjī Khalīfa, miscategorized this work as belonging to the genre of legal distinctions and that I am continuing this error by maintaining this assumption.

107 *Kashf al-ẓunūn* does not include any books with the title "*al-Naẓāʾir wa-l-furūq*," see Ḥājjī Khalīfa, *Kashf al-ẓunūn*, 2:1920.

108 Heinrichs, "Structuring the Law," 341; al-Bāḥusayn, *al-Furūq al-fiqhiyya*, 98–99; al-Sabīl, "*al-Muqaddima*," 1:29.

109 It is unlikely that this work was actually written by Ibn al-Turkumānī. This manuscript is a copy of the work that I call *Furūq*-A, see below pp. 188–89.

110 Ḥājjī Khalīfa, *Kashf al-ẓunūn*, s.v. "*al-Furūq fī furūʿ al-ḥanafiyya*," 2:1257; al-Qurashī, *al-Jawāhir al-muḍiyya*, 1:197–98, no. 139; al-ʿAsqalānī, *al-Durar al-kāmina*, 1:198; Ibn al-ʿImād, *Shadharāt al-dhahab*, 8:243; al-Tamīmī l-Dārī, *Ṭabaqāt al-saniyya*, 1:389, no. 240; *GAL* 2:64, S2:67–68; Ibn Quṭlūbughā, *Tāj al-tarājim*, 9, no. 30.

The Ḥanbalī *madhhab* saw one book of legal distinctions written in this century, *Īḍāḥ al-dalāʾil fī l-farq bayn al-masāʾil* by Abū Muḥammad Sharaf al-Dīn ʿAbd al-Raḥīm ibn ʿAbdallāh al-Zarīrānī l-Baghdādī l-Ḥanbalī (d. 741/1341).[111] Al-Zarīrānī was a Baghdadi jurist and hadith scholar who traveled to Damascus and Cairo. His *nisba* almost certainly connects him to Zarīrān, a small village south of Baghdad.[112] The edition of Ibn Rajab's *Dhayl al-ṭabaqāt* that I cite gives his name as ʿAbd al-Raḥīm al-Zarīrānī, but notes that the variant al-Zarīrātī is found on at least some of the manuscripts.[113] Other sources, such as *al-Durar al-kāmina* and *Shadharāt al-dhahab* refer to him as al-Zarīrānī.[114] The unicum manuscript in Princeton gives his name as ʿAbd al-Raḥmān al-Zarīrānī and is likely the source for the name given in the printed edition.[115] Further, this work is sometimes referred to as *Tanqīḥ al-Furūq*. This title alludes to the fact that this work is a commentary on and expansion of Ibn Sunayna's *Kitāb al-Furūq*. This self-conscious referencing suggests that writing works of legal distinctions had become a part of the Ḥanbalī legal-literary repertoire by this time.

The eighth/fourteenth century represents the high-water mark in the production of works of legal distinctions. Additionally, legal distinctions literature seems to have spread to many regions during this time. It was also during this century that ʿAlī ibn Yaḥyā ibn Rāshid al-Washlī l-Zaydī l-Yamanī wrote his *al-*

---

111 Heinrichs, "Structuring the Law," 343; al-Bāḥusayn, *al-Furūq al-fiqhiyya*, 97–98; Kızılkaya, *İslâm hukukunda farklar*, 171–72; al-Sabīl, "*al-Muqaddima*," 1:28. There is some uncertainty as to the name of this author. In "Structuring the Law," Heinrichs refers to him as al-Zarīrātī and says that in the introduction to al-Dimashqī's book of legal distinctions, this author's "name [is] wrongly given as ʿAbd al-Raḥmān al-Zarīrānī," although he amends his reading in "*Qawāʿid*," saying that the reading "ʻal-Zarīrātī' is apparently incorrect" (Heinrichs, "*Qawāʿid*" 383n37). Both *nisba*, however, are given to this author in the biographical sources. Kızılkaya refers to this author as al-Zurayrānī (lit: "Züreyrânî"). Wolfhart Heinrichs, "*Qawāʿid* as a Genre of Legal Literature," in *Studies in Islamic Legal Theory*, ed. Bernard Weiss (Leiden: Brill, 2002), 383n 37.

112 Shihāb al-Dīn Yāqūt ibn ʿAbdallāh al-Ḥamawī, *Muʿjam al-buldān*, 7 vols. No ed. (Beirut: Dār Ṣādir, 1397/1977), 3:140.

113 Ibn Rajab, *Dhayl Ṭabaqāt al-ḥanābila*, 5:104. Al-ʿUthaymīn says that this variant appears in the manuscript abbreviated "*ṭāʾ*," but in his introduction, does not label any manuscripts with this letter. See ʿAbd al-Raḥmān Muḥammad ibn Sulaymān al-ʿUthaymīn, "*Muqaddimat al-muḥaqqiq*," in *Dhayl Ṭabaqāt al-ḥanābila*, by Ibn Rajab, ed ʿAbd al-Raḥmān Muḥammad ibn Sulaymān al-ʿUthaymīn (Mecca: Maktabat al-ʿUbaykān, 1425/2005), 1:112–35.

114 Ibn al-ʿImād has his name as ʿAbd al-Raḥīm ibn ʿAbd al-Malik. This spelling likely reflects what was on the manuscripts since the editor notes that he is usually known as ʿAbd al-Raḥīm ibn ʿAbdallah. Ibn al-ʿImād, *Shadharāt al-dhahab*, 8:228.

115 MS Garrett 4577Y, Princeton University Library, Princeton, 2b.

Jamʿ wa-l-farq.[116] This work, discussed above, seems to have dealt with legal distinctions. Its title, *al-Jamʿ wa-l-farq*, is both a direct allusion to the work written by ʿAbdallāh al-Juwaynī and also seemingly places it in conversation with the Shāfiʿī tradition.[117] Apart from this work by ʿAlī ibn Yaḥyā, this title appears to be confined to works by Shāfiʿī authors.[118] Unfortunately, this work has not survived and other sources do not preserve excerpts from it.

The Ninth/Fifteenth Century

Production of works of *furūq* decreased in the following centuries. The ninth century saw only two works on legal distinctions, one from the Mālikī *madhhab* and one unusual Ḥanafī work. The Mālikī work is *al-Furūq* by Abū ʿAbdallāh Muḥammad ibn Yūsuf al-ʿAbdarī l-Gharnāṭī l-Mālikī, al-Mawwāq.[119] This work appears no longer to be extant, although a manuscript of a book of Mālikī distinctions at the Maktabat Āl Ibn ʿĀshūr al-Tūnisī in La Marsa is attributed to an author with a similar name, Muḥammad ibn Yūsuf al-Andalusī.[120] The manuscript in La Marsa is mentioned by Abū l-Ajfān and Abū Fāris, the editors of al-Dimashqī's *Furūq al-Dimashqī*, and consequently by both al-Bāḥusayn and Heinrichs. Abū l-Ajfān and Abū Fāris believed that this was a separate person because of the missing *nisba*s in the name given in the manuscript.[121] Al-Bāḥusayn agrees that the author of this manuscript is not al-Mawwāq. He mentions it at the end of his survey and treats it as an anonymous work because the name associated with it, Muḥammad ibn Yūsuf, is so common.[122] Heinrichs, meanwhile, finds it "highly unlikely" that the La Marsa manuscript is by someone other

116 Al-Bāḥusayn, *al-Furūq al-fiqhiyya*, 100; al-Sabīl, "*al-Muqaddima*," 1:38; Kaḥḥāla, 2:543, no. 10254.

117 Such a dialogue, between Zaydī scholars and Shāfiʿī scholars in Yemen in the eighth/fourteenth century, would not be unusual. See Bernard Haykel, *Revival and Reform in Islam: The Legacy of Muhammad al-Shawkānī* (Cambridge: Cambridge University Press), 12–15.

118 The main source of information on this work is a biographical dictionary by Muḥammad Zabāra. Muḥammad ibn Muḥammad ibn Zabāra al-Ḥasanī l-Yamanī, *Mulḥiq al-badr al-ṭāliʿ bi-maḥāsin man baʿd al-qarn al-sābiʿ*, 2 vols., no ed. (Beirut: Dār Maʿrifa, n.d.), 1:183–84.

119 Heinrichs, "Structuring the Law," 341; al-Bāḥusayn, *al-Furūq al-fiqhiyya*, 101–102; al-Sabīl, "*al-Muqaddima*," 1:31.

120 MS fāʾ-alif 98–90, Maktabat Āl Ibn ʿĀshūr al-Tūnisī, La Marsa.

121 Abū l-Ajfān and Abū Fāris, "*Dirāsa*," 40.

122 Al-Bāḥusayn, *al-Furūq al-fiqhiyya*, 105.

than al-Mawwāq, but nevertheless grants both works separate entries in his bibliography.[123]

There is, however, one mention of a Mālikī work of legal distinctions by an otherwise unknown Muḥammad ibn Yūsuf. In Najm al-Dīn al-Ṭūfī's *ʿAlam al-jadhal fī ʿilm al-jadal*, the author attributes a work of Mālikī legal distinctions to al-Shaykh Abū ʿAbdallāh Muḥammad ibn Yūsuf al-Andalusī l-Anṣārī l-Mālikī.[124] This may seem to refer to al-Mawwāq, but this is impossible, as al-Ṭūfī died in 716/1316, almost 180 years before the death of al-Mawwāq. Al-Ṭūfī could not have known of al-Mawwāq's work. This indicates that there were at least two scholars named Abū ʿAbdallāh Muḥammad ibn Yūsuf from al-Andalus who wrote works of Mālikī legal distinctions.[125]

Nevertheless, al-Mawwāq certainly wrote a work of legal distinctions. Aḥmad ibn ʿAlī l-Balawī (d. 938/1532), in his *Thabat*, mentions that Abū Jaʿfar Aḥmad al-Baqanī (*fl.* 9th/15th c.) received from al-Mawwāq himself a general license (*al-ijāza l-ʿāmma*) to transmit several works by al-Mawwāq, including *al-Furūq*.[126] If al-Mawwāq granted a license to teach his *Furūq*, he must have authored such a work, and the fact that the Arabo-Islamic heritage preserves this detail is strong evidence that he wrote this work and that it was well-known by other scholars.

The other work of legal distinctions from this century, entitled simply *al-Furūq*, was a peculiar work written in 802/1399–1400 by the Ḥanafī scholar Shaykh Bāyazīd ibn Isrāʾīl ibn Ḥājjī Dāwūd Marghāyatī(?) (d. early ninth/fifteenth c.). This work has only been discussed by modern authors. Al-Bāḥusayn, based on consultation of a microfilm version of the manuscript, says that it is thirty-two folios long, although the first ten folios of the manuscript are missing.[127] While he does not give any other information about the original manuscript, a complete copy of this work is found in MS Arabe 812 in the Bibliothèque nationale de France. Al-Sabīl says that Marghāyatī "is a minor author who fol-

---

123 Heinrichs, "Structuring the Law," 342.

124 Najm al-Dīn al-Ṭūfī, *ʿAlam al-jadhal fī ʿilm al-jadal*, ed. Wolfhart Heinrichs (Wiesbaden: Franz Steiner Verlag, 1408/1987), 73.

125 Based on this information, it seems likely to me that the La Marsa manuscript is not by al-Mawwāq, but only a study or edition of the text would help to answer this question.

126 See also Aḥmad ibn ʿAlī al-Balawī, *al-Thabat*, ed. ʿAbdallāh al-ʿImrānī (Beirut: Dār al-Gharb al-Islāmī, 1403/1983), 190. I thank Josef Ženka for this reference.

127 "*wa-huwa kitāb mūjiz yaqaʿa fī 32 waraqa saqaṭa min al-nuskha llatī aṭṭalaʿnā ʿalayhā ʿasharat awrāq min awwalihā.*" Al-Bāḥusayn, *al-Furūq al-fiqhiyya*, 101. It is not clear from his statement whether this manuscript was originally forty-two folio and only thirty-two survive, or if it was originally thirty-two folios and only twenty-two survive. The copy in the Bibliothèque nationale de France is copy takes up twenty folios, from 12b–32a.

lowed the style of Asʿad al-Karābīsī," and goes on to describe the work as "written by a foreigner with poor style and grammar (*uslūb al-kitāb rakīk wa-fīhi laknat al-aʿājim*)."[128] Marghāyātī is unknown aside from this text. The colophon of this work mentions that it was finished in Shaʿbān 802 / 28 March – 26 April 1400, a date that both al-Bāḥusayn and al-Sabīl mention. From its contents, it appears that Marghāyatī was a Ḥanafī scholar.[129]

The Tenth/Sixteenth Century

Furūq writing slowed significantly during the tenth/sixteenth century. Two works written during this century which are part of the tradition of *furūq*-literature: *al-Ashbāh wa-l-naẓāʾir* by Ibn Nujaym; and *ʿIddat al-burūq fī jamʿ mā fī l-madhhab min al-jumūʿ wa-l-furūq* by Abū l-ʿAbbās Aḥmad ibn Yaḥyā l-Wansharīsī l-Mālikī (d. 914/1508). Al-Wansharīsī's text is a book in the genre of legal distinctions; Ibn Nujaym's only has a section devoted to legal distinctions. Both of these works can be approached as an end-point for the tradition of distinctions writing.

ʿIddat al-burūq, a massive work of legal distinctions, was written by Aḥmad al-Wansharīsī, one of the most celebrated North African Mālikī scholars of the period. While it may not have eclipsed al-Qarāfī's work, which enjoyed great popularity and exercised tremendous influence, it was a very important work for the Mālikī *madhhab.* The title of al-Wansharīsī's book is a clear allusion to, and rhymes with, the title of al-Qarāfī's book *Anwār al-burūq fī anwāʾ al-furūq*, but these works are nonetheless fundamentally different. As discussed earlier, al-Qarāfī's book is not quite a work of legal distinctions, but a broader work encompassing applied linguistic distinctions, legal distinctions, legal maxims, and more. While there are traces of al-Qarāfī's style and presentation in Wansharīsī's *ʿIdda*, the *ʿIdda* is much more straightforwardly a work of legal distinctions. Stylistically, this later work differs slightly from other books in the distinctions tradition, most notably by omitting the standard phrase "the distinction between these is..." Despite this difference, *ʿIddat al-burūq* reads much like other works of legal distinctions.[130]

---

128 Al-Sabīl, "*al-Muqaddima*," 1:29.

129 Al-Bāḥusayn says that occasionally "he reveals the distinction by way of a question, as though it were a riddle or examination (*lughz wa-mtiḥān*)," al-Bāḥusayn, *al-Furūq al-fiqhiyya*, 101.

130 Interestingly, although the title of his work suggests a relationship between his work and that by al-Qarāfī, the introduction to this book has many resonances with the other Mālikī *furūq* texts, see Abū l-ʿAbbās Aḥmad ibn Yaḥyā l-Wansharīsī, *ʿIddat al-furūq fī jamʿ mā fī l-*

The other work from this century, by Ibn Nujaym, is entitled *al-Ashbāh wa-l-naẓāʾir.* It is not exclusively dedicated to legal distinctions, but it does include a chapter devoted to legal distinctions.[131] This chapter is essentially a small work of legal distinctions, not noticeably different from many of the other works on this list. This works is significant, however, for how Ibn Nujaym includes recognizable treatments of legal distinctions into broader conceptual legal organizations.

Both works from this century were written by figures who remained highly influential long after their deaths. It is intriguing that a genre so often characterized by little-known authors and texts of uncertain provenance terminates with works by two authors of such renown. Ibn Nujaym's work in particular became a cornerstone of Ḥanafī legal study in the Ottoman Empire, which officially adopted the Ḥanafī school, achieving a level of canonicity within Ottoman legal culture similar to that attained by al-Qarāfī for the Mālikīs a few centuries earlier. [132] There are numerous commentaries on Ibn Nujaym's text, which continued to be written well into the nineteenth century.[133]

Works of Indeterminate Date

In addition to the above, I found at least three separate works of legal distinctions that cannot be securely dated and that have an uncertain authorial attribution. One of these is a Shāfiʿī work of legal distinctions found in the British Library. The codex in the British Library, MS Or 6278, is an incomplete copy of a Shāfiʿī distinctions text that was finished on 18 Dhī al-Ḥijja, 854 / 22 January 1451.[134] Given the date this manuscript was copied and the repeated references to al-Rāfiʿī's *Muḥarrar* and al-Nawawī's *Sharḥ al-muhadhdhab*, this treatise was likely composed between 1300 and 1450.[135] Given this date, it is possible,

madhhab min al-jumūʿ wa-l-furūq, ed. Ḥamza Abū Fāris (Beirut: Dār al-Gharb al-Islāmī, 1990/1410), 79–80.

131 See the "Sixth Chapter" (*al-fann al-sādis*) of this work

132 According to Samy Ayoub, "the works, opinions, and *fatāwā* of [Ibn Nujaym] define the discussions of Ḥanafī legal development over the 17th–19th centuries"; see Samy Ayoub, "We're not in Kufa Anymore: The Construction of Late Ḥanafism in the Early Modern Ottoman Empire, 16th–19th Centuries CE" (Ph.D. Diss., University of Arizona, 2014), 24.

133 See Muḥammad Abū l-Fatḥ al-Ḥanafī, *Itḥāf al-abṣār wa-l-baṣāʾir bi-tabwīb Kitāb al-Ashbāh wa-l-naẓāʾir* (Alexandria: al-Maṭbaʿa al-Waṭaniyya, 1289[/1872–73]).

134 MS Oriental 6278, British Library, London, 108b.

135 The catalogue entry for this work states that it was "compiled about A.H. 700[/1300-01]." It is not clear to me what exactly led the catalogers to this conclusion, although perhaps it was a

though by no means certain, that this work is a copy of the *furūq* work of either Sirāj al-Dīn al-Armantī or Ibn al-Naqqāsh. The manuscript does not contain information on the author of the text, perhaps because the cover and introduction are missing.[136]

In addition, I also located two Ḥanafī works of distinctions, each with multiple manuscript witnesses. These two texts, which exist only in manuscript, are identified in the bibliographies complied by al-Bāḥusayn, al-Sabīl, and Kızılkaya. These texts have either no authorial attribution or are attributed to an otherwise unknown author. Because of the problems of attribution, the time and location from which these works originated is not easily discernable. Although the titles and authors vary, the indeterminate Ḥanafī works are all copies of one of two books, which I refer to as *Furūq*-A and *Furūq*-B.[137] The indeterminate Ḥanafī works include the following: *al-Furūq* by Aḥmad ibn Muḥammad al-Arzustānī (d. ?), *al-Furūq* by Aḥmad ibn Muḥammad al-Urdustānī (d. ?); *al-Furūq fī l-furūʿ* by Najm al-Dīn ʿAlī ibn al-Sayyid Abī Bakr al-Naysābūrī l-Ḥanafī (d. ?); and *al-Furūq ʿalā madhhab Abī Ḥanīfa*, which has no authorial attribution.

I have consulted all of the extant manuscripts of all of these works, save the one attributed to al-Urdustānī (MS 3677, Maktabat al-Awqāf, Baghdad). Al-Sabīl says that this work by al-Urdustānī exists in two copies, the manuscript in Baghdad and a manuscript in Berlin, MS Peterman II Nachtrag 4 at the Staatsbibliothek zu Berlin.[138] The manuscript in Germany is not attributed to any author, so "al-Urdustānī" must be mentioned in the manuscript in Baghdad. This Berlin manuscript, however, is a copy of *Furūq*-A.[139] If this Berlin and Baghdad manuscripts are copies of the same work, then the Baghdad manuscript attributed to al-Urdustānī must be a copy of *Furūq*-A as well.

similar set of assumptions. They also give the 854 [/1450–51] date as the date of composition of the manuscript. Alexander G. Ellis and Edward Edwards, *A Descriptive List of the Arabic Manuscripts Acquired by the Trustees of the British Museum since 1894* (London: British Museum, 1912), 25.

136 The manuscript has clearly marked quiration. Each quire, starting with the fourth (*al-rābiʿ*), is clearly marked and each of the following quires consists of ten folios, save the last one which only has six folios. The pages on which the second and third quire should be marked are missing the corner on which the quiration note is written. It seems, however, that this codex is missing most of the first quire, but is otherwise complete. The second quire starts on 2a, the third on 12a, and then quiration can be seen starting on 22a.

137 I discuss these works below.

138 I have been unable to ascertain the current name of the Baghdadi library in question. The Germany manuscript is often referred to as Berlin 4848, its number in the Ahlwardt catalog.

139 See below for a discussion of *Furūq*-A.

Finally, Chester Beatty 4507, *al-Furūq fī l-aḥkām ʿalā madhhab al-mālikiyya* is not attributed to an author and the Chester Beatty catalog lists no author. Al-Bāḥusayn and al-Sabīl treat this as a separate and otherwise unknown work of legal distinctions.[140] This manuscript is, however, a copy of Muslim al-Dimashqī's book of legal distinctions.[141]

Historical and Geographical Trends

There do not seem to be particular geographical trends in the composition of works of legal distinctions, although Baghdad in the fifth/eleventh century seems to have been a center of distinctions writing. The Mālikī jurist al-Qāḍī ʿAbd al-Wahhāb lived in Baghdad and Muslim al-Dimashqī was his student.[142] It was, however, a center for most kinds of legal writing and intellectual production and scholarly activity in general at this time. The Shāfiʿī scholars al-Ḥusayn al-Ṭabarī and ʿAbdallāh al-Juwaynī lived in Baghdad.[143] The genre of *furūq* crossed school, as both Mālikī and Shāfiʿī authors wrote these works. When ʿAbd al-Ḥaqq al-Ṣiqillī performed his pilgrimage, he is said to have met and had discussions with Imām al-Ḥaramayn al-Juwaynī, the son of ʿAbdallāh al-Juwaynī.[144] Baghdad was not, however, the only center of legal learning and distinctions writing. Several Ḥanafī and Shāfiʿī scholars spent time in Khurasan, notably in Nishapur, and Ibn al-Kātib lived in North Africa.[145] Thus, the centers of *furūq*-writing in the fifth century seem to reflect the centers of intellectual production more broadly and, like other intellectual activities, most works of legal

---

140 Al-Bāḥusayn, *al-Furūq al-fiqhiyya*, 103–104; al-Sabīl, "*al-Muqaddima*," 1:34.

141 It was used by Abū l-Ajfān and Abū Fāris in their edition of this work, Abū l-Ajfān and Abū Fāris, "*Dirāsa*," 49–50. A comparison between MS 4507, Chester Beatty Library, Dublin and the printed edition of Muslim al-Dimashqī's *Kitāb al-Furūq* make this evident.

142 For al-Qāḍī ʿAbd al-Wahhāb, see Shams al-Dīn Aḥmad ibn Muḥammad ibn Khallikān, *Wafāyāt al-aʿyān wa-anbāʾ abnāʾ al-zamān*, 8 vols., ed. Iḥsān ʿAbbās (Beirut: Dār Sādir, 1398/1978), 3:219–22, no. 400; Ibn al-ʿImād, *Shadharāt al-dhahab*, 5:112; Kaḥḥāla, *Muʿjam*, 2:344, no. 8711; Makhlūf, *Shajarat al-nūr al-zakiyya*, 103–104; al-Qāḍī ʿIyāḍ, *Tartīb al-madārik* 7:220–27. For Muslim al-Dimashqī, see Ibn Farḥūn, *al-Dībāj al-mudhahhab*, 2:347; al-Qāḍī ʿIyāḍ, *Tartīb al-madārik*, 8:57.

143 For al-Ḥusayn al-Ṭabarī, see Ibn Qāḍī Shuhba, *Ṭabaqāt*, 1:181, no. 142; al-Asnawī, *Ṭabaqāt*, 2:61–62 no. 767; al-Shīrāzī, *Ṭabaqāt*, 126. For ʿAbdallāh al-Juwaynī, see Ibn al-ʿImād, *Shadharāt al-dhahab*, 5:176–77; al-Asnawī, *Ṭabaqāt*, 1:165–66, no. 305; Ibn al-Subkī, *Ṭabaqāt*, 5:73–94, no. 439; al-Zarkashī, *al-Manthūr fī l-qawāʿid*, 69; Ibn Qāḍī Shuhba, *Ṭabaqāt*, 1:209–11, no. 171.

144 Ibn Farḥūn, *al-Dībāj*, 2:56; Makhlūf, *Shajarat al-nūr al-zakiyya*, 1:116.

145 Al-Qāḍī ʿIyāḍ, *Tartīb al-madārik*, 7:252; Makhlūf, *Shajarat al-nūr al-zakiyya*, 106.

distinctions emerged from large urban centers. In the eighth/fourteenth century, Cairo emerged as a center of distinctions-writing. Of the six works of legal distinctions composed during this period, four were written in Cairo.[146] The other two works are *Īḍāḥ al-dalāʾil* by Sharaf al-Dīn al-Zarīrānī and *al-Jamʿ wa-l-farq* by ʿAlī ibn Yaḥyā l-Zaydī. Although Sharaf al-Dīn al-Zarīrānī spent the majority of his life in Baghdad, the sources tell us that he also travelled to Cairo and Damascus.[147] Little is known about ʿAli ibn Yaḥyā, aside from the fact that he lived in Yemen; he does not appear to have had any connection to Cairo.[148]

The historical movement of these texts is not entirely clear. The results of this bibliographic survey demonstrate sustained interest in legal distinctions; manuscript copies of earlier works were produced with some regularity long after the sixteenth century.[149] These results also show a certain amount of geographic spread for individual texts, with a large grouping of Ḥanafī and Shāfiʿī texts in both Cairo and Istanbul.[150] The presence of texts in various imperial centers also suggests that works of legal distinctions were important enough to preserve in capital cities.

Some curiosities do emerge from an initial exploration of the manuscripts. The presence of al-Qarāfī's *al-Furūq* in Istanbul and al-Jurjānī's *al-Muʿāyāt* in Rabat is peculiar. Istanbul was not a center of Maliki law, nor was Rabat a hub for Shāfiʿī jurists. The preservation of these two works perhaps signals their historical importance or popularity. Al-Qarāfī's *al-Furūq* was perhaps the most important work of Mālikī law from the post-formative period, so it is perhaps not surprising to find it in Istanbul, but al-Jurjānī's work does not appear to have had a notable impact in the Shāfiʿī school. More research is needed to

---

146 These works are (i) *al-Jamʿ wa-l-farq* by Sirāj al-Dīn Yūnus ibn ʿAbd al-Mujīd ibn ʿAlī l-Hudhalī l-Armantī l-Shāfiʿī; (ii) *al-Furūq* by Tāj al-Dīn Aḥmad ibn ʿUthmān ibn Ibrāhīm ibn Muṣṭafā l-Turkumānī l-Mārdīnī l-Ḥanafī, also known as Ibn al-Turkumānī; (iii) *al-Furūq* by Abū Umāma Shams al-Dīn Muḥammad ibn ʿAlī ibn ʿAbd al-Wāḥid ibn Yaḥyā l-Dukkālī l-Maghribī l-Miṣrī l-Shāfiʿī, also known as Ibn al-Naqqāsh; (iv) and *Maṭāliʿ al-daqāʾiq fī taḥrīr al-jawāmiʿ wa-l-fawāriq* by Jamāl al-Dīn ʿAbd al-Raḥīm ibn al-Ḥasan al-Asnawī.

147 Ibn Rajab, *Dhayl Ṭabaqāt al-ḥanābila*, 5:104–15, no. 581; al-ʿAsqālānī, *al-Durar al-Kāmina*, 2:357, no. 2390; Ibn al-ʿImād, *Shadharāt al-dhahab* 8:228–29.

148 Kaḥḥāla, *Muʿjam*, 2:543, no. 10254; Muḥammad ibn Zabāra, *Mulḥiq al-badr al-ṭāliʿ*, 1:183–84.

149 See Appendix I for information on all of the manuscripts of these works.

150 Owing to the large number of manuscripts surveyed, this study has not taken ownership marks, reading notes, and other marginalia into consideration. This limits, to a great extent, my capacity to discuss geographic spread. Further study on the paratextual elements of these manuscripts will shed great light into the use and spread of these works.

understand the role of these works and the historical distribution of particular books of legal distinctions.

The lack of a clear early center of distinctions-writing may indicate that the prehistory of legal distinctions was robust and widespread. Otherwise, it would be surprising that early works emerging from disparate parts of the world are remarkably similar in style and content. In addition, distinctions-writing had currency throughout the premodern and Ottoman Muslim world. The reasons for its relevance have shifted over time and across geographies, from use in legal disputation to use as intellectual entertainment in literary salons, but the distinctions genre nevertheless remained enduringly relevant.

A Note on Manuscripts

As important as it is to understand the contexts in which new works of legal distinctions were written, it is necessary as well to determine their manuscript histories, or where these works were being copied and recreated. The history of the spread of these texts is an oft-overlooked aspect of the study of intellectual history but my analysis so far allows me to make some preliminary remarks on the spread and rewriting of legal distinctions manuscripts.[151] As Dagmar Riedel reminds us, "the reception of a work can be traced indirectly through its transmission and indicates how audiences utilized it, so that the evidence of its transmission documents its circulation and use."[152] The results of my survey into the material history of legal distinctions are echo the above review of the composition of works of legal distinctions.

The most interesting discovery I made through my survey of the material history of legal distinctions was not about material history at all. Generally speaking, it was easy to identify relevant works of legal distinctions based solely on the manuscript catalog. I did, however, consistently come across works of legal distinction cataloged under an ambiguous title, such as *Risāla fī l-fiqh*, or treatise on Islamic Law, and/or without authorial attribution. Many of these works are not catalogued completely, perhaps because some works do not pre-

151 My analysis is largely based on visits to the Bibliothèque nationale de France, Leiden University Libraries, the Princeton University Libraries, the Staatsbibliothek zu Berlin, and the Süleymaniye Library. In addition, I consulted scanned images of manuscripts or scanned microfilms from the website Jāmiʿ al-Makhṭūṭāt al-Islāmiyya. Jāmiʿ al-Makhṭūṭāt al-Islāmiyya, http://wqf.me, accessed May 2, 2019.

152 Dagmar A. Riedel, "Searching for the Islamic Episteme: The Status of Historical Information in Medieval Middle-Eastern Anthological Writing" (PhD Diss., Indiana University, 2004), 25.

serve enough information for proper cataloguing. Indeed, I noticed that upon closer examination, most of these works were actually different copies of the same two texts. These may be two different versions of a similar text, but the manuscript families can be identified with a fair degree of confidence. The first of these, which I label *Furūq*-A, I found in six different manuscript libraries.[153] The second, which I label *Furūq*-B, is found only in the Süleymaniye Library in Istanbul and in Leiden University.

The anonymous, untitled manuscripts on the topic of legal distinctions demand further study. Al-Bāḥusayn mentions these works in his survey, writing: "Finally, we know of no later works [after al-Wansharīsī] other than a few manuscripts with no known author (*mu'allifāt qalīla majhūlat al-mu'allaf*). It is unclear when they were written."[154] These manuscripts, however, are important works of legal distinctions. My research has revealed copies of these manuscripts in several major manuscript repositories. Moreover, I have discovered at least one anonymous work of legal distinctions in every major repository of Arabic manuscripts that I have consulted.[155] Because of the lack of information about these works or their authors, they are difficult to date or locate, although based on their content, page layout, and hands I suspect they were written in the Eastern Mediterranean and not before the seventh/thirteenth century. The results from this partial sample tell us a great deal about these two works and alerts us to the importance of the material history of legal distinctions. The widespread existence of manuscripts of two anonymous works on distinctions signals that they played an important role in Islamic legal culture.

I have found six witnesses for the distinctions text that I call *Furūq*-A: Halet Efendi 807 (HE 807), in the Süleymaniye Library in Istanbul; Peterman II Nachtrag 4 in the Staatsbibliothek zu Berlin; Garrett 4185Y (G 4185Y) in the Princeton University Library; Ẓāhiriyya 4501 in Damascus;[156] Fiqh Ḥanafī 2089 in the Maktabat al-Ḥaram al-Makkī in Mecca; and Khazā'in Kutub al-Awqāf 3677 in Bagh-

153 See below and Appendix I. Al-Sabīl and al-Bāḥusayn attribute this work to al-Urdustānī, presumably based on a manuscript in Baghdad. MS Garrett 4185Y, Princeton University Library, Princeton however, attributes the work to al-Arzustānī (MS Garrett 4185Y, 64b). The only trace remaining of these authors is their *nisbas*. I discuss this issue below. Al-Bāḥusayn, *al-Furūq al-fiqhiyya*, 103; al-Sabīl, "*al-Muqaddima*," 1:30.

154 Al-Bāḥusayn, *al-Furūq al-fiqhiyya*, 76.

155 I have found such manuscripts at the Bibliothèque Nationale de France, British Library, the Princeton University Library, the Staatsbibliothek zu Berlin, the Süleymaniye, and the University of Leiden Library.

156 MS Ẓāhiriyya 4501, Asadiyya Library, Damascus is heavily damaged, a fact which partly explains many of its large differences from the other MSS of this work.

dad.[157] These manuscripts share a common title, *Kitāb al-Furūq*, but otherwise display a high degree of variance.[158] Although they begin with similar chapter divisions, the manuscripts disagree on the placement of subdivisions and the ordering of subsections within the text, and on the number and ordering of distinctions within the text.[159] The Princeton manuscript also includes a unique section, not found in other manuscripts, *masāʾil farqiyya fiqhiyya* (issues of legal distinguishing). This suggests that the extant manuscripts are based on different manuscript stems for this work, but closer examination is required in order to understand the relationship between them.

In terms of content, *Furūq*-A is very reminiscent of other works of legal distinctions, particularly Asʿad al-Karābīsī's *Kitāb al-Furūq* and al-Maḥbūbī's *Talqīḥ al-ʿuqūl.* It is written in a very concise style that quickly presents each legal problem in the legal distinction and minimally explains the distinction between them. There are few references to other books of law or other scholars. Unsurprisingly, Abū Ḥanīfa, Muḥammad al-Shaybānī, and Abū Yūsuf, the three founding figures of the Ḥanafī school, are the three jurists who appear most often. The three founding figures are the only scholars mentioned in the Princeton manuscript, while the Sulaymaniye's HE 807 mentions both "Naṣīr ibn Yaḥyā [al-Balkhī (d. *ca.* 268/881–82)]"[160] and "Abū l-Layth [al-Samarqandī (d. *ca.* 383/993–94)?]."[161] The manuscripts also contain occasional references to passages from the Qur'an or to the hadith, as well as statements on the authority of unnamed individuals or the Ḥanafī school as a whole. The manuscripts of *Furūq*-A also demonstrate the permeability of the genre of legal distinctions; in particular the section on "Miscellaneous Legal Issues" (*masāʾil mutafarriqa*; *masāʾil mutashābiha*) contains some distinctions in the form of question and answer, and HE 807 ends with a section on legal stratagems, (*ḥīla*).[162] The final sections of HE 807 and G 4185Y are quite different, and seem to be works added appended to the end of each respective manuscript.

---

157 Of these, I have only been unable to consult the copy in Baghdad. I rely on the brief description given by al-Sabīl, "*al-Muqaddima*," 1:30.

158 The Princeton and Damascus manuscripts have this exact title. The Istanbul and Berlin copies are titled *Kitāb al-Furūq fī l-fiqh.*

159 See Appendix III for the tables of contents of these manuscripts.

160 MS Halet Efendi 807, Suleymaniye Library, Istanbul, 7b l.16. See also Abū l-Ḥasanāt Muḥammad ibn ʿAbd al-Ḥayy al-Laknawī, *al-Fawāʾid al-bahiyya fī tarājim al-ḥanafiyya*, ed. Muḥammad Badr al-Dīn Abū Firās al-Naʿsānī (Cairo: Aḥmad Nājī l-Jamālī wa-Muḥammad Amīn al-Khānjī, 1905), 221.

161 MS Halet Efendi 807, 19b l.3.

162 MS Halet Efendi 807, 30b–33b.

Furūq-B is work is a book of legal distinctions normally titled *Kitāb al-Furūq*, occasionally attributed to an Abū Bakr Najm al-Dīn al-Naysabūrī.[163] The manuscript of this work in Leiden, Leiden Or. 481 (LO481), is one of the two works that Joseph Schacht relies on in his article on distinctions.[164] Besides the Leiden copy, I have identified seven other copies, all of which are held at the Süleymaniye Library in Istanbul: Giresun Yazmalar 44 (GY44), Halet Efendi 780 (HE780), Esad Efendi 884 (EE884), Esad Efendi 542 (EE 542), Aşir Efendi 453 (AE453), Osman Huldi 50 (OH50),[165] and Yazma Bağışlar 1187 (YB1187). These manuscripts are all in good condition and complete, they start with the *basmala* and seem to end without any missing pages.[166] The manuscripts in the category of *Furūq*-B exhibit a much higher degree of completeness and similarity than those of *Furūq*-A.[167]

The text itself does not reveal much about its author, other than his having been a Ḥanafī. The title pages for these works similarly lack information about the author. Two of these manuscripts, GY44 and LO481, attribute this work to a certain Najm al-Dīn ʿAlī l-Naysābūrī,[168] who cannot be identified with confidence.[169] This name consists of an honorific (*laqab*), a patronym, and a geographic marker. Further, while the author's honorific and geographic origin are given in three manuscripts, his patronym is given alternatively as "ibn Abī Bakr" and "ibn Bakr."[170] His death date is never mentioned, even though the au-

163 It is most easily recognized from its opening phrase, "Praise be to God, who guides us with Islam and commands us to submit to Him (*al-ḥamd lillāh alladhī hadānā bi-l-islām wa-amaranā bi-l-istislām*)," and the first distinction in the book, which begins, "When a man prays wearing an impure garment that is in his possession … (*rajul ṣallā fī thawb kāna ʿindahu ghayr ṭāhir*)."
164 See Schacht, "*Furūq*-Büchern."
165 This is listed in the catalog as *Furūq Ibn Nujaym*, which is the title written on the outer and inner cover of the manuscript.
166 The only partial exception is OH50, of which the top of the first page is missing, affecting the first eight lines of the text on the first folio.
167 See Appendix IV for tables of contents of these manuscripts.
168 In the bibliographies compiled by al-Bāḥusayn and al-Sabīl, his first name (*ism*) is added, and given as ʿAlī. They do not cite a source for this, but it is likely from Ismāʿīl Pāshā l-Baghdādī, *Kitāb Īḍāḥ al-maknūn fī l-dhayl ʿalā Kashf al-ẓunūn* (Istanbul: Millî Eğtim Basımevi, 1972), 1:232 and 2:188.
169 Scholars who have discussed this manuscript have also been at a loss when attempting to identify this individual See Peter Voorhoeve, *Handlist of Arabic Manuscripts in the University of Leiden and Other Collections in the Netherlands*, 2nd ed. (The Hague; Boston: Leiden University Press, 1980), 85; *GAL* S2:956; P. De Jong and M.J. De Goeje, *Catalogus Codicum Orientalium Bibliothecae Academiae Luguno Batavae*, vol. 4 (Leiden: Brill, 1861), 155; Schacht "*Furūq*-Büchern," 506; Kızılkaya, *İslâm Hukukunda Farklar*, 196–98.
170 For "ibn Abi Bakr," see LO 481; for "ibn Bakr," see GY 44.

thor's name is sometimes written multiple times on a single manuscript.[171] It is possible that the author was well-known when these manuscripts were copied, although such a supposition also raises questions about the reliability of the bibliographic sources. It is surprising that a work which is seemingly so popular has almost entirely escaped recent notice. For now, however, the author of this text remains a mystery.

Furūq-A and *Furūq*-B overlap considerably. Both are terse works, and *Furūq*-B, like *Furūq*-A, mentions just a few jurists, primarily Abū Ḥanīfa (d. 150/767), Abū Yūsuf (d. 182/798), and Muḥammad ibn al-Ḥasan al-Shaybānī (d. 189/804), and, less frequently, Muḥammad ibn Muqātil al-Rāzī (d. 248/862),[172] al-Ṭaḥāwī (d. 321/933),[173] Abū Bakr al-Iskāfī (d. 333/944),[174] Naṣīr ibn Yaḥyā (d. *ca.* 250/864)[175] and "al-Faqīh Abū l-Layth," presumably al-Samarqandī (d. *ca.* 383/993).[176] There are noteworthy similarities in content between *Furūq*-A and *Furūq*-B. The mentions of Ḥanafī authorities or books are rare; these texts assume the reader is already familiar with Ḥanafī doctrine. The similarities may be due to the fact that they are both short works of Ḥanafī legal distinctions. Alternatively, their similarities may signify that these works were written in a similar cultural context; that is, it may be that the two works may have been composed around the same time and for similar purposes.

Conclusion

This chapter establishes the corpus of works of legal distinctions, identifies the authors of these works, and traces their remaining records. While the number of works of legal distinctions is relatively limited, these works were compiled for much of Islamic history. The genre's vitality was reflected in both the composition of new works and the production of manuscripts of existing books.

This survey further suggests avenues for future study. For example, why did interest in works of legal distinctions even with dubious attribution, as exempli-

171 See LO 481.

172 GY 44, 4b, l. 7. Muḥammad ibn Muqātil was a student of Muḥammad al-Shaybānī, see Fuat Sezgin, *Geschichte des Arabischen Schrifttums*, 9 vols., (Leiden: Brill, 1967), 1:436.

173 GY 44, 6a, l.13.

174 GY 44, 10a, ll.3–4. The passage in which Abū Bakr al-Iskāf appears is found in GY 44 and HE 807, although he is not mentioned in HE 807.

175 GY 44, 10a l.9. The passage in which Naṣir ibn Yaḥya appears is found in GY 44 and HE 807.

176 GY 44, 30a l.15. The passage in which Abū l-Layth appears is found in GY 44 and HE 807, see Sezgin, *Geschichte des Arabischen Schriftums*, 1:445–50.

fied in particular by *Furūq*-A, *Furūq*-B, and the *Kitāb al-Furūq* attributed to Muḥammad ibn Ṣāliḥ al-Karābīsī, have such staying power in the Ottoman context? Ironically, this interest dovetailed with an almost complete lack of new works of legal distinction. Such a study may also yield insights into larger issues pertaining to the role of Islamic law in Ottoman-era intellectual culture.

Ibn Nujaym seems to be a central figure in the story of legal distinctions in the Ottoman Empire. He was an outsider in the Ottoman legal system, not having graduated from the Ottoman madrasa system. Nevertheless, as Guy Burak writes, his "*al-Asbāh wa'l-naẓā'ir* ... drew the attention of senior members of the Ottoman learned hierarchy and was eventually incorporated into the imperial jurisprudential canon."[177] Ibn Nujaym's *al-Ashbāh wa-l-Naẓā'ir* was eventually sanctioned as a part of the Ottoman canon by the chief mufti, Ebû's-Su'ûd (d. 982/1574). After receiving his blessing, "the text entered circulation, which means that it was taught within ... the imperial madrasa system."[178] Nevertheless, Ibn Nujaym's text was not universally admired, however, as Burak notes, "several members of the Ottoman learned hierarchy remained perplexed as to the status of *al-Ashbāh wa'l-naẓā'ir* in the decades following its completion and its approbation by Ebû-S'ûd."[179] As a canonical text for the Ottoman educational system, the final work of Ḥanafī legal distinctions was disseminated widely by Ottoman scholars. A look at the reception of and commentaries on the *al-Ashbāh wa-l-naẓā'ir* and particularly the sixth section on distinctions would be worthwhile.

Another line of inquiry could analyze the manuscript record more intensively. A richer history than the one undertaken herein could look into the ownership history of several manuscripts, thereby identifying who was interested in them and where and when they moved. Combined with the bio-bibliographical record and the general history of legal distinctions uncovered in the present study, this avenue could yield insights into the later history of Islamic law. An intellectual history based largely on manuscript evidence could also help us understand the social role that these texts had. What were the motivations behind textual production and textual spread?

In particular, *Furūq*-A and *Furūq*-B deserve greater scrutiny. There seems to be two strands of inquiry relevant to these texts. The first involves the relationship between these two works. Have these always been separate works? Did their textual traditions merge? Although the manuscripts categorized as *Furūq*-A vary considerably, at this point, there is sufficient reason to believe that they comprise

---

177 Guy Burak, *The Second Formation of Islamic Law: The Ḥanafī School in the Early Modern Ottoman Empire* (Cambridge: Cambridge University Press, 2015), 136.
178 Burak, *Second Formation*, 138–39.
179 Burak, *Second Formation*, 136, see also 137–39.

one work. There seems clearly to be a relationship between these two texts, but what is the nature of this relationship? The second strand involves what seems to be the widespread popularity of these two woks. *Furūq*-A and *Furūq*-B are as popular as any other work of legal distinction, yet they seem to challenge our assumptions about the importance of authorship for the spread and popularity of intellectual production.

Conclusion

This study has focused on the history of the genre of legal distinctions. It has shown that this genre was a small but significant component of the literature of Islamic law. It also demonstrated the value of genre as a framework for Islamic legal research. Through our analysis of this genre, we gained a great deal of insight into Islamic legal history. Some of the findings of this study reinforce already understood facts about the development of Islamic law, such as the close formal connections between the disciplines of law and grammar, the importance of the fifth/eleventh century as a turning point in the development of legal literature, and the importance of formalized disputation in advancing legal thought and legal writing. At the same time, however, it has made several new contributions to the study of Islamic legal history and suggested a few lines of future inquiry.

Perhaps the primary finding of this study is the close connection between changes in the social uses of Islamic legal knowledge and in the intellectual production of legal scholars. A sustained analysis of treatises of legal distinction has revealed a close connection between social history and the rhetoric of Islamic legal texts; this can be seen both in the performance of legal knowledge at formal disputations and the connections with the rise of the distinctions genre and with the performance of legal knowledge in *majālis* and the proliferation of riddles and the rhetoric of riddles. It was through a sustained focus on the genre of legal distinctions that we gained this insight into Islamic legal history. In this way, this book has demonstrated the relevance of genre as a productive framework for Islamic legal research.

In studying the genre of legal distinctions, an understanding of genre as a kind of Wittgensteinian language game was productive. The idea of genre as a language game takes genre as a recurring activity that is structured by rules but open to change over time.[1] The first three chapters of this book laid down some of the rules that govern the particular game that is the genre of legal distinctions. Some of these rules are readily apparent: organization by legal topic, the comparison of two or more apparently similar but different legal problems, the disconnected narrative between one comparison and another, and the wording of book titles. Other rules, however, were more clearly tied to developments in the public demand for particular presentations of knowledge. In part, the legal logic of comparison found in works of legal distinctions is directly tied

1 I discuss this idea in the Introduction, pp. 7–8. See also R. Kevin Jaques, *Authority, Conflict and the Transmission of Diversity in Medieval Islamic Law* (Leiden: Brill, 2002), 17–23.

https://doi.org/10.1515/9783110605792-009

to the institution of formalized disputation, as shown by the handbooks of disputation studied in Chapter Three. Moreover, the logic of legal distinctions is closely connected to the popularization of formal disputation among Muslim jurists in the fifth/eleventh century and the need for resources to participate successfully in these disputations. Similarly, the convergence between riddles and distinctions was fueled by the popularization and spread of *majālis* and the changing aesthetic preferences that accompanied the spread of *majālis*.

At the same time, however, the focus on the genre has also helped us to understand legal distinctions more clearly. In particular, we have seen how they have a life independent of their relationship with the concepts of legal maxims (*al-qawāʿid al-fiqhiyya*), legal purposes (*maqāṣid al-sharīʿa*), or *al-ashbāh wa-l-naẓāʾir*.[2] In other words, the term *al-furūq al-fiqhiyya* is more than just another term for other genres or concepts in Islamic law. Musa's statement that *al-ashbāh wa-l-naẓāʾir* is synonymous with *furūq* is based on a statement of equivalency between both terms first by Jalāl al-Dīn al-Suyūṭī (d. 911/1505) and later by Shihāb al-Dīn al-Ḥamawī (d. 1098/1687).[3] It is clear that these authors under-

---

2 The specific meaning of the phrase *al-ashbāh wa-l-naẓāʾir* remains unclear to me. There are several legal books titled *al-Ashbāh wa-l-naẓāʾir*, primarily by Shāfiʿī scholars, among them: Ibn al-Wakīl (d. 716/1317), Tāj al-Dīn ibn al-Subkī (d. 771/1370), and Jalāl al-Dīn al-Suyūṭī (d. 911/1505). Ibn Nujaym also wrote a work with this title. Does this phrase indicate a particular kind of legal genre? If so, what separates this legal genre from works of legal maxims (*qawāʿid*)? Perhaps this phrase refers to a particular kind of intellectual activity, but if so, what does it entail and when did it gain currency? Finally, what is the relationship, if any, between these legal works and the other lexicographic and linguistic works with similar titles, such as: *al-Ashbāh wa-l-naẓāʾir fī l-Qurʾān al-karīm* by Muqātil ibn Sulaymān (d. 150/767), *Alfāẓ al-ashbāh wa-l-naẓāʾir* attributed to Ibn al-Anbārī (d. 577/1181), *Kitāb al-Ashbāh wa-l-naẓāʾir min ashʿār al-mutaqaddimīn wa-l-jāhiliyya wa-l-mukhaḍramīn* by Abū ʿUthmān Saʿīd al-Khālidī (d. 350/961) and Abū Bakr Muḥammad al-Khālidī (d. 380/990), also known as the *Ḥamāsat al-Khālidiyayn*, and *Kashf al-sarāʾir fī maʿnā al-wujūh wa-l-ashbāh wa-l-naẓāʾir* by Ibn al-ʿImad (d. 887/1482). It should not be taken for granted that these lexicographic works themselves form a coherent unit. It does, however, seem likely that al-Suyūṭī's four-volume *al-Ashbāh wa-l-naẓāʾir fī l-naḥw* has some relationship with his legal work. Nevertheless, there are many questions about these works that still need to be addressed.

3 Jalāl al-Dīn l-Suyūṭī, *al-Ashbāh wa-l-naẓāʾir fī qawāʿid wa furūʿ al-shāfiʿiyyah*, ed. ʿAbd al-Karīm al-Faḍīlī (Beirut: Dār al-Kutub al-ʿIlmiyya, 1411/1990), 7 and Aḥmad ibn Muḥammad al-Ḥamawī, *Ghamz ʿuyūn al-baṣāʾir: Sharḥ Kitāb al-Ashbāh wa-l-naẓāʾir*, 4 vols., no ed. (Beirut: Dār al-Kutub al-ʿIlmiyya, 1405/1985), 489. Khadiga Musa has recently cited these statements as proof that "*al-ashbāh wa'l-naẓāʾir* is actually the science of *al-furūq*." While this statement may be true by the ninth/sixteenth, the history of *al-ashbāh wa-l-naẓāʾir* and the connection of that discipline to that of legal distinctions. Khadiga Musa, "Part One: The Genre of *al-Qawāʿid al-fiqhiyya*," in *A Critical Edition of ʿUmdat al-Nāẓir ʿalā al-Ashbāh wa'l-Naẓāʾir* by Abū l-Suʿūd al-Husaynī, ed. Khadiga Musa (Sheffield: Equinox, 2018), 14; *idem*, "Legal Maxims

stood *al-ashbāh wa-l-naẓā'ir* to somehow be equivalent to *al-furūq al-fiqhiyya*. It remains, however, that works of *al-ashbāh wa-l-naẓā'ir* cover much more material than just legal distinctions and that at least until the time of al-Suyūṭī, legal distinctions are not commonly referred to as *al-ashbāh wa-l-naẓā'ir*. It is, perhaps, more accurate to state that by the time al-Suyūṭī wrote his *al-Ashbāh wa-l-naẓā'ir*, that genre had come to be inextricably linked to legal distinctions. Indeed neither the *al-Ashbāh wa-l-naẓā'ir* of Ibn al-Wakīl (d. 716/1317) nor that of Ibn al-Subkī contain a discussion of legal distinctions.[4] The reason for this discrepancy is likely, as Musa suggests, that "discipline of *al-ashbāh wa-l-naẓā'ir* was not fully developed in Ibn al-Subkī's time."[5] Indeed, she also suggests that *al-Ashbāh wa-l-naẓā'ir* could also be seen as "the science of *al-qawā'id al-fiqhiyya*."[6] It is clear that more research is needed to understand the identity, contours, and function of these genres, and that genres and the rules that governed them shifted across time, as we saw with the case of legal distinctions and legal riddles.

This study demonstrates this change clearly for legal distinctions and for legal riddles. It should not be surprising to see Islamic legal literature change in response to shifting demands from reading publics. The changes documented here, however, are changes in the presentation or packaging of legal information, not necessarily substantive changes to the legal content itself. The changes described here should not be understood as mere aesthetic changes, but rather the aesthetic changes inform us about shifts in the consumption of Islamic legal knowledge. These findings suggest that an increased focus on genre as a historically contingent phenomenon—looking at genre as a concept and changes within individual genres—would likely contribute greatly to our understanding of Islamic law and legal development. Genre, at least in the post-formative period (after the fifth/eleventh c.), responded to the demand of consumers of legal knowledge and their interests likely contributed to formal innovation of ideas, reasoning strategies, and the organization of knowledge.

---

as a Genre of Islamic Law: Origins, Development, and Significance of *al-Qawā'id al-Fiqhiyya*," Islamic Law and Society 21 (2014), 334.

4 Muḥammad ibn Makkī ibn al-Wakīl, *al-Ashbāh wa-l-naẓā'ir fī fiqh al-shāfi'iyya*, ed. Muḥammad Ḥasan Muḥammad Ḥasan Ismā'īl (Beirut: Dār al-Kutub al-'Ilmiyyah, 2002); Tāj al-Dīn ibn al-Subkī, *al-Ashbāh wa-l-naẓā'ir*, 2 vols., ed. 'Ādil Aḥmad 'Abd al-Mawjūd and 'Alī Muḥammad 'Awaḍ (Beirut: Dār al-Kutub al-'Ilmiyya, 1411/1991).

5 Musa, "Legal Maxims," 338. Of course, one could also understand that *al-ashbāh wa-l-naẓā'ir* was simply constituted in a different way in the time al-Subkī, without understanding this difference as a lack.

6 Musa, "Legal Maxims," 339.

This study also contains a brief survey of lexicographic distinctions. Lexicographic distinctions have not received much scholarly attention, yet they can shed light on many issues important for understanding the development of Arabic philological practices. A more thorough analysis of the *Kitāb al-Furūq al-lughawiyya* by Abū Hilāl al-ʿAskarī is desirable. It seems likely that a contextualization of al-ʿAskarī's work would help shed light on the important connections between lexicography and theology. Al-ʿAskarī is a well-known figure (today) about whom not much is known (historically); a study of his work on lexicographical distinctions could be helpful in further understanding his theological views, which in turn may shed light on his other writings, and grant us new insights into the linguistic worldview of Muʿtazilite theology at the end of the fourth/tenth century.

Similarly, the history of lexicographical distinctions deserves further scrutiny. As understood in Chapter Two, lexicographical distinctions could be seen in two ways: as theological treatises on synonymy and as thesauruses concerned with proper usage. That chapter speculates that the thesauric aspect gave the genre longevity; nevertheless, it may be that works of lexicographical distinctions retained their theological resonances throughout their history. A study of the lexicographic distinction books by Jalāl al-Dīn al-Suyūṭī and İsmail Hakkı Bursevi may help in understanding Sunni theological developments in the early modern period.

Finally, the critical bibliography of the genre of legal distinctions raises questions about our understandings of the written traditions of Islamic law. As concerns legal distinctions, the prevalence of works with dubious or unknown authorship is high. It is not clear to me whether the popularity of such works is something particular to the genre of legal distinctions, or if other genres of legal literature also have various popular works with unclear authorship. This is a question that should be pursued as it may help to clarify the role and and the relationship between authorship and the possible production of anonymous study texts. Chapter Five showed the importance of claims to authorship in the bio-bibliographical tradition. Certain claims known to be erroneous, such as the existence of a *Talqīḥ al-Maḥbūbī* attributed to Asʿad al-Karābīsī, were nevertheless preserved in the bibliographic tradition. It appears that there may be a tension between the importance of authorship and the prevalence of works with no known author.

Appendix I: Bibliography of *Furūq* Works by *Madhhab*

Below in outline form is a comprehensive list of works on legal distinctions, which is based on my research into the genre of *al-furūq al-fiqhiyya*. It contains all of the published editions and manuscripts known to me. The outline is arranged by legal school (*madhhab*), and then chronologically by author within each school. Authors for whom death dates are unknown are listed last within each legal school. The footnotes for each main entry contain the relevant bibliographical information about the author and/or the work described. If printed editions discuss particular manuscripts, I include a reference to the description for the manuscript in a footnote. For the reasons noted in the main text, this survey includes *al-Furūq* by al-Qarāfī and *al-Ashbāh wa-l-naẓā'ir* by Ibn al-Nujaym, but does not mention their manuscripts or editions. All other works are treated in detail.

Shāfiʿī

1. *Al-Furūq* by Abū l-ʿAbbās Aḥmad ibn ʿUmar ibn Surayj al-Shāfiʿī (d. 306/918).[1]
   a. Not extant.

---

1 Wolfhart Heinrichs, "Structuring the Law: Remarks on the *Furūq* Literature," in *Studies in Honour of Clifford Edmund Bosworth Volume I: Hunter of the East; Arabic and Semitic Studies*, ed. Ian Richard Netton (Leiden: Brill, 2000), 342; Yaʿqūb ibn ʿAbd al-Wahhāb al-Bāḥusayn, *al-Furūq al-fiqhiyya wa-l-uṣūliyya: muqawwamātuhā shurūṭuhā nash'atuhā taṭawwuruhā; dirāsa naẓariyya waṣfiyya tārīkhiyya* (Riyadh: Maktabat al-Rushd, 1419/1998), 68, 72–73, 84; ʿUmar ibn Muḥammad ibn ʿAbdallāh al-Sabīl, "*al-Muqaddima*," in ʿAbd al-Raḥīm ibn ʿAbdallāh al-Zarīrānī, *Īḍāḥ al-dalā'il fī l-farq bayn al-masā'il*, ed. ʿUmar ibn Muḥammad ibn ʿAbdallāh al-Sabīl (Mecca: Wizārat al-Taʿlīm al-ʿĀlī, Jāmiʿat Umm al-Qurā, Maʿhad al-Buḥūth al-ʿIlmiyya wa-Iḥyā' al-Turāth al-Islāmī, 1414/1993), 1:34; Ḥājjī Khalīfa, *Kashf al-ẓunūn ʿan asāmī l-kutub wa-l-funūn*, 2 vols., ed. Şerefettin Yaltkaya and Kilisi Rifat Bilge (Istanbul: Milli Eğitim Basımevi, 1971), s.v. "*al-Furūq fī furūʿ al-shāfiʿiyya*," 2:1257–58; Joseph Schacht, "Aus zwei arabischen *Furūq*-Büchern," *Islamica* 2 (1926), 509; ʿUmar Riḍā Kaḥḥāla, *Muʿjam al-mu'allifīn: Tarājim muṣannifī l-kutub al-ʿarabiyya*, 4 vols. (Damascus: Mu'assasat al-Risāla, 1376/1957), 1:218, no. 1596; Tāj al-Dīn al-Subkī, *Ṭabaqāt al-shāfiʿiyya l-kubrā*, 10 vols, ed. ʿAbd al-Fattāḥ Muḥammad Ḥulw and Maḥmūd Muḥammad al-Tannāḥī (Cairo: Dār Iḥyā' ʿUlūm al-ʿArabiyya, 1994), 3:21–39, no. 85; Abū Isḥāq al-Shīrāzī, *Ṭabaqāt al-fuqahā'*, ed. Iḥsān ʿAbbās (Beirut: Dār al-Rā'id al-ʿArabī, 1970), 108–109; Jamāl al-Dīn al-Asnawī, *Ṭabaqāt al-shāfiʿiyya*, 2 vols., ed. Kamāl Yūsuf al-Ḥūt (Beirut: Dār al-Kutub al-ʿIlmiyya, 1407/1987), 1:311, no. 593; Shihāb al-Dīn ʿAbd al-Ḥayy ibn Aḥmad ibn al-ʿImād, *Shadharāt al-dhahab fī akhbār man dhahab*, 10 vols., ed. ʿAbd al-Qādir al-Arnā'ūṭ and Maḥmūd al-Arnā'ūṭ (Damascus: Dār Ibn Kathīr, 1406/1986–1414/1993), 4:29–31; Ibn Qāḍī Shuhba, *Ṭabaqāt al-shāfiʿiyya*, 4 vols., ed. al-Ḥāfiẓ ʿAbd al-ʿAlīm Khān (Beirut: Dār al-Kutub al-ʿIlmiyya, 1407[/1986]), 1:89–91, no. 35.

https://doi.org/10.1515/9783110605792-010

2. *Kitāb al-masāʾil wa-l-ʿilal wa-l-furūq* by Abū l-Ḥasan ʿAlī ibn Aḥmad al-Nasawī (d. *ca* 320/932).[2]
   a. Not extant.

3. *Al-Kifāya fī l-furūq wa-l-laṭāʾif* by Abū ʿAbdallāh al-Ḥusayn ibn ʿAbdallāh al-Ṭabarī (d. *ca.* fifth/eleventh c.).[3]
   a. Not extant.

4. *Al-Jamʿ wa-l-farq* by Abū Muḥammad ʿAbdallāh ibn Yūsuf al-Juwaynī l-Shāfiʿī (d. 438/1047).[4]
   a. Alternate Titles:
      i. *Al-Furūq*
      ii. *Al-Wasāʾil fī furūq al-masāʾil.*[5]
   b. Editions:
      i. *Al-Jamʿ wa-l-farq*. Edited by ʿAbd al-Raḥmān ibn Salāma ibn ʿAbdallāh al-Mazīnī. 3 volumes. Beirut: Dār al-Jīl, 2004.
      ii. Partial edition: Edited by ʿAbd al-Raḥmān al-Mazīnī. MA Thesis, Sharīʿa College, Imām Muḥammad ibn Saʿūd Islamic University, 1405/1406.[6]
   c. MSS:

---

2 Heinrichs, "Structuring the Law," 342; Schacht, "*Furūq*-Büchern," 509; Ibn al-Nadīm, *al-Fihrist li-l-Nadīm*, 2 vols., ed. Ayman Fuʾād Sayyid (London: Muʾassasat al-Furqān li-l-Turāth al-ʿArabī, 1430/2009), 2.1:55.

3 The author of this work is Abū ʿAbdallāh al-Ḥusayn ibn ʿAbdallāh al-Ṭabarī. This is confirmed by all of the biographies of al-Ḥusayn ibn ʿAbdallāh, with the exception of that written by Abū Isḥāq al-Shīrāzī, who does not mention this work. See al-Bāḥusayn, *al-Furūq al-fiqhiyya*, 90–91; Ibn Qāḍī Shuhba, *Ṭabaqāt*, 1:181, no. 142; al-Asnawī, *Ṭabaqāt*, 2:61–62, no. 767; al-Shīrāzī, *Ṭabaqāt*, 126. Other sources, however, attribute this work to Abū ʿAbdallāh al-Ḥusayn ibn Muḥammad ibn al-Ḥasan al-Ḥannāṭī l-Ṭabarī (d. *ca* 495/1101–02), see al-Sabīl, "*al-Muqaddima*," 1:37; Kaḥḥāla, *Muʿjam al-muʾallifīn*, 1:636, no. 4795; Ḥājjī Khalīfa, *Kashf al-ẓunūn*, s.v. "*al-Furūq fī furūʿ al-shāfiʿiyya*," 2:1499; Ismāʿīl Bāshā l-Baghdādī, *Hadiyat al-ʿārifīn: Asmāʾ al-muʾallifīn wa-āthār al-muṣannifīn*, 2 vols. (Beirut: Dār Iḥyāʾ al-Turāth al-ʿArabī, n.d.), 1:311. These sources, however, are all late. Earlier biographies of al-Ḥannāṭī do not attribute this work to him, see Ibn Qāḍī Shuhba, *Ṭabaqāt*, 1:179–81, no. 141; al-Subkī, *Ṭabaqāt*, 4:367–71, no. 397; al-Asnawī, *Ṭabaqāt*, 1:193–94, no. 362; al-Shīrāzī, *Ṭabaqāt*, 118.

4 Heinrichs, "Structuring the Law," 342; al-Bāḥusayn, *al-Furūq al-fiqhiyya*, 87; al-Sabīl, "*al-Muqaddima*," 1:35–36; Najm al-Dīn al-Ṭūfī, *ʿAlam al-jadhal fī ʿilm al-jadal*, ed. Wolfhart Heinrichs (Wiesbaden: Franz Steiner Verlag, 1408/1987), 73; Ḥājjī Khalīfa, *Kashf al-ẓunūn*, s.v. "*al-Jamʿ wa-l-farq*," 1:601 and s.v. "*al-Furūq fī furūʿ al-shāfiʿiyya*," 2:1258; *GAL* 1:385–86, S1:667; Kaḥḥāla, *Muʿjam*, 2:307, no. 8443; Ibn al-ʿImād, *Shadharāt al-dhahab*, 5:176–77; al-Asnawī, *Ṭabaqāt*, 1:165–66, no. 305; Ibn al-Subkī, *Ṭabaqāt*, 5:73–94, no. 439; Badr al-Dīn al-Zarkashī, *al-Manthūr fī l-qawāʿid*, 3 vols., ed. Taysīr Fāʾiq Aḥmad Maḥmūd and ʿAbd al-Sattār Abū Ghudda (Kuwait: Wizārat al-Awqāf wa-l-Shuʾūn al-Islāmiyya, 1402/1982), 1:69; Ibn Qāḍī Shuhba, *Ṭabaqāt*, 1:209–11, no. 171.

5 MS Garrett 824H, Princeton University Library, Princeton.

6 Al-Bāḥusayn, *al-Furūq al-fiqhiyya*, 87.

i. Cairo, Dār al-Kutub al-Miṣriyya, 1504 Fiqh Shāfiʿī, n.d.[7]
ii. Cairo, al-Maktaba l-Azhariyya, 81 *fiqh shāfiʿī*, n.d.[8]
iii. Cairo, al-Maktaba l-Azhariyya, 890 *fiqh shāfiʿī*, n.d.[9]
iv. Dublin, Chester Beatty 4613, copied 786/1384.[10]
v. Istanbul, Süleymaniye Kütüphanesi, Aşir Efendi 146, n.d.[11]
vi. Istanbul, Suleymaniye Kutuphanesi, Turkhān v Sultan 146, eighth C / fourteenth C.[12]
vii. Princeton, Princeton University Library Garrett 824H, 1099/1687.

5. *Al-Wasāʾil fī furūq al-masāʾil* by Abū l-Khayr Salāma ibn Ismāʿīl ibn Jamāʿa l-Maqdisī l-Shāfiʿī (d. 480/1087–88).[13]
   a. Not extant.

6. *Al-Muʿāyāt* by Abū l-ʿAbbās Aḥmad ibn Muḥammad al-Jurjānī l-Shāfiʿī (d. 482/1089–90).[14]
   a. Alternate titles:
      i. *Al-Furūq*
      ii. *Al-Muʿāyāt fī l-ʿaql*
      iii. *Al-Muʿāyāt fī l-fiqh*
      iv. *Al-Muʿāyāt wa-l-imtiḥān*
   b. Editions:
      i. *Kitāb al-Muʿāyāt fī l-fiqh*. Edited by Ibrāhīm ibn Nāṣir al-Bashar. PhD Diss., Jāmiʿat Umm al-Qurā, 1415[/1994].
      ii. *Al-Muʿāyāt fī l-ʿaql aw al-Furūq*. Edited by Muḥammad Fāris. Beirut: Dār al-Kutub al-ʿIlmiyya, 1993.

---

7 ʿAbd al-Raḥmān ibn Salāma ibn ʿAbdallāh al-Mazīnī, "*al-Bāb al-thānī fī dirāsat al-kitāb*," in Abū Muḥammad ʿAbdallāh ibn Yūsuf al-Juwaynī, *al-Jamʿ wa-l-farq*, ed. ʿAbd al-Raḥmān ibn Salāma ibn ʿAbdallāh al-Mazīnī (Beirut: Dār al-Jīl, 2004), 1:35.

8 Al-Mazīnī, "*al-Bāb al-thānī*," 1:36.

9 Al-Mazīnī, "*al-Bāb al-thānī*," 1:36.

10 Al-Mazīnī, "*al-Bāb al-thānī*," 1:35–36.

11 In *GAL* S1:673 incorrectly attributed to Imām al-Ḥaramayn al-Juwaynī.

12 Al-Mazīnī, "*al-Bāb al-thānī*," 1:35.

13 Al-Bāḥusayn, *al-Furūq al-fiqhiyya*, 88–89; al-Sabīl, "*al-Muqaddima*," 1:36. *GAL* S1:505; Kaḥḥāla, *Muʿjam*, 1:772, no. 5741; al-Asnawī, *Ṭabaqāt*, 2:218, no. 1069; al-Zarkashī, *al-Manthūr*, 1:69; al-Ṭūfī, *ʿAlam al-jadhal*, 73; Ibn Qāḍī Shuhba, *Ṭabaqāt*, 1:245, no. 207; Ḥājjī Khalīfa, *Kashf al-ẓunūn*, 1:2007–2008; Ibn al-Subkī, *Ṭabaqāt*, 7:99, no. 794.

14 Heinrichs, "Structuring the Law," 342; al-Bāḥusayn, *al-Furūq al-fiqhiyya*, 89–90; al-Sabīl, "*al-Muqaddima*," 36–37; Kaḥḥāla, *Muʿjam*, 1:241, no. 1747; *GAL* S1:505; Ibn al-Subkī, *Ṭabaqāt*, 4:74–76, no. 271; al-Ziriklī, *Aʿlām* 1:214; Ḥājjī Khalīfa, *Kashf al-ẓunūn* s.v. "*al-Muʿāyāt fī l-ʿaql*," 2:1730; Ibn Qāḍī Shuhba *Ṭabaqāt* 1:260, no. 222; al-Asnawī, *Ṭabaqāt*, 1:165, no. 306.

c. MSS:
   i. Cairo, Dār al-Kutub al-Miṣriyya 915 *Fiqh Shāfiʿī*, Shaʿbān 586 / 3 September – 2 October 1190.[15]
   ii. Cairo, Dār al-Kutub al-Miṣriyya, Fiqh Shāfiʿī Ṭalaʿat 112, n.d.[16]
   iii. Rabat, al-Khizāna l-Malikiyya 913 *dāl*, n.d.

7. *Al-Furūq* by Abū l-Maḥāsin ʿAbd al-Wāḥid ibn Ismāʿīl al-Rūyānī l-Ṭabarī l-Shāfiʿī (d. 501/1107 or 502/1108).[17]
   a. Not Extant.

8. *Al-Fuṣūl wa-l-furūq* by Abū l-ʿAbbās Najm al-Dīn Aḥmad ibn Muḥammad ibn Khalaf ibn Rājiḥ al-Maqdisī l-Ḥanbalī, al-Shāfiʿī (d. 638/1241).[18]
   a. Not Extant.

9. *Al-Furūq* by Abū l-ʿAbbās Kamāl al-Dīn Aḥmad ibn Kashāsib al-Shāfiʿī l-Dizmārī (d. 643/1245).[19]
   a. Not Extant.

10. *Al-Jamʿ wa-l-farq* by Sirāj al-Dīn Yūnus ibn ʿAbd al-Majīd ibn ʿAlī l-Hudhalī l-Armantī l-Shāfiʿī (d. 725/1325).[20]
   a. Not Extant.

---

15 Ibrāhim ibn Nāṣir ibn Ibrāhīm al-Bashar, "*al-Muqaddima*," in Abū l-ʿAbbās Aḥmad ibn Muḥammad al-Jurjānī, *al-Muʿāyāt fī l-fiqh*, ed. Ibrāhīm ibn Nāṣir ibn Ibrāhīm al-Bashar (PhD Diss., Jāmiʿat Umm al-Qurā, 1415[/1994]), 109. This manuscript was previously cataloged under 1569 *ʿumūmī*, and 915 *khuṣūṣī*.

16 Al-Bashar, "*al-Muqaddima*," 110–11.

17 Al-Bāḥusayn, *al-Furūq al-fiqhiyya*, 92; al-Sabīl, "*al-Muqaddima*," 1:37. Al-Bāḥusayn says that this book must be similar to al-Jurjānī's *al-Muʿāyāt* since al-Subkī cites them together in his *al-Ashbāh w-al-naẓāʾir*. See also Ibn al-Subkī, *Ṭabaqāt*, 7:193–204, no. 901; al-Asnawī, *Ṭabaqāt*, 1:272, no. 518; Kaḥḥāla, *Muʿjam*, 2:332, no. 8626; Ibn al-ʿImād, *Shadharāt al-dhahab*, 6:8; al-Ziriklī, *al-Aʿlām*, 4:175; Ibn Qāḍī Shuhba, *Ṭabaqāt*, 1:287, no. 256.

18 Heinrichs, "Structuring the Law," 343; al-Bāḥusayn, *al-Furūq al-fiqhiyya*, 95; al-Sabīl, "*al-Muqaddima*," 1:37. This scholar was first a Ḥanbalī but later became a Shāfiʿī. This work seems not to be extant, but I believe it is a work in the Shāfiʿī tradition since it is cited in Badr al-Dīn al-Zarkashī, *al-Baḥr al-muḥīṭ fī uṣūl al-fiqh*, no ed. (Cairo: Dār al-Kutubī, 1414/1994), 7:220; 7:245; 7:394; and 8:38; See also al-Asnawī, *Ṭabaqāt*, 1:211–12, no. 404; Ibn Qādī Shuhba, *Ṭabaqāt*, 2:71, no. 371; Ibn al-ʿImād, *Shadharāt al-dhahab*, 7:331; Kaḥḥāla, *Muʿjam*, 1:262–63, no. 1896.

19 Al-Bāḥusayn, *al-Furūq al-fiqhiyya*, 95–96; al-Sabīl, "*al-Muqaddima*," 1:37; Ibn al-Subkī, *Ṭabaqāt*, 8:30, no. 1054; al-Asnawī, *Ṭabaqāt*, 1:152, no. 289; Ibn Qāḍī Shuhba, *Ṭabaqāt*, 2:100, no. 401; Kaḥḥāla, *Muʿjam*, 1:232, no. 1695.

20 Al-Bāḥusayn, *al-Furūq al-fiqhiyya*, 96–97; al-Sabīl, "*al-Muqaddima*," 1:37; Ibn al-Subkī, *Ṭabaqāt*, 10:430–33, no. 1419; al-Asnawī, *Ṭabaqāt*, 1:85–86, no. 149; Ibn al-ʿImād, *Shadharāt al-dhahab*, 8:125–26; Kaḥḥāla, *Muʿjam*, 2:193, no. 18608; Ḥājjī Khalīfa, *Kashf al-ẓunūn*, 1:601; Ibn Qāḍī Shuhba, *Ṭabaqāt*, 2:301–302, no. 574.

11. *Al-Furūq* by Abū Umāma Shams al-Dīn Muḥammad ibn ʿAlī ibn ʿAbd al-Wāḥid ibn Yaḥyā l-Dukkālī l-Maghribī l-Miṣrī l-Shāfiʿī, Ibn al-Naqqāsh (d. 763/1361).[21]
    a. Not Extant.
    b. Alternate Titles:
        i. *Kitāb al-Farq.*[22]
        ii. *Al-Naẓāʾir wa-l-furūq.*[23]

12. *Maṭāliʿ al-daqāʾiq fī taḥrīr al-jawāmiʿ wa-l-fawāriq* by Jamāl al-Dīn ʿAbd al-Raḥīm ibn al-Ḥasan al-Asnawī l-Shāfiʿī (d. 772/1370).[24]
    a. Editions:
        i. *Maṭāliʿ al-daqāʾiq fī taḥrīr al-jawāmiʿ wa-l-fawāriq.* Edited by Naṣr Farīd Muḥammad Wāṣil. Cairo: Dār al-Shurūq, 2007.[25]
    b. MSS:
        i. Baghdad, Maktabat al-Awqāf, 3959, n.d.[26]
        ii. Cairo, Dār al-Kutub al-Miṣriyya, 277 Fiqh Shāfiʿī, 19 Rabīʿ II 862 / 6 March 1457.[27]
        iii. Cairo, Dār al-Kutub al-Miṣriyya 901 Fiqh Shāfiʿī, n.d.[28]
        iv. Cairo, Dār al-Kutub al-Miṣriyya, 1431 Fiqh Shāfiʿī, n.d.[29]
        v. Cairo, Dār al-Kutub al-Miṣriyya, 372 Uṣūl al-fiqh, n.d.[30]

---

21 Heinrichs, "Structuring the Law," 342; al-Bāḥusayn, *al-Furūq al-fiqhiyya*, 99–100; al-Sabīl, "*al-Muqaddima*," 1:38; Ḥājjī Khalīfa, *Kashf al-ẓunūn*, s.v. "*al-Furūq fī furūʿ al-shāfiʿiyya*," 2:1258; Shihāb al-Dīn Aḥmad ibn ʿAlī ibn Muḥammad ibn Ḥajar al-ʿAsqalānī, *al-Durar al-Kāmina fī aʿyān al-miʾa l-thāmina*, no ed. (Beirut: Dār Iḥyāʾ al-Turāth al-ʿArabī, [197–]), 4:71–74; Ibn Qāḍī Shuhba, *Ṭabaqāt*, 3:131–32, no. 670; Ibn al-ʿImād, *Shadharāt al-dhahab*, 8:338; Kaḥḥāla, *Muʿjam*, 3:521, no. 14780; al-Ziriklī, *al-Aʿlām*, 6:286; al-Baghdādī, *Hadiyat al-ʿārifīn*, 2:162; *GAL* S2:348.

22 Al-Baghdādī, *Hadiyat al-ʿārifīn*, 2:162; Ibn al-ʿImād, *Shadharāt al-dhahab*, 8:338.

23 Ibn al-ʿImād, *Shadharāt al-dhahab*, 8:339; Ibn Qāḍī Shuhba, *Ṭabaqāt*, 3:132; Kaḥḥāla, *Muʿjam*, 3:521.

24 Heinrichs, "Structuring the Law," 343; al-Bāḥusayn, *al-Furūq al-fiqhiyya*, 100; al-Sabīl, "*al-Muqaddima*," 1:38; *GAL* 2:90–91, S2:107; Ḥājjī Khalīfa, *Kashf al-ẓunūn*, s.v. "*al-Furūq fī l-furūʿ al-shāfiʿiyya*," 2:1258; *ibid.* s.v. "*Maṭāliʿ al-daqāʾiq*," 2:1718; Ibn al-ʿImād, *Shadharāt al-dhahab*, 8:383–84; Schacht, "*Furūq*-Büchern," 510; Ibn Qāḍī Shuhba, *Ṭabaqāt*, 3:98–101, no. 648.

25 According to al-Bāḥusayn, Naṣr Farīd Muḥammad Wāṣil produced a study and edition of this work as his PhD Dissertation from al-Azhar University in 1392/1972–73 (al-Bāḥusayn, *al-Furūq al-fiqhiyya*, 100). The Dār al-Shurūq printing is likely the publication of his dissertation.

26 Abū l-Ajfān and Abū Fāris, "*Dirāsa*," 41.

27 Naṣr Farīd Muḥammad Wāṣil, "*Dirāsa*" in Jamāl al-Dīn ʿAbd al-Raḥīm ibn al-Ḥasan al-Asnawī, *Maṭāliʿ al-daqāʾiq fī taḥrīr al-jawāmiʿ wa-l-fawāriq*, 2 vols., ed. Naṣr Farīd Muḥammad Wāṣil (Cairo: Dār al-Shurūq, 2007), 1:17–18.

28 Wāṣil, "*Dirāsa*," 1:19–20.

29 Wāṣil, "*Dirāsa*," 1:18.

30 Wāṣil, "*Dirāsa*," 1:18–19.

vi. Cairo, Khizānat Makhṭūṭāt al-Jāmiʿ al-Azhar, 477 Fiqh Shāfiʿī, n.d.[31]
vii. Istanbul, Suleymaniye Kutuphanesi, Murat Molla 1054, 874/1469–70.

13. *Kitāb al-Furūq* by Anonymous (d. ?).
    a. MS:
        i. London, MS Oriental 6278, British Library, 18 Dhī l-Ḥijja, 854 / January 22, 1451.

Ḥanafī

1. *Al-Furūq* by Abū l-Faḍl Muḥammad ibn Ṣāliḥ al-Karābīsī l-Ḥanafī (d. 322/933–34).[32]
    a. Editions:
        i. *Kitāb al-Furūq*. Edited by ʿAbd al-Muḥsin Saʿīd Aḥmad al-Zahrānī. Ph.D Diss., Jāmiʿat Umm al-Qurā, 1418/1997.
    b. MSS:
        i. Baghdad, Maktabat al-Awqāf, 3533, n.d.[33]
        ii. Berlin, Staatsbibliothek zu Berlin, Or. 5013, 1025/1616.
        iii. Cairo, Dār al-Kutub al-Miṣriyya; Fiqh Ḥanafī 1923, after 1003/1595.
        iv. Cairo, Maktabat al-Azhar 2076 Rāfiʿī 26, Fiqh Ḥanafī 915, 1052/1642.
        v. Istanbul, Suleymaniye, Ahmet III 1181, 1003/1595.[34]
        vi. Istanbul, Suleymaniye, Feyzullah Efendi, 921, 9th/15th century (?).[35]

2. *Al-Ajnās wa-l-furūq* by Abū ʿAbbās Aḥmad ibn Muḥammad ibn ʿUmar al-Nāṭifī l-Ṭabarī l-Ḥanafī (d. 446/1054–55).[36]
    a. MSS:
        i. Istanbul, Suleymaniye Kutuphanesi, Esad Efendi 532.[37]
        ii. Istanbul, Suleymaniye Kutuphanesi, Nuruosmaniye 1372.[38]

---

31 Wāṣil, "*Dirāsa*," 1:20.

32 Heinrichs, "Structuring the Law," 341; al-Bāḥusayn, *al-Furūq al-fiqhiyya*, 69, 74, 84; al-Sabīl, "*al-Muqaddima*," 28; Ḥājjī Khalīfa, *Kashf al-ẓunūn* s.v. "*al-Furūq fī furūʿ al-ḥanafiyya*," 2:1257; *GAL* 1:442–43, S1:295; Kaḥḥāla, *Muʿjam*, 3:355, no. 13711; Schacht, "*Furūq*-Büchern," 508; al-Ziriklī, *al-Aʿlām*, 6:162; al-Baghdādī, *Hadiyat al-ʿārifīn*, 2:33.

33 Heinrichs, "Structuring the Law," 341.

34 Heinrichs, "Structuring the Law," 341.

35 Heinrichs, "Structuring the Law," 341.

36 Heinrichs, "Structuring the Law," 341; al-Bāḥusayn, *al-Furūq al-fiqhiyya*, 88; al-Sabīl, "*al-Muqaddima*," 1:28; al-Laknawī, *al-Fawāʾid al-bahiyya*, 36; Kaḥḥāla, *Muʿjam*, 1:287, no. 2086; Ḥājjī Khalīfa, *Kashf al-ẓunūn*, s.v. "*al-Ajnās fī l-furūʿ*," 1:11; *GAL* 1:372, S1:636; Ibn Quṭlūbughā, *Tāj al-tarājim*, 6–7, no. 12; al-Qurashī, *al-Jawāhir al-muḍiyya*, 1:297–98, no. 221; al-Ziriklī, *al-Aʿlām* 1:213; Taqī l-Dīn ibn ʿAbd al-Qādir al-Tamīmī l-Dārī, *al-Ṭabaqāt al-saniyya fī ṭabaqāt al-ḥanafiyya*, 4 vols., ed. ʿAbd al-Fattāḥ Muḥammad Ḥulw (Riyadh: Dār al-Rifāʿī, 1983), 2:71–72, no. 343.

37 Al-Sabīl, "*al-Muqaddima*," 1:28.

38 Al-Sabīl, "*al-Muqaddima*," 1:28.

3. *Al-Furūq* by Abū l-Muẓaffar As'ad ibn Muḥammad ibn al-Ḥusayn al-Naysābūrī l-Karābīsī l-Ḥanafī (d. 570/1174–75).[39]
   a. Editions:
      i. *Al-Furūq li-l-Karābīsī*. Muḥammad Ṭumūm and 'Abd al-Sattār Abū Ghudda. 2 vols. Kuwait: Wizārat al-Awqāf wa-l-Shu'ūn al-Islāmiyya, 1402/1982.
      ii. *Al-Furūq fī l-furū' fī fiqh al-Imām Abī Ḥanīfa l-Nu'mān raḍiya Allāh 'anhu*. Printed with *Ikhtilāf Abī Ḥanīfa wa-Ibn Abī Laylā* by Abū Yūsuf Ya'qūb ibn Ibrāhīm al-Anṣārī and *Tarjamat Abī Ḥanīfa wa-Abī Yūsuf wa-Muḥammad ibn al-Ḥasan al-Shaybānī* by Abū 'Abdallāh Muḥammad ibn Aḥmad al-Dhahabī. Edited by Aḥmad Farīd al-Mazīdī. Beirut: Dār al-Kutub al-'Ilmiyya, 1426/2005.
      iii. *Kitāb al-Furūq*. Edited by Muḥammad Ṭumūm. Cairo: Dār al-Salām, 1433/2012.
   b. MSS:
      i. Cairo, Dār al-Kutub al-Miṣriyya, 292 *fiqh ḥanafī*, n.d.[40]
      ii. Cairo, Dār al-Kutub al-Miṣriyya, 293 *fiqh ḥanafī*, 622/.[41]
      iii. Istanbul, Suleymaniye Kutuphanesi, Carullah 821, 1007/1598–99.[42]
      iv. Istanbul, Suleymaniye Kutuphanesi, Fatih 2039, 776/1374–75.

4. *Talqīḥ al-'uqūl fī furūq al-manqūl* by Aḥmad ibn 'Ubayd Allāh ibn Ibrāhīm al-Maḥbūbī l-Ḥanafī, also known as Ṣadr al-Sharī'a l-Awwal (d. 630/1232–33).[43]
   a. Alternate titles:
      i. *Kitāb talqīḥ al-'uqūl fī l-furūq bayn ahl al-nuqūl.*
   b. Editions:

---

39 Heinrichs, "Structuring the Law," 341; al-Bāḥusayn, *al-Furūq al-fiqhiyya*, 91–92; al-Sabīl, "*al-Muqaddima*," 1:28–29; Ḥājjī Khalīfa, *Kashf al-ẓunūn*, s.v. "*al-Furūq fī furū' al-ḥanafiyya*," 2:1257; *GAL* 1:375, S1:642; Kaḥḥāla, *Mu'jam*, 1:351, no. 2603; Schacht, "*Furūq*-Büchern," 506–508; al-Qurashī, *Jawāhir al-muḍiyya*, 1:386, no. 314; Ibn al-'Imād, *Shadharāt al-dhahab*, 4:4; al-Tamīmī l-Dārī, *Ṭabaqāt al-saniyya*, 2:181, no. 473; al-Baghdādī, *Hadiyat al-'ārifīn*, 1:204; Ibn Quṭlūbughā, *Tāj al-tarājim*, 12, no. 44.

40 Muḥammad Ṭumūm, "*Muqaddimat al-taḥqīq*," in *al-Furūq li-l-Karābīsī* by As'ad ibn Muḥammad al-Karābīsī, ed. Muḥammad Ṭumūm (Kuwait: Wizārat al-Awqāf wa-l-Shu'ūn al-Islāmiyya, 1982), 1:23–24.

41 Ṭumūm, "*Muqaddimat al-taḥqīq*," 23.

42 Schacht, "*Furūq*-Büchern," 508.

43 Heinrichs, "Structuring the Law," 341; al-Bāḥusayn, *al-Furūq al-fiqhiyya*, 94; al-Sabīl, "*al-Muqaddima*," 1:29; Ḥājjī Khalīfa, *Kashf al-ẓunūn*, s.v. "*Talqīḥ al-'uqūl fī furūq al-manqūl*," 1:481 and s.v. "*al-Furūq fī furū' al-ḥanafiyya*," 2:1257; *GAL* 1:380; Kaḥḥāla, *Mu'jam*, 1:191, no. 1415; Ibn Quṭlūbughā, *Tāj al-tarājim*, 9, no. 29; al-Qurashī, *Jawāhir al-muḍiyya* 1:196, no. 137; al-Tamīmī l-Dārī, *Ṭabaqāt al-saniyya*, 1:364, no. 208; al-Baghdādī, *Hadiyat al-'ārifīn* 1:204. Interestingly, *al-Ṭabaqāt al-saniyya* lists two works with this title by two different authors, Shihāb al-Dīn Aḥmad ibn 'Abdallāh ibn Ibrāhīm al-Maḥbūbī (al-Tamīmī l-Dārī, *Ṭabaqāt al-saniyya*, 1:364, no. 208) and Aḥmad ibn 'Ubayd Allāh ibn Ibrāhīm ibn Aḥmad ibn 'Abd al-Malik ibn 'Umar ibn 'Abd al-'Azīz ibn Muḥammad ibn Ja'far ibn Hārūn ibn Muḥammad ibn Aḥmad ibn Maḥbūb ibn al-Walīd ibn 'Ibāda, al-Imām Shams al-A'imma l-Maḥbūbī l-Bukhārī (al-Tamīmī l-Dārī, *Ṭabaqāt al-saniyya*, 1:376, no. 220).

i. *Kitāb Talqīḥ al-ʿuqūl fī furūq al-manqūl li-Shams al-Dīn Aḥmad ibn ʿUbayd Allāh al-Maḥbūbī Ṣadr al-Sharīʿa l-Awwal dirāsa wa-taḥqīq*, ed. ʿAbd al-Hādī Shīr al-Afghānī, MA Thesis, Cairo University, 1984.[44]

c. MSS:
   i. Berlin, Staatsbibliothek zu Berlin, Landberg 264, 1100/1688.[45]
   ii. Cairo, Dār al-Kutub al-Miṣriyya Fiqh Ḥanafī 982, n.d.
   iii. Istanbul, İstanbul Millet Kütüphanesi, Feyzullah Efendi 920, 1003/1594–95.
   iv. Istanbul, Suleymaniye Kutuphanesi, Beyazid 1903, n.d.
   v. Istanbul, Suleymaniye Kutuphanesi, Carullah 604, n.d.
   vi. Istanbul, Suleymaniye Kutuphanesi, Haci Mehmud Efendi 984, 995/1586–87.
   vii. Istanbul, Suleymaniye Kutuphanesi, Murat Molla 1009.
   viii. Istanbul, Suleymaniye Kutuphanesi, Şehid Ali Paşa 900.
   ix. Paris, Bibliothèque nationale de France, Arabe 923, n.d.
   x. Princeton, Princeton University Library, New Series, no. 298, n.d.

5. *Al-Furūq* by Tāj al-Dīn Aḥmad ibn ʿUthmān ibn Ibrāhīm ibn Muṣṭafā l-Turkumānī l-Mārdīnī l-Ḥanafī, Ibn al-Turkumānī (d. *ca.* 744/1343–44).[46]
   a. Not extant
   b. MSS:
      i. Damascus, al-Maktaba l-Asadiyya, Ẓāhiriyya 4501(?).[47]

6. *Al-Furūq* by Shaykh Bāyazīd ibn Isrāʾīl ibn Ḥājjī Dāwūd Marghāyatī (? d. early ninth/fifteenth c.).[48]
   a. MSS:
      i. Paris, Bibliothèque Nationale de France, Arabe 812.

---

44 Al-Bāḥusayn, *al-Furūq al-fiqhiyya*, 94; al-Sabīl, "*al-Muqaddima*," 1:29n2. Both of these sources say that this thesis was submitted to al-Azhar University, but it seems to be from Cairo University. See http://research.asu.edu.eg/handle/987654321/9953, accessed April 30, 2019.

45 Available online at http://resolver.staatsbibliothek-berlin.de/SBB00016C2300000000 accessed April 30, 2019.

46 Heinrichs, "Structuring the Law," 341; al-Bāḥusayn, *al-Furūq al-fiqhiyya*, 98–99; al-Sabīl, "*al-Muqaddima*," 1:29; Kaḥḥāla, *Muʿjam*, 1:192, no. 1420; Ḥājjī Khalīfa, *Kashf al-ẓunūn* s.v. "*al-Furūq fī furūʿ al-ḥanafiyya*," 2:1257; al-Qurashī, *al-Jawāhir al-muḍiyya*, 1:197–98, no. 139; al-ʿAsqalānī, *al-Durar al-Kāmina*, 1:198; Ibn al-ʿImād, *Shadharāt al-dhahab* 8:243; al-Tamīmī l-Dārī, *Ṭabaqāt*, 1:389, no. 240; *GAL* 2:64, S2:67–68; Ibn Quṭlūbughā *Tāj al-tarājim*, 9, no. 30.

47 Although this work is attributed to Ibn al-Turkumānī, this attribution seems erroneous. This is a copy of *Furūq*-A, which has been attributed to many different jurists, see above Chapter Five, pp. 188–89.

48 Al-Bāḥusayn, *al-Furūq al-fiqhiyya*, 101; al-Sabīl, "*al-Muqaddima*," 29. This text is also available in microfilm at the King Faisal Center for Research and Islamic Studies in Riyadh, microfilm 812. Neither al-Bāḥusayn nor al-Sabīl mention the manuscript reflected in the microfilm.

7. *Al-Ashbāh wa-l-naẓā'ir* by Zayn al-Dīn ibn Nujaym al-Miṣrī (d. 970/1563).[49]

8. *Furūq*-A; *al-Furūq ʿalā madhhab Abī Ḥanīfa.*[50]
   a. MSS:
      i. Baghdad, Khazā'in kutub al-awqāf, 3677, n.d.[51]
      ii. Berlin, Staatsbibliothek zu Berlin, Peterman II Nachtag 4 p2.
      iii. Damascus, Asadiyya Library, Ẓāhiriyya 4501, n.d.
      iv. Istanbul, Suleymaniye Kutuphanesi, Halet Efendi 807, n.d.
      v. Mecca, Maktabat al-Ḥaram al-Makkī, Fiqh Ḥanafī 2089, n.d.[52]
      vi. Princeton Garrett 4185Y, n.d.[53]

9. *Furūq*-B; *al-Furūq fī l-furūʿ* attributed to Najm al-Dīn ʿAlī ibn Abī Bakr al-Naysābūrī l-Ḥanafī (d. ?).[54]
   a. Alternate title
      i. *Taḥrīr al-furūq.*[55]
   b. MSS:
      i. Istanbul, Suleymaniye Kutuphanesi, Aşir Efendi 453.
      ii. Istanbul, Suleymaniye Kutuphanesi, Esad Efendi 542, 1057/1647–48.
      iii. Istanbul, Suleymaniye Kutuphanesi, Esad Efendi 884, 774/1372–73.
      iv. Istanbul, Suleymaniye Kutuphanesi, Giresun Yazmalar 44.
      v. Istanbul, Suleymaniye Kutuphanesi, Halet Efendi 780.
      vi. Istanbul, Suleymaniye Kutuphanesi, Osman Huldi 50, 1126/1714.[56]
      vii. Istanbul, Suleymaniye Kutuphanesi, Yazma Bağişlar 1187, 960/1552–53.
      viii. Leiden, Leiden University Library, Or. 481

Mālikī

1. *Furūq masā'il mushtabiha fī l-madhhab* by Abū l-Qāsim ʿAbd al-Raḥmān ibn ʿAlī ibn Muḥammad al-Kanānī l-Mālikī, also known as Ibn al-Kātib (d. 408/1017).[57]
   a. Not extant.

---

49 Al-Sabīl, "*al-Muqaddima*," 1:30; *GAL* 2:310–11, S2:425–27; Ḥajjī Khalīfa, *Kashf al-ẓunūn*, s.v. "*al-Ashbāh wa-l-naẓā'ir fī l-furūʿ*," 1:99–100; Ibn al-ʿImād, *Shadharāt al-dhahab* 10:523; al-Tamīmī l-Dārī, *Ṭabaqāt*, 3:275, no. 894.

50 Al-Bāḥusayn, *al-Furūq al-fiqhiyya*, 103–104; al-Sabīl, "*al-Muqaddima*," 1:30.

51 Attributed to Aḥmad ibn Muḥammad al-Urdustānī.

52 Attributed to Ismāʿīl Ḥaqqī.

53 Attributed to al-Arzustānī.

54 Al-Bāḥusayn, *al-Furūq al-fiqhiyya*, 103; al-Sabīl, "*al-Muqaddima*," 1:29; al-Baghdādī, *Īḍāḥ al-maknūn*, 1:232 and 2:188. *GAL* S2:956. See also excerpts in Schacht, "*Furūq*-Büchern," 515–24.

55 Al-Sabīl, "*al-Muqaddima*," 29.

56 This manuscript is attributed to Ibn Nujaym in the catalog.

57 Heinrichs, "Structuring the Law," 341; al-Bāḥusayn, *al-Furūq al-fiqhiyya*, 84–85; al-Qāḍī ʿIyāḍ, *Tartīb al-madārik*, 7:252; Makhlūf, *Shajarat al-nūr al-zakiyya*, 106.

2. *Al-Jumū' wa-l-furūq* by al-Qāḍī 'Abd al-Wahhāb ibn 'Alī l-Baghdādī l-Mālikī (d. 422/1031).[58]
   a. Alternate titles:
      i. *Kitāb al-Furūq fī masā'il al-fiqh.*[59]
      ii. *Al-Furūq al-fiqhiyya.*
   b. Editions:
      i. *Al-Furūq al-fiqhiyya.* Edited by Jalāl 'Alī l-Qadhdhāfī l-Jihānī. Dubai: Dār al-Buḥūth li-l-Dirāsāt al-Islāmiyya wa-Ihyā' al-Turāth, 1424/2003.
      ii. *Al-Furūq al-fiqhiyya li-l-Qāḍī 'Abd al-Wahhāb al-Baghdādī wa-'alāqatuhā bi-Furūq al-Dimashqī.* Edited by Maḥmūd Salāmah al-Ghiryānī. Beirut: Dār al-Gharb al-Islāmī, 1411/1991.[60]
      iii. *Al-Furūq al-fiqhiyya li-l-Qāḍī 'Abd al-Wahhāb al-Baghdādī wa-'alāqatuhā bi-Furūq al-Dimashqī.* Edited by Maḥmūd Salāmah al-Ghiryānī. Dubai: Dār al-Buḥūth li-l-Dirāsāt al-Islāmiyya wa-Ihyā' al-Turāth, 1424/2003.
   c. MSS:
      i. Tripoli, Libya, Markaz Dirāsāt al-Mujāhidīn al-Lībiyīn 588, n.d.[61]

3. *Al-Nukat wa-l-furūq li-masā'il al-Mudawwana* by Abū Muḥammad 'Abd al-Ḥaqq ibn Muḥammad ibn Hārūn al-Qurashī l-Sahmī l-Ṣiqillī l-Mālikī (d. 466/1073–74).[62]
   a. Editions:
      i. *Al-Nukat wa-l-furūq li-masā'il al-Mudawwana.* Edited by Aḥmad ibn Ibrāhīm ibn 'Abdallāh al-Ḥabīb. Ph.D. Diss., Jāmi'at Umm al-Qurā, 1416/1996.[63]
      ii. *Kitāb al-Nukat wa-l-furūq li-masā'il al-Mudawwana wa-l-Mukhtalaṭa.* 2 volumes. Edited by Abū Faḍl al-Dimyāṭī Aḥmad ibn 'Alī. Casablanca: Markaz al-Turāth al-Thaqāfī l-Maghribī; Beirut: Dār Ibn Ḥazm, 2009.

58 Heinrichs, "Structuring the Law," 341; al-Bāḥusayn, *al-Furūq al-fiqhiyya*, 85–86; al-Sabīl, "*al-Muqaddima*," 1:31; Ibn Farḥūn, *al-Dībāj*, 2:26–29; al-Mawwāq, *al-Tāj wa-l-iklīl*, 2:7; Ibn Khallikān, *Wafāyāt al-a'yān*, 2:387; Ibn al-'Imād, *Shadharāt al-dhahab*, 5:112; Kaḥḥāla, *Mu'jam*, 2:344, no. 8711; Makhlūf, *Shajarat al-nūr al-zakiyya*, 103–104; al-Qāḍī 'Iyāḍ, *Tartīb al-madārik*, 7:220–27; Najm al-Dīn al-Ṭūfī, *'Alam al-jadhal*, 73.

59 Heinrichs, "Structuring the Law," 341.

60 Although it appears that this edition is the original of the next edition, the Dubai volume includes numerous citations of works printed after 1991. I have been unable to consult this edition.

61 Neither edition of 'Abd al-Wahhāb's *Furūq* gives an accession number, al-Jihānī, "*Muqaddima*," 17–19 and al-Ghiryānī, "*al-Qism al-dirāsī*," 19–20. This is the same manuscript attributed al-Dimashqī by Abū l-Ajfān and Abū Fāris, which they refer to as *Maktabat al-Awqāf bi-Ṭarābulus* 588 (Abū al-Ajfān and Abū Fāris, "*Dirāsa*," 49). It is unclear to me whether the manuscript is now at the Markaz al-Lībī li-l-Maḥfūẓāt wa-l-Dirāsāt al-Tārīkhiyya or al-Hay'at al-'Āmma li-l-Awqāf wa-l-Shu'ūn al-Islamiyya.

62 Heinrichs, "Structuring the Law," 341; al-Bāḥusayn, *al-Furūq al-fiqhiyya*, 88; al-Sabīl, "*al-Muqaddima*," 1:31; *GAL* 1:471, S1:661; Kaḥḥāla, *Mu'jam*, 2:6635, no. 6635; al-Ziriklī, *al-A'lām* 3:282; Ibn Farḥūn, *al-Dībāj*, 2:56; Makhlūf, *Shajarat al-nūr al-zakiyya*, 1:116; al-Qāḍī 'Iyāḍ, *Tartīb al-madārik*, 8:71–74; Najm al-Dīn al-Ṭūfī, *'Alam al-jadhal*, 73.

63 See Abū l-Ajfān and Abū Fāris, "*Dirāsa*," 38.

b. MSS:
  i. Cairo, Maktabat al-Azhariyya, Rawwāq al-Maghāriba 3156, n.d.[64]
  ii. Madrid, Biblioteca Nacional de España 5231 (autograph copy), written 459/1067.[65]
  iii. Marrakesh, Khizānat Ibn Yūsuf 499, written 740/1339–40.[66]
  iv. Rabat, al-Khizāna l-Malikiyya 261, n.d.[67]
  v. Rabat, al-Khizāna l-Malikiyya 350 *qāf*/2, written 743/1342–43.[68]

4. *Al-Furūq al-fiqhiyya* by Abū l-Faḍl Muslim ibn ʿAlī l-Dimashqī l-Mālikī (d. fifth/eleventh c.).[69]
  a. Alternate titles:
    i. *Furūq muttafiq ẓāhirihā mukhtalif bāṭinihā*
  b. Editions:
    i. *Al-Furūq al-fiqhiyya*. Edited by Muḥammad Abū l-Ajfān and Ḥamza Abū Fāris. Beirut: Dār al-Gharb al-Islāmī, 1992.
  c. MSS:
    i. Dublin, Chester Beatty 4507, n.d.[70]
    ii. Fez, Khizānat al-Qarawiyīn, 1193, n.d.[71]
    iii. Tunis, Dār al-Kutub al-Waṭaniyya, 1692, Shaʿbān 1399[*sic*] / December 1978.[72]
    iv. Tunis, Dār al-Kutub al-Waṭaniyya, 1694, n.d.[73]
    v. Tunis, Dār al-Kutub al-Waṭaniyya, 14862, 1291/1874–75.[74]

64 Aḥmad ibn Ibrāhīm ibn ʿAbdallāh al-Ḥabīb "*al-Muqaddima*," to ʿAbd al-Ḥaqq al-Siqillī, Abū Muḥammad ibn Muḥammad ibn Hārūn al-Sahmī, *al-Nukat wa-l-furūq li-masāʾil al-Mudawwana*, ed. Aḥmad ibn Ibrāhīm ibn ʿAbdallāh al-Ḥabīb (Ph.D. Diss., Jāmiʿat Umm al-Qurā, 1416/1996), 127–28.

65 According to *GAL*, this is Madrid 78, but this appears to be an old designation. Aḥmad ibn Ibrāhīm ibn ʿAbdallāh al-Ḥabīb gives the new number based on his visit to the library, see Aḥmad al-Ḥabīb, "*al-Muqaddima*," 124–25. The manuscript can be accessed digitally, see http://bdh-rd.bne.es/viewer.vm?id=0000014499, accessed April 30, 2019.

66 Aḥmad al-Ḥabīb, "*al-Muqaddima*," 127–28.

67 Aḥmad al-Ḥabīb, "*al-Muqaddima*," 126.

68 Aḥmad al-Ḥabīb, "*al-Muqaddima*," 125.

69 Heinrichs, "Structuring the Law," 341; al-Bāḥusayn, *al-Furūq al-fiqhiyya*, 86–87; al-Sabīl, "*al-Muqaddima*," 31. See also al-Qāḍī ʿIyāḍ, *Tartīb al-madārik*, 2:765, 8:57; Ibn Farḥūn, *Dībāj al-mudhahhab*, 2:347.

70 Abū l-Ajfān and Abū Fāris, "*Dirāsa*," 49–50. This manuscript is identified by al-Bāḥusayn as *al-Furūq fī l-aḥkām ʿalā madhhab al-Mālikiyya* by an anonymous author since this is what appears on the title page of this manuscript (al-Bāḥusayn, *al-Furūq al-fiqhiyya*, 104). However, it is clearly identified by Abū l-Ajfān and Abū Fāris as a copy of Muslim al-Dimashqī's *Furūq*.

71 Abū l-Ajfān and Abū Fāris, "*Dirāsa*," 47.

72 Abū l-Ajfān and Abū Fāris, "*Dirāsa*," 48.

73 Abū l-Ajfān and Abū Fāris, "*Dirāsa*," 50.

74 Abū l-Ajfān and Abū Fāris, "*Dirāsa*," 48–49. According to Abū l-Ajfān and Abū Fāris, it was 3217 in (*min raṣīd*) the al-Maktaba al-Aḥmadiyya collection.

5. *Al-Furūq aw Anwār al-burūq fī anwāʾ al-furūq* by Abū l-ʿAbbās Shihāb al-Dīn Aḥmad ibn Idrīs ibn al-Raḥmān al-Qarāfī (d. 684/1285).[75]

6. *Al-Furūq* by Abū ʿAbdallāh Muḥammad ibn Yūsuf al-ʿAbdarī l-Gharnāṭī l-Mālikī, also known as al-Mawwāq (d. 897/1492).[76]
   a. MSS:
      i. La Marsa, Maktabat Āl Ibn ʿĀshūr al-Tūnisī *fāʾ-alif* 98–90, n.d.(?)[77]

7. *ʿIddat al-burūq fī jamʿ mā fī l-madhhab min al-furūq* by Abū l-ʿAbbās Aḥmad ibn Yaḥyā ibn Muḥammad al-Wansharīsī l-Mālikī (d. 914/1508).[78]
   a. Editions:
      i. *ʿIddat al-furūq fī jamʿ mā fī l-madhhab min al-jumūʿ wa-l-furūq*. Edited by Ḥamza Abū Fāris. Beirut: Dār al-Gharb al-Islāmī, 1990/1410.
      ii. *ʿIddat al-furūq fī jamʿ mā fī l-madhhab min al-jumūʿ wa-l-furūq fī madhhab al-Imām Mālik wa-yalīhi Īḍāḥ al-masālik ilā qawāʿid al-Imām Mālik kilāhumā taʾlīf al-ʿAbbās Aḥmad ibn Yaḥyā l-Wansharīsī l-Tilimsānī*. Edited by Aḥmad Farīd al-Mazyadī. Beirut: Dār al-Kutub al-ʿIlmiyya, 2005
      iii. Fez Lithograph edition.[79]
   b. MSS:
      i. Rabat, al-Khizāna l-Malikiyya 1563, n.d.[80]
      ii. Tunis, al-Maktaba l-Waṭaniyya 4725, n.d.[81]
      iii. Tunis, al-Maktaba l-Waṭaniyya 4859, 1288/1872–73.[82]
      iv. Tunis, al-Maktaba l-Waṭaniyya 14889, n.d.[83]

---

75 Heinrichs, "Structuring the Law," 341–42; al-Bāḥusayn, *al-Furūq al-fiqhiyya*, 152–54; al-Sabīl, "*al-Muqaddima*," 1:32–33; *GAL* 1:385, S1:665; Kaḥḥāla, *Muʿjam*, 1:100, no. 750; Schacht, "*Furūq*-Büchern," 509; Makhlūf, *Shajarat al-nūr al-zakiyya*, 188–89.
76 Heinrichs, "Structuring the Law," 341; al-Bāḥusayn, *al-Furūq al-fiqhiyya*, 101–102; al-Sabīl, "*al-Muqaddima*," 31; *GAL* S2:375–76; Kaḥḥāla, *Muʿjam*, 3:787, no. 16479; Makhlūf, *Shajarat al-nūr al-zakiyya*, 262. See also Aḥmad ibn ʿAlī al-Balawī, *al-Thabat*, Ed. ʿAbdallāh al-ʿImrānī. (Beirut: Dār al-Gharb al-Islāmī, 1403/1983), 190. I thank Josef Ženka for this last reference.
77 Heinrichs, "Structuring the Law," 342. This manuscript is likely not a copy of the work by al-Mawwāq, but is often attributed to him.
78 Heinrichs, "Structuring the Law," 342; al-Bāḥusayn, *al-Furūq al-fiqhiyya*, 102; al-Sabīl, "*al-Muqaddima*," 1:32; Kaḥḥāla, *Muʿjam*, 1:325, no. 2389; *GAL* 2:248, S2:348; Makhlūf, *Shajarat al-nūr al-zakiyya*, 274–75.
79 Abū Fāris mentions this edition in his introduction. He claims it is "the famous and widely circulated Fez lithograph edition (*ṭabaʿat Fās al-mashhūra l-mutadāwala*)," but I have not been able to find another reference to this work.
80 Ḥamza Abū Fāris, "al-Qism al-Dirāsī," in *ʿIddat al-furūq fī jamʿ mā fī l-madhhab min al-jumū ʿwa-l-furūq* by Abū l-ʿAbbās Aḥmad ibn Yaḥyā ibn Muḥammad al-Wansharīsī, ed. Ḥamza Abū-Fāris (Beirut: Dār al-Gharb al-Islāmī, 1990/1410), 56–57.
81 Abū Fāris, "*al-Qism al-Dirāsī*," 55.
82 Abū Fāris, "*al-Qism al-dirāsī*," 56.
83 Abū Fāris, "*al-Qism al-dirāsī*," 56.

v. Tunis, al-Maktaba l-Waṭaniyya 15087, n.d.[84]

8. *Furūq bayn masāʾil fiqhiyya mutashābihat al-aḥwāl mutakhālifat al-iʿtibār* by Abū ʿAbdallāh Muḥammad ibn Yūsuf (d. ?).[85]
   a. MSS:
      i. La Marsa, Maktabat Āl Ibn ʿĀshūr al-Tūnisī *fāʾ-alif* 98–90, n.d.[86]

Ḥanbalī

1. *Al-Furūq fī masāʾil al-fiqhiyya* by ʿImād al-Dīn Ibrāhīm ibn ʿAbd al-Wāḥid ibn ʿAlī ibn Surūr al-Maqdisī l-Ḥanbalī (d. 614/1218).[87]
   a. Not extant.

2. *Al-Furūq* by Muʿaẓẓam al-Dīn Abū ʿAbdallāh Muḥammad ibn ʿAbdallāh al-Sāmarrī l-Ḥanbalī, also known as Ibn Sunayna (d. 616/1219).[88]
   a. Alternate title:
      i. *Al-Furūq al-mushtabih ṣuwarihā l-mukhtalif aḥkāmihā.*
   b. Editions:
      i. *Kitāb al-Furūq ʿalā madhhab al-Imām Aḥmad ibn Ḥanbal.* Edited by Muḥammad ibn Ibrāhīm ibn Muḥammad al-Yaḥyā. Riyadh: Dār al-Ṣumayʿī, 1997.
      ii. *Al-Furūq min awwal kitāb al-jināyāt ilā nihāyat al-kitāb dirāsatan wa-taḥqīqan.* Edited by Anas ibn ʿUmar ibn Muḥammad al-Subayyil. MA Thesis, Jāmiʿat Umm al-Qurā, 1435/2014.
   c. MSS:
      i. Basra, ʿAbbāsiyya Library, 39 *jīm*, n.d.[89]

---

84 Abū Fāris, "*al-Qism al-dirāsī*," 55–56.

85 This is perhaps the author referred to by al-Ṭūfī in his *ʿAlam al-jadhal* as "al-Shaykh Abū ʿAbdallāh Muḥammad ibn Yūsuf al-Andalusī l-Anṣārī l-Mālikī" (al-Ṭūfī, *ʿAlam al-jadhal*, 73). Although this may appear at first glance to be a clear reference to al-Mawwāq, al-Ṭūfī died in 716/1316, while al-Mawwāq died almost two hundred years later, in 897/1492.

86 Heinrichs, "Structuring the Law," 342.

87 Al-Bāḥusayn, *al-Furūq al-fiqhiyya*, 94; al-Sabīl, "*al-Muqaddima*," 1:40; Ibn Rajab, *Dhayl Ṭabaqāt al-ḥanābila* 3:198–220; Kaḥḥāla, *Muʿjam*, 1:42, no. 312; al-ʿUlaymī, *al-Durr al-Munaḍḍad*, 1:339, no. 969; Ibn al-ʿImād, *Shadharāt al-dhahab*, 7:105–108.

88 Heinrichs, "Structuring the Law," 343; al-Bāḥusayn, *al-Furūq al-fiqhiyya*, 93–94; al-Sabīl, "*al-Muqaddima*," 1:40; *GAL* S1:689; Ibn al-ʿImād, *Shadharāt al-dhahab*, 7:126–27; Najm al-Dīn al-Ṭūfī, *ʿAlam al-jadhal*, 73; Ibn Rajab, *Dhayl Ṭabaqāt al-ḥanābila*, 3:249–51.

89 Muḥammad ibn Ibrāhīm ibn Muḥammad al-Yaḥyā, "*Muqaddima*," in Muʿaẓẓam al-Dīn Abū ʿAbdallāh Muḥammad ibn ʿAbdallāh al-Sāmarrī, *Kitāb al-Furūq ʿalā madhhab al-Imām Aḥmad ibn Ḥanbal*, ed. Muḥammad ibn Ibrāhīm ibn Muḥammad al-Yaḥyā (Riyadh: Dār al-Ṣumayʿī), 99; Anas ibn ʿUmar ibn Muḥammad al-Subayyil, "*al-Taḥqīq*" in *al-Furūq min awwal kitāb al-jināyāt ilā nihāyat al-kitāb dirāsatan wa-taḥqīqan*, Muʿaẓẓam al-Dīn Abū ʿAbdallāh Muḥammad

ii. Damascus, Asadiyya Library, Ẓāhiriyyah, 19 Muḥarram 856 / February 2, 1452.[90]
iii. Leipzig, Leipzig University Library, Vollers 389, n.d.[91]

3. *Al-Furūq* by Abū ʿAbdallāh Muḥammad ibn ʿAbd al-Qawī ibn Badrān al-Mardāwī l-Maqdisī l-Ḥanbalī (d. 699/1299–300).[92]
   a. Not extant.

4. *Īḍāḥ al-dalāʾil fī l-farq bayn al-masāʾil* by Abū Muḥammad Sharaf al-Dīn ʿAbd al-Raḥīm ibn ʿAbdallāh al-Zarīrānī l-Baghdādī l-Ḥanbalī (d. 741/1341).[93]
   a. Alternate title:
      i. *Tanqīḥ al-furūq.*[94]
   b. Editions:
      i. *Īḍāḥ al-dalāʾil fī l-farq bayn al-masāʾil.* Edited by ʿUmar ibn Muḥammad ibn ʿAbdallāh al-Sabīl. 2 volumes. Mecca: al-Mamlaka l-ʿArabiyya l-Saʿūdiyya, Wizārat al-Taʿlīm al-ʿĀlī, Jāmiʿat Umm al-Qurā, Maʿhad al-Buḥūth al-ʿIlmiyya wa-Iḥyāʾ al-Turāth al-Islāmī, Markaz Iḥyāʾ al-Turāth al-Islāmī, 1414[/1993–94].
      ii. *Īḍāḥ al-dalāʾil fī l-farq bayn al-masāʾil.* Edited by Muḥammad Ḥasan Muḥammad Ḥasan Ismāʿīl. Beirut: Dār al-Kutub al-ʿIlmiyya, 1424/2003.
      iii. *Īḍāḥ al-dalāʾil fī l-farq bayn al-masāʾil.* Edited by ʿUmar ibn Muḥammad al-Sabīl. Dammam, [Riyadh(?)]: Dār Ibn al-Jawzī, 1431[/2009–10].
   c. MSS:
      i. Princeton, Princeton University Library, Garrett 4577Y, n.d.[95]

---

ibn ʿAbdallāh al-Sāmarrī, ed. Anas ibn ʿUmar ibn Muḥammad al-Subayyil, (MA Thesis, Jāmiʿat Umm al-Qurā, 1435/2014), 90.

90 al-Yaḥyā "*Muqaddima*," 99. The editions of this book cite this manuscript but do not give its accession number.

91 Schacht, "*Furūq*-Büchern," 507–508; al-Subayyil, "*al-Taḥqīq*," 89. This manuscript is available digitally, http://www.refaiya.uni-leipzig.de/receive/RefaiyaBook_islamhs_00000858, accessed April 30, 2019.

92 Al-Bāḥusayn, *al-Furūq al-fiqhiyya*, 96; al-Sabīl, "*al-Muqaddima*," 1:40; Ibn Rajab, *Dhayl Ṭabaqāt al-ḥanābila*, 2:343; Ibn al-ʿImād, *Shadharāt al-dhahab*, 7:789–90; al-Ziriklī, *al-Aʿlām*, 6:214; al-ʿUlaymī, *al-Durr al-Munaḍḍad*, 442, no. 1176; al-Baghdādī, *Hadiyat al-ʿārifīn*, 2:139.

93 Heinrichs, "Structuring the Law," 343; al-Bāḥusayn, *al-Furūq al-fiqhiyya*, 97–98; al-Sabīl, "*al-Muqaddima*," 1:28; Kaḥḥāla, *Muʿjam*, 2:132, no. 7117; Ibn Rajab, *Dhayl*, 5:104–15, no. 581; al-ʿAsqalānī, *al-Durar al-Kāmina* 2:357, no. 2390; Ibn al-ʿImād, *Shadharāt al-dhahab*, 8:228–29.

94 This title is given on the cover page of Princeton University Library, Garrett 4577Y.

95 This is likely a unicum, as implied by the printed editions. See al-Sabīl, "*al-Muqaddima*," 1:126–27; Muḥammad Ḥasan Muḥammad Ḥasan Ismāʿīl, "*al-Dirāsa*" to Sharaf al-Dīn ʿAbd al-Raḥīm ibn ʿAbdallāh al-Zarīrānī, *Īḍāḥ al-dalāʾil fī l-farq bayn al-masāʾil*, ed. Muḥammad Ḥasan Muḥammad Ḥasan Ismāʿīl (Beirut: Dār al-Kutub al-ʿIlmiyya, 1424/2003), 9.

Shi'i Works

1. *Kitāb al-Furūq* by Aḥmad ibn Muḥammad al-Barqī (d. third/ninth c.).[96]
   a. Not extant.

2. *Al-Jamʿ wa-l-farq* by ʿAlī ibn Yaḥyā ibn Rāshid al-Washlī l-Zaydī l-Yamanī (d. 777/1375–76).[97]
   a. Not extant.

Works Incorrectly Said to Be of Legal Distinctions

1. *Al-Muskit* by al-Zubayr ibn Aḥmad ibn Sulaymān ibn ʿAbdallāh al-Zubayrī (d. 317/929–30).[98]
   a. There is not enough information to classify this work.

2. *Al-Furūq [wa-manʿ al-tarāduf]* by Abū ʿAbdallāh Muḥammad ibn ʿAlī l-Ḥakīm al-Tirmidhī (d. *ca.* 298/910).[99]
   a. This work is on lexicographic distinctions.

3. *Al-Muṭāraḥāt* by Aḥmad ibn Muḥammad ibn Aḥmad al-Baghdādī, also known as Ibn al-Qaṭṭān (d. 359/970).[100]
   a. This is a work of law, but not on distinctions.

---

96 Ibn al-Nadīm, *al-Fihrist*, 2.1:73.

97 Al-Bāḥusayn, *al-Furūq al-fiqhiyya*, 100; al-Sabīl, "*al-Muqaddima*," 1:38; Kaḥḥāla, *Muʿjam*, 2:543, no. 10254.

98 Al-Bāḥusayn *al-Furūq al-fiqhiyya*, 68, 73–74; al-Sabīl, "*al-Muqaddima*," 1:35; al-Shīrāzī, *Ṭabaqāt*, 108; Ibn Khallikān, *Wafāyāt al-aʿyān*, 2:69; Ḥājjī Khalīfa, *Kashf al-ẓunūn*, 2:1626; Ibn al-Subkī, *Ṭabaqāt*, 3:295; al-Asnawī, *Ṭabaqāt*, 1:606

99 Al-Bāḥusayn, *al-Furūq al-fiqhiyya*, 69–70; Ibn al-Subkī, *Ṭabaqāt*, 2:20; *GAL* S1:356; al-Ziriklī, *al-Aʿlām*, 6:272; Kaḥḥāla, *Muʿjam*, 3:502, no. 14648; Ḥājjī Khalīfa, *Kashf al-ẓunūn*, s.v. "*al-Furūq fī furūʿ al-shāfiʿiyya*," 2:1258. Al-Bāḥusayn also claims that the attribution of a book of legal distincitons to al-Tirmidhī is doubtful, but most likely a confusion stemming from his having written a book of lexicographic distinctions and having been considered a Shāfiʿī jurist.

100 Al-Bāḥusayn, *al-Furūq al-fiqhiyya*, 69, 71–72; al-Sabīl, "*al-Muqaddima*," 1:35; Ibn al-Subkī, *Ṭabaqāt*, 3:295; Ibn al-ʿImād, *Shadharāt al-dhahab*, 4:306; Hājjī Khalīfa, *Kashf al-ẓunūn* 2:1714. But also, see al-Zarkashī, *al-Manthūr*, 1:70. Al-Bāḥusayn says that it is erroneously attributed to this Ibn al-Qaṭṭān, but instead was by Abū ʿAbd ʿAllāh al-Ḥusayn ibn Muḥammad al-Qaṭṭān who died between the fifth and sixth centuries, and that it is not a work of *furūq*, but rather question and answer. See also al-Subkī, *Ṭabaqāt*, 3:163; and Asnawī, *Ṭabaqāt*, 2:146.

4. *Al-Iḥkām fī tamyīz al-fatāwā ʿan al-aḥkām wa-taṣarrufāt al-qāḍī wa-l-imām* by Abū l-ʿAbbās Aḥmad ibn Idrīs al-Qarāfī (d. 684/1285).[101]
   a. This is a work on fatwas and legal rulings.

5. *Al-Furūq* by al-Qāḍī Muḥammad ibn Kāmil ibn Muḥammad ibn Tammām al-Tadmurī l-Shāfiʿī (d. after 741/1340).[102]
   a. The only mention I could find for this work was in the *Muʿjam al-muʾallifīn.*

6. *Al-Furūq* by ʿUmar ibn Raslān al-Bulqīnī (d. 805/1403).[103]
   a. This is a work on Sufism.

7. *Furūq al-uṣūl* attributed to Kemalpaşazade (d. 940/1534).[104]
   a. This work is on applied linguistic distinctions in law.

8. *Qurrat al-ʿayn wa-l-samʿ fī bayān al-farq wa-l-jamʿ* by Badr al-Dīn ibn ʿUmar ibn Aḥmad ibn Muḥammad al-ʿĀdilī l-ʿAbbāsī l-Ḥuraythī(?) al-Shāfiʿī (d. *ca.* 970/1562–63).[105]
   a. This is a work on Sufism.

9. *Talqīḥ al-Karābīsī.*[106]
   a. This work does not exist, but was erroneously cited by Ibn Nujaym in his *al-Ashbāh wa-l-naẓāʾir*, at the beginning of section six (*al-fann al-sādis*).

10. *Al-Furūq al-fiqhiyya li-l-Imām Mālik* by Ibrāhīm Ismāʿīl Jalāl
    a. This is a work of legal distinctions, but compiled by a modern scholar from the works of Mālik.

101 Al-Sabīl, "*al-Muqaddima*," 1:34, Abū l-Ajfān and Abū Fāris, "*Dirāsa*," 39; Ḥājjī Khalīfa, *Kashf al-ẓunūn*, s.v. "*al-Iḥkām fī tamyīz al-fatāwā ʿan al-aḥkām wa-taṣarrufāt al-qāḍī wa-imām*," 1:21. See also Shihāb al-Dīn al-Qarāfī, *The Criterion for Distinguishing Legal Opinions from Judicial Rulings and the Administrative Acts of Judges and Rulers*, trans. Mohammad Fadel (New Haven: Yale University Press, 2017).

102 This work is only mentioned in Kaḥḥāla, *Muʿjam*, 3:606, no. 15326. This scholar has entries in al-ʿAsqalānī, *al-Durar al-Kāmina*, 5:411; and al-ʿUlaymī, *al-Uns al-jalīl bi-taʾrīkh al-Quds wa-l-Jalīl*, 2:140, but they do not mention this book.

103 Ibn al-ʿImād, *Shadharāt al-dhahab*, 9:80–81.

104 Ḥājjī Khalīfa, *Kashf al-ẓunūn* s.v. "*Furūq al-uṣūl*," 2:1257. He describes this work as "a useful (*mufīda*) treatise by a later jurist (*baʿḍ al-mutaʾakhkhirīn*)."

105 Al-Bāḥusayn, *al-Furūq al-fiqhiyya*, 104; al-Sabīl, "*al-Muqaddima*," 1:39; ʿAlī Abā Ḥusayn, ed., *Fihrist makhṭūṭāt al-baḥrayn*, 2 vols. (Manama: Markaz al-Wathāʾiq al-Tārīkhiyya, 1404/1983), 1:99; Kaḥḥāla, *Muʿjam*, 3:557, no. 14995. Al-Bāḥusayn says this is actually a work of sufism, not a legal work and therefore is not a work of legal distinctions. I have not been able to examine this work myself.

106 Ḥājjī Khalīfa, *Kashf al-ẓunūn*, s.v. "*Furūq al-Karābīsī*," 2:1258.

11. *Al-Furūq li-Ibn Qayyim al-Jawziyya: Muntazaʿ min aghlab kutub Ibn Qayyim raḥimahu Allāh taʿālā* by Yūsuf al-Ṣāliḥ.
    a. This is a work of legal distinctions, but compiled by a modern scholar from the works of Ibn Qayyim al-Jawziyya.

12. *Al-Furūq al-fiqhiyya ʿind Imām Ibn Qayyim al-Jawziyya jamʿan wa-l-dirāsa* by Abū ʿUmar Sayyid Ḥabīb ibn Aḥmad al-Madanī l-Afghānī.
    a. This is a work of legal distinctions, but compiled by a modern scholar from the works of Ibn Qayyim al-Jawziyya.

13. *Al-Furūq al-fiqhiyya ʿind al-Imām al-Shāfiʿī fī Kitāb al-Umm* by Sāmī Muḥammad Ṣubḥ.
    a. This is a work of legal distinctions, but compiled by a modern scholar from al-Shāfiʿī's *Kitāb al-Umm.*

14. *Al-Naẓāʾir al-fiqhiyya* by Abū ʿImrān Mūsā ibn ʿĪsā l-Fāsī l-Ṣanhājī l-Qayrawānī (d. ?).[107]
    a. This is a work of legal maxims.

107 Al-Bāḥusayn, *al-Furūq al-fiqhiyya*, 86.

Appendix II: Chronological *Furūq* Bibliography

This appendix includes a bibliography of all known works of legal distinctions, arranged chronologically by death date of author. For more information on a specific work or its author, refer to Appendix I.

Third/Ninth Century

1. *Kitāb al-Furūq* by Aḥmad ibn Muḥammad al-Barqī (Shiʿī, d. third/ninth c.).

Fourth/Tenth Century

2. *Al-Furūq* by Abū l-ʿAbbās Aḥmad ibn ʿUmar ibn Surayj (Shāfiʿī, d. 306/918).
3. *Kitāb al-masāʾil wa-l-ʿilal wa-l-furūq* by Abū l-Ḥasan ʿAlī ibn Aḥmad al-Nasawī (d. *ca* 320/932).
4. *Al-Furūq* by Abū l-Faḍl Muḥammad ibn Ṣāliḥ al-Karābīsī (Ḥanafī, d. 322/932–34).

Fifth/Eleventh Century

5. *Al-Kifāya fī l-furūq* by Abū ʿAbdallāh al-Ḥusayn ibn ʿAbdallāh al-Ṭabarī (Shāfiʿī, d. *ca.* fifth/eleventh c.).
6. *Furūq masāʾil mushtabiha fī l-madhhab* by Abū l-Qāsim ʿAbd al-Raḥmān ibn Muḥammad al-Kanānī, also known as Ibn al-Kātib (Mālikī, d. 408/1017).
7. *Al-Jumūʿ wa-l-furūq* by al-Qāḍī ʿAbd al-Wahhāb ibn ʿAlī l-Baghdādī (Mālikī, d. 422/1031).
8. *Al-Furūq al-fiqhiyya* by Abū l-Faḍl Muslim ibn ʿAlī l-Dimashqī (Mālikī, d. fifth/eleventh c.).
9. *Al-Jamʿ wa-l-farq* by Abū Muḥammad ʿAbdallāh ibn Yūsuf al-Juwaynī (Shāfiʿī, d. 438/1047).
10. *Al-Ajnās wa-l-furūq* by Abū ʿAbbās Aḥmad ibn Muḥammad al-Nāṭifī l-Ṭabarī (Ḥanafī, d. 446/1054–55).
11. *Al-Nukat wa-l-furūq li-masāʾil al-Mudawwana* by Abū Muḥammad ʿAbd al-Ḥaqq ibn Muḥammad ibn Hārūn al-Qurashī l-Ṣiqillī l-Mālikī (Mālikī, d. 466/1073–74).
12. *Al-Wasāʾil fī furūq al-masāʾil* by Abū l-Khayr Salāma ibn Ismāʿīl ibn Jamāʿa l-Maqdisī (Shāfiʿī, d. 480/1087–88).
13. *Al-Muʿāyāt* by Abū ʿAbbās Aḥmad ibn Muḥammad al-Jurjānī (Shāfiʿī, d. 482/1089–90).

https://doi.org/10.1515/9783110605792-011

Sixth/Twelfth Century

14. *Al-Furūq* by Abū l-Maḥāsin ʿAbd al-Wāḥid ibn Ismāʿīl al-Rūyānī l-Ṭabarī (Shāfiʿī, d. d. 501/1107 or 502/1108).
15. *Al-Furūq* by Abū l-Muẓaffar Asʿad ibn Muḥammad ibn al-Ḥusayn al-Naysābūrī l-Karābīsī (Ḥanafī, d. 570/1174–75).

Seventh/Thirteenth Century

16. *Al-Furūq fī masāʾil al-fiqhiyya* by ʿImād al-Dīn Ibrāhīm ibn ʿAbd al-Wāḥid ibn ʿAlī ibn Surūr al-Maqdisī (Ḥanbalī, d. 614/1218).
17. *Al-Furūq* by Abū ʿAbdallāh Muḥammad ibn ʿAbdallāh al-Sāmarrī, also known as Ibn Sunayna (Ḥanbalī, d. 616/1219).
18. *Al-Fuṣūl wa-l-furūq* by Abū l-ʿAbbās Najm al-Dīn Aḥmad ibn Muḥammad ibn Khalaf ibn Rājiḥ al-Maqdisī l-Ḥanbalī (Shāfiʿī, d. 638/1241).
19. *Talqīḥ al-ʿuqūl fī furūq al-manqūl* by Aḥmad ibn ʿUbayd Allāh al-Maḥbūbī, also known as Ṣadr al-Sharīʿa al-Awwal (Ḥanafī, d. 630/1232–33).
20. *Al-Furūq* by Abū l-ʿAbbās Kamāl al-Dīn Aḥmad ibn Kashāsib al-Shāfiʿī al-Dizmārī (Shāfiʿī, d. 643/1245).
21. *Al-Furūq aw Anwār al-burūq fī anwāʾ al-furūq* by Abū l-ʿAbbās Aḥmad ibn Idrīs al-Qarāfī (Mālikī, d. 684/1285).
22. *Al-Furūq* by Abū ʿAbdallāh Muḥammad ibn ʿAbd al-Qawī ibn Badrān al-Maqdisī (Ḥanbalī, d. 699/1299–1300).

Eighth/Fourteenth Century

23. *Al-Jamʿ wa-l-farq* by Sirāj al-Dīn Yūnus ibn ʿAbd al-Mujīd ibn ʿAlī al-Hudhalī l-Armantī (Shāfiʿī, d. 725/1325).
24. *Īḍāḥ al-dalāʾil fī al-farq bayn al-masāʾil* by Abū Muḥammad Sharaf al-Dīn ʿAbd al-Raḥīm ibn ʿAbdallāh al-Zarīrānī al-Baghdādī (Ḥanbalī, d. 741/1341).
25. *Al-Furūq* by Tāj al-Dīn Aḥmad ibn ʿUthmān ibn Ibrāhīm ibn Muṣṭafā l-Turkumānī l-Mārdīnī, also known as Ibn al-Turkumānī (Ḥanafī, d. *ca.* 744/1343–44).
26. *Al-Furūq* by Abū Umāma Shams al-Dīn Muḥammad ibn ʿAlī ibn ʿAbd al-Wāḥid ibn Yaḥyā l-Dukkālī l-Maghribī l-Miṣrī l-Shāfiʿī, also known as Ibn al-Naqqāsh (d. 763/1361).
27. *Maṭāliʿ al-daqāʾiq fī taḥrīr al-jawāmiʿ wa-l-fawāriq* by Jamāl al-Dīn ʿAbd al-Raḥīm ibn al-Ḥasan al-Asnawī (Shāfiʿī, d. 772/1370).
28. *Al-Jamʿ wa-l-farq* by ʿAlī ibn Yaḥyā ibn Rāshid al-Washlī l-Zaydī l-Yamanī (Zaydī, d. 777/1375–76).

Ninth/Fifteenth Century

29. *Al-Furūq* by Shaykh Bāyazīd ibn Isrāʾīl ibn Ḥājjī Dāwūd Marghāyatī? (Ḥanafī, d. early ninth/fifteenth c.).
30. *Al-Furūq* by Abū ʿAbdallāh Muḥammad ibn Yūsuf al-ʿAbdarī l-Mawwāq al-Gharnāṭī (Mālikī, d. 897/1492).

Tenth/Sixteenth Century

31. *ʿIddat al-burūq fī jamʿ mā fī al-madhhab min al-furūq* by Abū l-ʿAbbās Aḥmad ibn Yaḥyā al-Wansharīsī (Mālikī, d. 914/1508).
32. *Al-Ashbāh wa-l-naẓāʾir* by Zayn al-Dīn Ibn Nujaym al-Miṣrī (Ḥanafī, d. 970/1563)

Unknown

33. *Furūq*-A or *al-Furūq ʿalā madhhab Abī Ḥanīfa* by Anonymous (Ḥanafī).
34. *Furūq*-B or *al-Furūq fī al-furūʿ* attributed to Najm al-Dīn ʿAlī ibn al-Sayyid Abī Bakr al-Naysābūrī l-Ḥanafī (Ḥanafī, d. ?).
35. *Al-Furūq bayn masāʾil fiqhiyya mutashābihat al-aḥwāl mutakhālifat al-iʿtibār* by Muḥammad ibn Yūsuf al-Andalusī al-Anṣārī (Mālikī, d. ?).
36. *Kitāb al-Furūq* by Anonymous (Shāfiʿī).[1]

1 MS Oriental 6278, British Library, London.

Appendix III: The Manuscripts of *Furūq*-A: Table of Contents

https://doi.org/10.1515/9783110605792-012

Garrett 4185Y, Princeton University Library	Peterman II Nachtrag 4, Staatsbibliothek zu Berlin	Halet Efendi 807, Suleymaniye Library, Istanbul	Fiqh Ḥanafī 2089, Maktabat al-Haram al-Makki, Mecca	Ẓāhiriyya 4501, Damascus[a)]
Introduction	Introduction	Introduction	Introduction	Introduction
Kitāb al-Ṭahāra	Kitāb al-Ṭahāra	Kitāb al-Ṭahāra	Kitāb al-Ṭahāra	Kitāb al-Ṭahāra
Kitāb al-Ṣalāt	Kitāb al-Ṣalāt	Kitāb al-Ṣalāt	Kitāb al-Ṣalāt	Kitāb al-Ṣalāt
Kitāb al-Zakāt	Kitāb al-Zakāt	Kitāb al-Zakāt	Kitāb al-Zakāt	Kitāb al-Zakāt
Kitāb al-Ṣawm	Kitāb al-Ṣawm	Kitāb al-Ṣawm	Kitāb al-Ṣawm	Kitāb al-Ṣawm
Kitāb al-Ḥajj	Kitāb al-Ḥajj	Kitāb al-Ḥajj	Kitāb al-Ḥajj	Kitāb al-Ḥajj
Kitāb al-Nikāḥ	Kitāb al-Nikāḥ	Kitāb al-Nikāḥ	Kitāb al-Nikāḥ	Kitāb al-Nikāḥ
Kitāb al-Ṭalāq	Kitāb al-Ṭalāq	Kitāb al-Ṭalāq	Kitāb al-Ṭalāq	Kitāb al-Ṭalāq
Kitāb al-ʿItāq	Kitāb al-ʿItāq	Kitāb al-ʿItāq	Kitāb al-ʿItāq	Kitāb al-ʿItāq
Kitāb al-Aymān	Kitāb al-Aymān	Kitāb al-Aymān	Kitāb al-Aymān	Kitāb al-Ṣayd
Kitāb al-Buyūʿ	Kitāb al-Buyūʿ	Kitāb al-Buyūʿ	Kitāb al-Buyūʿ	Kitāb al-Buyūʿ
Kitāb al-Shufaʿa	Kitāb al-Shufaʿa	Kitāb al-Shufaʿa	Kitāb al-Shufaʿa	Kitāb al-Shufaʿa
Kitāb al-Rahn	Kitāb al-Rahn	Kitāb al-Rahn	Kitāb al-Rahn	Kitāb al-Rahn
Kitāb al-Ijāra	Kitāb al-Ijāra	Kitāb al-Ijāra	Kitāb al-Ijāra	Kitāb al-Ijāra
Kitāb al-Ṣayd	Kitāb al-Ṣayd	Kitāb al-Ṣayd	Kitāb al-Ṣayd	Kitāb al-Hiba
Kitāb al-Hiba	Kitāb al-Hiba	Kitāb al-Hiba	Kitāb al-Hiba	Kitāb al-Waṣāyā
Kitāb al-Waṣāyā	Kitāb al-Waṣāyā	Kitāb al-Waṣāyā	Kitāb al-Waṣāyā	
Kitāb al-Ḥudūd wa-l-saraqa	Kitāb al-Ḥudūd wa-l-saraqa	Kitāb al-Ḥudūd	Kitāb al-Ḥudūd wa-l-saraqa	

Continued

Garrett 4185Y, Princeton University Library	**Peterman II Nachtrag 4, Staatsbibliothek zu Berlin**	**Halet Efendi 807, Suleymaniye Library, Istanbul**	**Fiqh Ḥanafī 2089, Maktabat al-Haram al-Makki, Mecca**	**Ẓāhiriyya 4501, Damascus**[a]
Kitāb al-Wakāla	Kitāb al-Wakāla	Kitāb al-Wakāla	Kitāb al-Wakāla	
Kitāb al-Maʾdhūn	Kitāb al-Maʾdhūn	Kitāb al-Maʾdhūn	Kitāb al-Maʾdhūn	
Kitāb al-Ḥawāla wa-l-kafāla	Kitāb al-Ḥawāla wa-l-kafāla	Kitāb al-Ḥawāla wa-l-kafāla	Kitāb al-Ḥawāla	
Masāʾil mutafarriqa	Masāʾil mutafarriqa	Kitāb al-Daʿwā	Masāʾil mutafarriqa	
Kitāb al-Iqrār		Kitāb al-Shahāda		
Kitāb al-Diyāt		Kitāb al-Iqrār		
Masāʾil shattā		Kitāb al-Diyāt		
Masāʾil mutashābiha		Masāʾil shattā		
Masāʾil farqiyyah fiqhiyya		Kitāb al-Muḍāraba		
		Masāʾil mutashābiha		
		Masāʾil al-ḥīla		

[a] This manuscript has been heavily damaged. It has significant wear around the binding, the pages are out of order, and the end is missing.

Appendix IV: The Manuscripts of *Furūq*-B (Najm al-Dīn Naysābūrī, *attrib.*): Table of Contents

https://doi.org/10.1515/9783110605792-013

Giresun Yazmalar 44, Suleymaniye Library, Istanbul	**Halet Efendi 780, Suleymaniye Library, Istanbul**	**Leiden Or. 481, Leiden University Library**	**Esad Efendi 884, Suleymaniye Library, Istanbul**	**Esad Efendi 542 Suleymaniye Library, Istanbul**	**Aşir Efendi 453, Suleymaniye Library, Istanbul**	**Osman Huldi 50, Suleymaniye Library, Istanbul**	**Yazma Bağışlar 1187, Suleymaniye Library, Istanbul**
Introduction	Introduction	Introduction	Introduction	Introduction	Introduction	[missing]	Introduction
Ṣalāt	[Bāb al-Ṣalāt]	Ṣalāt	Masāʾil al-ṣalāt wa-l-zakāt	[Ṣalāṭ]	[Ṣalāt]	[title, if any, missing]	[ṣalāt]
Zakāt	Zakāt	Zakāt			Kitāb al-zakāt	Kitāb masāʾil al-ṣawm	Kitāb al-zakāt
Ṣawm	Ṣawm	Masāʾil al-ṣawm	Kitāb masāʾil al-ṣawm	Kitāb masāʾil al-ṣawm	Kitāb al-ṣawm	Kitāb al-ḥajj	Kitāb al-ṣawm
Ḥajj	Ḥajj	Masāʾil al-ḥajj	Kitāb al-ḥajj	Kitāb masāʾil al-ṣawm	Kitāb al-ḥajj	Kitāb al-nikāḥ	Kitāb al-ḥajj
Nikāḥ	Masāʾil al-nikāḥ	Masāʾil al-nikāḥ	Kitāb masāʾil al-nikāḥ	Kitāb masāʾil al-nikāḥ	Kitāb al-nikāḥ	Kitāb al-ṭalāq	Kitāb al-nikāḥ
Ṭalāq	Masāʾil al-ṭalāq	Masāʾil al-ṭalāq	Kitāb al-ṭalāq	Kitāb masāʾil al-ṭalāq	Kitāb al-ṭalāq	Kitāb masāʾil al-ʿitāq	
ʿItāq	Masāʾil al-ʿitāq	Masāʾil al-ʿitāq	Kitāb masāʾil al-ʿitāq	Kitāb masāʾil al-ʿitāq	Kitāb al-ʿitāq	Kitāb al-buyūʿ	
Aymān	Masāʾil al-aymān	Masāʾil al-aymān	Kitāb al-aymān	Kitāb masāʾil al-aymān	Kitāb al-aymān	Kitāb al-shufaʿa	
Buyūʿ	Buyūʿ	Buyūʿ	Kitāb masāʾil al-buyūʿ	Kitāb masāʾil al-buyūʿ	Kitāb al-buyūʿ	Kitāb masāʾil al-rahn	

Continued

Giresun Yazmalar 44, Suleymaniye Library, Istanbul	**Halet Efendi 780, Suleymaniye Library, Istanbul**	**Leiden Or. 481, Leiden University Library**	**Esad Efendi 884, Suleymaniye Library, Istanbul**	**Esad Efendi 542 Suleymaniye Library, Istanbul**	**Aşir Efendi 453, Suleymaniye Library, Istanbul**	**Osman Huldi 50, Suleymaniye Library, Istanbul**	**Yazma Bağışlar 1187, Suleymaniye Library, Istanbul**
Shufaʿa	Masāʾil al-shufaʿa	Masāʾil al-shufaʿa	Kitāb al-shufaʿa	Kitāb masāʾil al-shufaʿa	Kitāb al-shufaʿa	Kitāb masāʾil al-ijāra	
Rahn	Masāʾil al-rahn	Masāʾil al-rahn	Kitāb masāʾil al-rahn	Kitāb masāʾil al-rahn	Kitāb al-rahn	Kitāb masāʾil al-ṣayd	
Ijārāt	Masāʾil al-ijāra	Masāʾil al-ijāra	Kitāb masāʾil al-ijāra	Kitāb masāʾil al-rahn	Kitāb al-ijāra	Kitāb masāʾil al-hiba	
Ṣayd	Masāʾil al-ṣayd	Masāʾil al-ṣayd	Kitāb masāʾil al-ṣayd	Kitāb masāil al-ṣayd	Kitāb al-ṣayd	Kitāb masāʾil al-waṣāyā	
Hiba	Masāʾil al-hiba	Masāʾil al-hiba	Kitāb masāʾil al-hiba	Kitāb masāʾil al-hiba	Kitāb al-hiba	Kitāb masāʾil al-ḥudūd	
Waṣāyā	Masāʾil al-waṣāyā	Masāʾil al-waṣāyā	Kitāb masāʾil al-waṣāyā	Kitāb masāʾil al-waṣāyā	Kitāb al-waṣāyā	Kitāb al-wakāla	
Ḥudūd	Masāʾil al-ḥudūd wa-l-saraqa	Masāʾil al-ḥudūd wa-l-saraqa	Kitāb masāʾil al-ḥudūd	Kitāb masāʾil al-ḥudūd wa-l-saraqa	Kitāb al-ḥudūd	Kitāb masāʾil al-maʾdhūn	
Wakāla	Masāʾil al-wakāla	Masāʾil al-wakāla	Kitāb al-wakāla	Kitāb masāʾil al-wakāla	Kitāb al-wakāla	Kitāb al-ḥawāla wa-l-kafāla	
Maʾdhūn	Masāʾil al-maʾdhūn	Masāʾil al-maʾdhūn	Kitāb masāʾil al-maʾdhūn	Kitāb masāʾil al-maʾdhūn	Kitāb al-maʾdhūn	Kitāb masāʾi lal-daʿwā	

Continued

Giresun Yazmalar 44, Suleymaniye Library, Istanbul	Halet Efendi 780, Suleymaniye Library, Istanbul	Leiden Or. 481, Leiden University Library	Esad Efendi 884, Suleymaniye Library, Istanbul	Esad Efendi 542 Suleymaniye Library, Istanbul	Aşir Efendi 453, Suleymaniye Library, Istanbul	Osman Huldi 50, Suleymaniye Library, Istanbul	Yazma Bağışlar 1187, Suleymaniye Library, Istanbul
Ḥawāla wa-l-Kafāla	Masāʾil al-ḥawāla	Masāʾil al-kafāla wa-l-ḥawāla	Kitāb al-ḥawāla wa-l-kafāla	Kitāb masāʾil al-ḥawāla wa-l-kafāla	Kitāb al-ḥawāla	Kitāb masāʾil al-iqrār	
Daʿwā	Masāʾil al-daʿwā	Masāʾil al-daʿwā	Kitāb masāʾil al-daʿwā	Kitāb masāʾil al-daʿwā	Kitāb al-daʿwā	Kitāb masāʾil al-diyāt	
Iqrār	Masāʾil al-iqrār	Masāʾil al-iqrār	Kitāb masāʾil al-iqrār	Kitāb masāʾil al-iqrār	Kitāb al-iqrār	Kitāb masāʾil shattā	
Diyāt	Masāʾil al-diyāt	Masāʾil al-diyāt	Kitāb masāʾil al-diyāt	Kitāb masāʾil al-diyāt	Kitāb al-jināyāt	Kitāb masāʾil al-muḍāraba	
Masāʾil	Masāʾil shattā	Masāʾil shattā	Kitāb masāʾil shattā	Kitāb masāʾil al-muḍāraba	Kitāb al-muzāraʿa	Kitāb masāʾil mutashābiha	
Masāʾil ukhrā	Masāʾil al-muḍāraba	Al-Masāʾil al-mutāshabiha	Kitāb masāʾil al-muḍāraba	Kitāb masāʾil mutashābiha	Kitāb al-muḍāraba		
	Masāʾil al-mutāshabiha	Masāʾil al-ḥiyal	Kitāb masāʾil mutashābiha		Kitāb al-mushābiha		
					Kitāb al-ḥīla		
					Kitāb al-ḥiyal		

Works Cited

Manuscripts

Anonymous. *Al-Furūq fī l-fiqh*. MS Halet Efendi 807, Suleymaniye Library, Istanbul.
Anonymous. *Furūq Ibn Nujaym*. MS Osman Holdi 50, Suleymaniye Library, Istanbul.
Anonymous. *Kitāb al-Furūq*. MS Esad Efendi 884, Suleymaniye Library, Istanbul.
Anonymous. *Kitāb al-Farq*. MS Yazma Bağışlar 1187, Suleymaniye Library, Istanbul.
Anonymous. *Kitāb al-Furūq*. MS Halet Efendi 780, Suleymaniye Library, Istanbul.
Anonymous. *Masāʾil* [= *Kitāb al-Furūq*]. MS Oriental 6278, British Library, London.
Anonymous. *Risāla fī l-fiqh* [= *Kitāb al-Furūq*]. MS Halet Efendi 780, Suleymaniye Library, Istanbul.
Al-Arzustānī, Aḥmad ibn Muḥammad. *Kitāb al-Furūq*. MS Garrett 4577Y, Princeton University Library, Princeton.
Al-Dimashqī, Abū l-Faḍl Muslim ibn ʿAlī. *Al-Furūq al-fiqhiyya*. MS 4507, Chester Beatty Library, Dublin.
Al-Gharnāṭī, Abū ʿAbdallāh Muḥammad ibn Yūsuf al-ʿAbdarī l-Mālikī. *Al-Furūq*. MS fāʾ-alif 98–90, Maktabat Āl Ibn ʿĀshūr al-Tūnisī, La Marsa.
Ibn Ḥalwān al-Ṭabīb, Aḥmad. *Kitāb al-Furūq*. MS Ayasofya 4838, Suleymaniye Library, Istanbul.
Ibn al-Kutubī, Yūsuf ibn Ismāʿīl. *Kitāb fī l-farq bayn al-amrāḍ al-mushtabiha fī l-ṭibb*. MS Ahmet III 2120, Suleymaniye Library, Istanbul.
Ibn al-Kutubī, Yūsuf ibn Ismāʿīl. *Mā lā yasaʿu l-ṭabīb jahluhu*. MS Mansuri Collection R128.3.I127 1682, Library of Congress, Washington DC.
Ibn al-Turkumānī, Tāj al-Dīn Aḥmad ibn ʿUthmān ibn Ibrāhīm ibn Muṣṭafā. *Kitāb al-Furūq*. MS Ẓāhiriyya 4501, Asadiyya Library, Damascus.
Al-Jurjānī, Abū l-ʿAbbās Aḥmad ibn Muḥammad. *Kitāb al-Muʿāyāt fī l-fiqh ʿalā madhhab al-Imām al-Shāfiʿī*. MS Fiqh Shāfiʿī 915, Dār al-Kutub al-Miṣriyya, Cairo.
Marghāyatī(?), Shaykh Bāyazīd ibn Isrāʾīl ibn Ḥājjī Dāwūd. *Kitāb al-Furūq*. MS Arabe 812, Bibliothèque nationale de France, Paris.
Al-Nāṭifī, Abū ʿAbbās Aḥmad ibn Muḥammad. *Al-Ajnās wa-l-furūq*. MS Nuruosmaniye 1371, Suleymaniye Library, Istanbul.
Al-Nāṭifī, Abū ʿAbbās Aḥmad ibn Muḥammad. *Al-Ajnās wa-l-furūq*. MS Esad Efendi 542, Suleymaniye Library, Istanbul.
Al-Naysābūrī, Najm al-Dīn. *Kitāb al-Furūq*. MS Giresun Yazmalar 44, Suleymaniye Library, Istanbul.
Al-Naysābūrī, Najm al-Dīn. *Kitāb al-Furūq*. MS Or. 481, Leiden University Libraries, Leiden.
Al-Qāḍī ʿAbd al-Wahhāb ibn ʿAlī l-Baghdādī l-Mālikī. *Al-Jumūʿ wa-l-furūq*. MS 588, Markaz Dirāsāt al-Mujāhidīn al-Lībiyīn, Tripoli.
Al-Sharīf, Ḥusayn ibn Muḥammad. *Nafāʾis majālis al-sulṭāniyya fī ḥaqāʾiq asrār al-qurʾāniyya*. MS Ahmet III 2680, Topkapı Sarayı Müzesi Kütüphanesi, Istanbul.
Al-Zarīrānī, Abū Muḥammad Sharaf al-Dīn ʿAbd al-Raḥīm ibn ʿAbdallāh. *Kitāb Īḍāḥ al-dalāʾil fī l-farq bayn al-masāʾil*. MS Garrett 4577Y, Princeton University Library, Princeton.

https://doi.org/10.1515/9783110605792-014

Printed Sources

Abā Ḥusayn, ʿAlī, ed. *Fihrist makhṭūṭāt al-baḥrayn.* 2 vols. Manama: Markaz al-Wathāʾiq al-Tārīkhiyya, 1404/1983.

ʿAbd al-Tawwāb, Ramaḍān. "*Kitāb al-Farq li-Ibn Fāris wa-turāth al-farq fī l-ʿarabiyya*," In *Kitāb al-farq* by Ibn Fāris al-Lughawī. Edited by Ramaḍān ʿAbd al-Tawwāb, 39–43. Cairo: Maktabat al-Khātimī; Riyadh: Dār al-Rifāʿī, 1402/1982.

Abū l-Ajfān, Muḥammad and Ḥamza Abū Fāris. "*Al-Dirāsa.*" In *al-Furūq al-fiqhiyya* by Abū l-Faḍl Muslim al-Dimashqī. Edited by Muḥammad Abū l-Ajfān and Ḥamza Abū Fāris 9–58. Beirut: Dār al-Gharb al-Islāmī, 1992.

Abū l-Ajfān, Muḥammad and ʿUthmān Baṭīkh. "*Dirāsa tamhīdiyya.*" In *Durrat al-ghawāṣṣ fī muḥaḍārat al-khawāṣṣ* by Ibn Farḥūn. Edited by Muḥammad Abū l-Ajfān and ʿUthmān Baṭīkh, 5–53. Cairo: Dār al-Turāth; Tunis: al-Maktaba l-ʿAtīqa[, 1980].

Abū Fāris, Ḥamza. "*Al-Qism al-dirāsī.*" In *ʿIddat al-furūq fī jamʿ mā fī l-madhhab min al-jumūʿ wa-l-furūq* by Abū l-ʿAbbās Aḥmad ibn Yaḥyā ibn Muḥammad al-Wansharīsī. Edited by Ḥamza Abū Fāris, 9–76. Beirut: Dār al-Gharb al-Islāmī, 1990/1410.

Abū Shāma Shihāb al-Dīn ʿAbd al-Raḥmān al-Maqdisī. *Tarājim rijāl al-qarnayn al-sādis wa-l-sābiʿ al-maʿrūf bi-l-Dhayl ʿalā l-Rawḍatayn.* 5 vols. Edited by Ibrāhīm Shams al-Dīn. Dār al-Kutub al-ʿIlmiyya, 1422/2002.

Al-Afghānī, Abū ʿUmar Sayyid Ḥabīb ibn Aḥmad al-Madanī. *Al-Furūq al-fiqhiyya ʿind Imām Ibn Qayyim al-Jawziyya jamʿan wa-l-dirāsa.* 3 vols. Riyadh: Maktabat al-Rushd Nāshirūn, 2009.

Ahmad, Ahmad A. *Structural Interrelations of Theory and Practice in Islamic Law: A Study of Six Works of Medieval Islamic Jurisprudence.* Leiden: Brill, 2006.

Ali, Samer. *Arabic Literary Salons in the Islamic Middle Ages.* South Bend, IN.: Notre Dame University Press, 2010.

Al-ʿĀmilī, Muḥsin al-Ḥusaynī. *Aʿyān al-Shīʿa.* 28 vols. Edited by Ḥasan al-Amīn and Muḥsin al-Amīn. Beirut: Dār al-Taʿāruf, 1960–.

Aristotle. *On Sophistical Refutations. On Coming-to-be and Passing Away. On the Cosmos.* Edited and translated by E.S. Forster and D.J. Furley. Cambridge, MA: Harvard University Press, 1955.

Al-ʿAskarī, Abū Hilāl. *Al-Furūq al-lughawiyya.* Edited by Muḥammad Ibrāhīm Salīm. Cairo: Dār al-ʿIlm wa-l-Thaqāfa, 1998.

Al-ʿAskarī, Abū Hilāl. *Kitāb al-Awāʾil.* 2 vols. Edited by Muḥammad al-Miṣrī and Walīd Qaṣṣāb. Damascus: Wizārat al-Thaqāfa wa-l-Irshād al-Qawmī, 1975.

Al-ʿAskarī, Abū Hilāl. *Kitāb al-Ṣināʿatayn al-kitāba wa-l-shiʿr.* Edited by ʿAlī Muḥammad al-Bajāwī and Muḥammad Abū l-Faḍl Ibrāhīm. [Cairo:] Dār Iḥyāʾ al-Kutub al-ʿArabiyya, 1371/1952.

Al-Aṣmaʿī, ʿAbd al-Malik ibn Qurayb. *Kitāb al-Farq.* Edited by Ṣabīḥ al-Tamīmī. Beirut: Dār Usāmah, 1987.

Al-Asnawī, Jamāl al-Dīn ʿAbd al-Raḥīm ibn al-Ḥasan. *Al-Alghāz al-fiqhiyya wa-huwa l-kitāb al-musammā Ṭirāz al-mahāfil fī alghāz al-masāʾil.* Edited by Muḥammad ʿUthmān and Ṭaha ʿAbd al-Ruʾūf Saʿd. Cairo: al-Maktaba l-Azhariyya li-l-Turāth, 1433/2012.

Al-Asnawī, Jamāl al-Dīn ʿAbd al-Raḥīm ibn al-Ḥasan. *Maṭāliʿ al-daqāʾiq fī taḥrīr al-jawāmiʿ wa-l-fawāriq.* 2 vols. Edited by Naṣr al-Dīn Farīd Muḥammad Wāṣil. Cairo: Dār al-Shurūq, 2007.

Al-Asnawī, Jamāl al-Dīn ʿAbd al-Raḥīm ibn al-Ḥasan. *Ṭabaqāt al-shāfiʿiyya*. 2 vols. Edited by Kamāl Yūsuf al-Ḥūt. Beirut: Dār al-Kutub al-ʿIlmiyya, 1407/1987.

Al-ʿAsqalānī, Shihāb al-Dīn Aḥmad ibn ʿAlī ibn Muḥammad ibn Ḥajar. *Al-Durar al-kāmina fī aʿyān al-miʾa l-thāmina*. 4 vols. No ed. Beirut: Dār Iḥyāʾ al-Turāth al-ʿArabī, [197–].

Al-ʿAsqalānī, Shihāb al-Dīn Aḥmad ibn ʿAlī ibn Muḥammad ibn Ḥajar. *Fatḥ al-bārī*. 18 vols. Edited by ʿAbd al-ʿAzīz ibn Bāz. Beirut: Dār al-Maʿrifa, 1970.

Ayoub, Samy. "We're not in Kufa Anymore: The Construction of Late Ḥanafism in the Early Modern Ottoman Empire, 16th–19th Centuries CE." Ph.D. Diss., University of Arizona, 2014.

Al-Azem, Talal. *Rule-Formulation and Binding Precedent in the* Madhhab-*Law Tradition*. Leiden: Brill, 2016.

Baalbaki, Ramzi. *The Arabic Lexicographical Tradition: From the 2nd/8th to the 12th/18th Century*. Leiden: Brill, 2014.

Baalbaki, Ramzi. "*Kitāb al-ʿAyn* and *Jamharat al-Lugha*." In *Early Medieval Arabic: Studies on al-Khalīl ibn Aḥmad*, edited by Karin C. Ryding, 44–62. Washington D.C.: Georgetown University Press, 1998.

Badawi, Muhammad, ed. *Modern Arabic Literature: The Cambridge History of Arabic Literature*. Cambridge: Cambridge University Press, 1992.

Al-Baghdādī, Ismāʿīl Bāshā. *Hadiyat al-ʿārifīn asmāʾ al-muʿallifīn wa-āthār al-muṣannifīn*. 2 vols. 1951–55. Reprint, Beirut: Dār Iḥyāʾ al-Turāth al-ʿArabī, n.d.

Al-Baghdādī, Ismāʿīl Bāshā. *Kitāb Īḍāḥ al-maknūn fī l-dhayl ʿalā Kashf al-ẓunūn*. Istanbul: Millî Eğtim Basımevi, 1972.

Al-Bāḥusayn, Yaʿqūb ibn ʿAbd al-Wahhāb. *Al-Furūq al-fiqhiyya wa-l-uṣūliyya: muqawwamātuhā shurūṭuhā nashʾatuhā taṭawwuruhā; dirāsa naẓariyya waṣfiyya tārīkhiyya*. Riyadh: Maktabat al-Rushd, 1419/1998.

Al-Bājī, Sulaymān ibn Khalaf. *Kitāb al-Minhāj fī tartīb al-ḥijāj*. Edited by ʿAbd al-Majīd Turkī. Beirut: Dār al-Gharb al-Islāmī, 1987.

Al-Bakrī, ʿĀdil. "*Taqdīm al-kitāb*." In *al-Furūq bayn ishtibāhāt al-ʿilal* by Ibn al-Jazzār. Edited by Ramziyya l-Aṭraqjī, أ-ج. Baghdad: Wizārat al-Taʿlīm al-ʿĀlī wa-l-Baḥth al-ʿIlmī, Jāmiʿat Baghdād, Bayt al-Ḥikmah, 1989.

Al-Bakrī, Muḥammad ibn Abī Bakr. *Al-Istighnāʾ fī l-farq wa-l-istithnāʾ*. Edited by Saʿūd ibn Musʿad ibn Musāʿid al-Thubaytī. Mecca: al-Mamlaka l-ʿArabiyya l-Saʿūdiyya, Jāmiʿat Umm al-Qurā, Maʿhad al-Buḥūth al-ʿIlmiyya wa-Iḥyāʾ al-Turāth al-Islāmī, Markaz Iḥyāʾ al-Turāth al-Islāmī, 1988.

Al-Bakrī, Muḥammad ibn Abī Bakr. *Al-Iʿtināʾ fī l-farq wa-l-istihnāʾ kitāb yabḥathu fī qawāʿid al-fiqh al-islāmī wa-furūʿihi*. Edited by ʿĀdil Aḥmad ʿAbd al-Mawjūd and ʿAlī Muḥammad Muʿawwad. Beirut: Dār al-Kutub al-ʿIlmiyya, 1991.

Al-Baqqūrī, Muḥammad ibn Ibrāhīm. *Tartīb al-furūq wa-khtiṣārihā*. 2 vols. Edited by ʿUmar ibn ʿAbbād. Morocco: al-Mamlakah al-Maghribiyya Wizārat al-Awqāf wa-l-Shuʾūn al-Islāmiyya, 1414/1994.

Al-Barqī, Aḥmad ibn Muḥammad ibn Khālid. *Al-Maḥāsin*. 2 vols. Edited by al-Sayyid Jalāl al-Dīn al-Ḥusaynī. Tehran: Dār al-Kutub al-Islāmiyya 1370/1951.

Al-Bashar, Ibrāhīm ibn Nāṣir ibn Ibrāhīm. "*Al-Muqaddima*." In *Kitāb al-Muʿāyāt fī l-fiqh ʿalā madhhab al-Imām al-Shāfiʿī*, by Abū l-ʿAbbās Aḥmad ibn Muḥammad al-Jurjānī. Edited by Ibrāhīm ibn Nāṣir ibn Ibrāhīm al-Bashar, 3–106. PhD. Diss.: Jāmiʿat Umm al-Qurā, 1415[/1994].

Bauer, Thomas. "al-Azharī, Khālid ibn ʿAbdallāh." *Encyclopaedia of Islam, THREE.* Edited by Kate Fleet et al. Leiden: Brill 2008–.

Bauer, Thomas. *Die Kultur der Ambiguität: Eine Andere Geschichte des Islams.* Berlin: Verlag der Weltreligionen, 2011.

Becker, Carl H. "Christliche Polemik und islamische Dogmenbildung." *Zeitschrift für Assyriologie und verwandte Gebiete* 26 (1912): 171–95.

Bencheneb, Mohamed. "Lughz." Encyclopaedia of Islam, New Edition. Edited by H.A.R. Gibb et al. Leiden: Brill, 1960–2004.

Berkey, Jonathan P. "Popular Culture under the Mamluks: A Historiographical Survey." *Mamluk Studies Review* 9.2 (2005): 133–46.

Bernards, Monique. "Grammarians' Circle of Learning: A Social Network Analysis." In *ʿAbbasid Studies II: Occasional Papers of the School of ʿAbbasid Studies, Leuven, 28 June – 1 July 2004*, edited by John Nawas, 143–64. Leuven: Uitgeverij Peeters en Departement Oosterse Studies, 2010.

Bernards, Monique. "*Ṭalab al-ʿIlm* amongst the Linguists of Arabic during the ʿAbbāsid Period." In *ʿAbbasid Studies: Occassional Papers of the School of ʿAbbasid Studies, Cambridge, 6–10 July 2002*, edited by J.E. Montgomery, 111–28. Leuven: Uitgeverij Peeters en Departement Oosterse Studies, 2004.

Birnbaum, Eleazar. "Kātib Chelebi (1609–1657) and Alphabetization: A Methodological Investigation of the Autographs of his *Kashf al-Ẓunūn* and *Sullam al-Wuṣūl*." In *Scribes et manuscrits du Moyen-Orient*, edited by François Déroche and Francis Richard, 236–63. Paris: Bibliothèque nationale de France, 1997.

Blachère, Régis. *Un poète arabe du IVe siècle de l'Hégire (Xe siècle de J.-C.): Abou ṭ-Ṭayyib al-Motanabbî.* Paris: Adrien-Maissonneuve, 1935.

Blecher, Joel. "Ḥadīth Commentary in the Presence of Students, Patrons, and Rivals: Ibn Ḥajar and Ṣaḥīḥ al-Bukhārī in Mamluk Cairo." *Oriens* 41 (2013): 261–87.

Blecher, Joel. "In the Shade of the *Ṣaḥīḥ:* Politics, Culture and Innovation in an Islamic Commentary Tradition." Ph.D. Diss., Princeton University, 2013.

Blecher, Joel. *Said the Prophet of God: Hadith Commentary Across a Millenium.* Oakland: University of California Press, 2018.

Bosworth, C. E. "Muʿammā." Encyclopaedia of Islam, New Edition. Edited by H.A.R. Gibb et al. Leiden: Brill, 1960–2004.

Brockelmann, Carl. *Geschichte der arabischen Litteratur.* 2 vols and suppl. Second revised edition. Leiden: Brill, 1943.

Brookshaw, Dominic P. "Palaces, Pavilions, and Pleasure-Gardens: The Context and Setting of the Medieval *Majlis*." *Middle Eastern Literatures* 6.3 (2003): 199–223.

Brown, Jonathan A. C. "New Data on the Delateralization of *Ḍād* and its Merger with *Ẓāʾ* in Classical Arabic: Contributions from Old South Arabic and the Earliest Islamic Texts on Ḍ / Ẓ Minimal Pairs." *Journal of Semitic Studies* 52.2 (2007): 335–68.

Brunschvig, Robert. *La Berbérie orientale sous les Ḥafṣides des origines à la fin du XV siècle.* Paris: Adrien-Maisonneuve, 1940–47.

Burak, Guy. *The Second Formation of Islamic Law: The Ḥanafī School in the Early Modern Ottoman Empire.* Cambridge: Cambridge University Press, 2015.

Cahen, Claude and Charles Pellat. "Ibn ʿAbbād." Encyclopaedia of Islam, New Edition. Edited by H.A.R. Gibb et al. Leiden: Brill, 1960–2004.

Calder, Norman. *Islamic Jurisprudence in the Classical Era*. Edited by Colin Imber and Robert Gleave. Cambridge: Cambridge University Press, 2010.

Calder, Norman. "Al-Nawawi's Typology of Muftis and Its Significance for a General Theory of Islamic Law." *Islamic Law and Society* 3.2 (1996): 137–64.

Carter, Michael. "Arabic Grammar." In *Cambridge History of Arabic Literature: Religion, Learning and Science in the ʿAbbāsid Period*, edited by M.J.L. Young et al., 118–38. Cambridge: Cambridge University Press, 1990.

Carter, Michael. "Lexicography, Medieval." In *Encyclopedia of Arabic Literature*. 2 vols. Edited by Julie Scott Meisami and Paul Starkey. London: Ashgate, 1998.

Cavitch, Max. "Genre." In *The Princeton Encyclopedia of Poetry and Poetics*, 4th edition, edited by Roland Greene et al. Princeton: Princeton University Press, 2012.

Chaumont, Éric. "L'Autorité des textes au sein du šāfi'isme ancien." Paper presented at the conference "Rethinking Islamic Law: Can *Fiqh* be Applied Law?" Rabat, Morocco, 13 – 15 November, 2013.

Chaumont, Éric. "Préface." In *Kitāb al-Lumaʿ fī uṣūl al-fiqh; le Livre des Rais illuminant les fondements de la compréhsion de la Loi; Traité de théorie légale musulmane* by Muḥammad ibn Ibrāhīm al-Shīrāzī, 3–35. Translated by Éric Chaumont. Berkeley: Robbins Collection, 1999.

Cohen, David. "Koiné, langues communes et dialectes arabes." *Arabica* 9.2 (1962): 119–44.

Cook, Michael A. "The Origins of '*Kalām*.'" *Bulletin of the School of Oriental and African Studies* 43.1 (1980): 32–43.

Coulson, Noel J. *Succession in the Muslim Family*. Cambridge: Cambridge University Press, 1971.

Davidson, Arnold. *The Emergence of Sexuality: Historical Epistemology and the Formation of Concepts*. Cambridge, MA: Harvard University Press, 2002.

De Jong, Pieter and Michael Jan de Goeje. *Catalogus Codicum Orientalium Bibliothecae Academiae Lugduno Batavae*. Vol. 4. Leiden: Brill, 1861.

Al-Dhahabī, Shams al-Dīn Muḥammad ibn Aḥmad. *Siyar aʿlām al-nubalāʾ*. 25 vols. Edited by Shuʿayb al-Arnāʾūṭ, Ḥusayn Asad et al. Beirut: Muʾassasat al-Risāla, 1317/1996.

Al-Dhahabī, Shams al-Dīn Muḥammad ibn Aḥmad. *Taʾrīkh al-islām wa-wafayāt al-mashāhīr wa-l-aʿlām*. 53 vols. Edited by ʿUmar ʿAbd al-Salām Tadmurī. Beirut: Dār al-Kitāb al-ʿArabī, 1497/1987 – 1424/2004.

Al-Dimashqī, Abū l-Faḍl Muslim ibn ʿAlī. *Al-Furūq al-fiqhiyya*. Edited by Muḥammad Abū l-Ajfān and Ḥamza Abū Fāris. Beirut: Dār al-Gharb al-Islāmī, 1992.

El Shamsy, Ahmed. *The Canonization of Islamic Law: A Social and Intellectual History*. New York: Cambridge University Press, 2013.

El Shamsy, Ahmed. "The *Ḥāshiya* in Islamic Law: A Sketch of Shāfiʿī Literature." *Oriens* 41 (2013): 289–315.

El Shamsy, Ahmed. "Al-Shāfiʿī's Written Corpus: A Source-Critical Study." *Journal of the American Oriental Society* 132.2 (2012): 199–210.

Ellis, Alexander G. and Edward Edwards. *A Descriptive List of the Arabic Manuscripts Acquired by the Trustees of the British Museum since 1894*. London: British Museum, 1912.

Endress, Gerhard. "The Cycle of Knowledge: Intellectual Traditions and Encyclopaedias of the Rational Sciences in Arabic Islamic Hellenism." In *Organizing Knowledge: Encyclopaedic*

Activities in the Pre-Eighteenth Century Islamic World, edited by Gerhard Endress, 103–34. Leiden: Brill, 2006.

Escovitz, Joseph H. *The Office of Qāḍī al-Quḍāt in Cairo under the Baḥrī Mamlūks*. Berlin: Klaus Schwarz Verlag, 1984.

Fadel, Mohammad. "The Social Logic of *Taqlīd* and the Rise of the *Mukhtaṣar*." *Islamic Law and Society* 3.2 (1996): 193–223.

Feest, Uljana and Thomas Sturm. "What (Good) is Historical Epistemology? Editors' Introduction." *Erkenntnis* 75 (2011): 285–302.

Fowler, Alastair. "Genre." *Encyclopedia of Literature and Criticism*. Edited by Martin Cole. Detroit: Gale Research, 1990.

Frank, Richard M. *Beings and Their Attributes: The Teaching of the Basrian School of the Muʿtazila in the Classical Period*. Albany, NY: State University of New York Press, 1978.

Al-Ghazzī, Najm al-Dīn. *Luṭf al-samar wa-qaṭf al-thamar min tarājim aʿyān al-ṭabaqāt al-ūlā min al-qarn al-ḥādī ʿashr*. 2 vols. Edited by Maḥmūd al-Shaykh. Damascus: Wizārat al-Thaqāfa wa-l-Irshād al-Qawmī, 1981.

Al-Ghiryānī, Maḥmūd Salāmah. "*Al-Qism al-dirāsī*." In *al-Furūq al-fiqhiyya li-l-Qāḍī ʿAbd al-Wahhāb al-Baghdādī wa-ʿalāqatuhā bi-Furūq al-Dimashqī* by ʿAbd al-Wahhāb al-Baghdādī. Edited by Maḥmūd Salāmah al-Ghiryānī, 13–72. Dubai: Dār al-Buḥūth li-l-Dirāsāt al-Islāmiyya wa-Ihyāʾ al-Turāth, 1424/2003.

Gimaret, Daniel. "Muʿtazila." *Encyclopaedia of Islam, New Edition*. Edited by H.A.R. Gibb et al. Leiden: Brill, 1960–2004.

Goodmann, L.E. "Rāzī vs Rāzī – Philosophy in the *Majlis*." In *The* Majlis: *Interreligious Encounters in Medieval Islam*, edited by Hava Lazarus-Yafeh, Mark R. Cohen, Sasson Somekh, and Sidney Griffith, 84–107. Wiesbaden: Harrasowitz Verlag, 1999.

Griffel, Frank. "On the Character, Content, and Authorship of *Itmām Tatimmat Ṣiwān al-ḥikma* and the Identity of the Author of *Muntakhab Ṣiwān al-ḥikma*." *Journal of the American Oriental Society* 133.1 (2013): 1–20.

Gruendler, Beatrice. "Al-ʿAskarī, Abū Aḥmad." *Encyclopaedia of Islam, THREE*. Edited by Kate Fleet et al. Leiden: Brill, 2008–.

Gruendler, Beatrice. "Al-ʿAskarī, Abū Hilāl." *Encyclopaedia of Islam, THREE*. Edited by Kate Fleet et al. Leiden: Brill, 2008–.

Haarman, Ulrich. "Arabic in Speech, Turkish in Lineage: Mamluks and Their Sons in the Intellectual Life of Fourteenth-Century Egypt and Syria." *Journal of Semitic Studies* 33.1 (1988): 81–114.

Al-Ḥabīb, Aḥmad ibn Ibrāhīm ibn ʿAbdallāh. "*Al-Muqaddima*." In *al-Nukat wa-l-Furūq li-masāʾil al-Mudawwana qism al-ʿibādāt* by ʿAbd al-Ḥaqq ibn Muḥammad al-Ṣiqillī. Edited by Aḥmad ibn Ibrāhīm ibn ʿAbdallāh al-Ḥabīb, 1–147. PhD Diss., Jāmiʿat Umm al-Qurā, 1416/1996.

Hacking, Ian. *Historical Ontology*. Cambridge, MA: Harvard University Press, 2004.

Ḥājjī Khalīfa. *Kashf al-ẓunūn ʿan asāmī l-kutub wa-l-funūn*. 2 vols. Edited by Şerefettin Yaltkaya and Kilisli Rifat Bilge. Istanbul: Milli Eğitim Basımevi, 1971.

Ḥājjī Khalīfa. *Mīzān al-ḥaqq fī khtiyār al-aḥaqq*. Istanbul: Maṭbaʿat Abū l-Ḍiyāʾ, 1306/1889.

Al-Ḥakīm al-Tirmidhī, Muḥammad ibn ʿAlī. *Al-Furūq wa-manʿ al-tarāduf*. Edited by Muḥammad Ibrāhīm al-Juyūshī. Cairo: al-Nahār, 1998.

Halim, Fachrizal A. *Legal Authority in Premodern Islam: Yaḥyā ibn Sharaf al-Nawawī in the Shāfiʿī School of Law*. Abingdon, Oxon: Routledge, 2015.

Hallaq, Wael. *Authority, Continuity, and Change in Islamic Law.* Cambridge: Cambridge University Press, 2005.
Hallaq, Wael. "From *Fatwās* to *Furū'*: Growth and Change in Islamic Substantive Law." *Islamic Law and Society* 1 (1994): 29–65.
Hallaq, Wael. *The Origins and Evolution of Islamic Law.* Cambridge: Cambridge University Press. 2005.
Hallaq, Wael. *Sharī'a: Theory, Practice, Transformations.* Cambridge: Cambridge University Press, 2009.
Hallaq, Wael. "*Takhrīj* and the Construction of Juristic Authority." In *Studies in Islamic Legal Theory*, edited by Bernard Weiss, 317–35. Leiden: Brill, 2002.
Hallaq, Wael. "Was the Gate of Ijtihad Closed?" *International Journal of Middle Eastern Studies* 16 (1984): 3–41.
Al-Ḥamawī, Aḥmad ibn Muḥammad. *Ghamz 'uyūn al-baṣā'ir: Sharḥ Kitāb al-Ashbāh wa-l-naẓā'ir* printed with Ibrahīm ibn Nujaym al-Miṣrī, *al-Ashbāh wa-l-Naẓā'ir.* 4 vols. No ed. Beirut: Dār al-Kutub al-'Ilmiyya, 1405/1985.
Hämeen-Anttila, Jaakko. "Al-Aṣma'ī, Early Arabic Lexicography, and *Kutub al-Farq.*" *Zeitschrift für Geschichte der arabisch-islamischen Wissenschaften* 16 (2005): 141–48.
Hämeen-Anttila, Jaakko. *Maqama: A History of a Genre.* Wiesbaden: Harrassowitz, 2002.
Al-Ḥanafī, Muḥammad Abū l-Fatḥ. *Itḥāf al-abṣār wa-l-baṣā'ir bi-tabwīb Kitāb al-Ashbāh wa-l-naẓā'ir.* Alexandria: al-Maṭba'a al-Waṭaniyya, 1289[/1872–73].
Hanna, Nelly. *In Praise of Books: A Cultural History of Cairo's Middle Class, Sixteenth to Eighteenth Century.* Cairo: The American University in Cairo Press, 2004.
Al-Ḥarīrī, Abū Muḥammad al-Qāsim ibn 'Alī. *Maqāmāt al-Ḥarīrī.* No ed. Beirut: Maktabat al-Ma'ārif, 1873.
Haykel, Bernard. *Revival and Reform in Islam: The Legacy of Muhammad al-Shawkānī.* Cambridge: Cambridge University Press, 2003.
Haywood, John. *Arabic Lexicography: Its History and Its Place in the General History of Lexicography.* Leiden: Brill, 1965.
Heinrichs, Wolfhart. "*Qawā'id* as a Genre of Legal Literature." In *Studies in Islamic Legal Theory* edited by Bernard Weiss, 365–84. Leiden: Brill, 2002.
Heinrichs, Wolfhart. "Structuring the Law: Remarks on the *Furūq* Literature." In *Studies in Honour of Clifford Edmund Bosworth: Volume I, Hunter of the East; Arabic and Semitic Studies*, edited by Ian Richard Netton, 332–44. Leiden: Brill, 2000.
Hirschler, Konrad. *The Written Word in the Medieval Arabic Lands: A Social and Cultural History of Reading Practices.* Edinburgh: Edinburgh University Press, 2012.
Hodgson, Marshall G.S. *The Venture of Islam: Conscience and History in a World Civilization.* 3 vols. Chicago: University of Chicago Press, 1974.
Humphreys, Stephen. *Islamic History: A Framework for Inquiry.* Revised edition. Princeton: Princeton University Press, 2001.
Ḥunayn ibn Isḥāq. *Risāla fī l-farq bayn al-nafs wa-l-rūḥ.* Edited by Louis Cheikho, reprinted in *Ḥunain ibn Isḥāq: Texts and Studies*, edited by Fuat Sezgin et al. Frankfurt am Main: Institute for the History of Arabic-Islamic Science at the Johann Wolfgang Goethe University, 1999.
Ibn Abī Uṣaybi'a, Aḥmad ibn al-Qāsim. *'Uyūn al-anbā' fī ṭabaqāt al-aṭibbā'.* Edited by Nizār Riḍā. Beirut: Dār Maktabat al-Ḥayāt, [1965].

Ibn al-Akfānī, Muḥammad ibn Ibrāhīm ibn Sāʿid al-Anṣārī, al-Ḥakīm al-Mutaṭayyib. *Irshād al-qāṣid ilā asnā l-maqāṣid fī anwāʿ al-ʿulūm*. Edited by ʿAbd al-Munʿim Muḥammad ʿUmar and Aḥmad Ḥilmī ʿAbd al-Raḥmān. Cairo: Dār al-Fikr al-ʿArabī, [1990].
Ibn ʿAlī al-Balawī, Aḥmad. *Al-Thabat*. Edited by ʿAbdallāh al-ʿImrānī. Beirut: Dār al-Gharb al-Islāmī, 1403/1983.
Ibn Farḥūn, Ibrāhīm ibn ʿAlī. *Al-Dībāj al-mudhahhab fī maʿrifat aʿyān ʿulamāʾ al-madhhab*. 2 vols. No editor. Beirut: Dār al-Kutub al-ʿIlmiyya, 2004.
Ibn Farḥūn, Ibrāhīm ibn ʿAlī. *Durrat al-ghawāṣṣ fī muḥāḍarat al-khawāṣṣ*. Edited by Muḥammad Abū l-Ajfān and ʿUthmān Baṭīkh. Cairo: Dār al-Turāth; Tunis: al-Maktaba l-ʿAtīqa[, 1980].
Ibn Fāris al-Lughawī, Abū l-Ḥusayn Aḥmad. *Kitāb Futyā faqīh al-ʿarab*. Edited by Ḥusayn ʿAlī Maḥfūẓ in *Majallat al-Majmaʿ al-ʿIlmī l-ʿArabī* 33.3 (1377/1958): 441–66; 33.4 (1377/1958): 633–56.
Ibn Fūrak, Muḥammad ibn al-Ḥusayn. *Maqālāt al-Shaykh Abū l-Ḥasan al-Ashʿarī Imām Ahl al-Sunna*. Edited by Aḥmad ʿAbd al-Raḥīm al-Sāyiḥ. Cairo: Maktabat li-l-Thaqāfa l-Dīniyya, 1425/2005.
Ibn al-ʿImād, Shihāb al-Dīn ʿAbd al-Ḥayy ibn Aḥmad. *Shadharāt al-dhahab fī akhbār man dhahab*. 10 vols. Edited by ʿAbd al-Qādir al-Arnāʾūṭ and Maḥmūd al-Arnāʾūṭ. Damascus: Dār Ibn Kathīr, 1410/1989.
Ibn al-Jawzī, Abū l-Faraj ʿAbd al-Raḥmān ibn ʿAlī. *Al-Muntaẓam fī tawārīkh al-mulūk wa-l-umam*. 11 vols. Edited by Suhayl Zakkār. Beirut: Dār al-Fikr, 1415/1995–96.
Ibn al-Jawzī, Abū l-Faraj ʿAbd al-Raḥmān ibn ʿAlī. *Talbīs Iblīs*. No ed. Beirut: Dār al-Qalam, 1403[/1983].
Ibn al-Jazzār, Aḥmad ibn Jaʿfar. *Al-Furūq bayn ishtibāhāt al-ʿilal*. Edited by Ramziyya l-Aṭraqjī. Baghdad: Wizārat al-Taʿlīm al-ʿĀlī wa-l-Baḥth al-ʿIlmī, Jāmiʿat Baghdād, Bayt al-Ḥikmah, 1989.
Ibn Jinnī, Abū l-Fatḥ ʿUthmān. *Sirr ṣināʿat al-iʿrāb*. 2 vols. Edited by Ḥasan Hindāwī. Damascus: Dār al-Qalam, 1985.
Ibn Juljul, Sulaymān ibn Ḥassān. *Ṭabaqāt al-aṭibba wa-l-ḥukamāʾ*. Edited by Fuʾād Sayyid. Cairo: Imprimerie de l'Insitut Français d'Archéologie orientale, 1955.
Ibn Khālawayh, al-Ḥusayn ibn Aḥmad. *Names of the Lion*. Translated by David Larsen. Seattle: Wave Books, 2017.
Ibn Khaldūn. *Taʾrīkh Ibn Khaldūn al-musammā Dīwān al-mubtadaʾ wa-l-khabar fī taʾrīkh al-ʿarab wa-l-barbar wa-man ʿāṣarahum min dhawī l-shaʾn al-akbar*. 8 vols. Edited by Khalīl Shaḥāda and Suhayl Zakkār. Beirut: Dār al-Fikr, 1981–83.
Ibn Khaldūn. *The Muqaddimah: An Introduction to History*. 3 vols. Translated by Franz Rosenthal. New York: Pantheon Books, 1958.
Ibn Khallikān, Shams al-Dīn Aḥmad ibn Muḥammad. *Ibn Khallikan's Wafayat al-A'yan wa Anba' Abna' al-Zaman (M. de Slane's English Translation)*. Translated by Mac-Guckin de Slane. Edited by S Moinul Haq. Karachi: Pakistan Historical Society, 1961.
Ibn Khallikān, Shams al-Dīn Aḥmad ibn Muḥammad. *Wafayāt al-aʿyān wa-anbāʾ abnāʾ al-zamān*. 8 vols. Edited by Iḥsān ʿAbbās. Beirut: Dār Ṣādir, 1397/1977–1398/1978.
Ibn al-Nadīm, Muḥammad ibn Isḥāq. *Al-Fihrist li-l-Nadīm*. 2 vols. Edited by Ayman Fuʾād Sayyid. London: Muʾassasat al-Furqān li-l-Turāth al-ʿArabī, 1430/2009.

Ibn Nujaym al-Miṣrī, Zayn al-ʿĀbidīn Ibrāhīm. *Kitāb al-Ashbāh wa-l-naẓāʾir* printed with Aḥmad ibn Muḥammad al-Ḥamawī, *Ghamz ʿuyūn al-baṣāʾir sharḥ Kitāb al-Ashbāh wa-l-naẓāʾir.* No ed. Beirut: Dār al-Kutub al-ʿIlmiyya, 1405/1985.

Ibn Qāḍī Shuhba, Taqī l-Dīn Abū Bakr ibn Aḥmad. *Ṭabaqāt al-shāfiʿiyya.* 4 vols. Edited by al-Ḥāfiẓ ʿAbd al-ʿAlīm Khān. Beirut: Dār al-Kutub al-ʿIlmiyya, 1407[/1986].

Ibn al-Qifṭī, ʿAlī ibn Yūsuf. *Taʾrīkh al-ḥukamāʾ wa-huwa Mukhtaṣar al-zūzanī al-musammā bi-l-Muntakhabāt al-multaqaṭāt min Kitāb Ikhbār al-ʿulamāʾ bi-akhbār al-ḥukamāʾ.* Baghdad: Maktabat al-Muthannā, 196[?]; reprint of *Ibn al-Qifṭīs Taʾrīh al-ḥukamāʾ, auf Grund der Vorarbeiten Aug. Müllers.* Edited by Julius Lippert. Leipzig: Dieterich'sche Verlagsbuchhandlung, 1903.

Ibn Qutayba, ʿAbdallāh ibn Muslim. *Adab al-kātib.* Edited by Muḥammad al-Dālī. Beirut: Muʾassasat al-Risāla, 1967.

Ibn Quṭlūbughā, Zayn al-Dīn Qāsim. *Tāj al-tarājim fī ṭabaqāt al-ḥanafiyya, Die Krone der Lebensbescheibungen enthaltend die Classen der Hanefiten.* Edited by Gustav Flügel. Leipzig: In Commision bei F. A. Brockhaus, 1862.

Ibn Rajab, ʿAbd al-Raḥmān Muḥammad ibn Aḥmad al-Ḥanbalī. *Al-Dhayl ʿalā Ṭabaqāt al-ḥanābila.* 5 vols. Edited by ʿAbd al-Raḥmān Muḥammad ibn Sulaymān al-ʿUthaymīn. Mecca: Maktabat al-ʿUbaykān, 1425/2005.

Ibn Rajab, ʿAbd al-Raḥmān Muḥammad ibn Aḥmad al-Ḥanbalī. *Al-Farq bayn al-naṣīḥa wa-l-taʿyīr.* 3rd edition. Edited by Najam ʿAbd al-Raḥmān. Damascus, Beirut: Dār al-Maʾmūn li-l-Turāth, 1405[/1980].

Ibn al-Shiḥna, ʿAbd al-Birr ibn Muḥammad. *Alghāz al-ḥanafiyya li-Ibn al-Shiḥna l-musammā l-Dhakhāʾir al-ashrafiyya fī alghāz al-ḥanafiyya.* Edited by Fāṭima Shihāb. Cairo: al-Maktaba l-Azhariyya li-l-Turāth, 2014.

Ibn Sikkīt, Yaʿqūb ibn Isḥāq. *Kitāb al-Alfāẓ: aqdam muʿjam fī l-maʿānī.* Edited by Fakhr al-Dīn Qabbāwa. Beirut: Maktabat Lubnān, 1998.

Ibn al-Sunayna, Muʿaẓẓam al-Dīn Abū ʿAbdallāh al-Sāmarrī. *Al-Furūq min awwal kitāb al-jināyāt ilā nihāyat al-kitāb dirāsatan wa-taḥqīqan.* Edited by Anas ibn ʿUmar ibn Muḥammad al-Subayyil. MA Thesis, Jāmiʿat Umm al-Qurā University, 1435/2014.

Ibn al-Sunayna, Muʿaẓẓam al-Dīn Abū ʿAbdallāh al-Sāmarrī. *Kitāb al-Furūq ʿalā madhhab al-Imām Aḥmad ibn Ḥanbal.* Edited by Muḥammad ibn Ibrāhīm ibn Muḥammad al-Yaḥyā. Riyadh: Dār al-Ṣumayʿī, 1997.

Ibn al-Wakīl, Muḥammad ibn Makkī. *Al-Ashbāh wa-l-naẓāʾir fī fiqh al-shāfiʿiyya.* Edited by Muḥammad Ḥasan Muḥammad Ḥasan Ismāʿīl. Beirut: Dār al-Kutub al-ʿIlmiyyah, 2002.

Ibn al-Wazīr, Muḥammad ibn Ibrāhīm. *al-ʿAwāṣim wa-l-qawāṣim fī l-dhabb ʿan sunnat Abī Qāsim.* 9 vols. Edited by Shuʿayb al-Arnāʾūṭ. Beirut: Muʾassasat al-Risāla, 1415/1994.

Ibn Zabāra, Muḥammad ibn Muḥammad al-Ḥasanī l-Yamanī. *Mulḥiq al-Badr al-ṭāliʿ bi-maḥāsin man baʿd al-qarn al-sābiʿ.* 2 vols. Beirut: Dār al-Maʿrifa, n.d.

Ibrahim, Ahmed Fekry. "The Codification Episteme in Islamic Juristic Discourse between Inertia and Change." *Islamic Law and Society* 22 (2015): 157–220.

Ibrahim, Ahmed Fekry. *Pragmatism in Islamic Law: A Social and Intellectual History.* Syracuse, NY: Syracuse University Press, 2015.

Iskandar, A.Z. *A Catalogue of Arabic Manuscripts on Medicine in the Wellcome Historical Medical Library.* London: The Wellcome Historical Medical Library, 1967.

İsmail Hakkı Bursevi. *al-Furūq.* No ed. Dersaʿādet: Şirket-i Ṣaḥḥāfīye-'i ʿOsmānīye, 1308/1890–91.

Jackson, Sherman. *Islamic Law and the State: The Constitutional Jurisprudence of Shihāb al-Dīn al-Qarāfī*. Leiden: Brill, 1996.
Jackson, Sherman. "*Taqlīd*, Legal Scaffolding and the Scope of Legal Injunctions in Post-Formative Theory *Muṭlaq* and *ʿĀmm* in the Jurisprudence of Shihāb al-Dīn al-Qarāfī." *Islamic Law and Society* 3.2 (1996): 165–92.
Jalāl, Ibrāhīm Ismāʿīl. *Al-Furūq al-fiqhiyya li-l-Imām Mālik*. Beirut: Dār al-Kutub al-ʿIlmiyya, 2007.
Al-Jallad, Ahmad. "New Evidence from a Safaitic Inscription for a Late Velar/Uvular Realization of *ṣ in Aramaic." *Semitica* 58 (2016): 257–70.
Al-Jandārī, Aḥmad ibn ʿAbdallāh. *Tarājim al-rijāl al-madhkūra fī Sharḥ al-Azhār*. n.p.: Maṭbaʿat al-Tamaddun, 1913/1332.
Jaques, R. Kevin. *Authority, Conflict, and the Transmission of Diversity in Medieval Islamic Law*. Leiden: Brill, 2006.
Al-Jihānī, Jalāl. "*Muqaddima*." In *al-Furūq al-fiqhiyya* by Abū Muḥammad al-Qāḍī ʿAbd al-Wahhāb al-Baghdādī ibn ʿAlī. Edited by Jalāl ʿAlī l-Qadhdhāfī l-Jihānī, 9–26. Dubai: Dār al-Buʿūth li-l-Dirāsāt al-Islāmiyya wa-Ihyāʾ al-Turāth, 1424/2003.
Johansen, Baber. "The All-Embracing Town and Its Mosques." *Revue de l'Occident musulman et de la Mediterranée* 32 (1981): 139–61.
Johansen, Baber. *The Islamic Law on Land Tax and Rent: The Peasants' Loss of Property Rights under the Hanafite Doctrine*. London: Croom Helm, 1988.
Johansen, Baber. "Legal Literature and the Problem of Change." In *Islam and Public Law: Classical and Contemporary Studies*, edited by Chibli Mallat, 29–47. London: Graham and Trotman, 1993. Reprinted in Baber Johansen. *Contingency in a Sacred Law*, 446–64. Leiden: Brill, 1998.
Al-Jurjānī, Abū l-ʿAbbās Aḥmad ibn Muḥammad. *Al-Muʿāyāt fī l-ʿaql aw al-Furūq*. Edited by Muḥammad Fāris. Beirut: Dār al-Kutub al-ʿIlmiyya, 1993.
Al-Juwaynī, Abū Muḥammad ʿAbdallāh ibn Yūsuf. *Al-Jamʿ wa-l-farq*. 3 vols. Edited by ʿAbd al-Raḥmān ibn Salāmah ibn ʿAbdallāh al-Mazīnī. Beirut: Dār al-Jīl, 1424/2004.
Al-Juwaynī, Imām al-Ḥaramayn ʿAbd al-Malik ibn ʿAbdallāh. *Al-Kāfiya fī l-jadal*. Edited by Fawqiyya Ḥusayn Maḥmūd. Cairo: Maṭbaʿa ʿĪsā l-Bābī l-Ḥalabī wa-Shurakāʾuhu, 1399/1979.
Kaḥḥāla, ʿUmar Riḍā. *Muʿjam al-muʾallifīn: Tarājim muṣannifī l-kutub al-ʿarabiyya*. 4 vols. Damascus: Muʾassasat al-Risāla, 1376/1957.
Kanazi, George. *Studies in the Kitāb aṣ-Ṣināʿatayn of Abū Hilāl al-ʿAskarī*. Brill: Leiden, 1989.
Karabela, Mehmet. "The Development of Dialectic and Argumentation Theory in Post-Classical Islamic Intellectual History." PhD Diss., McGill University, 2011.
Al-Karābīsī, Asʿad ibn Muḥammad. *Al-Furūq li-l-Karābīsī*. 2 vols. Edited by Muḥammad Ṭumūm and ʿAbd al-Sattār Abū Ghudda. Kuwait: Wizārat al-Awqāf wa-l-Shuʾūn al-Islāmiyya, 1402/1982.
Al-Karābīsī, Muḥammad ibn Ṣāliḥ. *Kitāb al-Furūq*. Edited by ʿAbd al-Muḥsin Saʿīd Aḥmad al-Zahrāṇī. Ph.D Diss., Jāmiʿat Umm al-Qurā, 1418/1997.
Al-Kāsānī, ʿAlāʾ al-Dīn Abū Bakr ibn Masʿūd. *Badāʾiʿ al-ṣanāʾiʿ fī tartīb al-sharāʾiʿ*. 10 vols. Beirut: Dār al-Kutub al-ʿIlmiyya, 1406/1998.
Kemalpaşazade. *Furūq al-uṣūl*. Edited by Muḥammad ibn ʿAbd al-ʿAzīz al-Mubārak. Beirut: Dār Ibn Ḥazm, 2009.

Kızılkaya, Necmettin. *İslâm hukukunda farklar: Furûk literatürü üzerine bir inceleme*. Istanbul: İz Yayıncılık, 2016.

Kraus, Paul and George Vajda. "Ibn al-Rāwandī or al-Rēwendī." Encyclopaedia of Islam, New Edition. Edited by H.A.R. Gibb et al. Leiden: Brill, 1960–2004.

Al-Laknawī, Abū l-Ḥasanāt Muḥammad ibn ʿAbd al-Ḥayy. *Al-Fawāʾid al-bahiyya fī tarājim al-ḥanafiyya*. Edited by Muḥammad Badr al-Dīn Abū Firās al-Naʿsānī. Cairo: Aḥmad Nājī l-Jamālī wa-Muḥammad Amīn al-Khānjī, 1905.

Lane, Edward William. *An Arabic-English Lexicon in Eight Parts*. 8 vols. Beirut: Librarie du Liban, 1968.

Larkin, Margaret. "Popular Poetry in the Post-Classical Period." In *Cambridge History of Arabic Literature: Arabic Literature in the Post-Clasical Period*, edited by Roger Allen and D.S. Richards, 191–244. Cambridge: Cambridge University Press, 2006.

Lowry, Joseph E. "The First Islamic Legal Theory: Ibn al-Muqaffaʿ on Interpretation, Authority, and the Structure of the Law." *Journal of the American Oriental Society* 128 (2008): 25–40.

Lowry, Joseph E. Introduction to *The Epistle on Legal Theory* by Muḥammad ibn Idrīs al-Shāfiʿī, translated by Joseph E. Lowry, xv-xx. New York: New York University Press, 2013.

Lowry, Joseph E. "Is There Something Postmodern about *Uṣūl al-Fiqh? Ijmāʿ*, Constraint, and Interpretive Communities." In *Islamic Law in Theory: Studies on Jurisprudence in Honor of Bernard Weiss*. Edited by A. Kevin Reinhart and Robert Gleave, 285–315. Leiden: Brill, 2014.

Lowry, Joseph E. "The Legal Hermeneutics of al-Shāfiʿī and Ibn Qutayba: A Reconsideration." *Islamic Law and Society* 11 (2004): 1–41.

Lowry, Joseph E. and Devin J. Stewart, "Introduction," in *Essays in Arabic Literary Biography 1350–1850*, edited by Joseph E. Lowry and Devin Stewart, 1–11. Wiesbaden: Harrassowitz Verlag, 2009.

"*Madjlis*." *Encyclopaedia of Islam, New Edition*. Edited by H.A.R. Gibb et al. Leiden: Brill, 1960–2004.

Makdisi, George. *The Rise of Colleges: Institutions of Learning in Islam and the West*. Edinburgh: Edinburgh University Press, 1981.

Makdisi, George. *The Rise of Humanism in Classical Islam and the Christian West: With Special Reference to Scholasticism*. Edinburgh: Edinburgh University Press, 1990.

Makhlūf, Muḥammad ibn Muḥammad. *Shajarat al-nūr al-zakiyya fī ṭabaqāt al-mālikiyya*. 2 vols. Cairo: al-Maṭbaʿa l-Salafiyya wa-Maktabatihā, 1349[/1930–31].

Al-Mardāwī, Alāʾ al-Dīn Abū l-Ḥasan ʿAlī ibn Sulaymān. *Al-Inṣāf fī maʿrifat al-rājiḥ min al-khilāf ʿalā madhhab al-imām al-mubajjal Aḥmad ibn Ḥanbal*. 12 vols. Edited by Muḥammad Ḥāmid al-Faqī. Cairo: Maṭbūʿat al-Sunna l-Muḥammadiyyah, 1374/1955–1377/1958.

Marʿī, Yūsuf, ed. *Bayān al-farq bayn al-ṣadr wa-l-qalb wa-l-fuʾād wa-l-lubb al-mansūb li-Abī ʿAbdallāh Muḥammad ibn ʿAlī l-Ḥakīm al-Tirmidhī*, attributed to al-Ḥakīm al-Tirmidhī, Muḥammad ibn ʿAlī. Amman: al-Markaz al-Malikī li-l-Buḥūth wa-l-Dirāsāt al-Islāmiyya, 2009.

Markaz al-Malik al-Fayṣal li-l-Buḥūth wa-l-Dirāsāt al-Islāmiyyah. *Khizānat al-turāth: Fihris shāmil li-ʿanāwīn al-makhṭūṭāt wa-amākinihā wa-arqām ḥifẓihā fī maktabāt al-ʿālam*. n.d. CD-ROM.

Al-Mashāyikh, Amal. *Abū Hilāl al-ʿAskarī nāqidan.* Amman: Wizārat al-Thaqāfa, 2002.

Masud, Muhammad Khalid, Brinkley Messick, and David S. Powers. "Muftis, Fatwas, and Islamic Legal Interpretation." In *Islamic Legal Interpretation: Muftis and Their Fatwas.* Edited by Muhammad Khalid Masud, Brinkley Messick, and David S. Powers, 3–32. Cambridge, MA: Harvard University Press, 1996.

Al-Mazīnī, ʿAbd al-Raḥmān ibn Salāma ibn ʿAbdallāh. "*al-Bāb al-thānī fī dirāsat al-kitāb.*" In *al-Jamʿ wa-l-farq* by ʿAbdallāh al-Juwaynī. 3 vols. Edited by ʿAbd al-Raḥmān ibn Salāma ibn ʿAbdallāh al-Mazīnī, 1:19–36. Beirut: Dār al-Jīl, 1424/2004.

Melchert, Christopher. *The Formation of the Sunni Schools of Law: 9th – 10th Centuries C.E.* Leiden: Brill, 1997.

Miller, Larry B. "Islamic Disputation Theory: A Study in the Development of Dialectic in Islam from the Tenth through Fourteenth Centuries." PhD Diss., Princeton University, 1984.

Montgomery, James E. "Speech and Nature: al-Jāḥiẓ, *Kitāb al-Bayān wa-l-tabyīn*, 2.175–207," Parts 1–4, *Middle Eastern Literatures* 11.2 (2008): 169–91; 12.1 (2009): 1–25; 12.2 (2009): 107–25; 12.3 (2009): 213–32.

Muʾassasat Āl al-Bayt. *Al-Fihris al-shāmil li-l-turāth al-ʿarabī l-islāmī l-makhṭūṭ.* Second edition. Amman: Muʾassasat Āl al-Bayt, n.d.

Muranyi, Miklos. *Die Rechtsbücher der Qairawāners Saḥnūn B. Saʿīd: Entstehungsgeschichte und Werküberlieferung.* Stuttgart: Deutsche Morgenländische Gesellschaft; F. Steiner, 1999.

Musa, Khadiga. "Legal Maxims as a Genre of Islamic Law: Origins, Development, and Significance of *al-Qawāʿid al-Fiqhiyya.*" *Islamic Law and Society* 21 (2014): 325–65.

Musa, Khadiga. "Part One: The Genre of *al-Qawāʿid al-fiqhiyya.*" In *A Critical Edition of 'Umdat al-Nāẓir 'alā al-Ashbāh wa'l-Naẓā'ir* by Abū l-Suʿūd al-Husaynī. Edited by Khadiga Musa. Sheffield: Equinox, 2018.

Al-Musawi, Muhsin. "The Medieval Islamic Literary World-System: The Lexicographic Turn." *Mamluk Studies Review* 17 (2013): 43–71.

Al-Musawi, Muhsin. "Pre-Modern Belletristic Prose." In *Cambridge History of Arabic Literature: Arabic Literature in the Post-Clasical Period*, edited by Roger Allen and D.S. Richards, 101–33. Cambridge: Cambridge University Press, 2006.

Al-Nābulusī, ʿAbd al-Ghanī. *Taḥqīq al-qaḍiyya fī l-farq bayn al-rishwa wa-l-hadiya.* Edited by ʿAlī Muḥammad Muʿawwaḍ and ʿĀdil Aḥmad ʿAbd al-Mawjūd. Cairo: Maktabat al-Zahrāʾ, 1412/1991.

Najm al-Dīn al-Ṭūfī, Sulaymān ibn ʿAbd al-Qawī. *ʿAlam al-jadhal fī ʿilm al-jadal.* Edited by Wolfhart Heinrichs. Wiesbaden: Franz Steiner Verlag, 1408/1987.

Naṣṣār, Ḥusayn. *Al-Muʿjam al-ʿarabī: nashʾatuhu wa-taṭawwuruhu.* Expanded edition. 2 vols. Cairo: Dār Miṣr, 1408/1988.

Al-Nawawī, Abū Zakariyyāʾ Muḥyī l-Dīn ibn Sharaf. *Kitāb al-Majmūʿ sharḥ al-Muhadhdhab li-l-Shīrāzī.* 23 vols. Edited by Muḥammad Najīb al-Muṭīʿī. Jedda: Maktabat al-Irshād, 1992.

Neuberger, Max. "The Early History of Urology." Translated by David Riesman. *Bulletin of the Medical Library Association* 25.3 (1937): 147–65.

Nicholson, Reynold. *A Literary History of the Arabs.* Cambridge: Cambridge University Press, 1907.

Petry, Carl F. *The Civilian Elite of Cairo in the Later Middle Ages.* Princeton: Princeton University Press, 1981.

Pfeifer, Helen. "Encounter after the Conquest: Scholarly Gatherings in 16th-Century Ottoman Damascus." *International Journal of Middle East Studies* 47 (2015): 219 – 39.

Pomerantz, Maurice. "Ebn ʿAbbād, Emāʾīl, al-Ṣāheb Kāfī al-Kofāt." *Encyclopaedia Iranica.* Edited by Ehsan Yarshater. London: Routledge, 1982–.

Pomerantz, Maurice. *Licit Magic: The Life and Letters of al-Ṣāḥib ibn ʿAbbād (d. 385/995).* Leiden: Brill, 2017.

Pormann, Peter E. and Emilie Savage-Smith. *Medieval Islamic Medicine.* Edinburgh: Edinburgh University Press, 2007.

Powers, David S. *Law, Society, and Culture in the Maghrib, 1300 – 1500.* Cambridge: Cambridge University Press, 2002.

Al-Qāḍī ʿIyāḍ ibn Mūsā. *Tartīb al-madārik wa-taqrīb al-masālik li-maʿrifat aʿlām madhhab Mālik.* 8 vols. Edited by Saʿīd Aḥmad Aʿrāb. [Rabāt?:] al-Mamlaka l-Maghribiyya Wizārat al-Awqāf wa-l-Shuʾūn al-Islāmiyya, 1402/1982.

Qāḍīkhān, al-Ḥasan ibn Manṣūr. *Sharḥ al-Ziyādāt.* 6 vols. Edited by Qāsim Ashraf Nūr Aḥmad, Muḥammad Taqī l-ʿUthmānī, and Wahbat al-Zamīlī. Beirut: Dār Iḥyāʾ al-Turāth al-ʿArabī, 1426/2005.

Qaṭāya, Salman. "*Taṣdīr.*" In *Kitāb Mā l-fāriq aw al-Furūq aw Kalām fī l-furūq bayn al-amrāḍ* by Abū Bakr al-Rāzī. Edited by Salmān Qaṭāya, ج. Aleppo: Jāmiʿat Ḥalab, Maʿhad al-Turāth al-ʿIlmī l-ʿArabī, 1398/1978.

Al-Qarāfī, Abū l-ʿAbbās Aḥmad ibn Idrīs. *Al-Furūq aw Anwār al-burūq fī anwāʾ al-furūq.* Printed with *Idrār al-shurūq ʿalā Anwāʾ al-furūq* by Ibn al-Shāṭṭ; *Tahdhīb al-Furūq*; and *al-Qawāʿid al-sunniyya fī l-asrār al-fiqhiyya* by Muḥammad ʿAlī ibn Ḥusayn al-Makki. 4 vols. Edited by Khalīl Mansūr. Beirut: Dār al-Kutub al-ʿIlmiyya, 1418/1998.

Al-Qarāfī, Abū l-ʿAbbās Aḥmad ibn Idrīs. *The Criterion for Distinguishing Legal Opinions from Judicial Rulings and the Administrative Acts of Judges and Rulers.* Translated by Mohammad H. Fadel. New Haven, CT: Yale University Press, 2017.

Al-Qirqisānī, Yaʿqūb ibn Isḥāq. *Kitāb al-Anwār wal-marāqib: code of Karaite law.* 5 vols. Edited by Leon Nemoy. New York: Alexander Kohut Memorial Foundation, 1939 – 43.

Al-Qurashī, Abū Muḥammad ʿAbd al-Qādir ibn Muḥammad. *Al-Jawāhir al-muḍiyya fī ṭabaqāt al-ḥanafiyya.* 5 vols. Edited by ʿAbd al-Fattāḥ Muḥammad al-Ḥulw. Giza: Hajr, 1413/1993.

Qusṭā ibn Lūqā. *Risāla fī l-farq bayn al-rūḥ wa-l-nafs.* Edited by ʿAlī Muḥammad Isbir. Damascus: Dār al-Yanābīʿ, 2006.

Quṭrub, Abū ʿAlī Muḥammad ibn al-Mustanīr. *Kitāb al-Farq.* Edited by Khalīl Ibrāhīm al-ʿAṭiyya and Ramaḍān ʿAbd al-Tawwāb. Cairo: Maktabat al-Thaqāfa l-Dīniyya, 1987.

Quṭrub, Abū ʿAlī Muḥammad ibn al-Mustanīr. *Das Kitāb al-wuḥūsh mit einem Paralleltexts von Quṭrub.* Edited by Rudolf Geyer. Vienna: F. Tempksy 1888.

Rabb, Intisar. "Doubt's Benefit: Legal Maxims in Islamic Law, 7th–16th centuries." Ph.D. Diss., Princeton University, 2009.

Rabb, Intisar. *Doubt in Islamic Law: A History of Legal Maxims, Interpretation, and Islamic Criminal Law.* Cambridge: Cambridge University Press, 2014.

Rabb, Intisar. "Islamic Legal Maxims as Substantive Canons of Construction: *Ḥudūd*-Avoidance in Cases of Doubt." *Islamic Law and Society* 17 (2010): 63 – 125.

Al-Ramlī, Shams al-Dīn Muḥammad ibn Aḥmad. *Nihāyat al-muḥtāj ilā sharḥ al-Minhāj fī l-fiqh ʿalā madhhab al-Imām al-Shāfiʿī wa-maʿahu Ḥashiyat Abī l-Ḍiyāʾ Nūr al-Dīn ʿAlī l-Shabrāmallisī l-Qāhirī l-mutawaffī 1087 H [wa-] Ḥāshiyat Aḥmad ibn ʿAbd al-Razzāq ibn

Muḥammad ibn Aḥmad al-maʿrūf bi-l-Maghribī l-Rashīdī. 8 vols. No ed. Beirut: Dār al-Kutub al-ʿIlmiyya, 1424/2003.

Rapoport, Yossef. *Marriage, Money, and Divorce in Medieval Islamic Society.* Cambridge: Cambridge University Press, 2005.

Raz, Joseph. *The Concept of a Legal System: An Introduction to the Theory of Legal System.* 2nd edition. Oxford: Clarendon Press, 1980.

Al-Rāzī, Abū Bakr Muḥammad ibn Zakarīyāʾ. *Kitāb Mā l-fāriq aw al-Furūq aw Kalām fī l-furūq bayn al-amrāḍ.* Edited by Salmān Qaṭāya. Aleppo: Jāmiʿat Ḥalab, Maʿhad al-Turāth al-ʿIlmī l-ʿArabī, 1398/1978.

Riedel, Dagmar A. "Searching for the Islamic Episteme: The Status of Historical Information in Medieval Middle-Eastern Anthological Writing." Ph.D. Diss., Indiana University, 2004.

Rippin, Andrew. "Aaron." *Encyclopaedia of Islam, THREE.* Edited by Kate Fleet et al. Leiden: Brill, 2008–.

Robin, Christian Julien. "Les inscriptions de l'arabie antique et les études arabe." *Arabica* 68.4 (2001): 509–77.

Robinson, Chase F. *Islamic Historiography.* Cambridge: Cambridge University Press, 2003.

Rowson, Everett. "Alexandrian Age in Fourteenth-Century Damascus: Twin Commentaries on Two Celebrated Arabic Epistles." *Mamluk Studies Review* 8 (2003): 97–110.

Al-Sabīl, ʿUmar ibn Muḥammad ibn ʿAbdallāh. "*Al-Muqaddima.*" In *Īḍāḥ al-dalāʾil fī l-farq bayn al-masāʾil* by ʿAbd al-Raḥīm ʿAbdallāh Zarīrānī. Edited by ʿUmar ibn Muḥammad ibn ʿAbdallāh al-Sabīl, 1:17–121. Mecca: al-Mamlaka l-ʿArabiyya l-Saʿūdiyya, Wizārat al-Taʿlīm al-ʿĀlī, Jāmiʿat Umm al-Qurā, Maʿhad al-Buḥūth al-ʿIlmiyya wa-Iḥyāʾ al-Turāth al-Islāmī, 1414/1993.

Al-Ṣafadī, Khalīl ibn Aybak. *Ikhtirāʿ al-khurāʿ.* Edited by Fārūq Asalīm. Damacus: Ittiḥād al-Kuttāb al-ʿArab[, 2000].

Al-Ṣafadī, Khalīl ibn Aybak. *Al-Wāfī bi-l-wafāyāt.* 28 vols. Edited by Aḥmad al-Arnaʾūṭ and Turkī Muṣṭafā. Beirut: Dār Iḥyāʾ al-Turāth al-ʿArabī, 2000.

Al-Ṣāḥib ibn ʿAbbād, Abū l-Qāsim Ismāʿīl. *Al-Farq bayn al-ḍād wa-l-ẓāʾ.* Edited by Muḥammad Ḥasan Āl Yā Sīn. Baghdad: Maktabat al-Nahḍa; al-Maktaba l-ʿIlmiyya; Maṭbaʿa l-Maʿārif, 1377/1958.

Al-Ṣāliḥ, Yūsuf. *Al-Furūq al-fiqhiyya li-Ibn Qayyim al-Jawziyya muntazaʿ min aghlab kutub Ibn Qayyim raḥimahu Allāh taʿālā.* Riyadh: Yūsuf al-Ṣāliḥ, 2009.

Sālimān, Muḥammad. *Fann al-alghāz ʿind al-ʿarab wa-maʿhu l-Lafẓ al-lāʾiq wa-l-maʿnā l-rāʾiq [wa-]l-Alghāz al-naḥwiyya [wa-]l-Ṭāʾir al-maymūn fī ḥall lughz al-Kanz al-madfūn.* Edited by Muḥammad Sālimān. Cairo: al-Hayʾa l-Miṣriyya l-ʿĀmma li-l-Kitāb, 2012.

Schacht, Joseph. "Aus zwei arabischen *Furūq*-Büchern." *Islamica* 2 (1926): 505–37.

Schacht, Joseph. "Classicisme, traditionalisme et ankylose dans la loi religieuse de l'Islam." *Classicisme et decline culturel dans l'histoire de l'Islam.* Edited by R. Brunschvig and G.E. von Grunebaum, 141–61. Paris: G.P. Maisonneuve et Larose, 1977.

Schacht, Joseph. *An Introduction to Islamic Law.* Clarendon Press: Oxford, 1982.

Schacht, Joseph. "Ikhtilāf." *Encyclopaedia of Islam, New Edition.* Edited by H.A.R. Gibb et al. Leiden: Brill, 1960–2004.

Schoeler, Gregor. *The Genesis of Literature in Islam: From the Aural to the Read.* Translated by Shawkat M. Toorawa. Edinburgh: Edinburgh University Press, 2009.

Seidensticker, Tilman. "Lexicography: Classical Arabic." *Encyclopedia of Arabic Language and Linguistics.* Edited by Lutz Edzard et al. Leiden: Brill, 2007.

Seyed-Gohrab, A. A. "The Art of Riddling in Classical Persian Poetry." *Edebiyat* 12 (2001): 15–36.

Sezgin, Fuat. *Geschichte des arabischen Schrifttums.* 9 vols. Leiden: Brill, 1967–94.

Al-Shāfiʿī, Muḥammad ibn Idrīs. *The Epistle of Legal Theory.* Edited and translated by Joseph E. Lowry. New York: New York University Press, 2013.

Al-Shīrāzī, Abū Isḥāq. *Al-Muhadhdhab fī fiqh al-Imām al-Shāfiʿī.* 3 vols. Edited by Muḥammad al-Zuḥaylī. Damascus: Dār al-Qalam; Beirut: al-Dār al-Shāmiyya, 1416/1996.

Al-Shīrāzī, Abū Isḥāq. *Ṭabaqāt al-fuqahāʾ.* Edited by Iḥsān ʿAbbās. Beirut: Dār al-Rāʾid al-ʿArabī, 1970.

Shoshan, Boaz. *Popular Culture in Medieval Cairo.* Cambridge: Cambridge University Press, 1993.

Al-Ṣiqillī, ʿAbd al-Ḥaqq ibn Muḥammad. *Kitāb al-Nukat wa-l-furūq li-masāʾil al-Mudawwana wa-l-Mukhtalaṭa.* 2 vols. Edited by Aḥmad ibn ʿAlī. Casablanca: Markaz al-Turāth al-Thaqafī; Beirut: Dār Ibn Ḥazm, 2009.

Al-Ṣiqillī, ʿAbd al-Ḥaqq ibn Muḥammad. *Al-Nukat wa-l-furūq li-masāʾil al-mudawwana qism al-ʿibādāt.* Edited by Aḥmad ibn Ibrāhīm ibn ʿAbdallāh al-Ḥabīb. PhD Diss., Jāmiʿat Umm al-Qurā, 1416/1996.

Sluga, Hans. *Wittgenstein.* Malden, MA: Wiley-Blackwell, 2011.

Stetkevych, Suzanne P. *Abū Tammām and the Poetics of the ʿAbbāsid Age.* Leiden: Brill, 1991.

Stewart, Devin. "Muḥammad b. Dāʾūd al-Ẓāhirī's Manual of Jurisprudence: *Al-Wuṣūl ilā maʿrifat al-uṣūl.*" In *Studies in Islamic Legal Theory,* edited by Bernard G. Weiss, 99–158. Leiden: Brill, 2002.

Stewart, Devin. "Muḥammad b. Jarīr al-Ṭabarī's *al-Bayān ʿan uṣūl al-aḥkām* and the Genre of *Uṣūl al-Fiqh* in Ninth-Century Baghdad." In *ʿAbbasid Studies: Occasional Papers of the School of ʿAbbasid Studies, Cambridge 6–10 July 2002,* edited by James Montgomery, p. 321–49. Leuven: Peeters, 2004.

Al-Subayyil, Anas ibn ʿUmar ibn Muḥammad. "*al-Taḥqīq.*" In *al-Furūq min awwal kitāb al-jināyāt ilā nihāyat al-kitāb dirāsatan wa-taḥqīqan* by Muʿaẓẓam al-Dīn Abū ʿAbdallāh Muḥammad ibn ʿAbdallāh al-Sāmarrī. Edited by Anas ibn ʿUmar ibn Muḥammad al-Subayyil. MA Thesis: Jāmiʿat Umm al-Qurā, 1435/2014.

Al-Subkī, Tāj al-Dīn. *Al-Ashbāh wa-l-naẓāʾir.* 2 vols. Edited by ʿĀdil Aḥmad ʿAbd al-Mawjūd and ʿAlī Muḥammad ʿAwaḍ. Beirut: Dār al-Kutub al-ʿIlmiyya, 1411/1991.

Al-Subkī, Tāj al-Dīn. *Ṭabaqāt al-shāfiʿiyya l-kubrā.* 10 vols. Edited by ʿAbd al-Fattāḥ Muḥammad al-Ḥulw and Maḥmūd Muḥammad al-Tannāḥī. Cairo: Dār Iḥyāʾ al-Kutub al-ʿArabiyya, 1994.

Ṣubḥ, Sāmī Muḥammad. *Al-Furūq al-fiqhiyya ʿind al-Imām al-Shāfiʿī fī Kitāb al-Umm.* Beirut: Dār al-Muqtabas, 2018.

Al-Suyūṭī, Jalāl al-Dīn. *Al-Ashbāh wa-l-naẓāʾir fī qawāʿid wa-furūʿ al-shāfiʿiyyah.* Edited by ʿAbd al-Karīm al-Faḍīlī. Beirut: Dār al-Kutub al-ʿIlmiyya, 1411/1990.

Al-Suyūṭī, Jalāl al-Dīn. *Kutub Khalq al-insān maʿ taḥqīq kitāb Ghayāt al-iḥsān fī khalq al-insān li-l-Suyūṭī.* Edited by Nihād Ḥasūbī Ṣāliḥ. Baghdad: Wizārat al-Thaqāfa wa-l-Iʿlām, 1989.

Al-Suyūṭī, Jalāl al-Dīn. *Al-Muzhir fī ʿulūm al-lugha wa-anwāʿihā.* 2 vols. Edited by Muḥammad Aḥmad Jād al-Mawlā Bek, Muḥammad Abū l-Faḍl Ibrāhīm, and ʿAlī Muḥammad al-Bajāwī. Cairo: Maktabat Dār al-Turāth, n.d.

Al-Tamīmī l-Dārī, Taqī l-Dīn ibn ʿAbd al-Qādir. *Al-Ṭabaqāt al-saniyya fī ṭabaqāt al-ḥanafiyya.* 4 vols. Edited by ʿAbd al-Fattāḥ Muḥammad Ḥulw. Riyadh: Dār al-Rifāʿī, 1983.

Ṭaşköprüzāde, Aḥmad ibn Muṣṭafā. *Miftāḥ al-saʿāda wa-miṣbāḥ al-siyāda fī mawḍūʿāt al-ʿulūm.* 3 vols. No ed. Beirut: Dār al-Kutub al-ʿIlmiyya, 1405/1985.

Thābit ibn Abī Thābit. *Kitāb al-Farq.* Edited by Ḥātim Ṣaliḥ al-Ḍāmin. Beirut: Muʾassasat al-Risāla, 1408/1988.

Todorov, Tzvetan. *Genres in Discourse.* Edited and translated by Catherine Porter. Cambridge: Cambridge University Press, 1990.

Ṭumūm, Muḥammad. "*Muqaddimat al-taḥqīq.*" In *al-Furūq li-l-Karābīsī* by Asʿad ibn Muḥammad al-Karābīsī. Edited by Muḥammad Ṭumūm and ʿAbd al-Sattār Abu Ghudda, 5–29. Kuwait: Wizārat al-Awqāf wa-l-Shuʾūn al-Islāmiyya, 1982.

Tuttle, Kelly. "Expansion and Digression: A Study in Mamlūk Literary Commentary." PhD Diss., University of Pennsylvania, 2013.

Al-ʿUlaymī, Mujīr al-Dīn ʿAbd al-Raḥmān ibn Muḥammad. *Al-Durr al-munaḍḍad fī dhikr asḥāb al-imām Aḥmad.* 2 vols. Edited by ʿAbd al-Raḥmān ibn Sulaymān al-ʿUthaymīn. [Riyadh(?)]: Maktabat al-Tawba; Cairo: Maṭbaʿat al-Madanī, 1412/1992.

Al-ʿUthaymīn, ʿAbd al-Raḥmān Muḥammad ibn Sulaymān. "*Muqaddimat al-muḥaqqiq*" in *Dhayl Ṭabaqāt al-ḥanābila* by Ibn Rajab al-Ḥanbalī. Edited by ʿAbd al-Raḥmān Muḥammad ibn Sulaymān al-ʿUthaymīn, 1:11–135. Mecca: Maktabat al-ʿUbaykān, 1425/2005.

van Ess, Josef. *Theologie und Gesellschaft im 2. und 3. Jahrhundert Hidschra: Eine Geschichte des religiösen Denkens im frühen Islam.* 6 vols. Berlin: De Gruyter, 1991–97.

van Ess, Josef. "Wāṣil b. ʿAṭāʾ." *Encyclopaedia of Islam, New Edition.* Edited by H.A.R. Gibb et al. Leiden: Brill, 1960–2004.

van Gelder, Geert Jan. "al-Abīwardī, Abū al-Muẓaffar Muḥammad." *Encyclopaedia of Islam, THREE.* Edited by Kate Fleet et al. Leiden: Brill, 2008–.

van Gelder, Geert Jan "*Badīʿ*." *Encyclopaedia of Islam, THREE.* Edited by Kate Fleet et al. Leiden: Brill, 2008–.

Vishanoff, David R. "A Reader's Guide to al-Shāfiʿī's *Epistle on Legal Theory* (*al-Risāla*)." *Islam and Christian-Muslim Relations* 28.3, 145–69.

Voorhoeve, Peter. *Handlist of Arabic Manuscripts in the University of Leiden and Other Collections in the Netherlands.* 2nd edition. The Hague: Leiden University Press, 1980.

Walzer, Richard. Introduction to *Galen on Medical Experience. First Edition of the Arabic Version with English Translation and Notes by R. Walzer* by Galen. Edited and translated Richard Walzer. London: Pub. For the trustees of the late Sir Henry Wellcome by the Oxford University Press, [1947].

Al-Wansharīsī, Abū l-ʿAbbās Aḥmad ibn Yaḥyā. *ʿIddat al-furūq fī jamʿ mā fī l-madhhab min al-jumūʿ wa-l-furūq.* Edited by Ḥamza Abū Fāris. Beirut: Dār al-Gharb al-Islāmī, 1990/1410.

Wāṣil, Naṣr al-Dīn Farīd Muḥammad. "*Dirāsa.*" In *Maṭāliʿ al-daqāʾiq fī taḥrīr al-jawāmiʿ wa-l-fawāriq* by Jamāl al-Dīn al-Asnawī. Edited by Naṣr al-Dīn Farīd Muḥammad Wāṣil, vol. 1. Cairo: Dār al-Shurūq, 2007.

Weiss, Bernard et al. "Alta Discussion." In *Studies in Islamic Legal Theory.* Edited by Bernard Weiss, 385–429. Leiden: Brill, 2002.

Welsh, Andrew and Eric J. Rettberg. “Riddles.” In *The Princeton Encyclopedia of Poetry and Poetics*, 4th edition, edited by Roland Greene et al. Princeton: Princeton University Press, 2012.

Weninger, Stefan. “More Sabaic minuscule texts from Munich.” *Proceedings of the Seminar for Arabian Studies* 32 (2002): 217 – 23.

Wensinck, Arent Jan. *Concordance et indices de la tradition musulmane: les six livres, le Musnad d’al-Dārimī, le Muwatta’ de Mālik, le Musnad de Aḥmad ibn Ḥanbal.* 8 vols. Leiden: E.J. Brill, 1933 – 38.

Wild, Stefan. *Das Kitāb al-ʿain und die arabische Lexicographie.* Wiesbaden: Harrassowitz, 1965.

Witkam, Januarius Justus. *De Egyptische Arts Ibn al-Akfānī (gest. 749/1348) En Zijn Indeling Van de Wetenschappen.* Leiden: Ter Lugt Pers, 1989.

Witkam, Januarius Justus. “Ibn al-Akfānī (d. 749/1348) and His Bibliography of the Sciences.” *Manuscripts of the Middle East* 2 (1987): 37 – 41.

Wittgenstein, Ludwig. *Preliminary Studies for the “Philosophical Investigations”; Generally known as The Blue and Brown Books.* New York: Harper & Row, 1965.

Wittgenstein, Ludwig. *On Certainty.* Edited by G. E. M. Anscombe. Translated by Denis Paul and G. E. M. Anscombe. Oxford: Blackwell, 1969.

Woodward, Ian. *Understanding Material Culture.* London: Sage, 2007.

Al-Yaḥyā, Muḥammad ibn Ibrāhīm ibn Muḥammad. “*Muqaddima.*” In *Kitāb al-Furūq ʿalā madhhab al-Imām Aḥmad ibn Ḥanbal* by Muʿaẓẓam al-Dīn Abū ʿAbdallāh al-Sāmarrī, ibn Sunayna. Edited by Muḥammad ibn Ibrāhīm ibn Muḥammad al-Yaḥyā, 2 – 114. Riyad: Dār al-Ṣumayʿī, 1997.

Yāqūt al ibn ʿAbdallāh al-Ḥamawī, Shihāb al-Dīn. *Muʿjam al-buldān.* 7 vols. No ed. Beirut: Dār Ṣādir, 1397/1977.

Yāqūt al ibn ʿAbdallāh al-Ḥamawī, Shihāb al-Dīn. *Muʿjam al-udabāʾ: irshād al-arīb ilā maʿrifat al-adīb.* 7 vols. Edited by Iḥsān ʿAbbās. Beirut: Dār al-Gharb al-Islāmī, 1993.

Young, Walter E. *The Dialectical Forge: Juridical Disputation and the Evolution of Islamic Law.* Cham: Springer, 2017.

Young, Walter E. “The Dialectical Forge: Proto-System Juridical Disputation in the *Kitāb Ikhtilāf al-ʿIrāqiyyīn.*” 2 vols. PhD Diss., McGill University, 2012.

Al-Zabīdī, Muḥammad Murtaḍā l-Ḥusaynī. *Tāj al-ʿarūs min jawāhir al-Qāmūs.* 40 vols. Edited by ʿAbd al-Sattār Aḥmad Farrāj et al. Kuwait: Maṭbaʿat Ḥukūmat al-Kuwayt, 1384/1965 – 1422/2001.

Al-Zahrānī, ʿAbd al-Muḥsin Saʿīd ibn Aḥmad. “*Al-Dirāsa.*” In *Kitāb al-Furūq* by Muḥammad ibn Ṣāliḥ al-Karābīsī. Edited by ʿAbd al-Muḥsin Saʿīd ibn Aḥmad al-Zahrānī, 2 – 84. Ph.D. Diss., Jāmiʿat Umm al-Qurā, 1417[/1996].

Al-Zarkashī, Badr al-Dīn Muḥammad. *Al-Baḥr al-muḥīṭ fī uṣūl al-fiqh.* 8 vols. No ed. Cairo: Dār al-Kutubī, 1414/1994.

Al-Zarkashī, Badr al-Dīn Muḥammad. *Al-Manthūr fī l-qawāʿid.* 3 vols. Edited by Taysīr Fāʾiq Aḥmad Maḥmūd and ʿAbd al-Sattār Abū Ghudda. Kuwait: Wizārat al-Awqāf wa-l-Shuʾūn al-Islāmiyya, 1402/1982.

Al-Ziriklī, Khayr al-Dīn. *Al-Aʿlām qāmūs tarājim li-ashhar al-rijāl wa-l-nisāʾ min al-ʿarab wa-l-mustaʿribīn wa-l-mustashriqīn.* 15th printing, 8 vols. Beirut: Dār al-ʿIlm li-l-Malāyīn, 2002.

Zysow, Aron. *The Economy of Certainty: An Introduction to the Typology of Islamic Legal Theory.* Atlanta: Lockwood Press, 2013.

Index

Aaron 85–87
Abbasid 2, 9, 58, 60, 123, 127, 154
ʿAbdallāh ibn ʿUmar 133
ʿAbd al-Tawwāb, Ramaḍān 61–63
al-Abīwardī, Abū l-Muẓaffar Muḥammad ibn Abī l-ʿAbbās 66
al-Abīwardī, Abū Yaʿqūb 66
Abū l-Ajfān, Muḥammad 5, 31, 39, 43, 73, 132, 135, 159, 170, 180, 185, 202, 207 f., 213
Abū l-ʿAlāʾ Ṣāʿid ibn Muḥammad 172
Abū ʿAlī Muḥammad ibn ʿAbd al-Wahhāb 67
Abū ʿAlī Muḥammad ibn al-Mustanīr, see Quṭrub
Abū Bakr al-Abharī 24
Abū Bakr al-Iskāfī 191
Abū Bakr al-Khallāl 24
Abū Fāris, Ḥamza 5, 31, 39, 43, 73, 159, 170, 180, 183, 185, 202, 207–210, 213
Abū Ḥanīfa l-Nuʿmān ibn Thābit 24
Abū Hurayra 149
Abū ʿImrān al-Qayrawānī 161
Abū Jaʿfar al-Baqanī 181
Abū Naṣr 63
Abū l-Qāsim al-Ṭābithī 170
Abū Shāma 173
Abū Ṭayyib al-Lughawī 61
Abū ʿUbayd al-Qāsim ibn Salām 63
Abū Yūsuf Yaʿqūb ibn Ibrāhīm 204
Abū Ziyād al-Kilābī 63
adab 56, 62, 67, 112, 122–124, 135
Ahmad, Ahmad A. 8, 10 f., 24, 70
Aḥmad ibn ʿAlī al-Balawī 181, 209
Aḥmad ibn Ḥanbal 10, 24, 31, 39, 102 f., 139, 150, 177, 210
Aḥmad ibn Ḥubb Allāh 174
alghāz 5, 14, 119, 135, 143
ʿAlī ibn Abī Ṭālib 10, 132 f.
ʿAlī ibn Yaḥyā bn Rāshid al-Yamanī 2, 163, 179–80, 186, 212, 216
analogy 21, 33, 89, 93, 104
Anatolia 56
Andalus 24
Aristotle 75, 91 f.
Armant 177
al-Armantī, Sirāj al-Dīn Yūnus ibn ʿAbd al-Mujīd ibn ʿAlī l-Hudhalī 177, 184, 216
al-ashbāh wa-l-naẓāʾir 5 f., 8, 35, 119, 164, 195 f.
al-ʿAskarī, Abū Aḥmad al-Ḥasan ibn ʿAbdallāh 65–68
al-ʿAskarī, Abū Hilāl al-Ḥasan ibn ʿAbdallāh 55–57, 65–68, 113, 197
al-Aṣmaʿī 63–65
al-Asnawī, Jamāl al-Dīn 39 f., 148 f., 151–153, 167 f., 173, 177, 185 f., 198–202, 212, 216
al-ʿAsqalānī, Ibn Ḥajar 124, 128, 178, 202, 205, 211, 213
al-Aṭraqjī, Ramziyya 47
al-Azharī, Khālid ibn ʿAbdallāh 134
al-Arzustānī, Aḥmad ibn Muḥammad 184, 188, 206

Baalbaki, Ramzi 58–60, 65
Badr al-Dīn ibn ʿUmar al-Ḥuraythī 162
Baghdad 2 f., 9, 24, 46, 50, 66, 71, 173, 179, 184–186, 188 f., 202 f., 206
al-Baghdādī, Ismail Bāshā 170, 172 f., 202–204, 206 f., 211 f., 215 f.
al-Bāḥusayn, Yaʿqūb 5, 16 f., 31–35, 40, 158 f., 162, 166–170, 172–182, 184 f., 188, 190, 198–214
al-Bakhnasā 177
al-Bakrī, ʿĀdil 47 f.
al-Bakrī, Badr al-Dīn 32, 159
al-Balkhī, Abū l-Qāsim 189
al-Bāqillānī, Abū Bakr 43
al-Baqqūrī, Muḥammad 40
al-Barqī, Aḥmad ibn Muḥammad 2, 162, 212, 215
al-Bashar, Ibrāhīm ibn Nāṣir ibn Ibrāhīm 136, 144 f., 200 f.
Basra 68, 210

https://doi.org/10.1515/9783110605792-015

Berlin 3, 5, 68, 82, 98, 149, 184, 187–189, 203, 205 f., 219 f.
Bilbeis 177
biobibliographic writing. See *ṭabaqāt*
Blecher, Joel 5, 124, 128 f.
Brockelmann, Carl 98, 169
Brown, Jonathan 9, 69–72
al-Bukhārī 124, 128, 133, 149
al-Bulqīnī, ʿUmar ibn Raslān 162, 213
Bursevi, İsmail Hakkı 56, 197

Cairo 2, 14 f., 40, 49, 57 f., 63 f., 67, 85, 89, 100, 103, 110, 119–121, 124–128, 130–132, 134 f., 137, 141, 148 f., 151 f., 154, 166, 168 f., 171, 173, 177–179, 186, 189, 198, 200–205, 208

ḍābiṭ, ḍawābiṭ 30, 32, 145 f. , 155
Damascus 66, 70, 74, 76, 126 f., 150, 154, 167 f., 173, 176, 178 f., 186, 188 f., 198, 205 f., 211, 219 f.
al-Dhahabī, Shams al-Dīn 46, 68, 73, 204
diagnostics. See distinctions, differential diagnostics
dialectics. See disputation
al-Dimashqī, Abū l-Faḍl Muslim ibn ʿAlī 32, 38 f., 159, 170, 179 f, 185, 207 f., 215
al-Dimashqī, Aḥmad ibn Asʿad Ibn Ḥalwān 46
disputation 12–14, 16 f., 23, 25–30, 34, 38, 41 f., 46, 53, 80–87, 89–109, 114, 118, 120, 122, 124 f., 136, 145, 149, 151 f., 175, 187, 194 f.
distinctions 2, 5 f., 11–20, 22–45, 47, 49 f., 52–57, 60–65, 69, 73–75, 77, 79–81, 86, 103–105, 107 f., 110–114, 116–123, 131 f., 136 f., 141–149, 151–192, 194–198, 212–215
– applied lexicographic distinctions 13, 43, 45, 74, 76 f., 79, 144, 162, 175
– differential diagnostics, *see also* medicine 12, 43–50, 79, 112
– lexicographic distinctions 12 f., 43–45, 56 f., 75, 77, 79, 111 f., 116–118, 162, 197, 212

Egypt 26, 123, 125, 130, 134, 148, 153 f., 177
El Shamsy, Ahmed 8–11, 13, 27, 96, 149, 155
epistemology, historical 23, 44, 120
ethics 12, 45, 76 f.

fatwa 4 f., 135, 140, 175, 213
furūʿ al-fiqh 1 f., 11
furūq. See distinctions
Furūq-A 178, 184, 188–193, 205 f., 217
Furūq-B 184, 188, 190–193, 206, 217

Galen 45 f.
genre 1 f., 4–14, 16–18, 30 f., 34–41, 43–45, 47, 49, 51, 54–57, 61, 65, 70, 79, 81, 94–96, 103, 109 f., 114, 117–121, 125, 134–137, 140, 144 f., 149, 152–155, 157 f., 161–169, 171 f., 175, 178 f., 182 f., 185, 187, 189, 191, 194–198
grammar 43, 55, 58, 73, 111, 113 f., 148, 182, 194

hadith 10, 61, 66 f., 76 f., 85, 92, 111, 124, 128 f., 131–133, 135, 139, 149 f., 163, 179, 189
hajj 145 f.
Ḥājjī Khalīfa 73, 97–102, 134 f., 159–161, 166–169, 172, 174, 177 f., 198–205, 212 f.
al-Ḥakīm al-Tirmidhī 57, 65, 73, 162, 166
Hallaq, Wael 1, 4, 24 f., 36, 96, 140
Hama 178
Hamadan 66, 173
al-Ḥamawī, Aḥmad ibn Muḥammad 73, 142, 160 f., 179, 195
Ḥanafī school 24, 159, 172, 183, 189, 192
Hanna, Nelly 130
al-Harawī, Shams al-Dīn 128
al-Ḥarīrī 135
al-Ḥasan al-Būrīnī 127
al-Ḥasan ibn Maḥmūd al-Sarrād (or al-Zarrād) 162
ḥāshiya 9,

Heinrichs, Wolfhart 6, 17, 27, 29, 31, 34f., 43, 49, 158f., 166, 168–170, 172f., 175–181, 198–211
ḥīla 189, 220, 224

Ibn Abī Uṣaybiʿa 46, 49f.
Ibn al-Akfānī 98, 100–102, 160
Ibn al-ʿĀlima, see al-Dimashqī, Aḥmad ibn Asʿad Ibn Ḥalwān
Ibn ʿAsākir 126
Ibn Bābawayh Muḥammad ibn ʿAlī 68
Ibn Badrān, Abū ʿAbdallāh Muḥammad ibn ʿAbd al-Qawī l-Maqdisī 176, 211, 216
Ibn Farḥūn 38, 132f., 135f., 141, 153, 171, 185, 207f.
Ibn Fāris al-Lughawī 63, 135
Ibn Ḥazm 38, 77, 83, 162, 207
Ibn al-ʿIzz 137f.
Ibn al-Jawzī 67, 135, 211
Ibn al-Jazzār 46–49, 51–54, 73
Ibn Juljul 48–50
Ibn Kamāl Pāsha. See Kemalpaşazade
Ibn Kashāsib, Abū l-ʿAbbās Kamāl al-Dīn Aḥmad al-Dizmārī 173, 201, 216
Ibn Kathīr 168, 198
Ibn al-Kātib 170, 185, 206, 215
Ibn Khaldūn 100
Ibn Khallikān 66, 185, 207, 212
Ibn al-Kutubī, Yūsuf ibn Ismāʿīl 46f.
Ibn al-Nadīm 50, 63, 98, 162, 166, 199, 212
Ibn al-Naqqāsh, Shams al-Dīn Muḥammad ibn ʿAlī 177f., 184, 186, 202, 216
Ibn Nujaym 5, 33, 141–144, 155, 160f., 164, 182f., 190, 192, 195, 206, 213, 217
Ibn Qāḍī Shuhba 145, 148, 167f., 173, 178, 185, 198–202
Ibn al-Qāsim 37
Ibn al-Qaṭṭān, Abū ʿAbdallāh 152f., 161, 212
Ibn Qayyim al-Jawziyya 162, 214
Ibn al-Qifṭī 50, 73
Ibn Qudāmā, Muwaffaq al-Dīn 102–103
Ibn Qutayba 56, 62, 112f., 135
Ibn Quṭlūbughā 169, 172, 174, 178, 203–205
Ibn Rajab al-Ḥanbalī 76, 110
Ibn al-Rēwandī 82–84
Ibn al-Shiḥna 137f.
Ibn Shujāʿ, Muḥammad 115
Ibn al-Sikkīt 63f.
Ibn Sunayna, Muḥammad ibn ʿAbdallāh al-Sāmarrī 6, 31, 39, 176f., 179, 210f., 216
Ibn Surayj 24, 37, 165f., 168, 198, 215
Ibn Surūr, Ibrāhīm ibn ʿAbd al-Wāḥid al-Maqdisī 176, 210, 216
Ibn Taymiyya 31, 110
Ibn Ṭūlūn Mosque 148
Ibn al-Turkumānī, Tāj al-Dīn Aḥmad ibn ʿUthmān 178, 186, 205, 216
Ibn Zaydūn 154
Ikhmīm 177
Ikhtilāf. See *khilāf*
ʿilla 13, 42, 77, 87f., 90, 93, 95, 104f.
inheritance 147
Iraq 26
ʿĪsā ibn Dīnār 24
Isbir, ʿAlī Muḥammad 74f.
Isfahan 66
Istanbul 5, 35, 41, 46, 94, 97, 121, 129, 131f., 158–160, 169, 186, 188–190, 198, 200, 203–206, 219f., 222–224

jadal. See disputation
Jalāl, Ibrāhīm Ismāʿīl 162, 170, 195, 207, 213
Jammāʿīl 176
Jamma'in 176
al-Jarbādhqānī 71
al-Jihānī, Jalāl 170, 207
al-Jīlī, ʿAbd al-ʿAzīz 153
Johansen, Baber 4, 140, 151
al-Jurjānī, Abū l-ʿAbbās Aḥmad 136, 144–148, 152f., 155, 165, 168, 186, 200f., 215
al-Juwaynī, ʿAbdallāh 12, 17–30, 32, 35–37, 39, 81, 103–108, 145, 149, 152f., 168, 180, 185, 199f.
al-Juwaynī, Imām al-Ḥaramayn Abū l-Maʿālī 89f., 104, 108, 171, 185, 200

Kaḥḥāla, ʿUmar Riḍā 167–169, 172–174, 176–178, 180, 185 f., 198–205, 207, 209–213
Kanazi, George 65–68
al-Karābīsī, Asʿad ibn Muḥammad 32, 39, 115 f., 142, 160–161, 171 f., 174, 182, 189, 197, 204, 216
al-Karābīsī, Muḥammad ibn Ṣāliḥ 166 f., 171 f., 192, 203, 215
al-Karkhī, Abū l-Ḥasan 24
Kemalpaşazade 77–79
Khalīl ibn Aḥmad 58, 64 f.
khilāf 39, 81, 94–103, 109, 125
Khurasan 185

La Marsa 180 f., 209 f.
legal stratagem. See *ḥīla*
the Levant 178
lexicography 43, 45, 49, 51, 55, 58 f., 61, 64, 73, 79, 110 f., 114, 118, 161, 166, 197
Lowry, Joseph 3, 5, 13, 95 f., 135
lugha. See lexicography

mabsūṭ 140
madrasa 38, 122, 155, 192
al-Maḥbūbī, Aḥmad ibn ʿUbayd Allāh 142, 160 f., 173 f., 189, 204 f., 216
al-Maḥbūbī, ʿUbayd Allāh ibn Masʿūd ibn Aḥmad 174
majlis 122, 124 f., 127–131, 137, 146, 155
Makdisi, George 82, 91, 95, 97, 122
Mālik ibn Anas 10, 24, 37, 133
Mālikī school 24, 40, 153
maqāṣid al-sharīʿa 119, 195
al-Maqdisī, Abū l-Khayr ibn Jamāʿa 29, 152, 168, 200, 215
al-Maqdisī, Muṭahhar ibn Ṭāhir 83
al-Mardāwī, Abū l-Ḥasan ʿAlī ibn Sulaymān 102 f., 211
Marghāyatī(?), Bāyazīd ibn Isrāʾīl ibn Ḥājjī Dāwūd 181
al-Mawwāq 170, 180 f., 207, 209 f., 217
Mecca 32, 158, 171, 176 f., 179, 188, 198, 206, 211, 219 f.
medicine, *see also* distinctions, differential diagnostics 12, 43–45, 47–49, 51, 73, 112, 122
Miller, Larry B. 82–86, 89–93, 96, 101
Mongol 3, 126
Moses 85–87
Muḥammad ibn Muqātil al-Rāzī 191
Muḥammad ibn Yūsuf al-Andalusī l-Anṣārī l-Mālikī 181, 210
Muḥammad ibn Yūsuf al-Andalusī l-Anṣārī l-Mālikī l-Mawwāq. See al-Mawwāq
Muḥammad ibn Zabāra 163, 180, 186
Muḥammad (the Prophet) 9, 17 f., 28 f., 32 f., 38–40, 43, 46, 56 f., 61 f., 64, 66–68, 70 f., 74, 77, 85 f., 97, 100, 103, 110–112, 129, 133, 135–137, 139, 144 f., 149–152, 158 f., 162 f., 166–173, 175–181, 183, 185 f., 189, 191, 195 f., 198–204, 206–217
Muḥammad al-Shawkānī 163
mukhtaṣar 24, 50, 140, 166
Musa, Khadiga 8, 10 f., 195 f.
al-Musawi, Muhsin 129
Muslim 5, 31–34, 38 f., 43, 58, 66, 72, 76, 81–87, 97, 101, 112, 121, 126, 133, 138, 143, 147, 149, 152, 157, 159, 170, 185, 187, 195, 208
Muʿtazila 67 f.
al-Muzanī, Ismāʿīl ibn Yaḥyā 166

naḥw. See grammar
Najm al-Dīn Aḥmad ibn Muḥammad ibn Khalaf ibn Rājiḥ al-Maqdisī 173, 201, 216
al-Nasawī, Abū l-Ḥasan ʿAlī ibn Aḥmad 166, 199, 215
Naṣīr ibn Yaḥyā l-Balkhī 189, 191
Naṣṣār, Ḥusayn 58, 62
al-Nāṭifī, Abū ʿAbbās Aḥmad ibn Muḥammad al-Ṭabarī 169, 203, 215
al-Nawawī, Muḥyī l-Dīn ibn Sharaf 25, 149 f., 183
al-Naysābūrī, Najm al-Dīn ʿAlī ibn Bakr 6, 31, 40 f., 131, 171, 184, 204, 206, 216 f.
Nishapur 185
North Africa 157, 171, 182, 185

Ottoman 15, 101, 123, 126 f., 130, 140, 154, 159, 167, 183, 187, 192
Oxyrhynchus. See al-Bakhnasā

Pfeifer, Helen 126–128
philosophy 12 f., 45, 74, 77, 82, 101, 124
Plato 75
Powers, David 4 f., 25, 140, 175

al-Qāḍī 'Abd al-Wahhāb al-Baghdādī 169 f.
al-Qāḍī 'Iyāḍ 170, 185, 206–208
al-Qāḍī l-Nu'mān 48
al-Qanṣūh Ghawrī 129
al-Qarāfī, Shihāb al-Dīn 5, 24 f., 40, 153, 160, 164, 175, 182 f., 186, 198, 209, 213, 216
Qaṭāya, Salmān 46 f., 49–51
al-qawā'id al-fiqhiyya 8, 119, 175, 195 f.
al-Qazwīnī, Abū Ḥātim 153
Qipchak 125
al-Qirqisānī, Abū Yūsuf Ya'qūb 83–87
qiyās. See analogy
Qur'an 60, 67, 69, 78, 85, 110, 129, 135, 145 f., 189
Quṭrub 61–65
Qus 177
Qusṭā ibn Lūqā 74–77

Rabat 155, 170, 186, 201, 208 f.
Rabb, Intisar 8, 10 f.
al-Rabī' ibn Sulaymān 105
al-Rāfi'ī, 'Abd al-Karīm ibn Muḥammad 149 f., 183
al-Rāzī, Abū Bakr Zakariyyā' 46–54
al-Rāzī, Abū Ḥātim Aḥmad 124
al-Rāzī, Muḥammad ibn Zakariyyā' 124
riddles, see *alghāz*
al-Rūyānī, Abū l-Maḥāsin 'Abd al-Wāḥid ibn Ismā'īl al-Ṭabarī 168, 201, 216

al-Sabīl, 'Umar 158 f., 163, 166–170, 172–182, 184 f., 188–190, 198–213
al-Ṣadūq. See Ibn Bābawayh
al-Ṣafadī, Khalīl ibn Aybak 130, 154
al-Ṣāhib Ibn 'Abbād 71
Saḥnūn ibn Sa'īd 37
Sālimān, Muḥammad 135
Samarqand 172
al-Samarqandī, Abū l-Layth 189, 191
al-Sāmarrī, Abū 'Abdallāh Muḥammad ibn 'Abdallāh, *see* Ibn Sunayna
al-Sāmarrī, Mu'aẓẓam al-Dīn Abū l-Fatḥ 'Abdallāh ibn Hibat Allāh 176
al-Sarakhsī, Abū l-'Abbās Aḥmad ibn Muḥammad 43, 73
Schacht, Joseph 4–6, 17, 31, 34, 36, 41, 94, 96, 159, 166, 172, 176 f., 190, 198 f., 202–204, 206, 209, 211
Sezgin, Fuat 74, 191
Shāfi'ī school 2, 19, 22, 24, 29 f., 36 f., 149 f., 152, 159, 165, 168, 173, 177, 186
al-Shāfi'ī, Muḥammad ibn Idrīs 10, 13, 18–24, 26, 91, 95 f., 100, 121, 135 f., 150, 162, 173, 198, 201, 213 f., 216
Shahrastānī 98
al-Shaybānī, Abū 'Amr 58
al-Shaybānī, Muḥammad ibn al-Ḥasan 10, 189, 191, 204
Shi'i 2, 10, 68, 162 f., 165, 212
al-Shīrāzī, Abū Isḥāq 37, 93, 114, 150, 167 f., 185, 198 f., 212
al-Silafī, Abū Ṭāhir Aḥmad ibn Muḥammad 66
al-Ṣiqillī, 'Abd al-Ḥaqq 37 f., 94, 170 f., 185, 215
al-Subayyil, Anas ibn 'Umar ibn Muḥammad 177, 210 f.
al-Subkī, Tāj al-Dīn 166–168, 173, 177, 185, 195 f., 198–201, 212
Sufism 45, 159, 162, 213
sunna, see hadith
al-Suyūṭī, Jalāl al-Dīn 64, 164, 195–197

ṭabaqāt 46, 127, 153, 158, 169, 171, 179, 203
al-Ṭabarī, Abū l-'Abbās Aḥmad ibn 'Abdallāh 9, 150, 153, 167 f., 185, 199, 215 f.
al-Ṭaḥāwī 191
al-Tamīmī l-Dārī 169, 174
takhrīj 8, 23 f.
taqlīd 4 f., 24 f., 29
Ṭaşköprüzāde, 'Iṣām al-Dīn 98–103
al-Tha'ālabī 62
Thābit ibn Abī Thābit 60, 63
theology 13, 66–68, 73, 82–84, 96, 122, 197
Todorov, Tzvetan 6 f.

al-Ṭūfī, Najm al-Dīn 12, 17, 27–30, 181, 199 f., 207, 210

ʿUmar ibn al-Khaṭṭāb 133
al-Urdustānī, Aḥmad ibn Muḥammad 184, 188, 206
uṣūl al-fiqh 1 f., 5, 11, 30, 35, 96, 100, 111, 114, 173, 201 f.

al-Wansharīsī, Abū l-ʿAbbās Aḥmad 32, 182, 188, 209, 217
Wāṣil ibn ʿAṭāʾ 66
Wittgenstein, Ludwig 7, 9, 36

Yaḥyā ibn Yaḥyā l-Laythī 10, 24
al-Yaḥyā, Muḥammad ibn Ibrāhīm ibn Muḥammad 39, 176 f., 210 f.
Yāqūt al-Ḥamawī 66
Yemen 180, 186
Young, Walter E. 58, 81–84, 87 f., 91–94, 96, 101, 125, 174

al-Zahrānī, ʿAbd al-Muḥsin Saʿīd ibn Aḥmad 166 f., 203
Zarīrān 179
al-Zarīrānī, Sharaf al-Dīn ʿAbd al-Rahīm ibn ʿAbdallāh 32, 179, 186, 198, 211
al-Zarkashī, Badr al-Dīn 12, 17, 28–30, 168, 173, 185, 199–201, 212
Zaydī 2, 163, 179 f., 186
al-Ziriklī, Khayr al-Dīn 46, 73, 169, 200–203, 207, 211 f.
al-Zubayrī, al-Zubayr ibn Aḥmad 152 f., 161, 166, 212

www.ingramcontent.com/pod-product-compliance
Lightning Source LLC
Chambersburg PA
CBHW061937220426
43662CB00012B/1934
* 9 7 8 3 1 1 0 7 6 3 2 7 0 *